NEUROPSYCHOLOGICAL FUNDAMENTALS IN LEARNING DISABILITIES
REVISED EDITION

. . . Happiness is very important. It is more important than the achievement of some elementary scholarly goals. A happy child and a happy adult are preferred over a well instructed but unhappy child or adult. Humans are social beings.

. . . To possess "language" in its widest sense is to perceive the existence of things and direct oneself toward them; it is to experience them, to comprehend them in their objectivity and/or function, and to react mimically and gesturally.

NEUROPSYCHOLOGICAL FUNDAMENTALS IN LEARNING DISABILITIES
REVISED EDITION

Julio B. de Quirós, MD, PhD
Orlando L. Schrager, MD

ACADEMIC THERAPY PUBLICATIONS
NOVATO, CALIFORNIA

Academic Therapy Publications
20 Commercial Boulevard
Novato, California 94949-6191

Tests, books, and materials
for and about the learning disabled

2 1 0 9 8 7 6 5 4 3
3 2 1 0 9 8 7 6 5 4

Library of Congress Cataloging in Publication Data
Quiro's, Julio Bernaldo de.
  Neuropsychological fundamentals in learning disa-
bilities.
  Includes bibliographical references and index.
  1. Learning disabilities. 2. Neuropsychology.
I. Schrager, Orlando L., joint author. II. Title.
[DNLM: 1. Education, Special. 2. Learning disorders.
3. Neurophysiology—In infancy and childhood.
WS110 Q8n]
RJ506.L4Q57   1979   616.8   79-25106
ISBN: 0-87879-613-4

Preface

One of the greatest present problems in educational systems is related to defining "learning disability." Teachers, psychologists, speech therapists, physical therapists, and other specialized workers in the field have developed remedial techniques and therapies in regard to various conditions which manifest themselves as "learning disabilities." But in the United States and in many other countries it is very difficult to establish an interchange of ideas between educators, therapists, and doctors.

In general, physicians are much more concerned with the treatment of organic diseases and illnesses than treatment of learning disabilities. Moreover, the "language" of a doctor is quite different than the "language" of an educator. In the several contacts we have had in the United States with health and educational authorities, we have come to realize that a main question is how to use the medical approach in order to be practical for teachers and how to use the educational approach in order to be practical for doctors.

Our book is written not only for teachers, but also for psychologists, therapists, educational workers, and doctors—that is, for all professionals who contribute to the educational team. We want to examine how a teacher can be helped by a doctor, what kind of studies can help the doctor himself in order to provide useful data to the teacher, what a teacher can expect from a doctor dealing with learning disabilities, how the teacher can improve remedial techniques and therapies, and what kind of clinical diagnosis a teacher or a therapist can *suspect,* so that confirmation from the unified educational team may be requested.

At present, learning disabilities constitute a serious problem that challenges the diverse disciplines concerned with education. Probably the solution for learning-disabled children is the greatest task for our generation: Only if we improve our present approaches concerning these conditions, will it be feasible to minimize personal and social maladjustments in our children and teenagers. There are so many implications for the future of humanity in this solution, that combined treatments with several professions is critical.

It is always the same: Nature never realizes that humans work according to different specialized fields. Nature "mixes" many human "specializations" in the different conditions which constitute the broad field of learning disabilities.

We hope that better communication between professionals will lead to better lives among the learning disabled.

The authors want to express their appreciation to John Arena for his trust and support for the publication of this book, to James B. Preston for his handling of the manuscript, and to Mirian Tannhauser for her thoughtful final review of the project. Without their help, this original version in English would have never been possible.

Our deepest wishes are that the contents and goals of this book might be in the near future transformed into practical improvements within the field of children's education.

J. B. de Quirós
O. L. Schrager
Buenos Aires
March, 1977

This book is dedicated to learning-disabled children everywhere and to the future of humanity.

Contents

A CLASSIFICATION OF LEARNING DISABILITIES

Primary Learning Disabilities

Difficulties in *specific* human acquisitions (*Lingua*, language, reading, writing, mathematical calculation, and the like, are *primarily* disturbed.)

Compensated Cerebral Damages or Dysfunctions	Perceptual Handicaps	Abnormal Postural Afferences
Developmental Dyslexia	Auditorization Disturbances	Vestibular-Proprioceptive Dissociation
Developmental Dysphasia	Visualization Disturbances	Vestibular-Oculomotor Split
Developmental Apractognosia		

Secondary Learning Disabilities

Difficulties in *nonspecific* human achievements (*Lingua*, language, reading, writing, mathematical calculation, and the like, are *secondarily* disturbed.)

Biological Abnormalities		Psychic Disturbances	Socioeconomic Disadvantages. Ecological Factors
Central Nervous System Pathology	Sensory Impairments		
Diffuse Brain Damage	Hypoacusis	Reactive Behavior	Cultural Deprivations
Cerebral Palsies	Deafness	Neurotic Behavior	Malnutrition
Cerebral Lesions	Amblyopia	Psychotic Behavior	School Dropouts
	Blindness		Teaching Errors

Other labels, such as mental retardation, epilepsy, and so on.

CHAPTER I

Terminology and Concepts

(1) NEUROLOGY AND NEUROPSYCHOLOGY

We are very fortunate to be living in these times, because we are facing a deep change in human behavior and human sciences, in social structures and learning possibilities. Today, the most difficult things to teach and the most difficult things to learn are still "how to love" and "how to be loved." These are also questions without answers in modern education, although these questions concern themselves directly with happiness. But we are at the beginning of a new epoch in understanding ourselves and understanding young people (infants, children, teenagers). Only recently have people been replacing the "supreme" educational purposes of their parents with their own. Only recently have people come to feel that, much better than obtaining a "great" doctoral degree, is obtaining a "small" amount of happiness—with or without the doctoral degree. Certainly there are no general "prescriptions" for happiness: Everybody has his own "prescription." The only difficult task is to find it. Educational systems can aid in achieving this goal.

Several sciences contribute to a better understanding of behavior and learning abilities, both normal and abnormal. If we are able to understand why many school failures appear, we could prevent or ameliorate them. When learning-disabled children feel they and their problems are understood, they can have the opportunity to "discover" themselves, to "accept" themselves as simply being different (for better or worse) than their mates. This is important for their future . . . and their own happiness "prescription."

Neurology is one of those "helping" sciences, and it can be defined as the branch of medicine concerning the nervous system in its normal and diseased states. This science did not exist as a specialty until the last century, when Guillaume Benjamin Armand Duchenne (1806-1875), Jean-Martin Charcot (1825-1893), and John Hughlings Jackson (1834-1911), among others, established a solid background for modern neurology. Hughlings Jackson, particularly, is now internationally recognized as the "father" of modern neurology. His works are still being reprinted today, which is highly unusual in medicine.

Neurology began as a science which dealt with very definite and clear abnormalities. It described precisely many diseases, symptoms, and signs related to the nervous system; and it was successful in connecting these data to central nervous system damages or lesions. During the first half of this century, neuropediatrics (that is, neurology for infants and children) was very much developed. During the second half, neuropsychology began. Traditional neurology was effective in clear, definite lesions or damages, but it did not serve in diffuse, slight, or "minimal" nervous diseases. This was the main reason for the development of neuropsychology, a term which is rarely defined in medical treatises or dictionaries.

Some authors believe that neuropsychology is related to the acquisition of information (through psychological assessments) concerning general intelligence, academic achievement, auditory-visual and haptic perception, eye-hand and other similar coordinations, speech and language processes, attention and memory span, emotions, and (eventually) levels of motor activities and maturation.

Some other authors, nevertheless, during recent decades, have introduced the concept that neuropsychology is a new branch of health sciences which generally deals with basic medical approaches that study relationships between cerebral functions (and achievements) and human behavior.[1]

In adults, neuropsychology mainly concerns itself with behavior changes in patients with localized cerebral lesions. It therefore facilitates a better understanding of the importance that each cerebral region has among the complex functions and achievements that rule human behavior.[2]

In infants and children, neuropsychology is also directed to disturbances produced in specific human achievements (in general: symbolic disabilities). These disorders manifest themselves as speech, *lingua,* and/or language disturbances; reading, writing, spelling, and computational disabilities; dysgraphias; etc. Various other symptoms usually appear associated with such disorders, and are frequently recognized as "learning disabilities," "minimal brain (or cerebral) dysfunctions," "developmental dyslexia," "developmental aphasia," and so on. Often these syndromes also include hyperactivity; lack of attention span for visualizing and auditorizing, perceptual handicaps, and the like.

On these bases, neuropsychologists study the pathways which could intervene between objective disturbances (such as in behavior, movement, or perception) and the cerebral or central nervous system disorder from which such a disturbance originates.

The study of neuropsychology can delineate the essential steps and proper sequences which must be followed in order to obtain adequate rehabilitation.

(2) DEVELOPMENT: EVOLUTION, MATURATION, AND LEARNING

Certainly there are diverse criteria regarding these frequently used terms; definitions of these terms do not always agree. Definitions from a traditional point of view can be easily found in many specialized dictionaries and textbooks.[3] Our goal in this book is to emphasize some practical notions. Therefore, we will try to avoid "classical," but often confusing definitions of these (or other) terms. We should, therefore, define our terms.

"Development" refers to all the continuous changes that occur from conception itself to death or, in diseases, to degeneration of the tissues.

"Evolution" means the biological development of inherited behaviors. (Processes such as myelination or other biochemical modifications arising from aging; various metabolic changes: hormonic, electrolytic, and others; modifications of organ size, etc., are included in "evolution.")

"Maturation" means the externalization of biological and environmental developments seen through objective signs (e.g., sitting, crawling, walking, and so on). Maturation depends on biological development but also requires the presence of environmental influences or pressures.

"Learning" means the acquisition of developmental behaviors which depend on environmental influences.

Consequently, development is a broad term which includes evolution, maturation, and learning. In a word, it is the result of the interaction between evolution, maturation, and learning.

(3) HUMAN LEARNING AND LEARNING DISABILITIES

We should emphasize the fact that environmental influences are essential for the process of learning.

Primary learning processes allow adaptation and survival; they permit the maintenance of the species through time—if the environment does not change radically and abruptly. Animals and young children have primary learning processes.

Secondary learning processes allow the utilization of generational knowledge. Learning comes not only from the environment but also from experiences with many other members of the same species. Some animals and young children have secondary learning processes.

Tertiary learning processes imply the use of symbols which permit transmission and reception of knowledge through successive generations, that is to say, through *time*. Only human beings have the potential for tertiary learning processes. This type of learning is transmitted as *lingua*.

Quaternary learning processes are not only a symbolic communication; they also imply the ability to think with symbols and formulate (or create) diverse, different, or new patterns. Inventions, discoveries, and innovations* are included in this special type of symbolic communication that generally is recognized as language. Only human beings have quaternary

*What is *invented* did not previously exist. (The Chinese invented gun powder.) What is *discovered* already existed. (Columbus discovered America.) *Innovation* means the introduction of new expressions to the familiar *lingua*.

learning processes.

Primary and secondary learning processes are characteristic of animals and human beings. Tertiary and quaternary learning processes are specific to the human race. *Lingua* and language constitute the principal facets of human learning. Learning disabilities are caused mainly by problems in these two specific human processes.

(4) FUNCTIONS AND DYSFUNCTIONS

Learning disabilities are very much related to dysfunctions. This being so, we should discuss the meaning of "function" and "dysfunction."

Dorland's Medical Dictionary defines function as "the special, normal, or proper action of any part or organ."[4] A function may be, for example, "to see"; but, according to this definition, it is also the action of the occipital neurons, or the action of the ocular pathway axons, or the action produced by cone-like bodies of the retina. Function is hearing; function is audition; function is the action of the small bones in the middle ear. Function is the part and function is the whole. Function depends on the natural development of any part or organ. This development occurs spontaneously in the regular evolution and maturation of an organ or apparatus through physiological and environmental influences or pressures.

Dysfunction is the disturbance of a function (for instance, of breathing, of the lung, of the pulmonary alveolus, etc.) produced by such things as malformation, an illness, or negative environmental influence. Dysfunction is a term which is applied to the disturbance of any function (of any organ, or any apparatus). For instance, in brain-stem disorders many important central functions can be disturbed or disrupted (for example: directional audition); in cerebellar disorders muscular coordination is disturbed; and in cerebral disorders the higher functions of man are disturbed. If the disorder is a central lesion or damage, Jackson's Law is respected: The last functional acquisitions are the first which are lost.

In cerebral dysfunctions (in young children) there are slight or mild types of pathology; labels currently used, such as cerebral palsy, mental retardation, epilepsy, etc., are found in this group.

In minimal (or minor) cerebral dysfunctions there is only the loss of the last human acquisitions (Jackson's Law): in general, all the possibilities of symbolization (language, *lingua,* the ability to listen, think, speak, write, spell, or do mathematical calculations, according to each type of pathology). As we can see, "minimal cerebral dysfunctions" can be frequently observed as "causes" of the alleged *specific* learning disabilities. Nevertheless, the great question remains: What does the term "learning disability" really mean? In the United States Public Law 91-230, Section 602-15 (April 13, 1970), defines "children with specific learning disabilities" as those children who have a disorder in one or more of the basic psychological processes involved in understanding or using language, spoken or written, which disorder manifests itself in imperfect ability to listen, think, speak, write, spell, or do mathematical calculations. Among the learning disabled are mentioned those with such conditions as "perceptual handicaps, brain injury, minimal brain dysfunction, dyslexia, and developmental aphasia." In this law, not included were children who have learning problems which are primarily the result of visual, hearing, or motor handicaps, or mental retardation, or emotional disturbance, or of environmental disadvantage. Many aspects of the federal definition have been discussed in recent years; but in 1977, a new law, Public Law 94-142, has attempted to refine earlier efforts. Probably the main point to be established is always the same: a real definition of *learning disability*.

Some authors identify specific learning disabilities with "dyslexia" and with "minimal brain dysfunction"; but certainly in this group we can also include "vestibular-proprioceptive dissociations" (with cerebellar intervention after four years of age).

(5) FUNCTIONAL SYSTEMS AND SYSTEMIC DYSFUNCTIONS

We should remember that every learning ability stems from not only sufficient neurological development, but also from other environmental factors. All functions need environmental aids; in order to breathe, we need air; in order to walk, we need ground and gravitational forces; in order to see, we need light and things to be seen. Nature provides the indispensable environment in order for functions to develop. Humans do not need any other help (outside nature itself) in order to develop their functions.

But a different kind of function is the functional system. Nature does not provide the environmental aids for functional systems. The ability to read is a functional system; and reading requires written materials. These kinds of materials are produced only by human beings. When a function becomes evident only through human environmental help, we recognize it as a functional system. This notion is essential to an understanding of human learning processes.

In order to read, therefore, we need not only correct perceptual vision, but also many written materials. Without written materials it is not possible to teach reading. To see is a function; to read is a functional system. The concept of "functional system" was introduced by Russian authors, but it is possible to read some American comments on this subject.[5]

Actually "learning disabilities," "dyslexias," "minimal cerebral dysfunctions," "postural dysfunctions," and so on are "systemic dysfunctions," because (1) they are never exclusively bioneurological, and (2) they are always correlated with human environmental influences or pressures. In summary, they depend on functional systems.

(6) ABNORMALITIES IN HUMAN LEARNING

From a very simple point of view, "specific learning disabilities" seem to be labeled as "dyslexias," "dysgraphias," and "dyscalculias"—each one of these terms being related to reading, writing, and arithmetic. It is important to remember that the alleged "specific learning disabilities" actually are only symptoms, and not real clinical entities. For instance, besides a reading disorder, there can be many other symptoms which can lead to different diagnoses of learning disabilities, according to the results obtained through careful examination.

Also, there is confusion between dysgraphia and dyspraxia for hand movements. Dysgraphia means a disorder in correctly tracing shapes, sizes, directions, and pressures in writing, independent of symbolic or perceptual disabilities. On the one hand, dysgraphia exists, for instance (as a symptom) in cerebellar or basal ganglia damage. On the other hand, dysgraphia often appears in "specific learning disabilities" combined with dyslexia and/or other symptoms; it is very common to see distortion in the shape of letters, lack of observance of edges and lines, irregular sizes, and evident awkwardness in pressure applied to the pencil on the sheet of paper.

The fundamentals of human learning are established on symbolic abilities. These abilities demand (1) sufficient bioneurological development, (2) adequate environmental influences, and (3) noninterference of the body itself on higher cortical levels.

Sufficient bioneurological development depends on evolution and maturation, and finally permits the achievement of symbolic thought and formulation (symbolic creativity).

Adequate environmental influences act on maturation and learning, and depend on numerous psycho-socio-cultural factors.

The noninterference of the body itself on higher cortical levels is obtained through postural control by lower systems.

According to the greater or lesser influence of these three main possibilities of human learning, different syndromes related to "dyslexia," "dysgraphia," and "dyscalculia" may be determined. External manifestations such as "dyslexia," "dysgraphia," and "dyscalculia" do not provide basic elements for a clinical classification of learning disabilities. However, essential points of human learning permit a logical clinical classification, for practical purposes referred to as *prognosis* and *treatment.*

(7) AIMS OF THIS BOOK

We respect, very much, traditional neurology, but we also assume that through classical examinations we can only obtain classical diagnoses (i.e., related to definite central damage responding to clear lesions in different levels of the central nervous system).

Of course, we accept the traditional points of view which are extremely useful in our daily medical work. But today it is obvious that many factors are related not only to central nervous system damage but also to other causes. For example, developments in modern medicine allow many children, who were in other times destined to survive in unfortunate circumstances, now to remain apparently "normal," and usually be incorporated into regular schools. Also, the increasing use of alcohol, tobacco, and drugs among pregnant mothers can provide poor conditions for the correct development of their children. These factors should be added to other well-known factors which also can produce various central nervous system damage or pathological conditions: prematurity, asphyxia neonatorum, birth trauma, inheritance, genetic errors, infections, illnesses, etc.

Similarly, we cannot forget the various kinds of modern environmental pollution: air and water pollution, family instability, general stresses, tension living—to name a few—which transform the environment of children into a continuous state of anxiety and insecurity.

Society must react immediately in order to control the factors which disable the child from developing proper human learning processes. In some way we must insist on the crucial importance of this subject, hoping that authorities become sensitive to this tremendous danger to the future of humanity.

But one thing remains: we are facing more and more "new" conditions, or syndromes, which are not amenable to traditional forms of examination or description. Therefore, it is indispensable that we describe them through appropriate "new" clinical terminology and medical procedures. This book attempts to do just that. Only one goal, however, can justify its publication: to have fewer learning disabled today in order to have a better society tomorrow.

NOTES

1. A. L. Benton, "Developmental Dyslexia: Neurological Aspect," in W. J. Freidlander (ed.), *Advances in Neurology* (New York: Raven Press, 1975).
2. A. R. Luria, "Luria's Preface to the Spanish Version," in *El Cerebro en Accion* (M. Torres, trans.) (Barcelona, Spain: Ed. Fontanella, 1974).
3. J. P. Chaplin, *Dictionary of Psychology* (New York: Dell Publishing Co. Inc., 1968); H. B. Robinson and N. M. Robinson, *The Mentally Retarded Child: A Psychological Approach* (New York: McGraw-Hill, 1965): 179-180.
4. *Dorland's Medical Dictionary* (23rd ed.) (Philadelphia: W. B. Saunders Co., 1957).
5. P. K. Anohkin (also cited as "Anojin," "Anokhin," and "Anoxin"), "Problemy Centra i Periferii v Fiziologii Nervnoj dejat el'nosti," *Gor'kij* (1935) as cited by A. R. Luria, *Cerebro y Lenguaje* (L. Flaguer, trans.) (Barcelona, Spain: Ed. Fontanella, 1974); P. K. Anojin, *La Inhibicion Interna como Problema de Fisiologia* (Ciencia y Conocimiento, trans.) (Buenos Aires: Ediciones Nuestro Tiempo, 1963); A. R. Luria, *Higher Cortical Functions in Man* (London: Tavistock, 1966); A. R. Luria, "Meta-Principles in Luria's Neuro-Psychology," *Skolepsychology* [Copenhagen] 8 (1971): 407; A. R. Luria, *Cerebro y Lenguaje* (Luis Flaqüer, trans.) (Barcelona, Spain: Ed. Fontanella, 1974); A. R. Luria, *El Cerebro en Accion* (M. Torres, trans.) (Barcelona, Spain: Ed. Fontanella, 1974); D. M. Bowden, "The Functional System: Keystone to Luria's Neuro-Psychology," *Skolepsychology* [Copenhagen] 8 (1971): 409-417 (paper originally presented at the convention of the American Psychological Association, New York, 1966).

CHAPTER II

The Basis for

Human Learning Development

(8) SPEECH, LINGUA, AND LANGUAGE

As was stated in Chapter I, neuropsychology is the study of relationships between cerebral functions (or achievements) and human behavior.
Disorders such as speech, *lingua,* and/or language disturbances; reading,
writing, spelling, and mathematical-calculations disabilities; or dysgraphias,
etc., are one of the main groups related to neuropsychological approaches.
It is necessary for us to be aware that the alleged "learning disabilities"
are constituted by disorders in human behavior: Symbolic comprehension
is a fundamental human behavior, indispensable for developing speech.
Symbolic comprehension is also useful in many neuropsychological examinations, and it is included as an item in general batteries employed by
many authors. Therefore, we should clarify here—before going on—what
we mean by "speech," "*lingua,*" and "language."

"Speech" is the oral expression of *lingua* and language. For traditional linguists, speech (*parole*) is the individual part of language; and *langue*
is a store of conventional expressions used by a community (for instance,
wordlike signs or fixed phrases). Saussure's term *langue* belongs to traditional linguistics; and it must not be confused with *lingua,* which belongs to
clinical approaches. For us, as clinicians, our concepts of speech and *lingua*
are much more useful than the linguistic concepts of *parole* and *langue.*[1]

Symbolic creativity emerges from symbolic thought, from fantasy,
from inventions, from discoveries. Again, the example: What is invented did
not previously exist. The Chinese invented gunpowder; humans invented
language. What is discovered already existed: Columbus discovered America;
a child discovers many things in English (as a language). Fantasy means
originality in symbolic communication. Innovation means introduction of

new expressions to the familiar *lingua.* These new expressions can be created by the individual himself or learned in other *milieux* and then introduced into his own *lingua,* in order to obtain language.

It is possible to find *lingua* not only in children, but also in abnormal adult situations. In many circumstances an adult uses *lingua:* when one is tired, or when there is brain damage (some aphasics), or when serious behavior problems exist (some schizophrenics). In some pathological cases, patients maintain social possibilities for symbolic communication, but they are unable to use *lingua* as language: They can tell us perfectly what happened in a movie, but they cannot obtain personal conclusions from it. They cannot add, nor argue, nor discuss anything related to the movie outside the presented sequences. These patients are frequently considered "without language disturbances." We disagree: They do not use language, they use only symbolic communication (*lingua*). People who use *lingua* may employ familiar vocabulary and syntax, but have difficulties in understanding and/or responding to complex contextual structures. In some cases the "mechanism" works quite well: Thought, intention, speech, inner speech, and the grammatical pattern of the sentence are all quite correct; but the individual has difficulties in categorizing thoughts or in understanding who is "the brother's father," "the father's brother," or other similar things. Perhaps it is dangerous to think, however, that some specific localization is connected with this kind of difficulty (posterior damage or parietal occipital lesion?). We must not forget that language is creative use of a learning ability (*lingua*). *Lingua* is certainly a community's agreed-upon linguistic patterns of usage, but it is also a learning ability. In the United States the linguistic pattern is English and people *learn* English; in Germany, German; in Italy, Italian; etc. This is a main difference: *lingua* is learned, language is created from the previous existence of *lingua. Lingua* begins in the social community, and goes to the individual. Babies already receive its influence. Language begins with the individual and can be extended to the community. Language is individual creativity sometimes applied to the community. Difficulty in making discoveries is difficulty in the development from *lingua* to language; various kinds of brain damage can produce this symptom. Every patient who has disturbances in *lingua* also has disturbances in discoveries, inventions, and innovations. Causes that can produce language troubles are, in general, neither specific nor localized in a determined region of the brain.

(9) EXPRESSION, CONNECTION, AND COMMUNICATION

"Expression" is a term which has different meanings. Sometimes "expression" is used to mean symbolic externalizations of human beings: gestures, mimicry, speech, writing, etc. Also, the term is used to mean the emotional characteristic of speech ("expressive speech").

But there is a third meaning: All external manifestations and utterances in human or living beings are considered expressions. It is not new to anybody that infants externalize their needs through the whole body, relaxing it or contracting it, according to pleasant or unpleasant situations. Every mother knows perfectly well that "something is happening with the baby" only by feeling it—that is, through the body. Every living creature moves or utters "because of" or "in order to." For instance, an amoeba moves because of the changes of the environment (pH, temperature, etc.) or in order to procure food, to reproduce, etc.

When expressions are understood by an observer, it is possible to speak about "connection."[2] Babies are "connected" with their mothers when they are "normal," because their expressions are "interpreted" by mothers through repetition, experience, and conditioning.

When understanding is produced between at least two individuals (for instance, mother-baby and baby-mother), we may use the term "communication." Actually, communication consists of being able to understand what the other individual wants "to say" (or "to mean"), and/or being able to be understood by the other individual concerning what we are "saying" (or "meaning"). Without exception, in communication there is a purposeful behavior created or established by human or nonhuman beings. Communication belongs to practically all living creatures. Gestures, mimicry, and essentially the body itself, are naturally involved in the very basis of communication: The only thing is to know how to "understand" the message, recognizing the cue that every message has. Animals can communicate among themselves and with human beings, in a variety of ways; but speech, *lingua*, and language are specific types of communication which belong only to humans. We can make this differentiation clear enough if we remember that all animals live in dwellings; but huts, apartments, "houses" in general, are specific dwellings of human beings. The main components of language are symbolic creativity and innovation—capabilities which only human beings are able to reach and develop. These are some of the main reasons why we do not agree with the popular notion of "language of animals."

(10) POSTURE, EQUILIBRIUM, AND LEARNING

At the end of Section 8 in this chapter, we defined *lingua* as a learning ability upon which language is established. Learning ability depends on coordinated motor activities of some purposeful movement. Several authors have called attention to this.[3] "Intentionality" refers to purposeful movements (voluntary or nonvoluntary ones). Intentional movements can be defined as purposeful movements, consciously or unconsciously made by the individual. The bases of motor activities are posture and equilibrium (or balance). First, therefore, we should discuss posture, position, attitude, equilibrium, and purposeful equilibrium. Then we will briefly review these as they apply to motor activities and learning.

Posture is the reflex activity of the body in relation to space (i.e., flexed or extended tonic postures). Position is the characteristic posture of a species (e.g., sitting in dogs is different than sitting in humans). Attitude is related to reflexes (of some intentionality) that lead to the return to a species-specific position.

Equilibrium (or balance) is the interplay between various forces, particularly gravity, and the motor power of the skeletal muscles. An organism has achieved equilibrium when it can maintain and control postures, positions, and attitudes. It is necessary to emphasize, nevertheless, that equilibrium begins before birth.

Posture is based on muscular tonus: It is chiefly related to the body.

Equilibrium (or balance) is based on proprioception (deep sensitivity), vestibular function, and vision—the cerebellum being the principal coordinator of this information. Equilibrium is chiefly related to space.

Purposeful equilibrium is the position that allows the processes of "natural learning": those skills necessary for the survivial of the species and the internalization of a large amount of external information.

As stated previously, posture and equilibrium are the bases of motor activities, and these are the platform for learning processes.

Some years ago we presented a keynote address on motor activities and learning theories at the Tenth International Conference of the Association for Children with Learning Disabilities (1971) in Detroit, Michigan.[4] In our presentation, we reviewed some important international approaches in the study of motor activities. It could be worthwhile here to recapitulate them:

> Genetic epistemology states that knowledge is primarily "an action upon the object. . . . All the cognitive mechanisms are based on motor activity."[5] For Piaget, "To know does not consist in copying reality but in acting upon it to transform it. . . ."[6]
>
> It is significant that Piaget's statements are coincident with the principles already established by the Swiss-French specific literature. In the last book of Andre Rey, before his death, he wrote: "The whole externalization of actions is a typical manifestation of all the lower psychological levels. Efferences [*] produce contact with the external reality. . . . New afferences [*] are generated through this contact, and they allow the child to imagine action, and after this he stops, looking irresistibly for the external world."[7] Rey explains quite well here the earlier connections between motor activity and mental action.
>
> According to this theory, movements which are able to elicit knowledge "are not just any kind of movements, but they are systems of coordinated movements looking for a result or an intention."[8]
>
> Behaviorism and conditionings are strongly connected with knowledge through motor activity. In the past few years proponents of behaviorism, as well as neo-Pavlovianism, have insisted that movement can help language and learning processes.[9]
>
> Writers in the field of cybernetics also state that human beings must elaborate a strategy of activity during the solution of every complex problem.[10]
>
> Psycholinguistics emphasizes that, while motor activity exerts upon a physical reality that has its own laws, generative grammar allows structures that make communication possible through human laws. Motor activity must be con-

---

*Efference is centrifugal: actions moving away from a nervous center. Afference is centripetal: information moving toward a nervous center.

ditioned to external physical rules which do not depend on human criteria. The progressive displacement of the motor activities by the mental actions allow adaptation to pre-established human rules, which can partially be modified."[11]

Through all these theories one fact remains: motor activity is essential in order to learn. In pathological cases (for instance, the cerebral palsies) the therapist must stabilize the body and rule its movements in order to obtain real learning.

(11) THE CONTINUITY OF BODY SCHEMA AND BODY AWARENESS

The interrelation between motor activity and the formation of body schema was clearly described by H. Wallon, when he differentiated two opposite "forces" acting on the young baby: proprioception and exteroception. Through these two information inputs (as described by Sherrington: one coming from the body itself and the other from the environment), Wallon distinguished two "spaces": "corporal space" and "outside space." Projection of "corporal space" *to* and *in* "outside space"—through movement—is for Wallon the basic notion of body schema, since he defined it as "the motoric adaptation to outside space."[12]

The notion of "body schema" was introduced at the beginning of this century, in England, mainly by Henry Head, who developed ideas previously stated by himself and Gordon Holmes at the end of the nineteenth century with the name "postural model." He discussed the body's representation at the level of the cortex, and he connected this notion with the "phantom limb" in the amputees during World War I. Head's classical volumes can be consulted in all specialized libraries, not only through its first edition (1926) but also through the second one (1963).[13]

The neurophysiological point of view held by Head was developed by Paul Schilder during the 1920s. Gradually, through carefully sequenced research projects, through published writings, and through others' use of the ideas, these notions became more clear and more useful, not only for specific examinations and diagnosis, but also for therapeutic approaches. Schilder introduced a psychoanalytic and socio-psycho-neurological point of view. At present, Schilder's ideas concerning "body image" are implemented all over the world, and they are currently used in learning and rehabilitation. Lauretta Bender's summary of Schilder's ideas is probably one of the best and most understandable explanations of the subject.[14]

According to Schilder, "the image of the human body means the picture of our own body which we form in our mind. . . . the way in which the body appears to ourselves.[15] Lauretta Bender and Archie A. Silver continue: "This Gestalt of ourselves has as its matrix a pattern, biologically determined by laws of growth and development and constitutionally limited. This matrix. . . . is the most stable part of the body image. But upon this matrix is added a continuous flow of new experiences, of physical sensation and of emotional impact, all of which create, develop and continually modify the body image.[16]

As is possible to see in Bender's foregoing synthesis, body image has two different parts: (1) the constitutional biological pattern, and (2) the continuously modified pattern (new experiences). But Bender and Silver further clarify these notions:

> Part of these new experiences arise in the explorations of one's own body as a child and as an adult, through cutaneous, visceral, kinesthetic and special sensory impulses. Parts of one's own body assume libidinous values. But many of the new experiences are elaborated in relation to the actions and attitudes by others, by identification, by emphasis upon particular parts of the body by others, so that a social component of the body image is added to the individual one. . . . The body image then is not the sum total of perceptions and experience but it is the constellation of these experiences into a Gestalt of oneself. The above concept of body image includes the postural model of the body. . . . "[17]

Body schema and body image constitute a relevant first step to understanding body influences in the development of learning abilities. The notion of body schema is extremely important and teachers are very aware of it; but, although exercises in developing the child's body image (that is, a "gut-level" appreciation of his body schema) are important to the development of the child, many teachers keep children performing these exercises long after the need for them is past—because teachers themselves sometimes do not quite know what to do next.

At the present time body schema is understood as neuromuscular (functional) action resulting from all the deep parts and tissues which contribute to maintaining a position in a static or dynamic situation. Body image refers more to the feelings, information, or experiences provided by the body itself (haptic, sensory inputs, emotional and social influences, etc.). It is easy to see that these two concepts relate very much to Head's and Schilder's criteria.

"Body concept" relates to one's knowledge about one's own body. Body concept means that one is able to recognize, to identify and to name his body parts, for instance: "hand," "nose," "eye," and so on. It is possible to speak about "concept" only when knowledge reaches verbalization. Nevertheless, "body insight" (i.e., nonverbal knowledge of the body) is the very beginning of body concept: Through drawings, play, and other representational tasks, it is possible to obtain knowledge of the body through body insight.

As Marianne Frostig has pointed out, body image, body schema, and body concept are the tripartition (artificial to a certain degree) which consitute "body awareness."[18] In general, body awareness is the most frequently used term in special therapy.

Most teachers and therapists know how to work with body awareness, but they do not know how to go further. Many children attain acceptable body awareness, but they remain at that point without developing motor activities and learning abilities.

(12) POSTURAL SYSTEM INTEGRATION AND CORPORAL POTENTIALITY

A young normal child establishes body awareness during the second year of postnatal life. At the same time, the postural system is developing. Posture and equilibrium, both, constitute the postural system. The postural system is the conjunction of anatomical-functional structures, series of parts, organs, or apparatus as they relate to the maintenance of body relationships: (1) within the body itself, and (2) in space, in order to obtain positions which allow a definite and useful activity or which enable learning. The postural system is established on the interrelationships of primary body schema. It develops toward corporal potentiality.

Purposeful equilibrium, primary body schema, integration of the postural system, are basic for: (1) the use of instruments or objects; (2) the independence of both halves of the body; (3) the learning of noncondi-tioned language; (4) the possibility of developing creativity; and (5) the capacity for higher-level learning.

The body is continuously giving the individual information (through afferences to the higher centers) about the body's pain, temperature, move-ment, tension, and so on. The higher cortical levels can receive such informa-tion; but in order to develop human learning, the latter must be "inhibited" at the conscious level. That is why to think with language requires much more than purposeful equilibrium. It needs the noninterference (at the awareness level) of such afferences related to the body itself. If the indivi-dual is able to exclude (or "inhibit" from the conscious level) body affer-ences, human learning processes can develop properly. That is what we understand by corporal potentiality, which can therefore be defined as the possibility of excluding body information in order to obtain human learning processes. It is impossible to introduce human learning processes while corporal needs (physiological, survival, comfort) are not met. Human beings, after establishing a primary body schema and an integrated postural system, must displace the body's hierarchy in order to allow symbolic development and to introduce language as an instrument (*lingua*), and then to formulate language, making abstractions possible.

As we have already stated, in order to obtain these results, human awareness must set aside many stimuli supplied to the body. The informa-tion provided by these stimuli is not at all eliminated, but *potentially* con-tinues on the basis of automatic mechanisms of posture and position. The development of such a corporal potentiality clearly indicates that a great number of high-level mental skills can be used for purposes other than the control of the body itself. This implies the use of central nervous system structures in human cultural learning, which is far removed from the natural world of instincts and survival.

Postural systems are common to mankind and animals alike; yet, corporal potentiality implies a function of this postural system that is specifically human: It allows the definite symbolic orientation of one of the cerebral hemispheres (as it is more and more liberated from somatic information) and the hemispheric cerebral dominance of our species.

If we review the definition of a postural system, we can see that several parts which make up the postural system may act together from the very beginning; but others do not, because they are "immature" or have not finished their myelination. Simultaneous and coordinated action of the eyes, deep sensitity, vestibular organs, and the cerebellum, are necessary for allowing the movements which permit survival and learning. The primary integration of the postural system is obtained at the third year of age. A biological-developmental (that is, evolutional) milestone of this integration could be the staining of adult type in the ponto-cerebellar pathways.* A maturational (that is, externalized biological-developmental) milestone is the possibility in maintaining erect posture with closed eyes, feet together, and both arms hanging normally at the sides of the body (Romberg's test). Another maturational milestone is the possibility of avoiding synkinesis when the thumb of one hand touches successively the tips of the other four fingers (variously referred to as the orientation test, "pianotage," or the oppositional finger test). Only through developmental achievements can these clear signs be seen. Romberg's test, which can normally be given to children over three years old, indicates clearly that, without vision and only with proprioception and vestibular inputs, the child can perfectly control his balance. This is a tremendous step in the development of equilibrium, posture, tonus, and therefore intentional and coordinated motor activities which are the bases for human learning processes. The oppositional finger test also shows the possibility of acting independently with each side of the body. This is a necessary starting point in laterality: The child can move a hand without any kind of reaction in the motor activities of the other hand. Both signs (Romberg's test and the oppositional finger test) point out essential facts in the continuity of body awareness, and represent the external manifestation of postural system integration.

Consequently, in normal development, after obtaining body awareness, the child attains the integration of the postural system. In special education teaching, many times this normal pattern can be followed; and some exercises can be directed toward developing it (the therapist can introduce activities to develop body awareness, and then, activities to aid postural integration). This is not the moment to detail therapeutic procedures; but, in general, we can emphasize the importance of "dividing" the body into two halves and of excluding some parts of the body which intervene in postural system integration, in order to program series of motor activities.

The next step in the continuous development of body awareness is corporal potentiality, which we defined earlier as "the possibility of excluding the body in order to introduce human learning." Between the ages of four and six years, the child's language begins to direct motor activities, and symbolic thought begins to dominate the left cerebral hemisphere.

*General myelination progresses until the beginning of the third decade of life. Microscopic techniques use different staining procedures in order to see this evolution. Staining of adult type is the one which is obtained when myelination in a part of the nervous system attains the final features of its evolution. Over many years in a person's life, myelination of different parts of the nervous system is progressively reaching the adult features; and during all that time, stain characteristics change: Some parts of the central nervous system are already myelinated in newborn babies, other parts during infancy and childhood, and so on.

Also, laterality is much more developed; and the child is able to stand in tandem position (the toe-heel position, or Mann's test), and then can develop the ability to stand on one foot.

We believe that cerebral hemispheric dominance is a different concept than body laterality. Cerebral hemispheric dominance refers to the achievement of symbolic possibilities on one side of the brain. Body laterality refers chiefly to motor activity abilities and secondarily to sensory predominance: In general, there is more strength, dexterity, skill, eumetria, etc., on one side of the body than on the other. These abilities on one side of the body belong to different levels, and not only to the cortex itself: Various gray nuclei in the cerebrum, cerebellum, and brain-stem may take part in providing these different qualities on each side of the body. Meanwhile, the environment also acts, mainly in the externalization of handedness. Therefore, body laterality includes inputs of several levels acting together with inputs of peripheral receptors. In Chapter III we shall review the principal aspects of laterality and human learning. But, as a preface to that discussion, we should summarize the main neurological levels that control posture.

(13) NEUROLOGICAL LEVELS AND POSTURAL CONTROL

Since having accepted the works of Hughlings Jackson, the field of neurophysiology has become accustomed to admit the presence of low and high central levels of action. Although we can now recognize much more complex functional structures than those analyzed by Hughlings Jackson, the lower levels of action, as Hughlings Jackson described them, are useful in explaining motor activities.

Higher systemic functions involve different levels together. For instance, it is extremely difficult to organize a language test according to Hughlings Jackson's formulations. H. Schuell (in a lecture published after her death) reminded us that Dr. Joe R. Brown suggested to her the organization of a test for aphasics on levels comparable to Hughlings Jackson's formulations of levels of complexity of neural integration. "I wasn't very happy about this," she says, "but I allowed myself to be persuaded. It did not work very well. Patients were never inclined to stay on any level we could define. We abandoned the scheme a little later."[19] We must understand that neural levels of integration have much more to do with body, posture, tonus, etc., than with symbolic possibilities of language. *Lingua* depends essentially on environmental influences; and language (in our world) is predicated on *lingua*. Neural levels therefore cannot be really correlated with language as a result of the number of variables involved (many of which depend on the environment).

In a schematic way, in every motor activity we recognize a low, an intermediate, and a higher level of work. The low and intermediate levels allow maintenance of posture and tonus that, early in the child's life, permit motor activity and, later, facilitate any learning process that requires mental actions. If posture is not sufficiently maintained by those levels, the intervention of the higher level will be needed. When the higher levels are forced to enter into action in order to maintain posture, learning possibilities decrease: When the cerebral cortex is forcefully employed in maintaining posture, intentional coordinated motor activities or mental actions obviously decrease or fail. Learning processes, therefore, also decrease or fail altogether. It is evident that, in order to apply itself to proper human skills, the cerebral cortex "transfers" many of its initial motoric responsibilities to automatic levels.

Consequently, we must reason that, as intentional and coordinated motor activity allows the presence of learning processes, postural systems permit the development of motor activity. Thus, before facing motor activity, we must study the postural system.

Through vestibular-proprioceptive integration, the postural system begins its actions in the young child. Vestibular input and proprioception act together.[20] For this reason clinical information about infantile posture and equilibrium may be considered as information about vestibular-proprioceptive integration, and not merely functions of vestibular organs themselves. If it is true, however, that some other thing happens when we study vestibular organs or proprioception in a child or in an adult (where in general vestibular and proprioceptive inputs may act independently), we shall also see special postural conditions which include vestibular-proprioceptive reactions, which traditionally were assumed only for young children (for instance, certain tonic-neck reactions). But it is critical for us to accept that, in young children, not only is "language" quite different than in the adult (in young children *lingua* exists and language is developing), but also postural and vestibular-proprioceptive reactions are different (in young children, for instance, Meniere's disease doesn't exist). Obviously, laterality and hemispheric dominance are also different, as we shall see in Chapter III.

In order to summarize these notions, we should say that postural control in humans is produced in a schematic way through a lower level (spine), an intermediate level (brain stem and cerebellum), and a higher level (cerebrum). There are many afferent and efferent pathways (or "circuits") which take part in producing posture, equilibrium, motor activities, and learning.

NOTES

1. F. de Saussure [C. Bally and A. Sechehaye (eds.), 1915], *Cours de Linguistique Generale* (5e Reed) (Paris: Payot, 1955).

2. J. B. de Quirós, "La Comprension de la Palabra Hablada," *Fonoaudiologica* 8:2 (1962): 139-158; J. B. de Quirós, *Terapias de Conexion en los Relardos Mentales Severos* (Buenos Aires: CEMIFA, 1975).

3. R. Held, "Plasticity in Sensory Motor Systems," *Scientific American* 213:5 (1965): 84; M. L. J. Abercrombie, "Some Notes on Spatial Disability: Movement, Intelligence Quotient and Attentiveness," *Developmental Medicine and Child Neurology* 10 (1968): 206-213; H. Cashdan, "The Role of Movement in Language Learning," in P. H. Wolff and R. MacKeith, *Planning for Better Learning,* Clinics in Developmental Medicine 33 (London: Spastics International Medical Publications, 1969): 37-42; R. Held and J. A. Bauer, "Development of Sensorially-Guided Reaching in Infant Monkeys," *Brain Research* 71 (1974): 265.

4. J. B. de Quirós, "Exclusion in Learning-Disabled Children" (keynote address, presented before the Tenth International Conference of the Association for Children with Learning Disabilities; reproduced by the learning disabilities program staff, Center for Effecting Educational Change, Fairfax County Public Schools, March, 1973); J. B. de Quirós, "Basis for Neurological Examination in Children with Language Disorders," *Folia Phoniatrica* [Basel] 28 (1976): 282.

5. J. Piaget, "Perception, Motricite et Intelligence," *Enfance* 2 (1956): 9-14.

6. J. Piaget, *Biologie et Connaissance, Essai sur les Relations entre les Regulations Organiques et les Processus Cognitifs* (Paris: Ed. Gallimard, 1967).

7. A. Rey, *Psychologie Clinique et Neurologie* (Neuchatel, Switzerland: Delachaux and Niestle, 1969).

8. J. Piaget, "Les Praxies chez l'Enfant," *Revue Neurologique* 102 (1960): 551-565.

9. B. F. Skinner, *Verbal Behavior* (New York: Appleton-Century-Crofts, 1957); B. F. Skinner, "Operant Behavior," in W. K. Honig (ed.), *Operant Behavior: Areas of Research and Application* (New York: Appleton-Century-Crofts, 1966); B. F. Skinner, *Contingencies of Reinforcements: A Theoretical Analysis* (New York: Appleton-Century-Crofts, 1969); G. Sleigh, "A Study of Some Symbolic Processes in Young Children," *British Journal of Disorders of Communication* 7 (1972): 163-175; A. R. Luria, "Meta-Principles in Luria's Neuropsychology," *Skolepsychology* [Copenhagen] 8 (1971): 407; A. R. Luria, *The Role of Speech in the Regulation of, Normal and Abnormal Behavior* (London: Pergamon Press, 1961); A. R. Luria, *Higher Cortical Functions in Man* (London: Tavistock Publications, 1966); A. L. Christensen, *Luria's Neuropsychological Investigation Manual* (Copenhagen: Munksgaard, 1975).

10. N. M. Amosov, *La Modelacion del Pensamiento y de la Psique* (A. Vidal Roget, trans.) (Montevideo: Ediciones Pueblos Unidos, 1967); N. Bernstein, *The Co-ordination and Regulation of Movements* (Oxford: Pergamon Press, 1967); V. N. Pushkin, *Heuristica a Ciencia do Pensamento Criador* (V. Neverova, trans.) (Rio de Janeiro: Zahar Editores, 1967).

11. N. Chomsky, "Review of Skinner's Verbal Behavior," *Language* 35 (1959): 26-58; N. Chomsky, *Aspects of the Theory of Syntax* (Cambridge: M.I.T. Press, 1965); N. Chomsky, "The Formal Nature of Language," in E. H. Lenneberg, *Biological Foundations of Language* (New York: John Wiley and Sons, 1967); N. Chomsky, *El Lenguaje y el Entendimiento* (J. Ferrate, trans.) (Barcelona: Editorial Seix Barral, 1971).

12. H. Wallon, *Les Origines du Caractere chez l'Enfant* (Paris: Presses Universitaires de France, 1949).

13. H. Head, *Aphasia and Kindred Disorders* (1926; 2nd ed. [reprint], Cambridge, England: Cambridge University Press, 1963).

14. L. Bender and A. A. Silver, "Body Image Problems of the Brain-Damaged Child," in L. Bender *et al.*, *Psychopathology of Children with Organic Brain Disorders* (Springfield, Illinois: Charles C. Thomas, 1956): 97-113.

15. P. Schilder, *Image and Appearance of the Human Body* (New York: International University Press, 1951).

16. Bender and Silver, *op. cit.*

17. *Ibid.*

18. M. Frostig, *Movement Education: Theory and Practice* (Chicago: Follet Educational Corporation, 1970).

19. H. Schuell, *Aphasia Theory and Therapy: Selected Lectures and Papers* (Baltimore: University Park Press, 1974).

20. J. B. de Quirós, "Vestibular-proprioceptive Integration: Its Influence on Learning and Speech in Children," in *Proceedings of the Tenth International Congress of Psychology* (April 3-7, 1966, Lima, Peru; Mexico; Trillas, 1967): 194-202; J. B. de Quirós, "Disturbances in the Language of a Child: The Child Who Does Not Speak," *Clinical Proceedings of the Children's Hospital* [Washington, D.C.] 25:7 (1969): 192-205.

NEUROPSYCHOLOGICAL FUNDAMENTALS

CHAPTER III

Laterality and Human Learning

(14) HUMAN LATERALITY

There are many differences between animals and humans; but among the most prominent ones are those referred to as "symbolization abilities" (mainly language) and those referred to as "posture" (mainly laterality). In regard to laterality, there is quite a controversy regarding whether or not some apes are able to develop one side of the body more than the other. It is true, nevertheless, that animals in general do not reveal a clear predominance of one side of the body over the other. Certainly, we have seen some animals with greater development on one side of the body than on the other; but this was always the result of abnormal causes that produced atrophy or handicaps on the other side. These things also apply to human beings, but these conditions can be recognized as accidental laterality: When a person loses the principal functions of an arm or a hand, the other one acquires many of those functions. When we examine laterality in a patient, therefore, it is critical that we know if there were an abnormality or pathology which influenced the use of one or the other side of the body.

Before going further, we should identify what "laterality" means. In general, laterality refers to motoric prevalences and preferences of one side of the body. This motoric lateralization often coincides with sensory predominance of the same side and symbolic possibilities of the opposite cerebral hemisphere. It is thus possible to accept the idea that laterality not only manifests itself mainly through motor activity, but also that it exists through sensory and sensitive inputs and through functional differentiation of both halves of the brain. In humans, "equivalent unilateral lesions do not produce equivalent effects."[1]

Motoric abilities are the principal factors in establishing body laterality. These factors are apparently "connected" with (1) sensory inputs, (2) vestibular-proprioceptive inputs, and (3) cerebral hemispheric specialization. It might be worthwhile, however, to emphasize a commonly accepted statement: Handedness is not directly related to the opposite dominant hemisphere. As R. D. Currier wrote some years ago for students of medicine, "It is important to know the handedness of the patient, although if this cannot be ascertained, it is usually safe to assume that the left cerebral hemisphere is dominant."[2]

Probably one of the most outstanding contributions in regard to constancy of left hemisphere as the dominant one in right- or left-handedness, was the book written by W. Penfield and L. Roberts in 1959.[3] After them many other authors performed important studies and published works on the same subject.

The external manifestations of motor activities refer to conditions of power, accuracy, precision, speed, coordination, and directionality of movements. Tonus and distance are also included in this list. "Distance" is used in medical terminology to mean the length existing between two or more successive movements, or between two places on the body, or between an object and the body. If we review all these components of motor laterality, we can see that different levels of the central nervous system are involved in producing a prevalence and/or preference of one hand or one side of the body: cerebral cortex, striatum, basal ganglia, cerebellum, reticular system, vestibular organs, etc. *Potential* should not be confused with *preference:* Potential depends on neuromuscular conditions; preference depends on psycho-socio-cultural influences. For example, a person is born with left-hand potential; but, because of the pressure society exerts on the individual to become lateralized to the right (many things in daily living favor use of the right side: using scissors, writing at a student desk, etc.), he prefers for personal reasons to use the right hand in order to perform most activities. This person, therefore, uses the right hand in such a way that later he could be classified as having a "mixed" or "crossed" laterality.

As we have shown, it is indispensable for us to differentiate "cerebral dominance" and "body laterality." Cerebral dominance is related to the development of symbolic abilities in one or another hemisphere; body laterality is related to potential or preference of motoric, sensory, and sensitive functions in one or another side of the body. According to Currier, "About 98 percent of all people, including at least half of those who are left-handed, have left-hemisphere dominance."[5] Consequently, only some few cases are left handed with right cerebral dominance: Most left-handed people also have left cerebral dominance. These latter cases should be discussed. According to N. Geschwind, in the left-handed person with left-cerebral dominance, some activities (such as writing) begin on the left hemisphere with the formulation of the linguistic message.[6] This message is then transmitted to the right hemisphere where the motor act of writing primarily takes place. When the patient writes with the left hand, only one cross through the corpus callosum is needed. But if he writes with his right hand, information for motor action must be retransmitted through the corpus callosum toward the left side. Geschwind's ideas are extremely useful in gaining an understanding of some phenomena related to symbolic cerebral dominance and laterality of motor activities.

Another point that we should discuss concerns itself with motor activity of one or both sides of the body and the action of only one of the cerebral hemispheres. In connection with this, M. Bridge Denckla states (quoting Wyke, and Bowen *et al.*) that "speed of repetitive finger movements also appears to be left-hemisphere dependent, as studies of brain-injured adults indicate that bilateral slowing results from left-hemisphere damage, whereas contralateral slowing alone results from right-hemisphere damage."[8] According to Bridge Denckla, in "young, right-preferring children, not only the establishment of right-side superiority but also the rapid improvement of left-sided skill must be regarded as a feature of cerebral maturation."[9] Speaking about the rapidity of finger movements, the author continues: "Cerebral dominance in motor performance appears to be manifested in the left (non-preferred) side (of the body) coming under the control of the dominant hemisphere."[10] On the other hand, and also according to Bridge Denckla, in young, right-preferring children, improvement of the left-hand skills would depend on the transfer of motor learning from right to left, thus implying "that some neurophysiological substrate which develop with age makes such transfer possible."

Let us once more recall the fact that, in humans, the dominant hemisphere for language (symbolic hemisphere) is not always the hemisphere for body laterality.

(15) OUR RIGHT-SIDED WORLD

Many people do not realize that they are living in a traditionally right-sided world. In all the different races, the different cultures, and the different countries, humans use the right hand (in a vast majority of individuals) in order to do not only the most skilled, accurate, or stronger movements, but also the most "noble" and "good" motor actions.

In Old English the right hand was called the "strong" hand. "Strong" qualified one of its characteristics. In English the term "right" is very clear and means, as in many other languages, "correct" or "good." In Spanish, German, French, Slavic, etc., the same happens. In Spanish *"mano derecha"* or *"diestra"* is used. Certainly these terms come from the Latin *"directa"* and *"dextra,"* that means "right," and "decent or convenient."

An opposite meaning is used for the left hand (also called the "sinister hand" in English). In Latin (or Italian) the term *"sinistra"* is used. This corresponds to the Spanish *"siniestra,"* although *"izquierda"* is much more used through an euphemistic reaction against the meaning of "sinister" (threatening, evil, unfortunate). *"Izquierdo"* in Spanish comes from Basque *"escuerdi,"* which means "half of a hand." Therefore in Spanish (as in almost all modern languages) the rejective origin to designate the left hand still continues. In many languages the term to designate "left hand" originally meant "oblique," "twisted," "weak," or "bad," in opposition to "good" or "right."

In Sanskrit "right" is *"daks"* (i.e., being skilled, being capable, being useful). From *"daks"* comes *"daksina"* and *"daksinya"* (*"daksina"* evolved into the Latin *"dextera"*). *"Daksinakara"* means in Sanskrit "the one who acts with rightness, with loyalty."

Our culture is Indo-European; and our languages, which mainly come from Latin and Greek, have a great ancestor in Sanskrit. For this reason we find an interest in old Indian cultures. Hinduism, Buddhism, and other Indian religions and beliefs use signs and symbols in order to mean happiness, comfort: For instance, this was the meaning of the swastika cross that was much later adopted by Adolph Hitler. It is worth remembering that in the swastika cross the "wings" deviate toward the right side. But the above mentioned religions also use another cross with wings deviated toward the left side, which is called "sawastika." This sawastika cross symbolizes unhappiness and represents Kali, the death goddess. As can be seen, confusion between "swastika" and "sawastika" can occur very easily in lateral disturbances.

Many external manifestations of our present civilization are perhaps connected with ancient beliefs of our ancestors. Why is that, in America, almost everyone eats with the right hand exclusively, when in Europe most people eat with both hands? In the old Indo-European culture, people ate only with the fingers of the right hand, hanging the left hand between both legs. In America people put the left hand underneath the table on the lap. In Europe, both hands are on the table, since both hands are used.

Many things in our world continuously remind us of the dominion of the right hand: In restaurants the knife is placed on the right side of the table setting; at the front of houses the same thing often occurs with the doorbells; in many chairs for students the "table" is also included on the right side; the "place of honor" is to the right of the most important personage (president's right, director's right, etc.).

Several occidental rules of etiquette and diplomacy are strictly related to such a principle: a guest's reception, official or political ceremonies, etc.

Teachers or parents frequently do not realize the existence of a right-sided world that tends to impose use of the right hand on almost all the children.

All human beings possess factors of right-handedness and left-handedness, but with maturity in almost all the cases there is found a definite preponderance of right-handedness. The majority of children classified as ambidextrous at three years of age, come to be considered right handed at school age: Probably some of these children have been potentially left handed; but environmental influences impose the use of the right hand, at least in various basic activities.

(16) THE ONTOGENY AND PHYLOGENY OF HUMAN LATERALITY

It is well known that *ontogeny* is the complete developmental history of the individual organism, and that *phylogeny* is the complete developmental history of a race or group of animals.[12]

There are different theories explaining the development of cerebral dominance and body laterality in infancy and childhood. Probably none of these theories can—by itself—explain satisfactorily this sort of complex phenomena. Let us review some facts on this topic. In newborn babies both hemispheres are apparently genetically equipotential. But we should bear in mind that, during the period covering the end of the first year of postnatal life and the beginning of the second year, some clear manifestations of speech (conditioned vocabulary) and hand potential appear together. Nevertheless, clear differences between both sides of the body cannot be clearly established, although A. Gesell considered the existence of normal tonic-neck reflexes at that age in supine position as one of the determining factors in body laterality.[13]

Unilateral hemispheric damage in infancy is followed by the "transfer" of speech possibility to the other hemisphere, as we discussed it with J. de Ajuriaguerra in France during the 1950s. When damage is bilateral, no acquisition of speech or language (according to the localization of the lesion) can take place for years: In regard to the length, depth, and location of damages at both cerebral sides, in some cases the language acquisition facility can rebuild itself, however slowly. Only some conditioned words (which are specifically verbal) and a very small amount of symbolic communication (gestural and verbal expressions) can be acquired; this situation finally results in mental retardation.

Body laterality also develops during infancy and early childhood, and there is a certain developmental coincidence between the potential of handedness by one side, and the establishment of hemispheric dominance (i.e., symbolic possibilities and the leadership [or deictic] activity of the dominant cerebral hemisphere) by the other.

It seems reasonable to suppose that symbolic hierarchy is reached by the left cerebral hemisphere between the fifth and sixth years of age. We agree with H. Hécaen and R. Angelergues when they acknowledge child's symbolic ability forming sometime about the fifth year of life, and also with Luria when he describes a leadership (deictic) function of speech after the intense development that usually happens during the third and the fourth years of life.[14]

We should remember that ponto-cerebellar myelination obtains a staining of adult type during the fourth postnatal year, according to research conducted at Harvard Medical School.[15] Ponto-cerebellar myelination allows smooth coordination of skilled movements. As was discussed earlier, this kind of action strongly participates as one of the factors determining handedness. The anterior speech area, therefore, is not the only region that develops more or less simultaneously with handedness; various levels in the central nervous system develop in conjunction with hand potential.

We feel, however, that aphasia of the adult type can be observed after five to six years of age; also, we concur that probably the "final lateralization ... is reached only after full acquisition of language, at the age of about ten. Temporal speech area develops later than anterior speech area and in closer correlation with acoustic and possibly cognitive and conceptual aspects of language. It is terminated at the age of ten, together with the stabilization of word memory."[16]

If we compare humans with other animals, it seems that no other species has either hemispheric dominance or body laterality. The question is this: Who is more happy, humans with hemispheric dominance or animals without it? It appears that hemispheric dominance and body laterality constitute a rare "privilege" of the human race. As O. L. Zangwill states, "The effects in animals of lesions of the hemisphere, contralateral to the preferred forepaw are, so far as is known, no different from those of lesions of ipsilateral hemisphere. It appears then that what in man we call *cerebral dominance* is an evolutionary development peculiar to the human species."[17]

A main issue before us is the genetic determination of laterality. Freud was perhaps the first to support the theory that laterality was genetically determined; but even now, controversies regarding this abound.[18] Discussion on the same subject has included not only the participation of doctors, physiologists, and psychologists, but also anthropologists and paleontologists. According to R. A. Dart and D. Craig, laterality was already established in *australopithecus* in South Africa approximately one million years ago.[19] These authors studied the vascular irrigation of the inner wall of the skulls, supposing that the better irrigation belongs to the dominant hemisphere. Also, they studied some of the *australopithecus* habits: These primitive men ate a certain type of monkey (mandrill), which they killed by coming smoothly from behind and striking the monkey's head with a large bone they used as a weapon. Dart and his colleagues analyzed statistically the crushed side of the mandrills' skulls they found in the area, establishing a definite degree of laterality in the primitive human species. Dart's explanations about *australopithecus* allowed a tentative acceptance of Freud's theory on genetically determined laterality. The existence of laterality in the most primitive human being—for instance, the *zinjanthropus* (belonging to the *Paranthropus* group), who presently is considered to have lived about two million years ago—was recently assumed through different investigations. Body laterality, language, and intelligence are, nevertheless, extremely complex processes which depend not only upon eventual (i.e., not completely demonstrated) genetic determination but also, consistently, upon environmental influences.

Consequently, it seems that body laterality and hemispheric dominance, as well as language, are not genetically determined, despite the enthusiasm some authors have in supporting these ideas. We feel that body laterality, hemispheric dominance, and language are genetically *predetermined* in our species (i.e., the possibility of obtaining these capabilities does exist; but it takes time to obtain these specific human skills: Egyptians, Mayans, Hopi, and Chinese attained these possibilities, even though their cultures were geographically and temporally completely separated). This is a matter of fact which shows that in human beings laterality, symbolic hemisphere, and language can develop independently of the race and the culture.

These capabilities certainly required more time to develop in some human groups than in others. The acquisition of these capabilities now is very much related to the cultural development of the environment.

In summary, these capabilities appear only in human beings. They seem to appear as a result of the existence of genetic conditions in our species, although they seem to need relatively long periods of time to develop in different human groups. Nevertheless there are sufficient arguments for thinking that, in the first place, hereditary cause is admissible—probably in agreement with Mendel's laws. In this regard the early works of D. C. Rife are particularly important.[20] There seems to exist an undoubted genotypical factor, but the mechanism probably puts into play various genes.[21] The previously mentioned capabilities are easily acquired in well developed cultural environments, because social pressure and continuous environmental

NEUROPSYCHOLOGICAL FUNDAMENTALS

teaching facilitate the development of them. Right-handedness and left-handedness seem to proceed from different brain integrations (when damage does not exist).

(17) RIGHT AND LEFT: SOME DEVELOPMENTAL ASPECTS AND NOTIONS OF SPACE

As has already been established in Chapter II, Section 12, after the acquisition of body awareness, the child "divides" his body into two halves: He is able to perform skilled movements with one hand (the oppositional finger test) without imitative movements on the other hand. There, we emphasized that the "division" of the body into two halves takes place around the third year of age; and it is an external manifestation of the primary integration of the postural system. We pointed out also the fact that possibilities of acting independently with each side of the body indicate an essential step in the development of laterality.

Between four and six years of age, leadership (deictic) functions of language begin to command actions, and symbolization begins in the left cerebral hemisphere.

We might note here that Binet's test [*Stanford-Binet Tests of Intelligence*] pinpoints six years of age as the time at which a child can indicate his left hand and his right ear. In schools in Argentina, we find, it is evident that the majority of the children recognize their left and right around seven years of age.[22] According to J. Piaget, the acquisition of the notions of left and right, in the sense of relative notions, goes on through three stages corresponding to three "desubjectivations" (that is, to three progressive socializations of thought): the first stage (five to eight years), in the course of which left and right are only considered from the child's own point of view; the second stage (eight to eleven years), when they are also considered from the point of view of others and of the questioner; and the third stage (eleven to twelve years), which marks the time which left and right are considered increasingly from the point of view of things themselves.[23] Piaget faced the child and presented a coin and a pencil, and asked him where the coin was. A child seven years old was able to say that the coin was "to the left," speaking in absolute terms and referring explicitly or implicitly to the position of his own body. Given the same situation, an adult was able to say that the coin was "to the left of the pencil." According to Piaget, the different kinds of answers are not a question of verbal shades of meaning: They have essential importance from a logical point of view. Before eleven years of age the child cannot accomplish the test in which, facing three objects in a line, he must answer if one of them is to the left or right of each one of the others.

Actually, between the ages of six and seven years, the child's sense of right and left appears. As has already been mentioned, there is a sort of coincidence between symbolic cerebral dominance (formulated language) and the internal notion of right and left. Between seven and nine years of age, the child can recognize right and left not only in himself, but also in a person facing him, passing over the mirror projection of his laterality as he used to do. Finally, understanding of right and left in objects is reached at about eleven years of age.

Sometimes we read explanations or definitions of right and left which incorporate the concept of direction-in-space; that is, "up and down," or "in front of and behind." These notions are in reality quite different. On the one hand, space is connected to perceptual inputs (visual, tactile, and on some occasions, auditory and olfactory). On the other hand, right and left are established upon the continuity of body schema and body awareness, and after the integration of the postural system and the appearance of corporal potentiality. Right and left are therefore closely related to the inner information of the body, the development of the central nervous system, and the integration of neuromuscular, sensory, and somesthetic inputs.

Before explaining the importance of different inputs in the production of right and left, it would be useful to clarify the meaning of "somesthesis," "kinesthesis," "proprioception," and "haptic."

(18) SOMESTHESIS, KINESTHESIS, PROPRIOCEPTION, AND HAPTIC NOTIONS IN LATERALITY

According to W. L. Jenkins somesthesis refers to cutaneous, subcutaneous, or deep sensitivites, kinesthesis, and internal or organic sensitivities.[24] It might be important here to differentiate somesthesis clearly from kinesthesis and proprioception.

Kinesthesis belongs to somesthesis, but mainly in the sense of position and movement. It is the fundamental sensitivity for human beings. Only with kinesthesis can a person adopt specific postures and positions of the species, and can control his head in order to learn. The person learns when he is able to maintain an erect position or a sitting position, or when he can perform skilled motor activities, including talking (as phonoarticulatory motor coordination). In general, kinesthesis is sensitivity produced by muscular movements. Specifically, kinesthesis means sensitivity provided by proprioceptors. The term "proprioceptor" was created by C. S. Sherrington; and it refers to receptors placed in muscles, tendons, and joints (muscles spindles, Golgi tendon endings, Pacinian corpuscles being the most important), although Sherrington considered vestibular organs also as proprioceptors.[25] The difference between kinesthesis and proprioception is the presence—or absence—of motor activity. According to Sherrington, the term "proprioceptor" includes every nervous or sensory organ that provides information about body positions or movements. In a practical vein, one might say that proprioception refers more to body positions, while kinesthesis is more related to body movements.

Proprioception and kinesthesis are quite different from body schema, because the former is related to sensitivity, to information from the body; the latter, body schema (with Head's approach), is more connected with cortical reception, registration, and formation of traces (or engrams) at the cortical levels.

From a clinical point of view, it is important to separate the movements made in order to maintain dynamic equilibrium from the movements made with intentional or voluntary purposes. These two types of movements provide two different sorts of information. In the first situation (dynamic equilibrium), kinesthesis is acting much more as proprioception than as kinesthesis itself. Consequently, kinesthesis acts together with vestibular and visual inputs on one side, and according to gravitational forces on the other

NEUROPSYCHOLOGICAL FUNDAMENTALS

side, in producing the necessary postures that equilibrium needs at any moment during movement.

It is our belief that kinesthesis accomplished a quite different role in intentional or voluntary coordinated motor activities. Let us explain the essential differences that we can see in these two situations:

1. In dynamic equilibrium situations, the action of kinesthesis (plus vestibular and visual inputs) is produced against gravity; that is, the first impulse is kinesthetic (and vestibular and visual) and the result is postural equilibrium at any moment of such a dynamic situation.

2. In intentional or voluntary movements, the first impulse is given by motor activity itself, and the information to the central nervous system about such movements is given by kinesthesis.

Kinesthesis, therefore, is a structure that is able to participate actively in dynamic equilibrium and also is an internal-feedback (or retroactive) system. A question consequently emerges, whether one may use the same term in order to designate two probably different anatomical-functional structures. Naturally, this could be a controversial question; but we do not hesitate to consider that clinical examination procedures must be decidedly different for both situations: Kinesthesis can predominate on one side of the body in dynamic balance tests, and at the same time can predominate on the other side in intentional or voluntary coordinated movements. Kinesthetic inputs which are important for body laterality are those which refer to voluntary coordinated movements.

In recent years the term "haptic" has been introduced in order to involve simultaneously kinesthetic and skin sensitivity (cutaneous and subcutaneous inputs). The reason given for use of the term "haptic" instead of "kinesthetic and tactile" was a very practical one: It is impossible to make a movement without receiving at the same time tactual information. Also, it is very difficult to obtain only responses from the skin itself without performing any movement. For instance, when we put a common object on the palm of a blindfolded adult's hand, only some features are recognized (cold, warm, great, small, hard, soft); if we flex passively the person's fingers, he is still not able to recognize the object, but he can add other characteristics (for instance: "It seems to be a box . . . but I don't know what kind. . . ."). If we leave the person free to move his fingers, he can recognize the nature and the name of the object (i.e., stereognosis is achieved: "It's a matchbox."). This much is evident: The tactile sense is not useful without active movement. Sherrington stated that "tactile" is a tactile-muscle-labyrinthine relationship.[26]

Next, we shall discuss the importance of kinesthesis in some aspects of laterality. It is critical that we differentiate kinesthesis for movement and kinesthesis for balance. The latter has only a secondary influence on laterality; but kinesthesis for voluntary skilled movements is extremely important for learning purposes; and it strongly contributes to body lateralization.

(19) KINETIC OUTPUTS VERSUS KINESTHETIC INPUTS. DIFFERENT TYPES OF LATERALITY

All the terms we have mentioned are needed to explain different phenomena that contribute to "right" and "left." When we say that motor conditions that produce laterality determine the extent of power, accuracy, dexterity, and so on, on one side of the body, this is not related only to the "order" starting from the cerebral cortex and modified through different levels of the central nervous system; it is also the result of information coming from the same side as kinesthetic (or haptic) inputs. The "order" coming from the cerebral cortex is kinetic output. The information going from the hand and other parts of the body is a haptic input. Both are essential in the process of laterality; sensory inputs and cortical regulations of these paths of information are very important in determining lateralization.

Once again, we should point out the differences between lateral *prevalence* and lateral *preference*. It has been shown that prevalence is possibly genetically determined; but, as a result of several environmental, psychological, social, and cultural factors, preference means that certain skills are to be performed by one or the other side of the body.

Clinical tests of laterality must be carefully considered, since they frequently give data not only about side-prevalence but also about side-preference. Test items that could in some way escape environmental bias were suggested by several authors who wanted to avoid the mistakes inherent in almost all traditional motor tests. For instance, R. Zazzo described 15 items, including (for example) catching one hand with the other, putting an elbow on the opposite palm, shuffling and dealing playing cards, and so on.[27] Nevertheless, test items of this type are *always* influenced by environment; thus, it is frequent that results of "crossed laterality" are obtained through their use.

What happens during balance tests when kinetic outputs are prevalent on one side of the body and kinesthesic inputs are predominant on the other side? How can a person be right sided for his hand, and left sided for his foot and his eye? How can a person be ambilateral and ambidextrous? Is there any difference between ambilaterality and mixed or crossed laterality?

Many researchers have noted that several syndromes producing learning disabilities and communication disorders show a great proportion of left-handedness, ambilaterality, or other lateral conflicts. This could be the case in regard to lateral preference; but it is doubtful that this could statistically be found in regard to lateral potential. From the point of view of lateral potential, it seems to be that great differences do not exist between control groups and groups having these disturbances.[28] Let us review the questions that were formulated earlier.

When kinetic outputs are predominant on one side of the body and kinesthetic inputs are predominant on the other side, during balance tests, we are facing lateral dissociation. This fact is connected with vestibular-proprioceptive dissociation; and it disturbs balance and posture, thus producing problems in voluntary coordinated motor activities. As we have said, the latter constitute the bases of human learning abilities. From a clinical point of view, kinesthetic or proprioceptive inputs increment during balance tests, and kinesthetic or proprioceptive inputs increment during a voluntary movement, are quite different. The kinesthetic increment for voluntary coordinated motor activities has a closely defined interrelationship with tonus, skilled functions, and—therefore—laterality. Kinesthetic increment in balance tests has nothing to do *directly* with body laterality; and it is important to bear in mind that balance tests produce reflex reactions. In reflex reactions, kinetic (or motor) response does not obey voluntary high-level control. To the contrary, in such reactions, only low and intermediate levels of the central nervous system participate.

In regard to mixed or crossed laterality (right-handedness, and left-footness and eyedness; or vice versa; or still other combinations), we realize that many variables are acting together: Potential and preferences influence the final result. The most common combination is the earlier-mentioned right-handedness (preference) with left lateral potential. Probably the more acceptable explanation is to admit a left laterality influenced by psycho-socio-cultural environment pressures. It is important to realize that in these cases there are not "conflicting" situations, because the right hand for many social activities is only determined by the spontaneous impact of the environment—"our right-sided world." Many times this kind of laterality is confused with forced or imposed change of handedness, but it is really a typical type of crossed or mixed laterality. Crossed or mixed laterality consists in the use of the nonprevalent hand for almost all actions that need a dominant hand.

Mixed laterality emerges when a stress situation develops by imposition of the nonpotential hand (against the potential one) in order to perform skilled and coordinated or brute-strength movements. When the selection of the right hand depends on family, teachers, or other pressures, the result is called a forced or imposed change of handedness. Of course, this is usually considered to be responsible for several communication disorders and learning disabilities. It is our opinion, supported by many observations, that imposition of other-hand preference will not determine negative results— *if* the opposition against the potential hand is cautiously made; that is, according to psychological foundations and personal characteristics. It seems to us that the question of forced handedness and negative results was greatly exaggerated by many authors during the 1950s; however, we agree that compulsion in the change of handedness can elicit psychological disturbances and therefore negatively influence communication and learning abilities.

As strange as it may seem, the imposed change of handedness is not only directed against left-handedness, but sometimes against right-handedness too. As early as 1962 we had already discovered that among school children there was a group that was definitely right handed; but, resulting from the use of poorly designed tests, teachers had thought they were left handed, thus forcing them to write with their left hand—opposing their natural right-hand potential![29]

Ambilaterality or ambidexterity consist mainly in the use of one or the other hand for all the actions that require a dominant hand. It may be said that crossed laterality implies use of a preferred hand; ambilaterality implies indistinct use of both the potential and preferred hand.

But what determines that an individual decides to modify prevalence of one hand by preference for the other?

If characteristic factors of the predominance of one hand are reviewed, it can be seen that, among those factors, are outputs from the cerebral cortex, which receive: (1) modifications at the level of subcortical gray nuclei and basal ganglia; (2) transformations of different levels of the brain stem and cerebellum; and finally (3) changes in the skeletal muscles. The latter are due to tonic and vestibular reflexes which culminate in kinesthetic and haptic information. These pieces of afferent information reach higher cortical levels, coming from specific muscles, tendons, and joint endings, as well as from other visual information which also provides important data for accomplishment of movement. Consequently, possibilities for ambilaterality depend not only on environmental factors, but also on the individual's own manual interests which are directed to obtain more skills in one, or the other, or both hands, in accordance with his own and predetermined goals.

The most important thing will always be to establish which is the body's lateral preference. The second most important thing is to determine the extent to which the misuse of the lateral potential hand is able to generate neuropsychological conflicts which produce human communication disorders and learning disabilities.

(20) PERCEPTUAL MODALITY AND LATERALITY

Each individual seems to have a particular optimum sensory and perceptual channel (i.e., auditory, visual, tactile, or kinesthetic) for learning purposes. In the last century J. M. Charcot made the clinical observation that, in order to learn, individuals generally had a preferred mode by which one acquired sensory information; and he thus categorized people as "audile," "visile," or "tactile."[30]

According to J. Wepman, a perceptual modality is each one of the "channels" or "pathways" used to learn and to receive information.[31] At the same time, studies on biotypological preferences of perceptual modalities for learning purposes were being carried out in the U.S.S.R.[32] Russian authors considered that the domination of perceptual modalities follows a sequential evolution in each individual and, consequently, in learning development. The first phase consists of motor activity predominance; the second one is a perceptual predominance; and the third one is determined by verbal (or language) dominance (deictic or leadership function of language).[33]

At the beginning of the 1970s, in German-speaking areas the perceptual modality theory of F. Affolter appeared, which theory postulated a close interrelationship in the development of different perceptual modalities.[34] Affolter pointed out the importance in distinguishing at least three developmental phases:

1. The phase of specific modality
2. The phase of intermodality
3. The serial phase.

The specific modality phase consists of learning of the existence of different stimuli, developing of attention span for such stimuli, and finally, being able to shut out or ignore some stimuli. This phase ends when the individual develops the ability to pursue (i.e., to search and to follow up) the stimulus through a perceptual modality. For instance, in hearing, the first reaction is alertness; the second one is hearing; and the third is audition. The same occurs with the other sensory organs.

The intermodality phase consists of the interchange and integration of the information provided by different sensory fields. For instance, at six months of age, a normal infant turns towards a source of sound. That means that the infant has learned previously that, when sound exists, there is always something to see. After seeing it, he wants to grasp the object. This is a sort of chain already well established by Sherrington: Development is much more related to an progressively intensive integration among the different sensory inputs, than to an increasing number of sensory organs.[35]

The serial phase consists of the connection that the child establishes between the different isolated stimuli that he previously received. Because of this integration, the child can anticipate some facts. If the child knows that always when he receives A, this is followed by B, C, etc., he can expect that this A-B-C sequence might be produced.

Affolter's ideas are valuable in interpreting abnormalities in perceptual modalities; but we are here interested much more in body laterality. We should remember that one of the principal intentional coordinated motor activities is produced early through the possibility of fixation, accommodation, convergence, and tracking movements of the eyes (in regard to objects). We must realize that all perceptual modalities are very much connected to laterality. In the eyes also there is a correlation between visual movements and neck-head movements. All perceptual modalities, sequence modalities, and series of movements originated by perceptual modalities are essential in the final establishment of laterality; therefore, perceptual modality in infant development is extremely important, and probably is the very beginning of sensory predominance.

At this writing, nobody can satisfactorily explain how it is possible to mix two different images (information coming from two eyes with different fields) into a single image, and also how we reverse the final image at the level of the occipital cortex. Nevertheless, sensory laterality (in this case, eye predominance) can help us to understand the fusion of two images and—perhaps—the acceptance of a reversed right world. Tests could also emphasize these things.

As a matter of fact, the eye, the ear, and the vestibular organs are predominant on one side of the body (commonly, the right side). In general, there are no arguments against the eye and/or ear lateral predominance; but vestibular laterality is never mentioned. This is not the place to explain the different tests that can help us in recognizing sensory, motor, or body laterality; but we shall point out prima facie that vestibular tests related to equilibrium, or balance, established on changing-consistency boards, can give us a large volume of useful data. Vestibular organs are related chiefly to equilibrium; and the reactions that we can obtain through caloric tests area mainly connected with oculomotor pathways, more than postural balance.

The various sensory organs establish a perceptual modality that generally is right sided. When perceptual modalities conflict so that some sensory inputs have right predominance and others have left predominance, different disturbances related to the functions of those perceptual modalities appear. The same occurs with vestibular organs. For instance, when vestibular organs in a static position show a predominance to the right side, but in a dynamic situation show a predominance to the left side, it is reasonable to think that in the static situation the modality was dominated by proprioceptive inputs, while in the dynamic situation vestibular inputs predominate. This vestibular-proprioceptive dissociation will produce an equilibrium disorder, which will affect the acquisition and development of notions of space, disorientation in laterality, troubles in attention span, and finally and consequently, failure in learning abilities.

How many learning-disabled persons do we know who have this kind of disorder?

NOTES

1. O. L. Zangwill, "Dyslexia in Relation to Cerebral Dominance," in J. Money (ed.), *Reading Disability: Progress and Research Needs in Dyslexia* (Baltimore: The Johns Hopkins University Press, 1962): 103-114.

2. R. D. Currier, "Nervous System," in R. D. Judge and G. D. Zuidema (eds.), *Physical Diagnosis: A Physiologic Approach to Clinical Examination* (Boston: Little, Brown & Co., 1968): 397-429.

3. W. Penfield and L. Roberts, *Speech and Brain Mechanisms* (New Jersey: Princeton University Press, 1959).

4. Zangwill, *op. cit.*; H. Hecaen and J. de Ajuriaguerra, *Les Gauchers* (Paris: Presses Universitaires de France, 1963); M. Sǒvak, *Pedagogishe Probleme der Lateralitat* (Berlin: Veb Verlag Volk und Gesundheit, 1968); R. Kourilsky and P. Grapin (eds.), *Main Droite et Main Gauche—Norme et Lateralite* (Paris: Presses Universitaires de France, 1969).

5. Currier, *op. cit.*

6. N. Geschwind, "Biologia y Lenguaje Grafico" (Segundo Congreso Panamericano de Audicion y Lenguaje; Lima, Peru, October 21-24, 1973).

7. L. E. Travis, *Speech Pathology* (New York: Appleton, 1931); L. E. Travis (ed.), *Handbook of Speech Pathology* (London: Peter Owen Ltd., 1950).

8. M. Bridge Denckla, Development in Speed Repetitive and Successive Finger Movements in Normal Children. *Developmental Medicine Child Neurology* 15:5 (1973): 635-645; M. Wyke, "The Effect of Brain Lesions on the Performance of an Arm-Hand Precision Task," *Neuropsychologie* 6 (1968): 125; F. P. Bowen, M. M. Hoehn, and M. Yahr, "Cerebral Dominance in Relation to Tracking and Tapping Performance in Patients with Parkinsonism," *Neurology* 22 (1972): 32.

9. M. Bridge Denckla, *op. cit.*

10. *Ibid.*

11. *Ibid.*

12. *Dorland's Medical Dictionary* (23rd ed.) (Philadelphia: W. B. Saunders Co., 1957).

13. A. Gesell, "The Tonic Neck Reflex in the Human Infant," *Journal of Pediatrics* 13 (1938): 455; A. Gesell et al., *The First Five Years of Life* (New York: Harper & Bros., 1940).

14. H. Hecaen and R. Angelergues, *Pathologie du Langage* (Paris: Presses Universitaires de France, 1965); A. R. Luria and F. Ia. Yudovich, *Speech and Development of Mental Processes in Children* (Staples Press, trans.) (Harmondsworth, Middlessex, England: Penguin Books Ltd., 1959); A. R. Luria et al., *Lenguaje y Psiquiatria* (J. M. Arancibia, trans.) (Madrid: Editorial Fundamentos, 1973).

15. P. I. Yakovlev and A. R. Lecours, "The Myelogenetic Cycles of Regional Maturation of the Brain," in A. Minkowski (ed.), *Regional Development of the Brain in Early Life* (Oxford: Blackwell Scientific Publications, 1967).

16. E. Bay, "Ontogeny of Stable Speech Areas in the Human Brain," in E. H. Lenneberg and E. Lennegerg (eds.), *Foundations of Language Development,* Volume 2 (New York: Academic Press, 1975; Paris: UNESCO, 1975): 21-29.

17. O. L. Zangwill, "The Ontogeny of Cerebral Dominance in Man," in E. H. Lenneberg and E. Lenneberg (eds.), *Foundations of Language Development*, Volume 1 (New York: Academic Press, 1975; Paris: UNESCO, 1975): 137-147.

18. S. Freud, *Ueber Aphasie* (Bern Convention, Sigmund Freud Copyright, Ltd., 1899); *On Aphasia* (New York: International University Press, 1953).

19. R. A. Dart and D. Craig, *Adventures with the Missing Link* (New York: Harper & Bros., 1959).

20. D. C. Rife, "Heredity and Handedness," *Scientific Monographs* 73 (1951): 188-191.

21. R. Zazzo (ed.), *Manual pour l'Examen Psychologique de L'Enfant* (Neuchatel, Switzerland: Delachaux et Niestle S. A., 1960): 18-36.

22. J. B. de Quirós *et al., Estudios sobre la Dislexia Infantil* (Santa Fe, Argentina: Ministerio de Educacion y Cultura, 1962).

23. J. Piaget, "Perception, Motricite et Intelligence," *Enfance* 2 (1956): 9-14.

24. W. L. Jenkins, "Somesthesis," in S. S. Stevens (ed.), *Handbook of Experimental Psychology* (New York: John Wiley & Sons, 1966): 1172-1190.

25. C. S. Sherrington, *The Integrative Action of the Nervous System* (New York: Scribner's Sons, 1906; New Haven, Connecticut: Yale University Press, 1947).

26. *Ibid.*

27. Zazzo, *op. cit.*

28. J. B. De Quirós and M. Della Cella, *La Dislexia en la Ninez* (Buenos Aires: Paidos, 1965).

29. Quirós, *Estudios . . ., loc. cit.*

30. J. M. Charcot, *Oeuvres Completes* (publiees par J. P. Charcot) (in 3 vols.) (Paris: Lecrosnier et Babe, 1890).

31. J. Wepman, "The Modality Concept," in H. K. Smith (ed.), *Perception and Reading* (Newark, *Delaware: International Reading Association*, 1968): 1-6.

32. A. R. Luria, *Human Brain and Psychological Process* (New York: Harper & Bros., 1966).

33. Luria, *Lenguaje . . ., loc. cit.*

34. F. Affolter, "Developmental Aspects of Auditory and Visual Perception: An Experimental Investigation of Central Mechanisms of Auditory and Visual Processing" (Doctoral dissertation; Pennsylvania State University, 1970); F. Affolter, "Aspekte der Entwicklung und Pathologie von Wahrnemungs," in Gautier and Prod'hom (eds.), *Gehörstorungen beim kind,* Pädiatrische Fortbildungskurse fur die Praxis, Heft 34 (Basel: Karger, 1972): 41-49.

35. C. S. Sherrington, *Man on his Nature* (London: Cambridge University Press, 1951).

CHAPTER IV

Motor Activities
and Human Learning

(21) LATERALITY AND MOTOR ACTIVITY: BODY EXCLUSION

We discussed laterality in Chapter III, noting the importance of motor activities in determining better abilities on one side of the body. The better developmental potential of one side (in accurate, quick, strong, or skilled movements) is indicative of laterality (potential or preference) of that side of the body. More sophisticated motor development on one side of the body, therefore, is related to laterality and human learning. Motor activities are always connected with learning processes. Many learning theories and much physiological evidence in regard to motor activities support these criteria.

As we saw in Chapter II, Section 10, the most widely accepted learning theories in one way or another emphasize the importance of motor activity in human learning processes. It is not easy to accept completely any one of these theories. Surely all of them have great value and provide valid and useful contributions to our work; yet "empty spaces"—unanswered questions—remain. It is our good fortune that the researchers whose work has a bearing on the future of special education are now taking initial steps, based on firm biological facts, which will allow us a more in-depth study of learning-disabled children.

The fact that knowledge starts through intentional coordinated motor activities is no longer doubted. As is also well known, higher cortical levels play a part in every new coordinated motor activity. Let us recall some concepts already established in this book. As intentional or voluntary motor activities become self-governed, the higher cortical levels can be used for other learning processes which may or may not be related to motor activities themselves. The more that intentional or coordinated motor activities can be reproduced automatically in a satisfactory way, the greater and better developmental possibilities there are for knowledge. Learning and motor activity initially exist only in terms for potential achievement, although it might be said that one's first learning experiences are those in the realm of motor coordination. At the very beginning of life, motor activity anticipates mental action; then, both factors are coincident; later, they coexist; finally, mental action subordinates motor activity.

As stated in Chapter II, Section 12, corporal potentiality is the possibility that human beings have of "excluding" the body in order to allow processes of higher learning—that is to say, to allow processes of elaboration, transformation, and inclusion (symbolization) of the received information. We should emphasize here the difference between "function" and "learning." The development produced normally or spontaneously in any part or organ and manifested through action is called "function." Functions can be inhibited, but they reappear when the individual needs them. For instance, olfaction in humans is normally inhibited, but in many brain damaged and mentally retarded individuals it is exaggerated: Evidently, these patients "need" the help of such a primitive afference looking for a better way to receive information from, and to adapt to the environment.

The development produced by the environment is recognized as "learning." Learning can be destroyed through environmental pressures or pathological conditions, and many times it never reappears.

Both cerebral hemispheres have functions and learning processes. The symbolic hemisphere (generally the left) is the major hemisphere for symbolic processes: language, analysis, sequential processing. The postural hemisphere (generally the right) is the major hemisphere for processing corporal information. In recent years the terms "major hemisphere" (for the left one) and "minor hemisphere" (for the right) have been rejected by many authors because the "minor" hemisphere is also a "major" hemisphere for nonverbal, spatial, and holistic processing. Nevertheless, the fact remains that one hemisphere is initially concerned with learned symbolic acquisitions and the other to holistic information.[1]

It is evident that each cerebral hemisphere has a sort of "specialization," excluding many stimuli that anatomically and physiologically arrive at it. As we noted in Chapter III, Section 14, specialization of cerebral hemispheres does not have much correspondence with body laterality. The concept of body exclusion emerges from the inhibition of the holistic (or postural, or corporal) hemisphere (generally the right one) by the symbolic (linguistic) hemisphere (generally the left one). This idea has particular relevance to the learning of language and to one of its derivatives, reading and writing, which is an exclusively human type of learning.

For the purposes of the present discussion the dominant cerebral side, as we have said, is also recognized as the symbolic hemisphere, and the nondominant side is also termed the postural or corporal hemisphere. We have relabeled both hemispheres because discussion of "major" and "minor" can also be extended to "dominant" and "nondominant" with similar arguments.

In regard to learning processes and, particularly when seen in the light of symbolic and postural (or corporal) cerebral hemispheres, we have already found that a man's cerebrum is then distinguished from that of other animals.[2] In order to be able to dedicate itself to symbolic skills, the symbolic hemisphere transfers information coming from the body and its spatial relationships to the postural (nondominant) hemisphere. Undoubtedly, this phenomenon must have important implications for body laterality. When unusual or very strong corporal-spatial information finds its way into the higher cortical levels, the symbolic hemisphere necessarily dedicates itself to processing this information. In such circumstances symbolic processes will be displaced or superseded by urgent vital needs. In cybernetic terms, it could be said that, if the available circuits for a lower-level program cannot process the information, thus requiring the intervention of other circuits ordinarily used for a higher-level program, these higher-level circuits will fail to execute their own functions. That is why language and learning will not develop properly if the postural and lateral "program" is not yet established. This is why we believe that, in the acquisition of human learning, examination of the postural system and corporal potentiality are of great significance.

(22) NEUROLOGICAL BASES FOR TONUS AND POSTURAL CONTROL

As we saw in our discussion of motor laterality, laterality can be influenced by various factors such as muscular tonus, greater strength, capabilities of making skilled, coordinated, accurate, and eumetric movements (i.e., smoothly executed voluntary movements). The environment acts upon these, imposing greater work on one side of the body.

At this point, let use review some anatomical and physiological concepts in regard to several of the factors just mentioned.

Sherrington discovered the stretch reflex or "myotatic" reflex (from Greek: *myos,* muscle; *tatos,* stretch), which represents the basic structure of tonus. Later, other authors (notably, J. Laporte and D. P. C. Lloyd) carefully analyzed this reflex.[3] Let us briefly describe the stretch reflex.

From the muscle endings which are arranged in the form of spirals and flower sprays within the muscle spindles, the myotatic or stretch reflex reaches the dorsal root ganglion and through it its axon enters the dorsal horn (from Latin: *cornu,* horn) of the spine, forming a synapse with the ventral horn motor neuron. From here the corresponding axon goes to the skeletal muscle fiber. Therefore, this is a monosynaptic reflex with "relays" in the spine, starting from some muscular fibers (rich in sarcoplasm) which contain the muscle spindle (i.e., intrafusal muscle fibers); after the synapsis at the anterior horn, it reaches the striated muscle fibers in skeletal muscles. Through this mechanism the intrafusal stretching generates the increase of tonus in skeletal muscles. This is shown in Figure 1.

It is evident that such a control of muscular tonus cannot follow a simple scheme. What happens when contraction is very great? What happens when the stimulus is very weak? How can it be possible to maintain tonus independently of contraction in such different circumstances? Let us address the first condition, when skeletal muscular contraction is very great.

After a certain level of contraction, Golgi tendon organs are stimulated, thus generating a reflex known as Laporte and Lloyd's reflex, which is generally considered as opposite to the myotatic one.[4] Laporte and Lloyd's reflex, starting from Golgi tendon organs (in the form of spirals around the

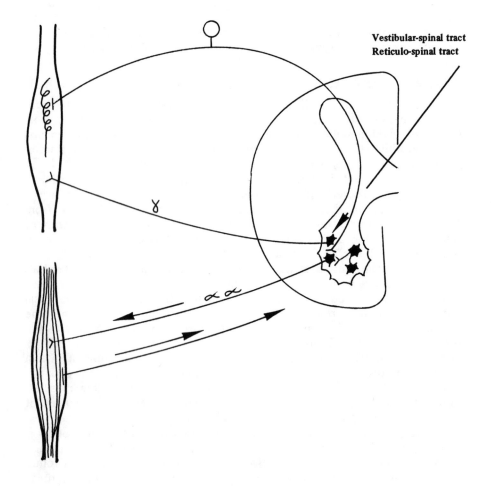

Figure 1. Stretch and Reflex: Action, Retroaction, Feedback.

end of the tendons, where they attach themselves to muscles), goes through several neurons until attaining the anterior spinal horn and diminishing or abolishing the tonus effect produced by the stretching of muscle spindles. Therefore, while the myotatic reflex increases the agonist tonus, the retroactive reflex (that is, Laporte and Lloyd's reflex) inhibits the agonist tonus. These two reflexes (myotatic and retroactive) act on a low level (spine); but they are modified by other higher levels.

The second condition, when the stimulus is very weak, is related to the assumption that the myotatic reflex could be handicapped in order to maintain tonus. Tonus modification produces postural instability, and therefore it elicits abrupt changes in head position. This kind of head movement becomes a specific vestibular stimulus. Then a compensatory action goes through reticular formation (reticular-spinal pathways) and gamma fibers toward muscle spindles and through the direct vestibular-spinal pathway toward the skeletal muscle fibers. The vestibular-spinal action is exerted upon neurons which send fibers which are called "alpha." Through these actions, vestibular organs can modify the results obtained through Sherrington's and Laporte and Lloyd's reflexes.[5] See Figure 1.

On the other hand, "gamma" fibers, which also leave from anterior horn neurons, finally go to the muscle spindle instead of arriving at the skeletal muscle fibers. The gamma system (which is constituted by these specialized fibers) acts in rapid and coordinated movements, improving the outputs coming from the central nervous system. Gamma fibers are connected mainly with the spine; and numerically speaking, there are twice as many alpha fibers as gamma fibers. Gamma fibers are also activated by proprioceptive influences and stimuli from several other parts of the brain. See Figure 1.

Other nonspinal reflexes also start from muscle spindles, with cerebellar and some cerebral basal ganglia involvement. These reflexes go through dorsal (direct) and ventral (indirect) spino-cerebellar tracts (Flechsig's and Gowers' tracts), first arriving at the cerebellar cortex, then connecting with other cerebellar grey nuclei, and arriving through the superior cerebellar peduncle at the opposite red nucleus. From the red nucleus some fibers continue their way up in order to reach higher central levels; but, as can be seen in Figure 2, the most important contingent goes down, crossing again the middle line and attaining the anterior horn motor neurons of the spine (rubro-spinal tract) and, through alpha fibers, the skeletal muscles. In summary, the role of the cerebellum in this circuit is as follows:

1. Muscle-spindle / posterior horn of the spine
2. Spino-cerebellar tracts
3. Cerebellar-rubro pathway
4. Rubro-spinal tract
5. Anterior horn of the spine / skeletal muscle

If this unconscious proprioceptive circuit fails in tonus and postural regulation, other higher central levels intervene through the information arriving at the cerebral cortex from the cerebellum through the red nucleus and thalamus. Feedback in these circumstances is obtained by visual and vestibular correction.

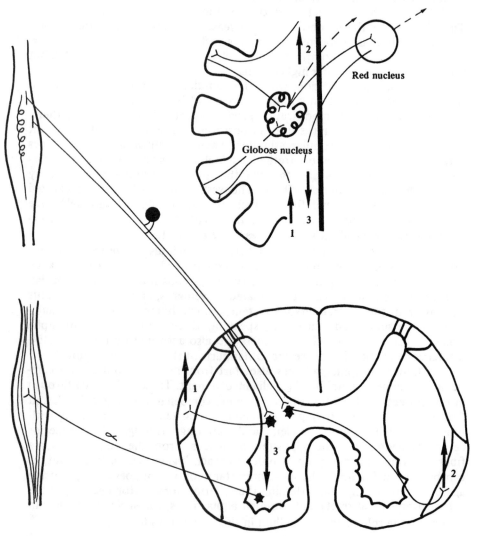

Figure 2. Neuromuscular Circuits with Cerebellar Participation. (1) Direct or dorsal spino-cerebellar tract (Flechsig's tract). (2) Indirect or ventral spino-cerebellar tract (Gowers' tract). (3) Rubro-spinal tract.

NEUROPSYCHOLOGICAL FUNDAMENTALS

Conscious proprioceptive circuits start from all proprioceptive receptors and reach Goll's and Burdach's columns (fasciculus gracilis and fasciculus cuneatus). The second neuron is in the inferior part of the medulla; and, after crossing the middle line, its fibers arrive at the thalamus through the medial lemniscus. From the thalamus they attain the cerebral cortex (particularly, the ascending parietal gyrus). At the cortical level, multiple types of cortical and subcortical connections are made mainly with frontal, parietal, and temporal zones. From these three zones different descending pathways originate, mainly the cortico-ponto-cerebellar-rubro-spinal tract, which connects with the anterior horn of the spine, and, through alpha fibers, with skeletal muscle fibers. See Figure 3.

We have just explained in brief form some elements of tonus and postural control in an adult individual. But in infants and young children the situation is different. In newborn infants, information to the cerebral cortex does not take place as it does in the adult, because in normal newborn babies myelination reaches the inferior thalamic laminae. Consequently, the tonic and postural system works exclusively with Sherrington's and Laporte and Lloyd's reflexes, intercalated neurons, proprioception, and vestibular apparatus, these structures being functional at time of birth. That is why the maneuver of holding a newborn normal baby in ventral suspension determines the direct stimulus on the otoliths provided by the head-hanging position, plus the stretching of muscle spindles of the neck muscles, thus generating antigravitational reaction through spinal reflexes and vestibular-spinal discharges which produce head straightening and dorsal muscular contractions. Similar explanations can be given for the placing response and stepping movements in newborn babies. (The placing response is the response that newborn babies have, when their feet are placed on a hard surface, of reacting with straightening of the whole body.)

(23) FEEDBACK, INTERNAL FEEDBACK, AND RETROACTION

We have just seen some of the principal central "circuits" which take part in tonus and posture. The idea of "circuit" is very much related to the "feedback" concept introduced by N. Wiener, a mathematician from Massachusetts.[6] At the end of the 1940s he created *cybernetics* as the science of government. We must think in terms of servo-mechanisms (for example, a simple electric elevator), and self-controlled machines, to understand the type of "government" referred to by Wiener. Among cybernetic principles, here we shall concern ourselves only with the notion of "feedback." Wiener described feedback as "the perceptual reactions of a person to his own responses; as a process by which goal directed responses are checked and corrected." According to Wiener it is clear enough that a voluntary motor activity or a movement is continuously checked and corrected by the higher levels of the central nervous system: When a person wants to take a book which is on a table, he must make very complicated, skilled movements in order to be successful in his goal. The hand is continuously moved in different directions. In the meantime the higher centers "correct" the kinetic order as kinesthetic inputs are providing information. Finally, the eyes control the movement toward the book, "correcting" again if it is necessary (for instance, when the person's hand goes away from or near the pursued

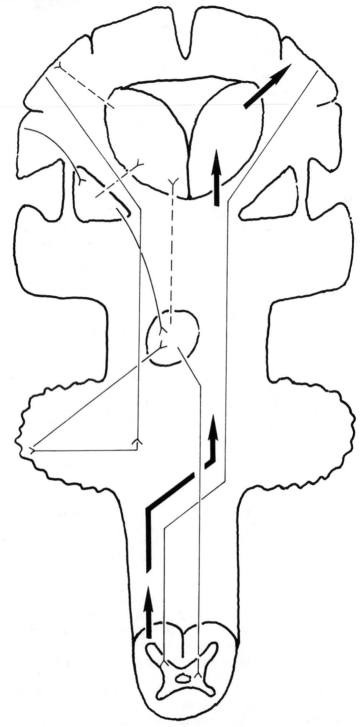

Figure 3. Neuromuscular Circuits with Cerebral Cortex Participation. Heavy lines: ascending tracts. Light lines: descending tracts. Dotted lines: information pathways to cortex.

NEUROPSYCHOLOGICAL FUNDAMENTALS

object, as commonly occurs in patients having cerebellar abnormalities).

As can be seen from this example, there is an "internal feedback" and an "external feedback." The permanent information of the movement of the arm and the hand, until the book is grasped, was essentially provided by kinesthetic and tactual inputs ("haptic" inputs) (see Chapter III, Section 18). These inputs constitute the internal feedback. The information provided by the eyes constitutes the external feedback.

"Retroaction" is a notion very similar to that of internal feedback. Nevertheless, the two are differentiated from a neurophysiological point of view. While internal feedback provides information about all receptors that participate in the movements for obtaining the book (first kinesthetic, and tactual, and finally—when the book is taken—also pressure receptors), retroaction is related only to the information about the specific kinetic order (kinesthetic information). Retroaction is connected with the action itself. In order to obtain a skilled movement, specific information must be continuously provided: These "specifics" are called "retroaction."

Internal and external feedback, however, are also related to the results obtained with such an action. Receptors which take part in feedback are specific and nonspecific ones. They are giving information about the obtained goals.

These notions are very important also in rehabilitation. If the goals expected through a movement are obtained, the movement is successful from a rehabilitative point of view. But it so happens that sometimes the movement is not well "programed" in regard to action and retroaction (kinetic-kinesthetic circuits).

We should emphasize that, from a rehabilitative point of view, many times the correct movement cannot be reached; in these cases, therapists must introduce only useful or adequate movements. These movements do not generally approach correct normal movement; but they can serve effectively personal wishes and objectives; and that is better than if the patient simply remained in bed.

As a general principle to be considered in learning disabilities and rehabilitative goals, we might mention that, the more intensive the environmental learning exigencies, and the more severe the individual's handicaps, the higher will be the central nervous system level requirements and greater the retroaction and feedback needs.

(24) THE EFFERENT THEORY IN VOLUNTARY MOVEMENTS

In the preceding Sections 22 and 23, the existence of neurological "circuits" for tonus and postural and movement control were analyzed. Accordingly, all muscular interventions (in posture, in equilibrium, in motor activities) deal with feedback and retroactive influences.

But it should be pointed out that a theory concerning efferent outputs as prevailing for motor activities was established as an opposite notion in regard to tonus and postural and movement control. In our discussion of theory, the arrival of information (related to movement) at the cortical level was considered indispensable for proper functioning. The opposite "efferent" theory (or "motor outflow" theory) assumes that the central nervous system has the essential "knowledge" of the features of all voluntary movements, and also that the central nervous system can control perfectly, and according to its previous "knowledge," the efferent signals going toward the muscles.

The central nervous system could be able to send an "order" or certain temporal sequence (Jones' timing) of outputs, and to maintain a "copy" of such an order.[7] The integration of "timing" in the nervous impulses is considered essential in order to obtain a pattern of skilled movements, but this pattern depends on the central nervous system's previous knowledge of the direction and extent of voluntary movements through monitoring its own efferent signals to the muscles.

According to this theory, retroaction, internal feedback, and external feedback could all be "functional" for skilled motor acquisitions or achievements; but they are useless in free voluntary movements.

E. Taub and A. T. Berman's research on bilateral spinal deafferentiation in monkeys support these statements.[8] They proved that peripheral afferences from receptors on the limbs were not necessary for patterns of complex movements. Taub, P. N. Perella, and G. Barro performed similar experiments with newborn monkeys four years later, and discovered that those deafferentiated animals were able to make skilled movements.[9]

From the physiological point of view, the efferent theory could have as a basic mechanism a cortical-to-cerebellar loop "around which efferent impulses are shunted at the time of transmission to the muscles."[10] The loop function could refer to the central nervous system "copy," and the interrelationship between these elements could serve to obtain impulse control of the voluntary movement.

According to the efferent theory (or "motor outflow" theory), proprioception would not be necessary for voluntary motor control, because of three main reasons:

1. Joint-receptors only transmit impulses from passive movements informing the central nervous system about the angles produced by the two joint-segments.
2. Muscle spindles could inform the central nervous system about the length of the muscle.[11]
3. Joint-receptors would not be necessary for perception of voluntary movements.[12]

Therefore, in order for sequences to be achieved at the central nervous system level, energy must be expended on motor control, rather than on processing incoming stimuli from the muscle spindles.

Because the fundamentals of this theory are quite different than those supporting the majority of the motor therapies used today, this theory is contrary to present rehabilitative methods and techniques used for a variety of motor disorders and handicaps.

(25) POSTURE, LINGUA, LANGUAGE, AND LEARNING

Several years ago we proposed that all the central nervous structures (including the spine) directly or indirectly intervene in language acquisition through sensory-motor circuits of permanent interaction.[13] The greater the requirements of the body, and the more that energy is expended in processsing incoming corporal stimuli, the longer will be the delay in language acquisition. We consider the early stages of language acquisition (*lingua*) as learning processes. For an organism to learn, it must be able, through proper amplification and inhibition of received stimuli, to process information and to act. For instance, if the constituent elements of the speech message and the environmental noises cannot be simultaneously amplified and inhibited, respectively, learning of speech becomes impossible. This simultaneous amplification and inhibition of oral messages is also obtained when there are no corporal interferences or exigencies.

If handicaps are severe, high levels of the central nervous system ("high-level programs") will be needed in order to maintain the postural system in "action." The higher the level of the central nervous system used to maintain the "service" of the body, the greater will be the difficulty in concentrating the higher skills on learning processes. Therefore, internalization of language will be very difficult to achieve when such handicaps are present.

The interference of the postural hemisphere with the symbolic work of the dominant hemisphere can be avoided by various normal or abnormal circumstances:

1. Reaching postures and positions that allow the proper development of corporal potentiality. This can be attained when body interferences such as afferent inputs (due to corporal disturbances), pain, fatigue, etc., are not present.
2. Under certain situations of great environmental or tensional pressure.
3. Inducing activities in the nondominant hemisphere (for example: putting it at the command of servo-mechanisms of automatic movements).

In regard to the third of these three points, it is well known that many times, particularly when fatigue is present or during intellectual emergencies, better concentration and symbolization are achieved when automatic walking is initiated. This makes it possible for the postural hemisphere to keep "busy," thus making the work of the symbolic or dominant hemisphere easier. When intellectual work must continue, and symptoms of physical or psychic tiredness appear, drowsiness included, the production of pain, or walking, or other motor activities can keep the individual awake and allow him to continue work. Conversely, if the individual adopts a comfortable position when tired, sleep overcomes him. However, the same position at times of mental alertness would allow him to continue efficient intellectual work. The opposite case is also true: If danger threatens, many body afferences are absolutely excluded, and the "life emergency services" (vision, hearing, locomotor apparatus, sometimes quick thinking—all of them based on neuro-endocrine reactions) are brought into action. In physical emergencies, the postural "program" prevails. In social or intellectual emergencies, the action belongs to the symbolic "program."

Symptoms showing the proper symbolic hemisphere dominance will not be considered here. We only call attention to the fact that, in language pathology, a lack of adequate dominance of the symbolic hemisphere is revealed through echolalic or perseverative speech, or through stereotypic writing. When these symptoms are transitory, they can be considered as results of fatigue or body interferences; but if they are constant, they show the existence of disturbed hemispheric symbolization.

(26) STRUCTURAL MATURATION AND LEARNING

The importance of motor activities in learning abilities should never be underestimated. Certainly motor activities, vision, and *lingua* and language are essential, preconditional functional systems necessary for the acquisition of specific human learning processes. In Chapter I, Section 5, it was established that reading and writing are functional systems because, without human environmental intervention, those skills are not learned. In order to be produced, reading and writing need complex structural maturation in motor activities, vision, and *lingua* and language levels. Normal *lingua* and language maturational levels are reached principally through audition.

Human tissues, organs, apparatus, and systems evolve through inherited behaviors, and mature through the externalization of biological and environmental developments by means of objective signs. Structural maturation refers to specific human externalizations related to the acquisition of some functions which are fundamental for such achievements. For instance, vision can be perfectly developed; but, in order for a person to learn to read and write, it is important to surpass vision itself and to achieve specific visual perception, visual discrimination, "visualization." Recognition and differentiation of *p, q, d, b,* establishing correspondences with diverse and different phonetic symbols, is a structural maturational level in vision.

We should say a few words on structural maturation in some of the basic developments of human learning.

It is commonly stated (from a medical point of view) that eye fixation, accommodation, and convergence are attained at the end of the second and during the third month of postnatal life.* This statement can be accepted as a general frame of reference. It can also be stated that, between the second and third months of postnatal life, visual structural maturation is beginning. This kind of maturation arrives to its apex with the possibility of correlating graphisms or symbols to language. As P. Niesel says, the first stage of visual development extends up to the end of the fifth year of age, the period in which spatial organization, visual-acuity evolution, and visual correlation with language, prevail.[14] Later on, visual development encompasses reading/writing.

Initially, vision works mainly as a perception, strongly connected with motor activity and haptic inputs from the mouth. The infant increases his visual knowledge, grasping objects and taking them to the mouth. During the first half of the second year of life (12 to 18 months of age), vision begins to have greater impact upon motor activities; but, on the other hand, many relationships with environmental *lingua* are not yet established at all.

---

*For the sake of practicality in settling the point at which life begins, we take as our baseline the point of conception.

NEUROPSYCHOLOGICAL FUNDAMENTALS

A. R. Luria performed an experiment related to this point.[15] He asked an infant 14 months of age to give him a toy well known by the baby. The infant was able to give him the toy if another more brilliant or nearer toy was not present. If such a circumstance occurred the infant would give the most brilliant or nearest toy, instead of the one first asked for. The question analyzed by Luria was that the word mentioned to the infant (and well known by the baby) had no correspondence with the response given by him. The latter was related to visual perception and was not connected at all with the verbal order.

Luria performed a similar experiment with children two years of age.[16] Each child was placed in front of nontransparent upside-down cup cup and a glass. A coin was then placed beneath the cup while the infant was seeing the action. The researcher then asked the child to look for the coin; the child picked up the cup and took the coin. The maneuver was repeated several times in a play modality; but suddenly it was modified: The coin was instead placed beneath the glass (always within the sight of the infant). In spite of the fact that the infant was seeing where the coin was placed (under the glass), when he was asked to search for the coin, he first picked up the cup; that is, he repeated the previous action. This behavior was considered by Luria as "motor inertia" because, at that age, motor action is predominant over visual information. Other experiments of that kind were also performed by Russian researchers.[17] Let us make reference here to one of them. Children of three and four years old were asked (1) to press a small rubber ball at any time a red light was switched on in front of them, and (2) not to press that ball when a blue light was switched on. But in order to facilitate the action, the children were instructed to say "yes" when pressing the ball (red light), and to say "no" when they must not do so (blue light). What happened was as follows:

1. Red light: The children said "yes" and pressed the ball.
2. Blue light: The children said "no" and automatically they
   pressed the ball again (the opposite of what they were
   saying).

This striking result was interpreted to mean that the leadership (or deictic) role of speech did not control motor and perceptual activities at that age. It must therefore be reasoned that, from the point of view of "language" acquisition and development, during the first five years of life, different predominances occur: initially motor activities, then perceptual skills, and finally symbolic processes.

This point of view has medical, diagnostic, and therapeutic implications: Effective rehabilitation must differentiate sensory or symbolic stages according to leadership possibilities in children's learning processes.

Many variables play a part in structural maturation. Positive or negative social environments are important in the results finally obtained. J. Cravioto, in Mexico City, made a follow-up on the influence of social classes in the possibilities of (1) visual-perceptual discrimination, (2) audio-visual symbolic identification, and (3) analytic-synthetic visual capabilities.[18] Different tests were employed in children six, seven, and eight years of age, belonging to low and middle socioeconomic groups. According to Cravioto, there was a consistent learning delay of one to two years in lower-class children (compared to middle-class children). If we bear in mind that those assessments concerned themselves with fundamental factors for learning reading and writing, it seems reasonable to accept the idea that acquisition in reading and writing language can be delayed by different environmental factors which influence (positively or negatively) physiological possibilities of the species.

The functional evolution of organisms can be modified according to neurophysiological and biological principles; but functional systems relate not only to organisms, but also to greater or lesser developmental pressures provided by the human environment in order to obtain structural "maturations" for human learning.

According to these criteria, it is possible to explain why in certain abnormalities some Piagetian "conservations" can be satisfactorily accomplished.* This fact does not allow the observer to assume that the child has attained real possibilities of reading and writing acquisition. In order to read and write "language," the existence of logical thought is not sufficient; its leadership function upon visual perception and motor activities is also necessary. As a matter of fact, postural-motor dominance is succeeded by visual-perceptual dominance, and the latter, by verbal symbolic dominance. These dominances act independently of multisensory influences of "sensory-motor" stages or "objective-symbolic period"; all these epistemologic terms described by Piaget can eventually represent real developmental steps in some children.[19] But until the time that functional systems of language reach the necessary structural maturation, it seems unreasonable to pretend that acquisition of reading and writing language has taken place.

(27) POSTURE, MOTOR ACTIVITY, MENTAL ACTION, AND LEARNING PROCESSES

As we have pointed out, every learning process is established through personal motor activities. Knowledge is first gained from personal motor experiences and follows through relationships between the individual and the environment. According to H. Wallon, emotional life interacts with tonic and spasmodic reactions.[20] Emotional life belongs to environmental influences; tonus and spasms belong to body reactions. Emotions influence motor life and vice versa. Movements, gestures, speech, reading, writing, and motor externalizations act on the environment and receive emotional influences. In this context we consider "reading" as a motor externalization: In order to read it is necessary to have skilled, coordinated movements of the eyes. Nevertheless, motor activities can also be represented by emotional reactions (environmental stimuli) or with mental actions (thoughts with language). On this subject one statement by Pierre Vayer seems worth mentioning: "Motor activity does not exist."[21] Really, motor activity cannot exist without emotional and environmental influences, which allow its appearance and externalization.

*Piaget's conservations refer to the possibility of acting with reversible thought upon objects. Piaget differentiates *substance, weight,* and *volume* conservations. For instance, a normal child five or six years old can identify as similar in quantity a file of six closely grouped buttons with another file of six separated buttons.

NEUROPSYCHOLOGICAL FUNDAMENTALS

Researchers working with children and animals agree that knowledge begins through motor activities, but researchers working with human learning processes many times do not consider motor activity to be the basis of knowledge. Probably this fact is due to the transformation of knowledge into mental actions. As knowledge attains higher levels, motor activities (for learning purposes) become more and more restricted, and mental actions progressively increase. The motor work with concrete objects begins to be used simply as verifications of hypotheses formulated by mental actions. Such researchers manage to put the cart before the horse.

In young children there are inherited patterns of motor activities which are already established at birth, and which progressively develop. This development occurs through factors of inheritance as well as through learning. Every new motor activity "requires, before anything else, a disrupting of some preexisting functional units, then a selective choice of the useful motor combinations, and finally their assembling into a new working unit."[22]

In coordinated and intentional motor activities, higher levels of the central nervous system are undoubtedly involved. When motor activity can be supported by other subcortical levels, higher levels can be used for other motor or nonmotor learning processes. When automatic motor activities can be satisfactorily produced, knowledge processes have better and greater developmental possibilities.

Certainly this background is not exactly the same which produced Getman's, Kephart's and others' ideas in the United States.[23] It is, instead, much more related to European approaches, and particularly to the work begun by Wallon and developed by Rey and Piaget, among others.[24]

Posture and motor activities are relevant for development of knowledge. Then, when knowledge is established, knowledge itself is used in order to obtain new acquisitions. For instance, at the beginning language is learned as *lingua,* but it is then generally transformed into an effective instrument in order to obtain higher achievements. Motor activities precede mental actions: then both act together; and finally motor activity is subordinate to mental action.

NOTES

1. S. J. Dimond and J. G. Beaumont, "Experimental Studies of Hemisphere Function in Normal and Brain Damaged Individuals," in S. J. Dimond and J. G. Beaumont (eds.), *Hemisphere Functions of the Human Brain* (London: Halstead Press, 1974); M. Kinsbourne and W. L. Smith, *Hemispheric Disconnection and Cerebral Function* (Springfield, Illinois: Charles C Thomas, 1974); R. M. Knights and D. J. Bakker (eds.), *The Neuropsychology of Learning Disorders* (Baltimore: University Park Press, 1976).

2. J. B. de Quirós and O. L. Schrager, "Postural System, Corporal Potentiality and Language," in E. H. Lenneberg and E. Lenneberg (eds.), *Foundations of Language Development,* Volume 2 (New York: Academic Press, 1975; Paris: UNESCO, 1975): 297-307.

3. C. S. Sherrington, *The Integrative Action of the Nervous System* (New York: Scribner's Sons, 1906; New Haven, Connecticut: Yale University Press, 1947); J. Laporte and D. P. C. Lloyd, *American Journal of Physiology* 169 (1952): 609ff.

4. *Ibid.*

5. *Ibid.*

6. N. Wiener, *The Human Use of Human Beings* (New York: Doubleday, 1946); N. Wiener, *Cybernetics* (New York: John Wiley, 1948); N. Wiener, *Cybernetics or Control and Communication in the Animal and Machine* (New York: John Wiley and Sons, 1961).

7. E. V. Holst, "Relations between the Central Nervous System and the Peripheral Organs," *British Journal of Animal Behaviour* 2 (1954): 89; B. Jones, "The Importance of Memory Traces of Motor Efferent Discharges for Learning Skill Movements," *Developmental Medicine and Child Neurology* 16:5 (1974): 620-628; R. W. Sperry, "Neural Basis of the Spontaneous Optokinetic Response Produced by Visual Neural Inversion," *Journal of Comparative and Physiology Psychology* 43 (1960): 482.

8. E. Taub and A. J. Berman, "Movement Learning in the Absence of Sensory Feedback," in S. J. Freeman (ed.), *The Neuropsychology of Spatially Orientated Behavior* (Homewood, Illinois: Dorsey Press, 1968).

9. E. Taub, P. N. Perella, and G. Barro, "Behavioral Development in Monkeys, Following Bilateral Forelimb Deafferentiation on the First Day of Life," in *Transactions of the American Neurological Association,* 1972, as cited by Jones, *op. cit.*

10. T. C. Ruch, "Basal Ganglia and Cerebellum," in T. C. Ruch and H. D. Patton (eds.), *Physiology and Biophysics* (Philadelphia: W. B. Saunders, 1965).

11. I. A. Boyd and T. D. M. Roberts, "Proprioceptive Discharges from Stretch-Receptors in the Knee-Joint of the Cat," *Journal of Physiology* 122 (1953): 38.

12. K. Browne, J. Lee, and P. A. Ring, "The Sensation of Passive Movement in the Metatarso-Phalangeal Joint of the Great Toe in Man," *Journal of Physiology* 126 (1954): 448.

13. J. B. de Quiro's and R. Gotter, *El Lenguaje en el Nino* (Buenos Aires: CEMIFA, 1963); J. B. de Quiro's and G. Ruiz Moreno, "Bases Neurologicas de la Foniatria," *Revista de la Asociacion Medica Argentina* [Buenos Aires] 71: 4 (1957): 101-108; O. L. Schrager, "Accion, Retroaccion y Realimentacion: Sus Interacciones en el Habla," *Actas de las Ias Jornadas Nacionales de Fonoaudiologia* (Buenos Aires, Argentina, 1972): 102-106.

14. P. Niesel, "Entwicklung und Optischeabstimmen Storungen," in E. Kong (ed.), *Zerebrale Bewegungsstorungen beim Kind* (Basel: Karger, 1974): 206-213.

15. A. R. Luria *et al., Lenguaje y Psiquitria* (J. M. Arancibia, trans.) (Madrid: Ed. Fundamentos, 1973).

16. *Ibid.*

17. O. K. Tikhomirow, and S. V. Jakovleva, as cited by Luria, *op. cit.*

18. J. Cravioto, "Mecanismos de Aprendizaje de la Lectura en Funcion de Clase Socio-Economica," (Segundo Congreso Hispanoamericano de Dificultades en el Aprendizaje de la Lectura y Escritura; Direccion de Ensenanza Especializada, Ministerio de Educacion y Cultura, Mexico, DF, May 7-14, 1974).

19. J. Piaget, "Les Praxies chez l'Enfant," *Revue Neurologique* 102 (1960): 551-565; J. Piaget, *Biologie et Connaissance—Essai sur les Relations entre les Regulations Organiques et les Processus Cognitifs* (Paris: Ed. Gallimard, 1967).

20. H. Wallon, *Les Origines du Caractere chez l'Enfant* (Paris: Presses Universitaires de France, 1949).

21. P. Vayer, personal communication, 1974.

22. J. Paillard, "The patterning of Skilled Movements," in J. Field, N. W. Magoun, and V. E. Hall (eds.), *Handbook of Physiology;* Section I: Neurophysiology, Volume III (Washington D. C.: American Physiological Society, 1960): 1679-1708.

23. G. N. Getman, *How to Develop your Child's Intelligence* (7th ed.) (Luverne, Minnesota: Announcers Press, 1962); N. C. Kephart, *The Slow Learner in the Classroom* (Columbus, Ohio: Charles E. Merrill, 1960).

24. Browne, *op. cit.;* Piaget, "Les Praxies . . .," *loc. cit.;* Piaget, *Biologie . . ., loc. cit.;* A. Rey, *Psychologie Clinique et Neurologie* (Neuchatel, Switzerland: Delachaux et Niestle, 1969); Wallon, *op. cit.*

CHAPTER V

Posture, Movement, and Learning

(28) BASIC ANATOMICAL CONCEPTS IN REGARD TO POSTURAL ACHIEVEMENTS

(29) FIRST PHYSIOLOGICAL CONCEPTS ABOUT POSTURE

(30) VESTIBULAR APPARATUS AND POSTURE

(31) CEREBELLAR AND RETICULAR INFLUENCES ON POSTURE

(32) VESTIBULAR-PROPRIOCEPTIVE INTEGRATION AND POSTURAL CONTROL

(28) BASIC ANATOMICAL CONCEPTS IN REGARD TO POSTURAL ACHIEVEMENTS

Everyone who is in any way concerned with posture and its influence on human acquisition of knowledge should be familiar with such names as Flechsig, von Monakow, Bechterew, Sherrington, Magnus, and others.

At this point in our discussion we will refer mainly to the important work of Paul Emil Flechsig (1847-1929) and Constantin von Monakow (1853-1930) as it relates to the anatomical basis of posture. Both authors must be placed within the framework of philosophical-scientific thinking (that is, positivism) which was predominant in Germany during the second half of the nineteenth century. Positivism, it should be noted, is a philosophical and scientific theory which considers knowledge to be derived from experience and direct observation. Other phenomena which escape observable reality were not considered scientific by nineteenth-century positivists.

The controversy between those who believe only in observation and those who believe that besides these direct observations and experiences there are other deducible phenomena, has existed throughout the history of humanity. In the twentieth century forms of positivism can be identified, for example, in behaviorism, structuralism, and others.

During the second half of the last century, Flechsig's ideas ran counter to those of his contemporary, Sigmund Freud (1856-1939), who believed in the existence of subjective and relatively unverifiable phenomena. Let us not be sidetracked, however, into judging whether Flechsig was "right" and Freud was "wrong," or vice versa. Science does not pose or answer questions in terms of "good" and "bad." Opposite points of view can converge in clarifying our knowledge and contributing to produce scientific progress.

Flechsig's and von Monakow's works are essential for the knowledge of nervous anatomo-physiology. Both of them made solid contributions in regard to postural evolution in human beings.

Flechsig discovered relationships between myelogeny (i.e., the evolution of the myelin sheets of nerve fibers in the development of the central nervous system) and the successive functions of the central nervous system.[1] Flechsig described three main myelogenic "laws" which are now accepted in scientific practice. The core concepts of these laws state that: (1) myelination of the nerve fibers of the developing brain takes place in a definite sequence; (2) fibers belonging to particular functional systems mature at the same time; (3) myelin formation temporarily repeats the previous formation of the axon; (4) myelination occurs at different rates, being complete around 20 years of age; and (5) there is a relationship between myelogeny and embryological development of the nervous system (thus "repeating" phylogenetic periods).

While these myelogenetic laws constitute an important contribution to neurology and psychology, Flechsig also introduced other important knowledge about human functions when he stated that sensitive fibers myelinate earlier than motor fibers, and that these myelinate earlier than associative fibers. We know now that higher human functions depend upon cerebral interconnections; but regarding some aspects of maturation, Flechsig's laws still retain their value because the developmental sequence he established represents a cue in the functional structure of the different brain regions.

In 1876 Flechsig's earlier descriptions showed that the first sensory nerves to develop (i.e., myelinate) were the central pathways related to tactile and olfactory functions; then the optic; and last, the auditory pathways. At that time he did not clarify what happened with the myelination of the vestibular pathways. Later on, W. von Bechterew differentiated myelogeny of the cochlear and vestibular branches of the eighth cranial nerve; and in 1921 Flechsig attracted international medical attention when he stated that the vestibular nerve was the first among all the sensory nerves to be myelinated.[2]

Flechsig was a pioneer in supposing that gravitational forces were able to act upon vestibular organs of the fetus between the fifth and the sixth month of pregnancy, this being one of the main causes in determining the early myelination of the fibers of the vestibular nerve.

When Flechsig was able to determine the extremely early myelination of the utricle and the saccule on the one hand and the simultaneous myelination of the ventral roots of the cervical spine (which controls neck muscles) on the other, he related neck muscles and utricle, stating that the principle vestibular function was the regulation of the head position in regard to body trunk and limbs. We must emphasize this statement: It is important to realize that vestibular inputs are extremely closely connected with head position, and that this is essential if humans are to receive information, to introduce knowledge and, certainly, *to learn*.

In connection with auditory (cochlear) fibers, our present knowledge is based in Flechsig's myelogenic research, including his finding that the auditory pathway is the last among all the sensory pathways to be myelinated.

Flechsig's other important contribution was his description of the dorsal spino-cerebellar tract, which myelinates earlier than the pyramidal tract. The importance of the spino-cerebellar tract in regard to skeletal muscles was determined by Flechsig when he established that cerebellar myelination continues until heterolateral reticular formation (at the level of the pons), and that from the reticular formation, myelination proceeds to the spinal anterior horns, and from there to skeletal muscles.

In summary, Flechsig's work holds that the formation of the postural system is very primitive: The vestibular pathway is the first sensory (or proprioceptive) pathway to myelinate. Flechsig called attention to the fact that every organ or structure corresponding to primary functions myelinates early: sucking, swallowing, peristaltic movements, breathing, shrieking, and crying are vital, complex functions, and are already established at birth. Processes of human communication depend on these functions.

At the same time that Flechsig made these outstanding contributions, Constantin von Monakow was studying the development of cerebral functions in children. In 1897 von Monakow understood that an extensive amount of stimuli arriving from peripheral receptors to the centers were able to produce an "energy" that was not retained, but that was transformed into coordinated movements. He thus considered spastic palsy to be the result of pyramidal tract damage, because the concentration of that "energy" in the central nervous system was not transformed into motor activity.[3]

Von Monakow related the basic activity in children to the myelination of the vestibular and auditory systems: This vestibular-auditory "soldering" (as von Monakow called it) should normally be accomplished within the period between the third month of gestation up to the twelfth month of postnatal life.

In 1914 von Monakow published an important work on brain localization, stating that brain functions in vertebrates are established within an ascending pattern toward the anterior zone of the medulla oblongata.[4]

In passing, we might note that Hughlings Jackson's ideas influenced von Monakow to state his concept of ascending levels of morphological and functional development at the central nervous system, which he used to call "cronogenic localization."

In 1930 von Monakow and R. Mourgue (according to A. Peiper) established the principle that the last genetic achievements were the most vulnerable, thus reinforcing Hughlings Jackson's law: In case of damage of the central nervous system, functions which appear latest in evolution are lost first.[5] Also, they believed that right-left information from body schema could be integrated in only one of the cerebral hemispheres. Von Monakow's and Mourgue's contributions were essential to the development of our ideas of laterality and learning.

(29) FIRST PHYSIOLOGICAL CONCEPTS ABOUT POSTURE

Let us, here, review some of the most outstanding works of Sherrington and of Magnus in relation to postural control.

C. S. Sherrington divided body sensitivity into three types: extero-ceptive, proprioceptive, and interoceptive.[6] While the first of these provides information from the external environment, both of the others provide information from the internal environment. Interoceptive sensitivity refers to information coming from nerve endings localized at the visceral level. Proprioception is the awareness of information coming from sensitive nerve endings localized at the level of the muscles, tendons, and joints (related to movements and body positions, and allied with labyrinthine functions. Visual perception (according to Sherrington) could be recognized as visuo-muscular-labyrinthine perception; and tactile perception could be recognized as tactual-muscular-labyrinthine perception.

Sherrington's other main contribution was the description of the stretch reflex analyzed in Chapter IV, Section 22. It could be also convenient to consult a good textbook on physiology in regard to tonus and posture: Both definitions and concepts are now interpreted according to Sherrington's accepted points of view. The term "postural function" was understood by him as both corporal attitudes and visceral movements together, which are maintained by tonic activity. Sherrington spoke not only about skel-etal, but also about visceral muscles in regard to the general tonicity of the body.

The most outstanding experiments in regard to animal postures were carried out by Magnus, and by Magnus and A. de Kleijn.[7] According to these authors, posture responds to "static reactions" and "dynamic reactions." The first type of such reaction was observed when partial or total support was given to the body. The second type of reaction was ob-served as the fundamental basis of movement. Clinically, static reactions are more interesting, mainly in babies and young children. Static reactions, according to Magnus, can be differentiated into local, segmentary, and general categories.

Local static reactions involve only a part of the body (for instance, a limb). Magnus described a "positive support reaction" and a "negative support reaction." In order to realize what kind of reactions we are speak-ing about, try taking a domestic cat or dog, and place the dorsum of one paw of the animal on a hard surface (for instance, an edge of a table). If the animal reacts by *stretching* its limb and supporting the paw on the table, this is called "positive support reaction." It occurs in intact animals as well as in decerebrated or decerebellated ones because it mainly depends on stretch reflexes and joint fixation. If the animal reacts by *flexing* its paw, this is called "negative support reaction"; and it depends on active processes which disrupt the "positive reaction."

"Segmentary static reactions" refers to the response of a large segment of the body (and not only a limb) to certain stimuli. For instance, if we produce pain on a limb of an animal supported so it is standing on its hind legs, it is possible to observe "positive support reactions" (i.e., tonus increase) on the other three legs, chiefly in the similar heterolateral one.

Magnus described other types of "segmentary reactions" as well; but here let us discuss the third type of reaction—"general static reactions"—

which were studied in decerebrated and mesencephalic animals. Magnus produced (in those animals) extension of the "facial" limbs and flexion of the "occipital" limbs when he rotated the animal head: He described the asymmetric tonic-neck reflex in experimental animals. He performed many other experiments involving general static reactions as well; later, de Kleijn and he made a significant contribution to our knowledge about tonic-neck and labyrinthine reflexes according to the law of reciprocal innervation (that is, when flexor tonus increases, extensor tonus diminishes, and vice versa).

In regard to righting labyrinthine reflexes, Magnus described the movements of the head in the animal in what has been called "the zero condition" (i.e., a mesencephalic or thalamic animal, without labyrinths). Magnus held the animal freely in the air and observed its reactions in such a situation: rabbits and guinea pigs did not raise their heads, probably because they did not use their eyes for righting responses. But cats, dogs, and monkeys showed righting reactions of the head if their eyes were opened; if vision was suppressed, the righting reaction did not appear. When labyrinths were involved, those animals were always able to maintain their heads in a normal position in spite of the movements imposed on the rest of their bodies.

Through these experiments Magnus concluded that righting reactions depend on visual reflexes and brain-stem centers. It is accepted that cortical centers only act in optical righting reflexes, while other centers are independent of direct voluntary influences because they are placed in brain-stem levels.

Righting reactions for head positions respond to labyrinthine, optic, and tactile stimuli, while righting reactions for body positions respond to proprioceptive and tactile inputs. Head and body orientations are related to gravity, supporting surfaces, distant environment (optic), and parts of the body.

Finally, Magnus and de Kleijn established that labyrinths and limbs have a double relationship: (1) a direct relation through the tonic labyrinthine reflex, and (2) an indirect relation, when labyrinths act upon neck muscles and then the latter act upon tonus and posture of the limbs.[8]

Sherrington, Magnus, and de Kleijn were pioneers in the study of posture, tonus, motor activity, and labyrinthine influences in animals. Their contributions to our knowledge of the possible mechanisms of many human postural abnormalities deserves our highest respect.

(30) VESTIBULAR APPARATUS AND POSTURE

The inner ear in humans has auditory and nonauditory organs. The cochlea is the auditory organ dedicated to hearing while the vestibular apparatus is the nonauditory organ dedicated to posture, equilibrium, muscular tonus, and spatial orientation. The vestibule in humans is a cavity in the middle of the labyrinth containing the saccule and the utricle. The vestibule communicates at the anterior end with the cochlea and at the posterior end with the semicircular canals. The utricle, the saccule, and the semicircular canals form the vestibular apparatus (or labyrinth). The vestibular nerve conducts impulses originating in the utricle, the saccule, and the semicircular canals. Vestibular nerves are related not only to posture and equilibrium; they also control the movements of the eyes and many other functions connected with intentional and coordinated movements.

This apparatus specifically responds to gravitational forces and accelerated or retarded movements. Receptor organs are located in the ampullae of the semicircular canals (cristae ampullares) and the maculae of the utricle and saccule. The maculae are covered by a gelatinous substance containing some prisms of calcium corbonate which are called "otoliths" or "otoconia." Impulses originate in these peripheral receptors (1) through the stimulation produced by movements, mainly the angular acceleratory one (turning or rotatory movements); (2) through gravitational forces, mainly related to linear acceleration, to body orientation, and to head position in space; and (3) through bone vibration of the head. See Figure 4.

From peripheral receptors, vestibular nerves are connected to centers on each medullar side. From the medulla some ascending fibers follow the medial longitudinal fasciculus, ending finally in the nuclei of the oculomotor nerves of both sides, ipsilateral and heterolateral. Other descending tracts connect vestibular nuclei with primary motoneurons of both sides in the cervical region of the spinal cord and with the ipsilateral side in all the levels of the spine. This vestibular action is much more important in the spinal levels corresponding to the upper part of the trunk and upper limbs.

Descending fibers participate with proprioception in posture and locomotion. It is currently being debated whether or not vestibular peripheral receptors act as proprioceptors, but certainly otoliths in the vestibular apparatus and proprioceptors of the neck muscles provide tonic laby-

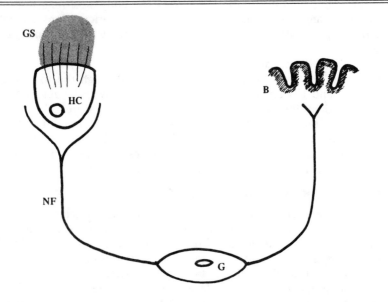

Figure 4. Reception and Transmission of Vestibular Stimuli. GS: gelatinous substance. HC: hair cell. NF: nerve fiber. G: ganglion. B: brain.

NEUROPSYCHOLOGICAL FUNDAMENTALS

rinthine reflexes and tonic neck reflexes which "sum algebraically" its effects in order to obtain compensatory movements of the limbs. Those effects can be clinically observed in normal persons.

Vestibular nuclei and cerebellar nuclei also are strongly connected with each other through vestibular-cerebellar and cerebellar-vestibular fibers. Vestibular-cerebellar fibers go together with direct root fibers to the tectum nuclei. From the tectum some fibers return to vestibular nuclei as well as to the reticular formation (i.e., a special structure formed by many different and very thin fibers, mainly at the brain stem) and spinal cord.

The vestibular apparatus connects with the cerebellum through many pathways. The cerebellum gains preponderance during childhood, the vestibular apparatus apparently being more important during infancy and early childhood. Vestibular and cerebellar data can both be obtained through clinical examination. In order to differentiate vestibular and cerebellar abnormalities, one must keep in mind the diverse signs that the labyrinth and cerebellum can provide.

From vestibular nuclei there are also cortical and subcortical projections (mainly contralateral) which seem to be already well established. These projections explain cortical participation in many postures and movements and also the final vestibular-visual motor coordination, which governs skilled movements essential for many learning abilities.

In summary, the vestibular apparatus plays an important role in posture, acting chiefly through vestibular-oculomotor pathways (in order to control eye movements) and through vestibular-spinal tracts (in order to control equilibrium).

As a final word, we should reiterate that reading requires skilled movements of the eyes, and that it is difficult to pay attention and to learn without natural or artificially created equilibrium.

(31) CEREBELLAR AND RETICULAR INFLUENCES ON POSTURE

Cerebellar action upon postural control is well accepted. This concept was originally established by L. Luciani and then developed by J. F. Fulton.[9] At the beginning of the twentieth century, Sherrington considered the cerebellum to be a "cephalic ganglion of proprioceptive system."[10] By the middle of the century, there was no further objection concerning the role of the cerebellum as the principal organ for the coordination of muscular activity. R. S. Sneider in 1950 called the cerebellum "the great modulator of neurologic function" in consideration of its influence on motor and sensory centers in the cerebrum, diencephalon, mesencephalon, and medulla.[11]

According to I. Esente, during the sixth month of gestation lateral cerebellar lobes are developed simultaneously with vestibular connections and striatum. These organs regulate muscular reactions, posture, and equilibrium in normal newborn babies and in premature infants.[12]

Myelination of the cerebellum was very carefully studied by L. B. Rorke and H. E. Riggs.[13] It is important to recall that, in newborn babies and infants, most of the cerebellum is already myelinated, starting with vestibular-cerebellar and cerebellar-vestibular interconnections. But only during the fourth year of age do the ponto-cerebellar tracts attain a staining of adult type.[14]

As a matter of fact, equilibrium maintained with both feet together and eyes closed is seldom, if ever, achieved until the fourth year of age. This is followed by the ability to stand on one leg. Both possibilities are surely related to the myelination of ponto-cerebellar pathways.

In newborn babies there are many responses that can be considered as synergies: for instance, the turning of the head in order to breathe in prone position; the displacement of the face against mother's breast in order to find the nipple; and also the head movements in order to avoid objects. The development of posture and equilibrium, nevertheless provokes a natural disruption of the mother-child dyad.[15] Postural, tonic, and righting reactions are milestones which differentiate several stages in maturation prior to the achievement of standing position: Following that come motor independence, space apprehension, and sufficient knowledge in order to be oneself.[16]

From birth through the first year of life, many types of cerebellar lesions or damage cannot be clinically diagnosed because the cerebellum is still "immature." A very frequent finding in examinations of babies (during the first months of postnatal life) is the presence of hypotonia and dysmetria in the head and the extremities. At that age these signs are difficult to differentiate from those provided by cerebellar lesions or definite athetosis. In other circumstances it is possible to observe an active hypertonia like that experimentally seen by G. G. J. Rademaker in animals.[17]

Cerebellar abnormalities produce a modification of the reflexes which are basic for equilibrium and coordination; but they can be properly diagnosed when the child must use his equilibrium (balance) and must make movements with directionality.

The cerebellum and vestibular nuclei act upon the reticular formation. The cerebellum exerts a tonic inhibitory action upon labyrinthine reflexes, and this action is produced through the reticular formation.

Many papers have been written in regard to the vestibular-reticular interconnections which take part not only in posture and equilibrium but also in the "ascending activating system." When natural vestibular stimulation (gravity, angular acceleration) is produced, simple activity in the reticular formation can be registered.[18]

In summary the cerebellum, vestibular apparatus, and reticular formation are acting together in many postural, tonic, and equilibrium functions.

(32) VESTIBULAR-PROPRIOCEPTIVE INTEGRATION AND POSTURAL CONTROL

In order to achieve posture, positions, purposeful equilibrium, and—eventually—locomotion and skilled movements, and in order to develop learning, normal persons must have vestibular impulses integrated with spinal motor activity.

Vestibular nerves exert spontaneous influence through a strong facilitating action upon the "pool" of spinal motor activity (i.e., upon the actions coming from different centers which at the level of the spine finally converge to produce motor activity). Vestibular stimulation can elicit spinal responses from ventral as well as dorsal roots. Vestibular-spinal fibers are connected with interneurons which project themselves to motoneurons and also to some presynaptic fibers of the dorsal roots.

Vestibular effect upon motoneurons can be excitatory or inhibitory effect is obtained through cerebellar and reticular actions.

Vestibular responses registered at the cervical level are more complex and important than vestibular responses obtained from lumbosacral levels. It seems reasonable to believe that vestibular apparatus controls the higher levels of the trunk and upper limbs much more than it does the lower limbs. Vestibular influences can then produce a more precise postural adjustment on the upper limbs than on the lower limbs. This influence is provoked through three descending tracts: (1) vestibular-spinal; (2) reticular-spinal; and (3) medial longitudinal fasciculus, the latter being of lesser importance, according to B. E. Gernandt and S. Gilman.[19]

Vestibular descending tracts influence gamma and alpha responses. When vestibular-spinal fibers do not function or are impaired, impulses upon gamma fibers do not arrive to produce muscular contraction or only attain poor or delayed contraction (because alpha fibers provide a supplementary action).

This situation can also produce a general hypotonia, mainly when vestibular-proprioceptive system is impaired. In general, hypotonia is greater in lower limbs; this is so because the connections of vestibular-spinal tracts are greater in upper limbs, as we said before.

We should be aware that vestibular stimulation can initiate the necessary series of muscular contractions which are able to maintain posture and to control equilibrium. Subsequent muscular control is governed by the effector itself.

As we have discussed, Sherrington, Magnus, and Rademaker were among those who pointed out the importance of neck proprioceptors in postural reactions. It is therefore understandable that, when pressure is exerted on neck muscles, it is possible to produce a greater inhibition of vestibular responses.

Actually, tonic-neck reflexes are not very easily seen in normal newborn babies in the supine position. This finding does not conform with A. Gesell's earlier statements, but it is in accord with many other more recent writers.[20] Nevertheless, it is possible to observe the tonic-neck reflex in other positions, in infants as well as in older children: This kind of reflex can be elicited until eight to nine years of age in "quadruped" position.[21] In other positions (e.g., "one-leg position") it is possible to see similar reactions not only in childhood but also in the adult life. Normally, vestibular-proprioceptive integration allows the production of such a reaction.

There are several discrete stages in vestibular-proprioceptive integration. We have previously discussed vestibular receptors being considered as proprioceptors: In newborn babies and in young children proprioception and vestibular apparatus act together. Vestibular-proprioceptive integration consists of "informing" the higher levels about body posture. Certainly, "balance" or "equilibrium" is quite different in babies than in young children. After the achievement of the standing position, vestibular-proprioceptive integration changes; and, for some tasks, the vestibular apparatus reacts inadequately in regard to proprioceptive inputs, and vice versa. Step by step, vestibular-proprioceptive integration develops, and cerebellar and reticular influences become very important for the production of equilibrium of an adult type. When the child is able to maintain himself on one leg, vestibular-proprioceptive integration is established as an important fact of the future body laterality: When proprioceptive action increases on one side of the body, vestibular reaction also increases on the same side; and when vestibular action increases on one side of the body, proprioceptive reaction also increases on the same side. When vestibular-proprioceptive dissociation disrupts this kind of integration those actions and reactions cannot be seen.

In summary, vestibular-proprioceptive integration is one of the most important factors in postural control. Other central nervous system levels participate in such a complex integration, mainly the cerebellum and reticular formation. To achieve postural control is to develop attention span, to open exteroceptors (particularly eyes and ears), and to allow more skilled movements.

Let us recall K. Lorenz' statement that the beginning of conceptualization was determined by knowledge of one's own body. He proposed that, when primitive man was able to grasp an object and simultaneously to see not only the object which he wanted but also his own hand grasping the object, he was able to become aware of his movements and to form the first conceptualizations.[22] It is not necessary to review our previous discussion in order to identify the importance of vestibular-proprioceptive integration with the possibility of body conceptualization. Lorenz' statement analyzes the starting point of the phylogenetic achievement of human learning. After this, only one step was missing for verbal conceptualization.

NOTES

1. P. E. Flechsig, *Die Leitungsbahnen im Gehirn und Ruckenmark auf Grund Entwicklungsge sichtlicher untersuchungen* (Leipzig: W. Engelmann, 1876); P. E. Flechsig, *Anatomie des menshlichen Gehirns uns Ruckenmarks auf myelogenetisher Grundlage* (Leipzig: G. Thieme, 1920); P. E. Flechsig, *Meine Myelogenetische Hirnlehre mit biographischer Einleitung* (Berlin: Julius Springer, 1927).
2. W. von Bechterew, "Ueber eine bisher unbekannte Verbindung der grosse Oliven mit dem Grosshirn," *Neurologische Centralband* 9 (1885); W. von Bechterew, *Die Leitungsbahnen im Gehirn un Ruckenmark* (Leipzig: Besold, 1894); P. E. Flechsig, "Die myelogenetische Gleiderung de Leitungs bahnen des lisenkerns beim Menschen," *Berliner sachsiner Akademie fur Wissenschaft* [Leipzig] 73 (1921): 295.
3. C. von Monakow, "Gehirnpathologie in Nithnagels," *Spezielle Pathologie und Therapie* [Wien] 9 (1897): 1.
4. C. von Monakow, *Die Lokalisation im Grosshirn* (Woesbaden: Herde, 1914).
5. C. von Monakow and R. Mourgue, "Biologische Einfuhrung in das Studium der Psychopathologie" (Stuttgart und Leipzig, 1930), cited by A. Peiper, *Die Eigenart der Kindlichen Hirntatigkeit* (Leipzig: VEB. Georg Thieme, 1961).
6. C. S. Sherrington, *The Integrative Action of the Nervous System* (New York: Scribner's Sons, 1906); C. S. Sherrington, *The Integrative Action of the Nervous System* (London: Constable and Co., 1911); C. S. Sherrington, *Selected Writings* (recompiled by Denny Brown) (London: Hamish, Hamilton Medical Books, 1939).
7. R. Magnus, *Korperstellung* (Berlin: Springer, 1924); R. Magnus, "Some Results of Studies in the Physiology of Posture," *Lancet* 211:2 (September 11, 1926): 531-536; 211:2 (September 18, 1926): 585-588; R. Magnus and A. de Kleijn, "Experimentelle Physiologie des Vestibulapparates," *Handbuch der Neurologie des Ohresheilkunde* 1 (1924).

8. Magnus and de Kleijn, *op. cit.*

9. J. F. Fulton, Commented in R. C. Truex, *Neuroanatomia Humana* (A. Mosovich, trans.) (Buenos Aires: El Ateneo, 1961).

10. Sherrington, *The Integrative Action* (1906), *loc. cit.*

11. R. S. Sneider, "Recent Contributions to the Anatomy and Physiology of the Cerebellum," *Archives of Neurology and Psychiatry* 64 (1950): 196-219.

12. I. Esente, *Physiologie de la Vision chez le Premature et le Nourrison Normal* (Paris: G. Doin et Cie, 1958).

13. L. Balian Rorke and H. E. Riggs, *Myelination of the Brain in the Newborn* (Philadelphia: J. B. Lippincott Company, 1969).

14. P. I. Yakovlev and A. R. Lecours, "The Myelogenetic Cycles of Regional Maturation of the Brain," in A. Minkowski (ed.), *Regional Development of the Brain in Early Life* (Oxford: Blackwell Scientific Publications, 1967): 3-70.

15. H. Wallon, *Les Origins du Caractere chez l'Enfant* (Paris: Presses Universitaires de France, 1949).

16. J. B. de Quirós, L. F. Coriat, and L. Benasayag, "Hacia el Encuentro del Esquema Corporal a traves de las Respuestas Neurologicas Vestibulares," *Fonoaudiologica* [Buenos Aires] 7 (1961): 27-55.

17. G. G. J. Rademaker, *Reaction Labyrinthique et Equilibre* (Paris: Masson, 1935).

18. B. E. Gernandt and C. A. Thulin, "Vestibular Connection of the Brain Stem," *American Journal of Physiology* 171 (1952): 121-127.

19. B. E. Gernandt and S. Gilman, "Descending Vestibular Activity and its Modulation by Proprioceptive, Cerebellar and Reticular Influence," *Experimental Neurology* 1 (1959): 274-304.

20. A. Gesell, "The Tonic Neck Reflex in the Human Infant," *Journal of Pediatrics* 13 (1928): 455; R. S. Paine and T. E. Oppe, *Neurological Examination of Children* Clinics in Developmental Medicine 20/21 (London: The Spastics Society in Association with William Heinemann Medical Books Ltd., 1966).

21. F. A. Hellebrandt, M. Schade, and M. L. Carns, "Methods of Evoking the Tonic-Neck Reflexes in Normal Human Subjects," *American Journal of Physical Medicine* 41 (1962): 90.

22. K. Lorenz, "The Innate Bases of Learning," in K. H. Pribram (ed.), *On the Biology of Learning* (New York: Harcourt, Brace and World, 1968).

NEUROPSYCHOLOGICAL FUNDAMENTALS

CHAPTER VI

Visual and Auditory
Foundations of Learning

(33) PERCEPTUAL MODALITIES DURING INFANCY
AND EARLY CHILDHOOD

We must try to explain some aspects of the development of different perceptual modalities during infancy and early childhood. Among these, visual and auditory inputs are perhaps the most important ones.

Classically, the word "perception" refers to the recognition of sensory information produced by different stimuli coming from the outside world. According to D. Katz, there is no firm delineation between the terms "sensation" and "perception."[1] Nevertheless, a more recent criterion considers perception as the resultant sensory-motor patterns produced by sensory stimulation. Perception, therefore, could be considered an acquired skill; and this concept opens new horizons in learning.

It is true that some people can learn best through the visual modality and others through the auditory modality. But it is also true that, in accordance with the development already achieved by the child, he may prefer to introduce knowledge through vision, through hearing/audition, or through haptic (tactile plus kinesthetic) receptors. Those situations indicate preferences for one or another perceptual input in order to learn. These perceptual inputs are called modalities, as was discussed in Chapter III, Section 20.

In abnormal children the choice of a perceptual modality is regularly determined by their own handicaps: in blind children, the ears; in deaf children, the eyes; and so on. Likewise, in learning-disabled children there are different preferred perceptual modalities.

In specific learning disabilities it was outlined by H. R. Myklebust and D. Johnson and by Quirós that, in order to learn, a visual or auditory predominant modality could exist ("auditorization" or "visualization").[2] Later on, Elena Boder extended our subtypes to include a third one: combining visual and auditory handicaps and therefore constituting virtual alexia.[3] According to her, those handicapped in auditorizing (in dyslexics) are recognized as "dysphonetics"; those handicapped in visualizing are recognized as "dyseidetics"; and those handicapped in both auditorizing and visualizing are recognized as "dysphonetics-dyseidetics."

Certain differences can be established between Boder's and our own singular view. Boder speaks much more than we do about the importance of perceptual modalities, analysis-synthesis skills, and correlated patterns of reading and spelling Gestalten. Earlier authors considered, as do we, the perceptual modality in dyslexia as constituting part of a total syndrome with many variables.[4]

Perceptual modalities also have much influence upon postural and motor development in children. In newborn babies the vestibular-proprioceptive system determines asymmetrical postures and, later on, head control. During the third month after birth visual perception begins to dominate, symmetrical postures are observed, and balance develops quickly until the baby can sit up at the age of six months. Vision generally includes the existence of coordinated movements. It is clear that eye movements must be coordinated with head movements in order to be effective. Then the baby begins to develop new perceptual modalities: auditory-visual-kinesthetic behaviors start establishing sequences of perceptual interrelationships which are useful for assessment and remediation.[5] An example of auditory-visual-kinesthetic behavior is seen when a baby reacts by turning his head toward a sound source, looking for an object (auditory-visual behavior); then he wants to grasp it (visual-kinesthetic behavior), and so on.

When a baby of this age (six months) hears a noise, he directs his eyes and head in order to see the object; and when he sees it, he tries to grasp it in order to take it to his mouth. The baby is discovering the "facing space." At the end of the first year of life crawling, standing up, and walking permit the development of new interactions of perceptual modalities which allow him to "discover" the "surrounding space." This sensory integration produces the necessary possibility for the appearance of speech as an imitation of the environment (*lingua*).

During the second year of life, the action of gravitational forces produces reinforcement and development of body schema through experimental walking, falling, brushing against objects, and so on—thus developing the control of "purposeful equilibrium." All these factors act within a "limiting space," while *lingua* continues its development as a result of the combination of the child's abilities and stresses from the outside environment: The child realizes that the use of *lingua* can help him communicate his needs, desires, fears, etc., to others.

During the third and fourth years of life, posture, positions, and equilibrium develop from the integration of the postural system. The body divides into two halves in order to coordinate different motor activities on both body sides (one side can do one skilled movement while the other is doing another movement); and Romberg's test can be performed without visual help. The space of the child becomes "environmental."

During the fifth and sixth years of life, corporal potentiality and body laterality are definitely established; standing on one leg is feasible;

and preference and prevalence in the use of one side of the body is finally achieved. This allows the possibility of symbolization because of the definite establishment of cerebral hemispheric symbolic dominance (generally the left) which may permit the development of language and also read and written language.

Perceptual modalities development can be seen in Table 1. These modalities are presented together with postural and motor development in children. It is particularly noteworthy to see how position, movement, and different kinds of "spaces" are sequenced according to the stage that predominates in child development.

(34) SENSORY-MOTOR RELATIONSHIPS AND PERCEPTUAL MODAL-ITIES (OVERLOADED AND EXTRACHARGED SYSTEMS)

Some of the most significant examples of the importance of motor activity for the proper achievement of perception can be found in some papers by R. Held.[6] According to M. L. T. Abercrombie, the fundamental conclusions of Held's works are: (1) that active body movements are important for the development of perceptual skills and (2) that the ability to compensate distorted visual or auditive perceptions depends on movement.[7] Held's ideas also support the idea that visual information and auditory information both require normal movements in order to be normally achieved. This suggests the existence of significant changes in the way that information coming from eyes and ears is processed in the sensory parts of the central nervous system. These processes take place within the general mechanisms of perceptual adaptation to the environment. It is therefore obvious that muscles, as well as the motor parts of the central nervous system, are included in this adaptive process.

The relationship between sensory and motor activities in the general process of adaptation to the environment also becomes evident when certain mammals (including humans) have, or are experimentally submitted to, motor or sensory deprivation: Their achievement in perceptual and motor skills greatly diminishes, and behavioral development is consequently distorted.

Adaptation to reorientation of perceptual receptors, and continuous dependence on contact with the environment in order to obtain appropriate motor coordination, are facts which imply sensory-motor and motor-sensory interrelationships.[8] These interrelationships, in our opinion, conform closely to the principles of action-retroaction and feedback which were analyzed in Chapter IV, Section 23.

According mainly to Johnson and Myklebust, any perceptual modality can function in three different ways:

1. Semi-independently of the other modalities, or "intra-neurosensory."
2. Helping another perceptual modality, or "interneuro-sensory."
3. Integrating a total system of information, or "integrative."[9]

These notions are connected with the concept of "extracharges" and

TABLE 1

Perceptual Modalities, Postural and Motor Development in Children

Age	Eliciting factors	Milestones	Attained function or acquisition
First Quarter	Vestibular-proprioceptive system	Tonic-neck posture Asymmetries Flexion-adduction Sucking	Head control
Second Quarter	Perceptual vision Coordinated movements	Symmetrical postures	Sitting position (balance)
Third Quarter	Objects Auditory-visual-kinesthetic modality	Grasping Flexion-abduction Extension-abduction Rolling	Facing space
Fourth Quarter	Crawling Standing up	Displacements First walking	Surrounding space
		SPEECH	
Second Year	Gravitation Body schema	Experimental walking Purposeful equilibrium	Limiting space

			LINGUA
Third and Fourth Years	Posture and equilibrium Integration of the postural system	Division of the body in two halves Romberg's test with eyes closed	Environmental space
Fifth and Sixth Years	Corporal potentiality	Standing on one leg	Reading/Writing
		LANGUAGE	
	Laterality	Preference by one side of the body	Symbolization
Seventh and Eighth Years	Diadochokinesis Alternating movements (cerebellum)	Motor dexterity Rules of games and sports	Skilled voluntary coordinated movements

"overloads." When some channels or pathways are dedicated not only to their specific functions, but also to a nonspecific function, we say that they have "extracharges." An example of an extracharge is the notion of space conveyed by audition in a blind person. A variety of experiments confirm beyond doubt the spatial function of hearing and audition in the blind. Perhaps one of the most interesting investigations was the one carried out by R. J. Schwartz under the supervision of M. D. Steer. Schwartz called attention to the fact that the standard number of words spoken by the congenitally blind adult was less than the standard number of words spoken by normal adults.[10] This was interpreted to mean that blind individuals, when speaking, were using hearing not only to control speech, but also to gain other information that commonly enters through the visual modality.

When a channel or pathway receives multiple stimuli at the same time, we speak of the "overloaded" system. For instance, in some children with learning disabilities, inhibition of several different stimuli together becomes impossible. Stimuli interfere with each other, and learning does not take place or is very difficult in such a situation.

The "overload" notion is closely related to the interneurosensory modality. The difference between "extracharge" and "overload" lies in the fact that overload refers to a learning pattern that can exist in normal situations, while extracharge always refers to abnormal situations (impairment or failure of a channel or pathway with the "help" of another modality in order to obtain the necessary information). In some abnormal cases the intraneurosensory modality can exist (for instance, a deaf child can learn through vision but not through audition): In these cases extracharges can help the handicapped modality; overload is produced in one or several pathways. In abnormal cases the integration of all the modalities is very difficult or impossible.

Visual and auditory perception must be considered within the general framework of sensory information integrated at the higher levels of the central nervous system. It is neither convenient nor justified to separate or isolate visual or auditory perception from the total sensory integration (including vestibular inputs). Nor is it possible to separate visual or auditory perception from body information, mainly from posture and movement. All types of learning rely on intentional coordinated motor activities and on sensory integration, vision and audition being extremely important. Visual and auditory perception in normal individuals undoubtedly constitute an important element in order for one to "grasp" the outside world, but it must be kept in mind that every perceptual learning requires use of the body and movement. There is no doubt that the knowledge we have from ourselves and from our environment, as well as the recognition of what we *could* do—with all that information—depends mainly on sensory integration. All sensory inputs provide the necessary information in order to allow adequate responses through afferential synthesis.[11]

(35) DEVELOPMENT OF HUMAN VISION

Vision needs the stimulation of light in order to develop and in order to establish the progressive myelination of the optic nerve. When normal babies receive proper light stimulation, visual skills already exist at the fourth month after birth.

Between the end of the second and the beginning of the third month after a baby is born, three principal functions of vision are established: fixation, accommodation, and convergence. "Fixation" means the possibility of directing the gaze so that the image of the object looked at falls on the fovea centralis (the point of clearest vision and most visual acuity at the center of the retina). "Accommodation" means the adjustment of the eye for several distances. "Convergence" means the coordinated movement of the two eyeballs toward a common near point of fixation. These three functions are extremely important in the development of vision; and they allow the development of other achievements: symmetric positions, outside-world cognition, intentional grasping, and so on.

Fixation, accommodation, and convergence constitute a milestone in human visual development; but the difference between this stage of development and that of using the eyes for reading and writing is enormous.

There are many well written, valuable works on the subject of vision development; however, the scope of this book requires that we limit our discussion to those three writers whose contributions are most relevant for our purposes: Esente, Niesel, and Fichsel.[12]

According to I. Esente, the development of visual apparatus occurs at three levels: The first one, of clear motor predominance, is essentially ruled by vestibular-optic reflex; the second one has its beginning in the optic-autonomic reflex (subcortical reflex) and it develops through optical-cortical reflex; the third one has a clear perceptual predominance, attaining its peak with the appearance of the fixation reflex.

P. Niesel considers the "visual system" extremely significant in a child's general development. This author calls our attention to the fact that the basic development of perception of (1) objects and (2) movements is produced during the first six months of life. The coordination of ocular movements with those of the head and upper limbs is ready by that period. Between the seventh and twelfth month after birth, accommodation, convergence, and coordination of both eyes' movements are developed to the point at which the first stages of binocular spatial vision are attained. Binocular spatial vision is reinforced with visual acuity up to the fifth year of life (as cited in Chapter IV, Section 26). According to Niesel, the entire accommodation process is always obtained at the tenth year of life. The association between the two factors just mentioned and the acquisition of language is of great significance.

H. Fichsel worked with visual evoked potentials. The notion of evoked potential implies the electrophysiological modification in several parts of the brain, produced by different deliberate sensory stimulations (for instance: EEG waves are modified through specific deliberate stimulations, like sounds, light, etc., those EEG modifications being identified by a computer in order to differentiate them from other EEG modifications). Fichsel says that visual evoked potentials on the registered waves of the cerebral cortex can be obtained in human fetuses as early as the three last months of gestation. He also states that these visual evoked potentials can be correlated to cerebral morphological variations, thus considering that, at the sixth or seventh year of age, maturation of the visual cerebral cortex is reached, since from that age onward the obtained visual evoked potentials are similar to those of adults.

Niesel's and Fichsel's conclusions give important foundational support to the existence of a consistent biological basis of structural maturation for reading/writing.[13]

According to some of T. G. R. Bower's studies, it seems that formation of the notion of "object" in infants occurs rather early.[14] In the beginning, this notion of "object" is merely visual and not directly related to general tactual or proprioceptive information. In order to be integrated as practical knowledge, such an early notion needs, then, other contributions, such as those coming from vestibular-visual, vestibular-oculomotor inputs, as well as those provided by the proprioceptive impulses of oculomotor muscles.[15]

(36) DEVELOPMENT OF VISUAL PERCEPTION

A practical definition of visual perception was stated by N. A. Buktenica, who said that "visual perception is literally the capacity to interpret, or give meaning to, what is seen."[16] This definition includes recognition, insight, and interpretation at the higher levels of the central nervous system of what is seen.

Several studies on visual perception in young children seem to corroborate the hypothesis, connecting visual perception with a variety of functions and capacities. These functions and capacities have an interdependent relationship.[17]

Let us stop for a moment to consider eye-hand coordination. In infancy, the functions of the hand and eye cooperate closely (that is, grasping and manipulation are in tune with motor, sensory, and perceptual vision). This functional relationship could be considered the beginning of the baseline of spatial organization. From the first month of life until the third, vision and grasping have independent maturational patterns. In the third month after birth it is possible to see in the infant some early specific combined reactions, because the infant—when facing some attractive object—produces reflex movements at the proximal segments of the upper limbs.[18] This early eye and upper-limb reaction implies future visuo-manual coordination, because voluntary grasping is maturationally established from it. Grasping depends not only on visuo-motor coordination, but also on vestibular-proprioceptive regulation. Some examples can clarify this statement: In congenitally blind children it is not possible to obtain appropriate use of the hands without lengthy proprioceptive training (postural, labyrinthine, and kinesthetic). In spite of intensive work, skilled hand movements are barely obtained, and they cannot write with common handwriting. They must use the Braille system of writing or, at least, typewriters—both requiring very special training. An opposite situation is produced in almost all cerebral-palsied children who—because of their postural and motor impairments—cannot grasp efficiently in spite of having efficient vision.

M. Frostig, W. Lefever, and J. R. B. Whittlesey assessed the development of visual perception according to five areas, operationally defined. These areas are: (1) visuo-motor coordination; (2) figure-ground; (3) constancy of shape; (4) position in space; and (5) spatial relationships.[19] These

NEUROPSYCHOLOGICAL FUNDAMENTALS

authors did not accept these five areas as the *only* ones pertaining to visual perception, but they considered these areas as those of particular relevance for academic achievement. Without doubt, these areas are extremely important for visual learning: We just spoke about visuo-motor (or eye-hand) coordination. With figure-ground, a sufficient capacity to differentiate figure and ground is necessary in order to obtain analysis and synthesis referred to words and sentences in reading. Constancy of shape permits recognition of letters and words in text. Position in space and spatial relationships relate to the ability to differentiate letters and sequences of letters in a word or in a sentence.

The use of perceptual abilities in academic learning is directly related to perceptual development—and particularly to visual development. There is a fundamental sequential correlation between motor activity, perception, thought, and language. In general terms, the field of visual development can be divided into four major areas: (1) visuo-motor coordination and space localization; (2) visual discrimination; (3) visual preferences and selective responses to visual stimuli; and (4) visual retentiveness of visual information.

Visuo-motor coordination is the primary factor of space localization and of precise directional responses. Visual discrimination is the primary factor of visual information. Both, visuo-motor coordination and visual discrimination, can be combined into visual information. Visual selectiveness depends on both of these factors. Visual experience is the result of visual exploration since birth. The newborn infant is able to process visual information long before the baby is actively physically able to explore the surrounding environment. All these factors must be sufficiently developed in normal children before school entrance. Sensory-motor and motor-sensory processes must be fully integrated, interrelated, and automatized in order to allow the achievement of symbolization and the learning of reading, writing, and their further developments.

Tests such as the *Bender Visual-Motor Gestalt Test,* the *Illinois Test of Psycholinguistic Abilities* (ITPA), the *Revised Visual Retention Test,* the *Visual Motor Integration Test,* and others, are extremely useful in order to assess different abilities in visual perception.[20]

A major problem in physiology of vision is how human beings can see the outside world as a stable world, always in the same "upright" position. Actually, that upright position of the outside world is permanent in spite of (1) the continuous movements of the eyes, (2) the different positions and movements of the head, (3) the several positions and movements of the body, and (4) the adoption of unusual positions, such as the upside-down position of the head.

Another associated problem faced by several authors with different explanations is the question of why we can see the world in the upright position and not in the reverse position. This is understandable if we recall the successive crossings of the visual pathways. It undoubtedly seems that central processes are able to correct visual inputs and to stabilize "inner" images in order to permit the necessary body movements for survival and development. This notwithstanding, explanations by different authors seldom coincide in clarifying this main point in physiology.

Summarizing our thoughts, we can say that:

1. An early capacity exists to form visual patterns, which is associated with visuo-motor coordination and vestibular-proprioceptive regulation.
2. Selective visual attention span influences developmental patterns in general, and particularly sensory patterns during the first stages of perceptual development.
3. Specific selectivity is continuously changing according to the level of maturation, but its influence is constant and remains during all the stages.
4 The problem of apparent stability of the visual world (in spite of the movements of the eyes) in normal individuals, needs much more research in order to be clarified.

(37) VESTIBULAR INFLUENCES ON VISUO-MOTOR COORDINATION

Numerous researchers have made important neurophysiological discoveries related to this subject. Vestibular influences upon eye movements were established during the end of the last century. As early as 1865, H. Aubert observed vestibular influences in vertical vision.[21] At the beginning of the twentieth century C. S. Sherrington on the one hand, and R. Magnus on the other, studied relations between proprioceptive and vestibular inputs.[22] At the level of the vestibular organs some reflexes were established: (1) static vestibular-ocular reflexes were elicited by otoliths; (2) stato-kinetic reflexes were elicited by semicircular canals. By about 1950 many facts about vestibular influences on visuo-motor coordination were already well established and accepted by the scientific world.

M. Minkowski wrote in 1948:

... Movements of the eyeballs exist in the fetus, even before the opening of the eyelids. These movements depend on outputs coming from vestibular centers. During the fifth gestational month myelination of vestibular central pathways and of posterior longitudinal fasciculus is already finished. Ocular movements, therefore, when produced by vestibular influences, occur several months earlier than do the ocular movements elicited by light stimulations acting at different points of the retina after birth.[23]

During the 1950s some important discoveries were made, which have subsequently been accepted by the medical community: (1) the first movements of the eyeballs in newborn babies are connected only with vestibular and postural centers; (2) after birth, eye movements rapidly increase because of the influence of new postural reflexes, auditory-tactile reflexes, and luminous reflexes.

Ocular movements are essential in the process of learning. All the reflexes just mentioned, therefore, take part in the development of learning processes. A main question to be solved was why visual perception remains the same in spite of the different head positions. At the end of the 1950s it was discovered that functional convergence in the primary visual cerebral cortex of vestibular and retinal inputs may be one of the most important mechanisms for sensory integration.[24] Other relevant psychophysiological contributions deal with specific vestibular-visual coordination in reticular formation (with projection to the visual cerebral cortex).[25] The visual world remains apparently the same during eye movements and body movements. In order to maintain stability of space, retino-cortical projections and vestibular-cortical projections are not static, but depend on continuous control—especially on oculo-vestibular coordination of the eye and body movements.

We might note in passing that during the 1960s it was demonstrated that almost all the visual cortex neurons were activated by labyrinthine inputs. When the visual cortex was receiving an input produced by luminous stimulation of the eyes, the activation of vestibular discharges was able to disturb or disrupt the visual area responses.[26] It was clearly determined that conjugate movements of the eyes (at least in monkeys) depend on vestibular inputs.[27] Conjugate movements of the eyes are those by which both eyeballs move in unison in the same direction. In order to stabilize the outside visual world, vestibular organs, in mammals, work together with head position and eye movements. In this, they are helped by the action of the neck receptors.[28] It was also shown that neck proprioceptors (located in vertebral joints and muscles) not only act upon body balance but also upon the regulation of eye movements.[29]

Many other recent authors insisted on the same fact: Labyrinthine (vestibular) inputs, oculomotor inputs, and neck proprioceptor inputs continuously interact in order to obtain, to develop, and to control body postures and positions, equilibrium, and space stabilization.[30]

The cerebellum does not seem to exert a direct control upon eye movements; it acts indirectly in modifying and influencing them. On the other hand, some authors believe in a sort of representation of ocular movements in some cerebellar regions.[31]

(38) VESTIBULAR-PROPRIOCEPTICE INTEGRATION, VISION, POSTURE, AND MOVEMENT

As stated in Chapter V, Section 32, vestibular-proprioceptive integration is part of a complex process by which postural control is attained, which in turn facilitates the development of attention span through perceptual modalities and learning. Vision is one of the most important perceptual modalities, and in Section 37 we reviewed some relevant questions in regard to the stability of space through vision.

Now we must confront another great neuropsychological question: How is it possible to have two different visual images (one from each eye) and to "feel" that only one image is produced? This question is extensively discussed all over the world. Certainly, vision in humans is binocular: Coordination between the function of both eyes produces a sole visual image. This process requires an extremely sensitive system of regulation, especially through oculomotor and vestibular visual coordination mechanisms.[32]

It is indispensable to realize that visual perception of movements is the result of a complex regulation among different inputs coming from retina, vestibular organs, proprioceptive receptors and, sometimes, auditory and tactual inputs—all of them related to attention span. This regulation is primarily coordinated at the brain-stem level and then elaborated at the cerebral cortex. In this sense it seems that some cortical neurons have specific responses to directional movements of objects.[33] In human beings the complex processing of visual information (such as axes detection, directional orientation, directional selectiveness, and so on) takes place at higher levels of the central nervous system. On the other hand, convergences of multisensory inputs are produced at various levels of the central nervous system, thus constituting one of the most prominent mechanisms of sensory integration.[34]

Some of the most outstanding psycho-neurophysiological findings on vestibular-proprioceptive and visuo-motor integration can be summarized as follows:

1. Vestibular organs play a fundamental role in the regulation of eyes and head position.
2. Vestibular-cortical, vestibular-oculomotor, vestibular-cerebellar, vestibular-spinal, vestibular-reticular, and vestibular visual interrelationships can be clearly distinguished.
3. Vestibular-oculomotor interrelationships are mainly stimulated by gravitational forces, and they could be useful for correct visual perception, with the participation of thalamic-cortical control.
4. Vestibular-spinal interrelationships are divided into two groups, which are affected by different inputs coming from muscles, joints, and skin.
5. Vestibular-visual interrelationships (through vestibular nuclei, reticular formation of the pons, some thalamic nuclei, some external geniculate body nuclei, and visual cerebral cortex), seem to function as visuo-spatial coordinators of vestibular and visual inputs coming from vertical and horizontal axes.

Posture and equilibrium fundamentally respond to three different sensory afferences coming from several peripheral receptors (proprioceptive, vestibular, and visual inputs). These three afferences working together constitute an afferential synthesis which gives to the individual the functional ability to develop the postural system through action-retroaction and feedback mechanisms.[35] Certainly afferent synthesis is coordinated by the cerebellum and the reticular formation when both structures have attained sufficient evolution to permit such a function.

Learning of one's own body and immediate space must precede learning language. Individuals need to develop a perceptual pattern, initially responding to their own vital needs. This pattern is accomplished through the development of behaviors. In a second stage, individuals need to develop according to their own abilities and interests: learning is extremely important for this development and for achieving acquired behaviors. Both processes (inherited and acquired behaviors) are intimately associated; and they follow a well recognized, sequenced pattern in normal individuals. When such a normal pattern is distorted, all the allied functions are also disturbed. When vision fails, proprioceptive and vestibular inputs must be reinforced; when the labyrinthine system fails, proprioceptive and visual inputs must be reinforced; and so on.

When visual, proprioceptive, and vestibular afferences are adequate, they must remain in balance with other sensitive and sensory afferences, integrating with them to form the total information to the higher levels of the central nervous system.* The adequate balance among these different inputs permits correct emotional, perceptual, and motor development in infants and children.

It is presently accepted that receptors at visceral organs (interoceptors) have a clear influence upon muscular tonus, mainly in infants and young children. In some monkeys straightening reflexes start from mesenteric and visceral receptors. The influence that corporal and visceral pain have upon posture is very well known.[36]

(39) DEVELOPMENT OF HUMAN HEARING

Development of hearing in humans begins much earlier than development of vision and finishes much later. The end organ begins its structural differentiation at three and one-half months of fetal life. It is worth pointing out that, at the same time, the myelination of the fibers of the semicircular canals is becoming complete. As can be seen, hearing is strongly connected with tonus and equilibrium. We already spoke in Chapter V, Section 28, about von Monakow's studies on myelination of the vestibular and auditory systems. Actually, connections between both systems are phylogenically and ontogenically very great. Fish and other animals which live in water, for example, have superior development of vestibular organs. If we think that the reception of vibrations transmitted by water can save the creature's life by helping it avoid the attack of an enemy, we can understand why vestibular organs in fish are so important.

In humans, Corti's organ attains complete development in the sixth month of fetal life. Only in passing, we might mention that in cats and rabbits auditory end organs begin to function between the first and second week of postnatal life. Nevertheless, these animals seem to have greater auditory acuity than humans.

At the level of the human brain stem, myelination of vestibular and auditory fibers occurs very early. As P. I. Yakovlev pointed out, both types of fibers constitute the "stato-acoustic" system, which is already developed and therefore recognized in all the microscopic preparations made during the sixth month of fetal life.[37] In newborn babies, stato-acoustic system fibers have finished their myelination at the level of the brain stem. In general, it is accepted that the three first neurons of auditory pathways are already myelinated between the sixth and seventh months of fetal life; before birth, myelination of acoustic radiations (which connect the medial geniculate body with the temporal auditory cortex) is beginning.

---

*The term "sensitive" mainly concerns itself with inner body information; the term "sensory" mainly concerns outside or external information. For instance, vision or hearing are sensory inputs, while pain, body temperature, and so on, are sensitive inputs.

In newborn babies there are some myelinated fibers at Heschl's convolution (area 41); and myelination progresses excentrically during the three first months of postnatal life toward the second and third temporal convolutions.

According to J. C. Lafon there is a slow reaction toward a near sound source during the first month of postnatal life.[38] These reactions require some meaning or significance in the sounds presented to the baby one month of age. For instance, the child is spontaneously conditioned to sounds meaning nourishment. When he is hungry these sounds can elicit a very clear reaction in the baby.

In the preceding example, the baby reacts to some acoustic signals which can satisfy his needs. Nevertheless, utterances in babies are spontaneous and do not respond to imitations of the environmental *lingua* until the ninth month of postnatal life. Deaf babies and hearing babies produce similar spontaneous reflex utterances until the third quarter of the first year of life. When auditory discrimination is achieved, phonic imitations of some of the heard environmental *lingua* sounds are then produced.

Auditory myelination is different in immature or premature newborn babies.[39] To say "different" means that auditory abilities will also be different; and, consequently, developmental auditory stages will not follow standard patterns.

We ought to consider this last concept in light of the various levels of ability children have in "introducing" symbolic learning through auditory information. Certainly, the child who is not able to learn symbolic systems of communication is commonly labeled as "aphasic," "autistic," and so on. Such children exist, they are a *reality,* despite how deeply we may disagree with the use of such labels. The causes that can produce these clinical pictures are various, but we want to emphasize here one of those causes: the disability in auditory discrimination.

(40) HUMAN HEARING AND AUDITION

Every teacher recognizes the word "deafness" and is able to relate this word to some learning difficulties. It is less common to recognize children who are able to hear but who have defective auditory discrimination. The ability to discriminate sounds permits learning. When this ability does not exist, or when it is disturbed, some learning disabilities can occur. In these children hearing and end organs are apparently normal. The brain is not processing the information that comes from the ear. Sometimes children cannot discriminate different sounds from one another. Sometimes, the sounds can be extremely different (for instance, those produced by several musical instruments), or they can belong to common words in the environment. Other times, the children do not easily recognize where the syllabic accent is placed in a word, or the major accent is in a sentence. Other children can hear the words perfectly well and they can repeat them echolalically, but their meaning cannot be grasped. In still other circumstances some children cannot differentiate pitch, melody, sound-sequences, rhythm, or other acoustic information such as sound-source and direction of the sound.

Our personal experiences with children in relation to auditory

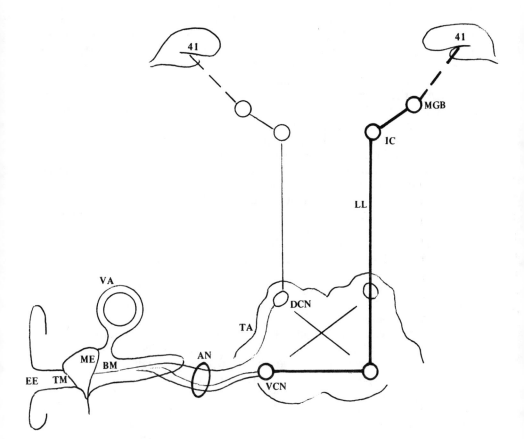

Figure 5. Auditory Pathways and Heschl's Area (Area 41). Area 41 is a small part of the cortex which receives auditory radiations and is located at the temporal inner side of the Sylvian fissure (or lateral cerebral fissure). EE: external ear. ME: middle ear. TM: tympanic membrane. VA: vestibular apparatus. BM: basilar membrane (supporting Corti's organ or end organ). AN: auditory nerve. VCN: ventral cochlear nucleus. DCN: dorsal cochlear nucleus. TA: tuberculum acusticum. LL: lateral lemniscus. IC: inferior colliculus. MGB: medial geniculate body. 41: gyrus temporalis transversus, Heschl's area, or area 41. Dotted line: auditory radiations. First neuron: Corti's ganglion. Second neuron: ventral and dorsal cochlear nuclei. Third neuron: inferior colliculus. Fourth neuron: medial geniculate body.

directionality (in a special acoustic chamber) allowed us to begin some sort of diagnostic differentiation in young children and to establish maturational stages in directional audition. Our conclusions were published some years ago, but in summary we know that in young children directional sound localization is made from sources placed at the same plane of the ears on each side of the body or in front. Between six and seven years of age, auditory directional localization permits the child to localize all the sound-sources existing at the level of the ear plane (both sides of the body, and in front and behind). In normal adults localization takes place not only at the same plane of the ear, but also at different levels of space. Directional audition is not correct in brain-stem disorders.[40]

American writers long ago recognized two different auditory functions: one related to auditory acuity, or *hearing,* and the other related to auditory perception, or *audition.* If we analyze all the acoustic factors that can be confused by a child, we will realize that all the preceding factors can be included in those two main auditory functions.

Let us remember that, for Myklebust, acceptable auditory perception was the ability to "structure the auditory world and select those sounds which are immediately pertinent to adjustment."[41]

For American writers, "auditory perception" is to give meaning to a heard message, and "auditory discrimination" is only one of the auditory perceptual abilities. According to N. A. Buktenica, auditory discrimination is defined as "the ability to discern differences among sounds .... But this skill overlaps with so many other perceptual skills—auditory awareness, auditory memory, sequencing of sounds, and understanding the meaning of sounds—that it seems to be one of the most useful skills on which to base a test for young children."[42]

There is one maturation for hearing and another for audition. From the point of view of learning we are much more interested in audition than in hearing: a child with poor hearing but with much training of audition in his residual hearing has much the greater possibility of integrating symbolic communication and harnessing it to personal creativity. There are different tests to check auditory discrimination, J. M. Wepman's *Auditory Discrimination Test* and Buktenica's *Test of Nonverbal Auditory Discrimination* being perhaps the two instruments best known in America.[43]

When auditory discrimination is distorted (but is not severely handicapped) the child goes to school, the handicap sometimes not having been identified at the preschool level. These children undoubtedly have learning disabilities, and many times they are considered as "dyslexics."

(41) AUDITORY SKILLS AND PERCEPTUAL MODALITIES

It is indispensable to realize that learning-disabled children can have disorders in their auditory skills. At the present time it is possible to measure, through the many available assessment instruments, the existence of perceptual auditory disabilities or, more precisely, disorders in auditory discrimination.

In 1960 J. M. Tato and J. B. de Quirós published a nosological approach supported by special procedures to measure audition in adults and children.[44] * Each procedure was based on specific disorders related to perceptual auditory modalities: (1) characteristics of the sound or voice (pitch, loudness, and timbre); (2) rhythmic characteristics of speech (movements, sound sequences, accent disposition); and (3) higher characteristics of language (message length, meaning and clarity of message, individual characteristics of the message). Many tests (European, American, and our own) were included in this taxonomic approach. These tests require sophisticated apparatus, materials, and techniques. We have personally studied in depth some procedures in brain tumors and lesions.[45]

Since our first studies in this area we have also investigated children having speech and learning handicaps, and have been able to compare results obtained through these tests in brain-damaged adults with those obtained from subjects who have what has sometimes been called "minimal brain dysfunctions."

It is well known that for many authors "minimal brain dysfunction" is synonymous to "dyslexia." In the next chapter we shall discuss different points of view about that. Nevertheless, we can admit already that some children having learning disabilities also have auditory discrimination impairment and other auditory difficulties discernible through sophisticated tests.

Auditory input, together with other afferences, inform the brain about stimuli that have produced excitation of peripheral receptors. As we have stated in this chapter, all these afferential syntheses facilitate the formation of inner "images" which will constitute the experience of the individual. Formation of those images normally requires a total integration of all the participant sensory-motor components. This concept is quite comparable to that of J. Barbizet's "meta-circuits."[46] If sensory integration fails, all sequences (maturational, functional, experiential) will be disrupted according to the degree of the handicap, thus determining an unusual developmental pattern. If only one sensory modality is disturbed, development is not halted but it is distorted, because other sensory modalities must help to construct an abnormal model which at least must try in some way to compensate the primary unisensorial deficit. It is obvious that the case in which two or more sensory modalities are disturbed is far more serious.[47]

NOTES

1. D. Katz, R. Katz, et al., Manual de Psicologia (A. Serrate, trans.) (Madrid: Ed. Morata, 1963).
2. H. R. Myklebust and D. Johnson, "Dyslexia in Children," Exceptional Children 29:1 (1962): 14-25; J. B. de Quirós and M. Della Cella, "La Dislexia como Sintoma y como Sindrome," Acta Neuropsiquiatrica Argentina 15:2 (1959): 178-193; J. B. de Quirós et al., Estudios Sobre la Dislexia Infantil (Santa Fe, Argentina: Ministerio de Educacion y Cultura, 1962); J. B. de Quirós, "Dysphasia and Dyslexia in School Children," Folia Phoniatrica 16 (1964): 201.
3. E. Boder, "Developmental Dyslexia: A Diagnostic Approach Based on Three Atypical Reading-Spelling Patterns." Developmental Medicine and Child Neurology 15:5 (1973): 663-687.

*The word "nosology" means medical classification (i.e., what can be medically classified as a distinct condition or clinical entity).

4. Quirós, "Dysphasia . . .," *loc. cit.*; H. R. Myklebust, *Development and Disorders of Written Language: Picture Story Language Test* (New York: Grune & Stratton, 1965); D. J. Johnson and H. R. Myklebust, *Learning Disabilities: Educational Principles and Practices* (New York: Grune & Stratton, 1967).

5. F. Affolter, "Aspekte der Entwicklung und Pathologie von Wahrnemungs," in Gautier und Prod'hom (eds.), *Gehörstorungen beim Kind,* Pediatrische Vorbildungskurse fur die Praxis Heft 34 (Basel: Karger, 1972): 41-49.

6. R. Held and J. Bossom, "Neonatal Deprivation and Adult Rearrangement: Complementary Techniques for Analyzing Plastic Sensori-motor Coordination," *The Journal of Compared Physiology and Psychology* 54:1 (1961): 33-37; R. Held and A. Hein, "Movement-Produced Stimulation in the Development of Visually Guided Behavior," *The Journal of Compared Physiology and Psychology* 56:5 (1963): 872-876; R. Held, F. Held, and J. Sandford, *Science* 142 (1963): 455-462, cited by M. L. J. Abercrombie, "Some Notes on Spatial Disabilities," *Developmental Medicine and Child Neurology* 10 (1968): 206-213.

7. Abercrombie, *op. cit.*

8. R. Held, "Plasticity of Sensori-Motor Systems," cited by Abercrombie, *op. cit.*

9. *Ibid.*

10. R. J. Schwartz, "Vocal Responses to Delayed Auditory Feedback in Congenitally Blind Adults" (mimeographed; Lafayette, Indiana: Purdue University, January, 1958).

11. P. K. Anokhin, "Cibernetique, Neurophysiologie et Psychologie," *Informations sur les Sciences Sociales* [Paris] 7:1 (1968): 169-197; A. J. Ayres, "Reading—A Product of Sensory Integrative Process," in H. K. Smith (ed.), *Perception and Reading* (Newark, Delaware: International Reading Association, 1968): 77-82; A. J. Ayres, "Sensorimotor Foundations of Academic Ability," in W. M. Cruickshank and D. P. Hallahan (eds.), *Perception and Learning Disability in Children,* Volume 2 (Syracuse, New York: Syracuse University Press, 1975).

12. I. Esente, *Physiologie de la Vision chez le Premature et le Nourrison Normal* (Paris: G. Doin et Cie., 1958); H. Fichsel, "Las Modificaciones de los Potenciales Visuales Evocados en la Maduracion de la Corteza Cerebral Humana," *Medicina Alemana* 15:6 (1974): 1020-1023 [translation from *Deutsche Medizinische Wochenschrift* 98:6 (1973): 209]; P. Niesel, "Entwicklung und optischeabstimmen Storungen," in E. Kong *et al., Zerebrale Bewegungstorungen beim Kind* (Basel: Karger, 1974): 206-213.

13. J. B. de Quirós, "Exclusions in Learning Disabled Children" (keynote address, Tenth Annual International Conference of the Association for Children with Learning Disabilities, Detroit; reproduced by learning disabilities program staff, Fairfax County Schools, March 1973).

14. T. G. R. Bower, "The Object in the World of the Infant," *Scientific American* 225:4 (1971): 30-38.

15. O. L. Schrager, "Vision, Sistema Postural y Aprendizaje," *Fonoaudiologica* [Buenos Aires], 20: 2-3 (1974): 67-81.

16. N. A. Buktenica, *Visual Learning* (San Rafael, California: Dimensions, 1968).

17. D. Notor and L. Stark, "Eye Movements and Visual Perception," *Scientific American* 224:6 (1971): 34-43; P. A. Merton, "How We Control the Contraction of Our Muscles," *Scientific American* 226:5 (1972): 30-37.

18. H. Baruk, "Neuropsychiatrie Infantile," in R. Debre, E. Lesne, et P. Rohmer, *Pathologie Infantile,* Volume 2 (Paris: G. Doin et Cie., 1946); H. Baruk, "Les Etapes du Developpement Psychomoteur et de la Prehension Volontaire chez le Nourrisson," *Archives Francaises de Pediatrie* 10:4 (1953): 425-432.

19. M. Frostig, W. Lefever, and J. R. B. Whittlesey, *Administration and Scoring Manual for the Marianne Frostig Developmental Test of Visual Perception* (Palo Alto: Consulting Psychologists Press, 1966).

20. L. Bender, *A Visual Motor Gestalt Test and Its Clinical Use* (New York: American

Orthopsychiatry Association, 1938); J. J. McCarthy and S. A. Kirk, *Illinois Test of Psycholinguistic Abilities,* Examiner's Manual (Urbana, Illinois: University of Illinois Press, 1961); A. L. Benton, *The Revised Visual Retention Test* (3rd ed.) (Iowa: The State University of Iowa; New York: The Psychological Corporation, 1973); K. E. Beery and N. A. Buktenica, *Developmental Test of Visual Motor Integration* (Chicago: Follett, 1967).

21. H. Aubert, *Physiologie der Netzhaut* (Breslau: E. Morgenstern, 1865).

22. C. S. Sherrington, *The Integrative Action of the Nervous System* (New York: Scribner's Sons, 1906); R. Magnus, *Korperstellung* (Berlin: Springer, 1924).

23. M. Minkowski, "Sull 'Evoluzione o la Localizzazione delle Funzione Nervose, supratutto dei Movimenti e dei Riflessi nel Feto e nel Neonato," *Atti del Convenio Italoswizzero* (Clinica Pediatrica dell' Universita di Milano; Bologna: Editoriale Capelli, 1948).

24. R. Jung, "Coordination of Specific and Non-Specific Afferent Impulses at Single Neurons of the Visual Cortex," in H. H. Jasper *et al.* (eds.), *Reticular Formation of the Brain* (Boston: Little, Brown, 1958); 423-434; O. J. Grusser, U. Grusser-Cornehls, and G. Saur, "Reaktionen einzelner Neuronen im optischen Cortex der Katze nach elektrischer Polarization des Labyrinths," *Pflugers Archiv Gesant Physiologie* 269 (1959): 593-612; O. J. Grusser and J. Grusser-Cornehls, "Mikroelektrodenuntersuchungen zur Konvergenz vestibularer and retinalier Afferenzen an einzelnen Neuronen des optischen Cortex der Katze," *Pflugers Archiv Gesant Physiologie* 270 (1960): 227-238.

25. G. Moruzzi, "The Physiological Properties of the Brain Stem Reticular System," in J. F. Delafresnaye (ed.), *Brain Mechanisms and Consiousness* (Oxford: Blackwell, 1954).

26. Grusser and Grusser-Cornehls, "Mikrodektrodenuntersuchungen ...," *loc. cit.*; R. Jung, "Korrelationen von Neuronentattigkeit und Sehen," in R. Jung and H. Kornhuber (ed.), *Neurophysiologie und Psychophysik des Visuallen Systems,* Symposium Freiburg (Berlin, Gottingen, Heilderberg; Springer, 1961): 410-434; R. Jung, "Neuronal Integration in the Visual Cortex and its Significance for Visual Information," in W. A. Rosenblith (ed.), *Sensory Communication* (Cambridge, Massachusetts: The M.I.T. Press, 1961).

27. M. B. Carpenter, "Ascending Vestibular Projections and Conjugate Horizontal Eye Movements," in W. S. Fields and B. K. Alford (eds.), *Neurological Aspects of Auditory and Vestibular Disorders* (Springfield, Illinois: Charles C. Thomas, 1964).

28. H. H. Kornhuber, "Vestibular Influences on the Vestibular and Somatosensory Cortex," in A. Brodal and O. Pompeiano (eds.), *Basic Aspects of Central Vestibular Mechanisms,* Progress in Brain Research, Volume 37 (London: Elsevier Publishing Company, 1972).

29. O. Pompeiano, "Spinovestibular Relations: Anatomical and Physiological Aspects," in Brodal and Pompeiano (eds.), *op. cit.*

30. A. Brodal, "Anatomy of Commissural Connections"; P. Bach-Y-Rita, "Structural and Functional Aspects of Extraocular Muscles in Relation to Vestibulo-Ocular Function"; J. Dichgans, C. L. Schmidt, and E. R. Wist, "Saccadic Discharges in Vestibular Nerve"; H. Shimazu, "Physiology of Commissural Connections"; E. Tarlow, "Anatomy of the Two Vestibulo-Oculomotor Projection Systems"; all in Brodal and Pompeiano (eds.), *op. cit.*

31. R. S. Dow and E. Manni, "The Relationship of the Cerebellum to Extraocular Movements," in M. B. Bender (ed.), *The Oculomotor System* (New York: Hoeber Med. Div., Harper & Row, 1964); B. Cohen and S. M. Highstein, "Vestibular Pathways to Oculomotor Neurons," in Brodal and Pompeiano (eds.), *op. cit.*

32. D. Godde-Jolly, A. Larmande, *et al., Les Nystagmus,* Volume I [Societe Francaise d'Ophtalmologie] (Paris: Masson et Cie., 1973).

33. D. H. Hubel, "Cortical Unit Responses to Visual Stimuli in Nonanesthetized Cats," *American Journal of Ophthalmology,* 46 (1958): 110-122.

34. Jung, *op. cit.*; C. R. Michael, "Retinal Processing of Visual Images," *Scientific American* 220 (1969): 104.

35. Anohkin, *op. cit.*

36. T. Ito and Y. Sanada, *Japan Journal of Physiology* 15 (1965): 235-242; J. B. de Quirós and O. L. Schrager, "Postural System, Corporal Potentiality, and Language," in E. H. Lenneberg and E. Lenneberg (eds.) *Foundations of Language Development* (New York: Academic Press; Paris: UNESCO Press, 1975): Volume 2, 297-307.

37. P. I. Yakovlev and A. R. Lecours, "The Myelogenetic Cycles of Regional Maturation of the Brain," in A. Minkowski (ed.), *Regional Development of the Brain in Early Life* (Oxford: Blackwell Scientific Publications, 1967): 3-70.

38. J. C. Lafon *et al., La Surdite du Premier Age* (Besancon: Camponovo, 1969): 46.

39. L. B. Rorke and H. E. Riggs, *Myelination of the Brain in the Newborn* (Philadelphia and Toronto: J. B. Lippincott, 1969).

40. J. B. de Quirós and N. D'Elia, *La Audiometria del Adulto y del Nino* (Buenos Aires: Editorial Paidos, 1974).

41. H. R. Myklebust, *Auditory Disorders in Children: A Manual for Differential Diagnosis* (New York: Grune & Stratton, 1954).

42. N. A. Buktenica, *Test of Nonverbal Auditory Discrimination (TENVAD)* (Chicago: Follett, 1975).

43. J. M. Wepman, *Auditory Discrimination Test* (Chicago: Author, 1958); Buktenica, *Test . . ., loc. cit.*

44. J. M. Tato and J. B. de Quirós, "Die sensibilisierte Sprachaudiometrie," *Acta Otolaringologica* [Stockholm] 51:6 (1960): 593-614.

45. J. B. de Quiros, "Accelerated Speech Audiometry, an Examination of Test Results," *Translations of the Beltone Institute for Hearing Research* Number 17 (Chicago, June 1964).

46. J. Barbizet, *Etudes sur la Memoire* (Paris: L'Expansion Scientifique Francaise, 1964); J. Barbizet, *Etudes sur la Memoire,* Deuxieme Serie (Paris: L'Expansion Scientifique Francaise, 1966).

47. O. L. Schrager, "Importancia de la Vision en la Estructuracion de la Postura y el Espacio en el Nino," *Revista Argentina de Tiflologia* [Buenos Aires] 2:2 (1973): 26-40; O. L. Schrager, "Consideraciones Medico-Recuperativas sobre la Comunicacion–Lenguaje en el Nino Sordo," *Revista Pedagogia Terapeutica* [Buenos Aires] 3:5 (1974): 4-23.

CHAPTER VII

Primary Learning Disabilities

(42) DYSLEXIA VERSUS MINIMAL BRAIN DYSFUNCTION— HISTORICAL FACTS

In Chapter I, Section 6, we remarked that, from a very simple point of view, "specific" or "primary learning disabilities" seem to be labeled as "dyslexias," "dysgraphias," and "dyscalculias." We also said that the external manifestations of these labels do not provide basic elements for a clinical classification of learning disabilities, which must be essentially related to *prognosis* and *treatment*.

The main problem to be faced is the tremendous confusion existing over meanings of different terms. What does "dyslexia" mean? What does "minimal brain dysfunction" mean? Are the terms synonymous?

In certain circumstances they *can be* virtually synonymous, but other times we believe they have different meanings. Something similar happens in many diseases: As doctors, we recognize diffuse brain damages in adults (for instance, cerebral sclerosis) and we identify this symptomatology with aphasic symptomatology; but in many other instances these clinical pictures have nothing to do with each other.

Possibly the study of the origin and evolution of the terms "dyslexia" and "minimal brain dysfunction" can clarify their meanings. Consequently we shall review here the history of both terms as labels currently used in educational and scientific environments.

It is surprising when we realize that many writers seem to ignore the fact that "dyslexia" was initially recognized as an aphasic symptom in adults, and then ask themselves why dyslexia (as a symptom) is always neurologically located in the left cerebral hemisphere: "This situation may result from an implicit assumption by the researchers of the importance of linguistic processing in reading, or it may result from an implicit assumption that the basic cognitive deficit in dyslexia is a language deficit."[1]

Since 1861 international scientific interest in regard to adult aphasia has been very great, and during the last century several descriptions of aphasic-alexic and aphasic-dyslexic cases have been written. As a matter of fact, area 39 of the left cerebral hemisphere (gyrus angularis) was considered to be the cause of "dyslexia" in aphasics. This assumption corresponds with our present neurological knowledge. The adult who has had area 39 damaged on the left side manifests dyslexic symptomatology. The adult who has had area 39 destroyed on the left side manifests alexic symtomatology. (The term "alexia" comes from Greek *a,* without; and *lexein,* to read.)

S. Kussmaul was the first to describe reading disabilities in order to designate these cases. Later Professor Berlin, from Stuttgart, created (according to M. Critchley) the term "dyslexia" to replace "word blindness" with the other "more correct" label.[2]

From the very beginning, "word blindness" or "dyslexia" was related to aphasia in adults. Near the end of the nineteenth century, pure "dyslexias" or "alexias" were considered very rare in adults; but several cases were described by a variety of authors in Europe and America. During the first half of the twentieth century researchers all over the world agreed that Some symptoms related to reading and writing can appear in isolation or allied with other aphasic symptoms in adults. Various zones of the brain were described as having a great connection with these processes.

Around the turn of the century some medical papers appeared, mainly in England, relating to a "new" condition which was assumed to be "congenital word-blindness": W. Pringle Morgan, James Kerr, O. Wernicke, James Hinshelwood, S. T. Orton, among others, published pioneer works on the subject.[3] With the exception of Orton (American) and Wernicke (Argentine), all the others were English.

The development of the concepts about the condition first recognized as "congenital word-blindness" was as follows:

1. At the outset it was associated with some forms of aphasia in adults (word blindness, dyslexia).

2. After World War I the conviction arose that a "specific" condition existed related to academic learning processes. From such a belief, Orton introduced a new term—"strephosymbolia" (from Greek *strephein,* to twist; and *symbolos,* symbols)—calling scientific attention only to dysgraphias exhibited by children having learning disorders. He refused to accept contemporary psychological interpretations of these conditions.[4]

3. Dyslexia was considered—mainly in Denmark and Sweden—as a "constitutional" or genetic (inherited) condition.[5]

4. Dyslexia was related to some psychomotor syndromes.[6] Many times it was coincident with the presence of the Strauss syndrome (hyperactivity, disinhibition, and perseveration).

5. During the 1960s dyslexia was identified by some authors as synonymous with minimal brain dysfunction, Strauss syndrome, and perceptual handicap.[7]

6. Other authors have accepted a much broader term (i.e., "learning disabilities"), and included dyslexia within this term. This is the criterion of American law when it mentions, among learning disabilities, different conditions (perceptual handicaps, brain injury, minimal brain dysfunction and developmental aphasia—see Chapter I, Section 4).

The concept of "minimal brain dysfunction" has also developed considerably in the last 35 years. A. A. Strauss and H. Werner were pioneers in describing the symptomatology of brain-injured children.[8] Because many of those children had no specific neurological symptoms pointing out the existence of brain injury, their statements were debated—and dismissed—in several medical circles. Strauss then changed the expression "brain-injured child" into "minimal brain-injured child." In different parts of the world, during the 1950s, divers symposia were held on the subject.[9] The main question was: Could brain damage be so subtle, so minimal, that it could not be registered by contemporary standards of assessment? Some doctors tried to introduce the expression "minimal cerebral palsy"—but the diagnosis was worse than the disease. Some others, such as W. Cruickshank and his colleagues, preferred to mention one of the oustanding symptoms of the brain-injured: "hyperactivity."[10] Finally, in 1962, the expression "minimal brain dysfunction" was accepted by most medical specialists throughout the world. The term emerged as a conclusion of Ronald Mac Keith after the International Study Group held at Oxford in 1962. He wrote as Conclusion Number 4: "The diagnosis is made on symptoms, so there are reasons for using the convenient but possibly illogical term of 'minimal brain dysfunction' rather than the anatomical term 'minimal brain damage.'"[11]

Minimal brain dysfunctions were very understandable if one followed the medical approach of B. C. L. Touwen and H. F. R. Prechtl or the remedial approach of Cruickshank.[12] "Dyslexia" is still a confusing term because some authors use it synonymously with "learning disabilities," and because others use it as a special category of learning disability. It is in the latter restrictive sense that we will employ the term here.

(43) THE TERM "LEARNING DISABILITIES"

The term "learning disabilities" has appeared as a necessity, because the children "diagnosed" as having "dyslexia," "minimal brain dysfunction," and so on (by means of other similar labels), were in some cases so different from one another that professional people began to assume that several clinical entities might be described within the general group showing some common symptomatology, especially the one referred to as difficulty in developing learning abilities.

In the United States S. A. Kirk was probably the first to call attention to the necessity of studying "learning disabilities" as a group. In 1962 he related a learning disability to a "retardation disorder, or delayed development in one or more of the processes of speech, language, reading, spelling, writing, or arithmetic," associating these symptoms with "a possible cerebral dysfunction and/or emotional or behavioral disturbance and not from mental retardation, sensory deprivation, or cultural or instructional factors."[13] It was easier—paraphrasing Kirk—to define a learning disability in 1962 than in 1977. Many people who fifteen years ago were almost sure about the meaning of the expression "learning disabilities," today might easily disagree with their own former definitions of the subject.

During the 1960s many American writers considered learning disabilities to be a group closely connected with "dyslexia," "minimal brain dysfunction," "Strauss syndrome," and "perceptual handicaps," considering all these terms so similar as to be practically synonymous.

According to a work sponsored by the National Society for Crippled Children and Adults, Inc., and the National Institute for Neurological Diseases and Blindness of the National Institute of Health, the deviations found in minimal brain dysfunctions "may manifest themselves by various combinations of impairment in perception, conceptualization, language, memory, and control of attention, impulse or motor function."[14]

Actually, it is a very difficult task to describe a sole symptomatology for all these syndromes. Certainly, it is not easy to explain that hyperactivity is an outstanding symptom in minimal brain dysfunction. On the other hand, it must be borne in mind that such a symptom may not be found in some learning disabilities where, to the contrary, it is feasible to find "hypoactivity."

Our opinion is that "learning disabilities" can manifest—or not manifest—symptoms of minimal brain dysfunction. We agree, however, that, generally, symptomatology of learning disabilities coincides with that of minimal brain dysfunction.

In 1968 the National Advisory Committee to the Bureau of Education for the Handicapped, Office of Education, defined learning disabilities as follows:

> Children with special learning disabilities exhibit a disorder in one or more of the basic psychological processes involved in understanding or using speech or written language. These may be manifested in disorders of listening, thinking, talking, reading, writing, spelling or arithmetic. They include conditions which have been referred to as perceptual handicaps, brain injury, minimal brain dysfunction, dyslexia, developmental aphasia, etc. They do not include learning problems which are due primarily to visual, hearing or motor handicaps, to mental retardation, emotional disturbance or environmental deprivation.[15]

This definition was the basis for developing the concept of learning disabilities which was introduced in Public Law 94-142, already commented upon in this book (see Chapter I, Section 4).

(44) PRIMARY VERSUS SECONDARY LEARNING DISABILITIES

There are some learning abilities that can be qualified as *specifically* human: symbolic communication, language, reading, writing, mathematical calculation.

In Chapter I, Section 3, we recognized tertiary and quaternary learning achievements as specific to the human race. We must repeat here that *lingua* and language constitute the principal facets of human learning. When these human abilities are disturbed, we may then speak about "learning disabilities." It is essential to realize that, at the same time, other learning abilities can remain intact and can be developed quite well.

Let us reiterate a commonly accepted statement in regard to the acquisition of a symbolic hemisphere in humans. It seems that left cerebral hemisphere dominance for symbolic processing (language) is present "at least by five years of age according to studies of brain damaged children and of normal children."[16] As can be seen, recent investigations apparently agree with previous assumptions made by A. R. Luria and F. Ia. Yudovich and by H. Hecaen and R. Angelergues, which were discussed in Chapter III, Section 16.

Learning disabilities can begin between three and five years of age. After five years of age, the incidence of learning disabilities in school children increases greatly because there are new human goals to be achieved.

Some clinical conditions producing learning disabilities are only seen in human beings. These conditions are recognized as *specific* or *primary* learning disabilities (for instance, "developmental aphasia," "dyslexia," and so on). There are other clinical conditions producing learning disabilities in humans that can also be seen (although without "learning disabilities") in experimental animals (for instance, cerebral palsy, mental retardation, deafness, and so on).

In *primary* learning disabilities specific *human* acquisitions (i.e., language, reading, writing, or mathematical calculation) are disturbed, but the other achievements (i.e., motor, sensory, intellectual skills, social adjustment) can be potentially normal. If the latter are disturbed, they manifest only slight or "minimal" impairments which are frequently not measurable through traditional neurological or psychological examination.

In *secondary* learning disabilities nonspecific human achievements are primarily disturbed. Many labels such as cerebral palsy, blindness, deafness, mental retardation, emotional disturbance, social maladjustment, and so on, are used. Learning disabilities in these cases are the secondary consequence of underlying nervous, sensory, psychic, or environmental abnormalities.

Causes that can produce primary or secondary learning disabilities are diverse and often very confusing. Several theories attempt to explain the causes of primary learning disabilities. They can be divided as follows:

1. Congenital disability ("developmental lag")
2. Inherited disability
3. Deficit-as-disability
4. Biochemical disability
5. Past-pathology disability

Recently (1978) we are discovering a significant correlation between high-risk factors and primary learning disabilities. Almost all the aforementioned theories, nevertheless, can be related to high risk. Let us analyze briefly those theories.

Congenital disability ("developmental lag"). W. Pringle Morgan was probably not only the first to publish a case history of "word blindness" in a child (14 years old), but also the first to interpret the cause of such a condition as "congenital."[17] According to him, the lack of development of the cerebral cortical area then recognized as "reading center" was responsible for such a disorder. Actually, his paper was stimulated very much by J. Hinshelwood's report in 1895 on acquired word blindness in adults.[18]

After Morgan, many other writers supported the idea of a developmental disorder in what is now recognized as "primary learning disability."[19] This statement was maintained despite the lack of neurological evidence, and it has developed into the notion of "developmental lag" described by P. Satz and G. K. Van Nostrand in 1973.[20] These two authors considered reading retardation to be produced by a lag in brain maturation, and their approach is similar in many respects to the approach of the earliest authors to write on the subject of dyslexia. Developmental lag assumes a disorder in maturation of the cerebral cortex, mainly in the left hemisphere.

Inherited disability. This theory was initially presented by C. J. Thomas and J. H. Fisher, both in 1905. It was also outlined by J. Hinshelwood in 1917. During the 1940s and 1950s this theory gained followers through "statistical verifications" made mainly by H. R. Skydsgaard in 1942 and B. Hallgren in 1950. In 1960 T. T. S. Ingram mentioned a dominant autosomic gene as responsible for some specific learning disabilities.[21]

Deficit-as-disability. The "deficit" notion assumes the existence of some "cerebral dysfunction" as the basis of reading retardation. The idea was developed during the 1960s. The first step in this tradition of thought was offered by authors who believed that minimal brain dysfunctions were syndromes similar to dyslexia.[22]

The next step was to accept that, in developmental dyslexia, "there is some sort of cerebral dysfunction underlying the acquisition of age-appropriate reading skills."[23]

Biochemical disability. This notion is related to the other theories: the congenital, the deficit, the inherited or genetic, and the past-pathology notions. All these theories of causation of learning disabilities can be related to a biochemical abnormality, which often produces minimal brain dysfunction symptomatology. Biochemical abnormalities can also be produced by causes we do not understand. One of the assumptions accepted by many authors is that attention span is severely disturbed by the abnormality in monoamine metabolism, "which is genetically transmitted." As a matter of fact, it is now fully admitted that nervous transmission in the central nervous system is made biochemically through "neurotransmitters." Different substances are used by the central nervous system as neurotransmitters: Probably in one percent of the brain several "amines" are able to act (serotonines, dopamines, and norepinephrine). The stimulant drugs currently used in minimal brain dysfunctions "probably act upon all three monoamines."[24] This notwithstanding, the same drugs sometimes produce opposite results in apparently similar abnormal children. It is indispensable, therefore, that we accept that there are different "learning disabilities" or different "minimal brain dysfunctions" which need also different medical classification (nosology) and therapeutic approaches. At the present time, nevertheless, the possible biochemical damage of whatever type in the brain can be assumed (and only assumed) through the exact knowledge of the mechanism of action of these different drugs.

Past-pathology disability. As was stated earlier, traditional neurological examination techniques in primary learning disabilities do not show any disturbances reasonably accepted as related to them.

Nevertheless, all writers address themselves to the present physical situation of the learning disabled. It seems that many doctors do not consider that some abnormalities can occur in early periods of life. When the abnormality is greatly ameliorated, doctors usually do not have precise procedures in order to determine that such an abnormality previously existed.

Every doctor knows that there are some children born with a hemiplegic syndrome. They cannot move the arm or the leg of one side of the body. These symptoms allow us to suppose that damage has occurred in the brain opposite the side of the hemiplegia. This notwithstanding, some of these cases ameliorate so much that, after a certain period, functions are reestablished in the hemiplegic limbs; and after a few years nobody can show medically that some brain damage existed during the early periods of life, although that damage undoubtedly existed.

For this reason we were some years ago extremely attracted by a new notion: past pathology (i.e., how neurological abnormal situations which occurred in the past can be clinically determined at examination time). At first we thought that through sophisticated advances in medicine (for instance, a scintillogram with special isotopes) it could be possible to locate precise brain regions that could have suffered slight damages in early years of life. Difficulties in such a procedure and problems in the obtained results prevented us from accepting the available conclusions. At the same time, Quirós suggested the comparison between static and dynamic responses in a child. The assumption was that, when static asymmetries disappear during dynamic situations, past pathology could be suspected. For instance, B. Bobath and K. Bobath noted that some children nine months of age, or older, may move themselves about in a sitting position (scooting, or "shuffling") instead of "crawling." This movement is considered by those authors as indicative or symptomatic of prior hypotonia.[25] We agree with such a conclusion; but, in order to accept the existence of past pathology (or previous central nervous system damage, or abnormal tonus evolution), we must look for asymmetries that the child has in static positions, we must observe whether they disappear during whole body movements (i.e., moving about in a sitting position [shuffling], crawling, or—later on—walking). If this happens, then we can assume the existence of past pathology.

We believe that the notion of past pathology is very important in regard to developmental lag because it can explain for us why many symptoms can appear. In other words, it can "justify" the existence of a syndrome with hyper- or hypokinesis, poor attention span, disinhibition, and perseveration that commonly result from brain damage: In the past, brain damage existed.

In regard to the theory of inherited or genetic disability, it is our belief that it is very difficult to speak about genetics without a clinical entity or very definite condition. Nobody knows which are the exact symptoms that permit one to diagnose a child as having dyslexia. Some authors emphasize psychological tests; others, visual tests; others, auditory and visual tests; still others, neurologically obtained data; and so on. How is it possible to speak about genetics in connection with a disease that for many authors is not a disease, or a condition that for many authors is not a condition? The same occurs in relation to statistical studies. What kind of confidence and reliability can we find in data which are obtained through studies that cannot be precise about what dyslexia means?

All this aside, the main question before us is: Does dyslexia belong to language abnormalities or to perceptual handicaps? We believe that it can be assumed that dyslexia has nothing to do with language and has very much to do with space directionality only when historical facts and adult pathology in regard to dyslexia are not taken into consideration. When we rejected the application of adult neuropathology to child neuropathology we spoke mainly about infants and young children. If the child is five or more years old, we must accept (according to our previous statements) that a child can have many of the adult symptoms. We believe that aphasia and dyslexia exist in childhood. We do *not* believe aphasia and dyslexia exist in infancy and early childhood.[26]

It is our opinion that *lingua* is an acquisition and language is a formulation that develops from such an acquisition. The question that we might ask ourselves is: Is language innate, or not? Noam Chomsky's position in regard to language is well known. According to him, language is obtained through the underlying inherited or innate disposition that exists in the human being. If this is so, language does not depend primarily upon the environment. Our own concepts in regard to *lingua* and language are adapted from some of Chomsky's statements.

The notion of deficit-as-disability is very closely connected with the procedure that an examiner can follow with a child. We can ask ourselves if examinations related to dyslexia are similar in different centers or in different countries. We are discussing here neither any specific test name, nor whether an examination is required; but we doubt very much that examinations called by the same name in several places are carried out with similar procedures and with similar interpretations. Another point of interest is that the deficit need not necessarily be a cerebral one. It could also result, for instance, from vestibular dysfunction. In a word, each of the five notions about primary learning disabilities discussed here have positive and negative aspects. All of them can be true, but all of them also can confuse the researcher when he accepts only one causation of such a disability. We believe that it is healthy to accept all these theories. Many causes can produce a primary learning disability, just as many causes can produce, for instance, deafness. The essential step needed to be taken is to develop examination procedures in order to determine the existence of one or more etiological variables, and to be able to adopt the necessary measures to improve differential diagnosis and to orient adequate treatment.

In relation to secondary learning disabilities, the causes that can produce these different conditions are very well known; and they will merit special attention in the next chapter.

Factors like prematurity, birth anoxia, infectious or viral disease, some inborn errors of metabolism, trauma, and other causes involving—directly or indirectly—the central nervous system, can produce different sensory, motor, or central nervous system impairments which necessarily evolve into a sort of secondary learning disability.

Secondary learning disabilities, however, do not apparently appear as a consequence of such factors because the latter usually produce clinical pictures such as brain damage, cerebral palsy, mental retardation, and so on. Secondary learning disabilities are more commonly related to other medical factors which can be briefly mentioned as follows:

1. Sensory handicaps, chiefly, hearing and visual deficits.
2. Intellectual handicaps, depending on many factors acting upon the IQ level.
3. Chronic or long-term diseases, which act through a lack of contact with the school environment, and through psychological problems.

Other factors that produce secondary learning disabilities are more related to psychological, pedagogical, and socioeconomic fields such as pedagogical errors, school dropouts, psychological disturbances, socioeconomic maladjustments, and nutritional and ecological factors.

(45) AN OVERVIEW OF PRIMARY LEARNING DISABILITIES

As we established in Chapter I, it is clear that quaternary learning abilities concern themselves with skills which are specific to humans. Primary or specific learning disabilities are related to the principal difficulty that a child has and the reason why he is brought to the doctor for consultation: "I'm here, doctor, because my child does not talk." Or, "I'm here, doctor, because my child doesn't learn at school." Almost always, when the main complaint concerns human achievements, we are faced with a primary learning disability. This notwithstanding, sometimes a learning disability is produced by secondary causes—in spite of the belief of parents who "do not know" the origin of such a difficulty, and in spite of the "diagnosis" of a teacher (or relative) who is assuming the existence of "dyslexia." Many times, those "dyslexics" really are hard of hearing, epileptic, and so on.

In our opinion, primary learning disabilities can result from compensated brain damages (or dysfunctions), from perceptual handicaps (mainly, auditory and visual), and from faulty postural afferences (chiefly, vestibular and proprioceptive). These three groups are related to the three levels commented upon in Chapter I, Section 6. The group responding to the higher level includes developmental dysphasia, developmental dyslexia, and developmental apractognosia.

Developmental dysphasia always must be assumed through a diagnosis of compensated damage, lesion, or past-pathology symptoms in Wernicke's zone in the left cerebral hemisphere. Wernicke's zone mainly corresponds to the posterior part of the first temporal convolution, and includes other neighboring areas of occipital and parietal lobes. This condition can sometimes be diagnosed through careful study of case histories made at the time of delivery or during the first period of postnatal life. In other instances, diagnosis is obtained through careful examination with neuropsychological procedures and through special tests. The main symptom is speech delay and difficulty in comprehension of speech. Developmental aphasia is not directly related to academic achievements, and it has been carefully treated in another of our books.[27]

Dyslexia may be traced to compensated damage or dysfunction of the angular gyrus at the left cerebral hemisphere. The angular gyrus corresponds to area 39, which is located in the union of parietal and temporal lobes at the end of the Sylvian fissure (or lateral cerebral fissure). The main dyslexic characteristic is a visual-perceptual handicap, and it is connected with audition and language on the one hand, and with visual-perceptual-cognitive processes on the other.

It is important to realize that each hemisphere is connected with the other through many associative pathways. One cerebral hemisphere, therefore, cannot work isolated from the other. Troubles in reading and writing can correspond to disorders in body schema and spatial relationships. Knowledge of body schema and spatial relationships are more related to the right cerebral hemisphere. Auditory and visual discrimination are more related to the left hemisphere. The same occurs with right-left orientation and reading and writing.

In dyslexic syndromes the main symptom is the difficulty in recognizing symbols for reading and writing. This is allied to right-left disorientation. Minor symptomatology is related to body schema and spatial relationships.

The opposite is observed in developmental apractognosia, which

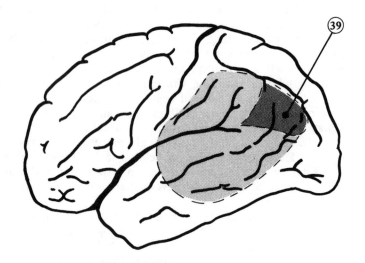

Figure 6. Wernicke's Area. Area 39 belongs to Wernicke's area.

NEUROPSYCHOLOGICAL FUNDAMENTALS

corresponds to compensated damage or dysfunction of the equivalent to Wernicke's zone in the right cerebral hemisphere. When developmental apractognosia occurs in children the main symptoms are difficulties in perceptual abilities, spatial relationships, and poor integration of the body schema. Allied minor symptoms are right-left disorientation, delay in the acquisition of speech with an adequate level of comprehension, and reading and writing disorders.[28]

The second group of primary learning disabilities corresponds to auditory discrimination and visual discrimination disturbances. The child can hear and see perfectly, but he cannot differentiate one sound from another or one graphism from another (mainly, when both stimuli are rather similar). Graphisms refer, for instance, to letters (*b, d, p, q,* and so on), to other graphic images (such as a series of chairs of different sizes, and in different positions), or to even more profound visual disturbances. Some tests have been specially created for investigating perceptual discrimination difficulties. The basic difference between dyslexia and perceptual handicaps is that dyslexia is a failure in the integration of auditory and visual discriminations into read/written language skills, while perceptual handicaps are failures in cognitive processes which are prior to that of language integration. Nevertheless, from a practical point of view, differential diagnosis between dyslexia and perceptual handicaps is frequently very difficult because these disturbances could be considered extremely similar from a clinical approach. That is why perceptual handicaps and developmental dyslexia are many times not distinguished from each other, and why their designative terms are frequently used as if they were synonymous.

The third group of primary learning disabilities consists in poor postural information feeding through poorly integrated vestibular and proprioceptive inputs. Vestibular nuclei at the medulla control skilled movements of the eyes as well as posture and equilibrium through deep information coming from muscles, joints, and tendons of the limbs. This was discussed in Chapter V, Section 30.

When vestibular-oculomotor pathways functionally fail, fixation and skilled movements of the eyes (like those used to follow sequenced patterns, which are essential for reading) are seldom produced; and reading abilities are consequently disrupted.

When vestibular-spinal pathways functionally fail, or when vestibular-proprioceptive information is not well integrated, posture, equilibrium, and body movements (specially skilled movements, like those of the hand which are essential for writing) are disturbed; and writing capabilities are consequently interfered with. In this last situation, the lack of control of posture and body movements generates disturbances in attention span and produces restlessness.

(46) PRIMARY LEARNING DISABILITIES AND DYSLERIA. DYSGRAPHIA AND DYSCALCULIA.

According to the aforementioned criteria, it is possible for us to accept that certain abnormalities at the cortical level can produce disturbances in (1) *lingua* and language (which is recognized as developmental dysphasia); (2) read/written language (which is recognized as developmental dyslexia); and (3) spatial-body schema (which is recognized as developmental apractognosia).

Perceptual handicaps create primary learning disabilities through difficulties in auditory and visual cognition (which are recognized as difficulties in the mechanisms of reading and writing). From a practical point of view, perceptual handicaps and developmental dyslexia can be investigated by means of similar clinical procedures.

Vestibular and proprioceptive abnormalities can produce primary learning disabilities through postural instability and imbalance (which are recognized as disturbances in attention span and production of restlessness).

Consequently, summarizing the five clinical syndromes that we accept as primary learning disabilities, we can mention them as follows:

1. Developmental dysphasia
2. Developmental dyslexia, perceptual handicaps
3. Developmental apractognosia
4. Vestibular-oculomotor split
5. Vestibular-proprioceptive dissociation

Another syndrome which is closely related to primary learning disabilities consists in the delay of maturation for reading and writing. Everybody knows that, from five to eight years of age, a child's reading and writing skills should develop. Also, every experienced teacher can remember some children who were not able to learn reading and writing at six years of age; but at seven or eight years of age, after a delay of one or two years, they were able not only to read and write, but also to follow the academic program with no more difficulties than other children. This sort of reading retardation seems to be maturational, because it is more or less spontaneously and rapidly compensated by development. This kind of child, therefore, can initially be confused with the dyslexic child when examination procedures are not very sophisticated.

We hesitate to label these children as belonging to the group of those who have primary learning disabilities; but we accept their existence; and we call them "dyslerics," and the syndrome, "dysleria."

We are even more hesitant to incorporate dysgraphia and dyscalculia within the group of primary learning disabilities. Every condition we have mentioned belonging to this group may or may not show dysgraphia, dyscalculia, or a combination of the two. Also, secondary learning disabilities may or may not present allied symptoms. Other central nervous system abnormalities (cerebral palsy, mental retardation syndrome, etc.) can manifest such symptoms among other more specific features.

As was stated in Chapter I, Section 6, dysgraphia means a disorder in correctly tracing shapes, forming letters of the proper size, using efficient strokes in forming letters, using comfortable pressure in grasping—independent of symbolic or perceptual disabilities. It might be important to emphasize that confusion of letters that can be similar in shape (for instance, *b, d, p, q*), or in articulation (for instance, *m, n; b, p*), cannot be called dysgraphias. This confusion can belong to perceptual handicaps (auditorizing, visualizing) or to dyslexia. Many of the errors in writing which have been called "dyslexic" must not be confused with dysgraphias. Some of them are visual or auditory errors of discrimination; others are visual and auditory errors (as Boder pointed out); and yet others can perhaps be diagnosed as associated dyspraxic movements of the hand. In neuropsychological examinations there are several tests investigating this kind of abnormal movement of the hands.

Something similar can be said in regard to dyscalculia. It is necessary to differentiate several causes that can produce computational difficulties. First, numbers can be confused, or they can be drawn in mirror-writing. Generally we can think of this kind of mistake as visual-perceptual handicap. Second, it can exist as a visual or auditory difficulty in cognition of the numbers. This symptom can be related to dyslexia or dysphasia syndromes. Third, the child seems to be unable to understand oral or written language concerning mathematical problems. The difficulty must be related to language disorders and, mainly, to developmental dysphasia or dyslexia. Finally, in arithmetical operations the concept of place value is essential for obtaining correct results. In an addition problem, for instance, if we put the numbers in wrong places, the result will also be wrong. This variety of mistake seems to be strongly connected with spatial relationships.

We agree with the Piagetian concept of operational thought which permits an individual to perform mathematical calculations correctly after the achievement of certain "genetic" (or developmental) levels. It seems to us that the achievement of such operational thought is rather coincident with the establishment of symbolization in what some call the dominant hemisphere. Let us recall that computational abilities are also symbolic achievements.

Our collaborator in another work, J. Feldman, considers seven different types of errors in mathematical calculation, mentioning them as follows:

1. Lack of number concepts:
   a. Inability to perform mental calculations—always needing concrete help.
   b. Difficulty in manipulating ones, tens, hundreds, etc., and in "carrying" in addition and subtraction.
   c. Difficulty in establishing operations of arithmetical problems (not resulting from reading difficulties).
   d. Difficulty in understanding numeral relationships: finding the numeral which has "more" or "less," the numeral which comes "after" or "before" another one; arranging numerals in ascending or descending order.
2. Spatial-temporal difficulties:
   a. Reversal in numerals when writing: ∂ instead of 5
   b. Reversal of numeral order: 75 instead of 57
   c. Failure in setting numerals in their proper spatial relationship:

$$\begin{array}{c} 85 \\ +4 \\ \hline \end{array} \qquad \text{instead of} \qquad \begin{array}{c} 85 \\ +\ 4 \\ \hline \end{array}$$

   d. Operating in a reversed order:

$$\begin{array}{c} 35 \\ +82 \\ \hline \downarrow \end{array} \qquad \text{instead of} \qquad \begin{array}{c} 35 \\ +82 \\ \hline \uparrow \end{array}$$

3. Figure-ground difficulties:
   a. Adding instead of subtracting, etc., are the traditional so-called "careless errors." That is, the child confuses the operational signs. Nevertheless, the mechanical operations of computations are correct. The child understands the concepts of addition, subtraction, etc. On closer inspection, the child *can* catch such errors.

4. Linguistic failures:
   a. Difficulties in understanding a written problem. This is overcome when the teacher reads the problem to the pupil.

5. Bizarre or strange mistakes:
   a. Mistakes resulting from lack of concrete cognition of the relationships involved in an arithmetical operation. This is seen even in disabled teenagers who, in performing simple operations, have been thought to have completely mastered and automatized them:

7	Child's explanation: "You can't take any-
805	thing away from the zero because it has no-
-309	thing to give. I'd better take from the 8."

6. Overstimulation difficulties:
   a. The operation is full of mistakes just because of its length; the child is able to perform well in short operations:

(good)	749	(bad)	85,697
	x 38		x 683

7. Mnesic failures:
   a. Difficulties in remembering addition, subtraction, and multiplication tables, despite existing number concepts and cognition of these operations. For example, the child understands and he is able to explain in a concrete form, that 2 x 3 is like •• •• •• or ⋮⋮ but he is not able to remember the result automatically (i.e., 6).[29]

As we have seen, it seems that all dysgraphias and dyscalculias are symptoms of other clinical entities. We agree, nevertheless, that in some rare cases, dyscalculias and dysgraphias can appear as apparently isolated entities. From a theoretical point of view this is perfectly acceptable; but in practice it is very difficult to find dyscalculias or dysgraphias as isolated conditions, belonging to primary learning disabilities. They are much more *symptoms* allied with primary or secondary learning disabilities.

(47) HYPERKINESIS, HYPERACTIVITY, AND RESTLESSNESS

Many writers consider the main symptom in minimal brain dysfunction to be hyperactivity. As we said before, many authors also believe that minimal brain dysfunctions and learning disabilities are synonymous. Consequently, it could be assumed that hyperactivity is the main symptom in primary learning disabilities.

In our view, hyperactivity, hypoactivity, and restlessness are three symptoms that commonly appear in learning disabilities. These three terms are quite different. Hyperactivity and restlessness can both be included within the concept of hyperkinesis (from Greek, *hyper,* more; *kinesis,* movement). This is to say, hyperkinesis is externalized by two eifferent symptoms: hyperactivity and restlessness. Hyperactivity depends on a great amount of motor disinhibition elicited by external stimuli. It is mainly connected with minimal brain dysfunction. Restlessness depends on a great amount of postural disinhibition elicited by poor body information (or internal stimuli). It is mainly connected with vestibular-proprioceptive dissociation.

As is very well known, vestibular centers and proprioceptive pathways have a broad relationship with the cerebellum. Because of the strong interconnection between vestibular and cerebellar centers, some authors speak more about vestibular-cerebellar dysfunction than about vestibular-proprioceptive dissociation. As was stated earlier in this book, cerebellar action in postural integration occurs at the age of three or four years (see Chapter II, Section 12). But, after the age of five years, the child's cerebellum also takes part in vestibular-proprioceptive actions which implies skilled coordination of hand movements (for instance, writing). This is one of the reasons why the cerebellum is important in school children.

It is also important to realize that motor awkwardness in children (the so-called "clumsy child") can frequently elicit a learning disability. The same can be said for hyperactivity, hypoactivity, and restlessness. Hyperactivity generally is associated (as a symptom) with brain injury, brain damage, and cerebral dysfunction. Among these three symptoms, hyperactivity is the most commonly found in the learning disabled.

Hypoactivity many times corresponds with cerebral cortex inhibition. Among the three symptoms this is the least frequently found in the learning disabled.

Restlessness corresponds with vestibular or proprioceptive (postural) disorders.

(48) VESTIBULAR-PROPRIOCEPTIVE DISSOCIATION AND VESTIBULAR-OCULOMOTOR SPLIT

As was pointed out in Chapter V, Section 30, vestibular organs act in establishing posture and equilibrium. Vestibular action takes place together with proprioception, which sends data about body movements (kinesthesis) from receptors located in deep structures (muscles, tendons, and joints).

When vestibular organs act mainly upon one side of the body, proprioception generally increases its action upon the same body side. Nevertheless, in some abnormalities it happens that proprioception predominates on one side of the body and vestibular organs on the other side of the body. When this phenomenon occurs, we speak about vestibular-proprioceptive dis-associations.[30] Through special neuropsychological and vestibular examinations we can discover the existence of vestibular-proprioceptive dissociation, which will be considered further in Chapter X.

It is clear that, when a child has vestibular-proprioceptive dissociation, attention span for the purposes of learning is very badly disturbed. Suppose you were in a bus whose route entailed many stops, restarts, and abrupt turns; you would have a feeling of instability that can be compared with that of vestibular-proprioceptive dissociation. If in such circumstances you wanted to learn something, you would have much difficulty in doing so. A child with vestibular-proprioceptive dissociation cannot maintain sufficient attention span in academically oriented situations, and cannot follow the learning rhythm of his classmates. If he has normal intelligence, he will realize the differences between him and his peers; and, therefore, he will react negatively to schoolwork.

We have also discussed in Chapter V, Section 30, that vestibular organs are connected with the extrinsic muscles of the eyes. This connection permits skilled movements of the eyes. Voluntary skilled movements of the eyes are, therefore, strongly related to vestibular inputs coming from vestibular-oculomotor pathways. When head-vestibular-ocular coordination fails, a reading disability can occur. When eye-head-hand coordination fails, a writing disability can appear. When both coordinations are disturbed, reading and writing disabilities are produced.

We call "vestibular-oculomotor split" the lack of appropriate vestibular-ocular coordination. In vestibular-oculomotor splits several symptoms are found: disturbances in ocular fixation and in skilled movements of the eyes being the most frequent ones. Among other signs and symptoms, provoked nystagmus examination (for instance, through rotatory, turning, or caloric tests—see Chapter IX, Section 66) can provide medical data in regard to vestibular-oculomotor pathways. Similarly, in the other primary learning disabilities, the child is aware of the fact that he cannot learn as quickly or as well as his classmates do.

It is indispensable that we not confuse vestibular-oculomotor splits with other learning disabilities, because correct diagnosis will permit proper prognosis, proper therapy, and proper remediation.

(49) COMMENTS ON PRIMARY LEARNING DISABILITIES

Our criteria for primary learning disabilities are rather different than those followed by other authors.

First of all, we must emphasize that learning disabilities are connected with specific human skills such as symbolic communication, language, reading, writing, or mathematics.

Primary learning disabilities mean that apparently these human skills are exclusively (or almost exclusively) disturbed.

Diagnosis of primary learning disabilities requires sophisticated tests in order to obtain useful data. It must be clear that, even with sophisticated examination techniques and procedures, the outstanding symptoms are always the ones related to disturbances of specific human skills. Other symptoms are not so evident as the symbolic disturbance is.

Parents come to the doctor because of their children's symbolic disturbances, and they believe that in other ways their children must be normal. Many times the doctor finds little or no abnormality through traditional neuropediatric and sensory examinations, and only psychoeducational assessments inform him about the existence of a symbolic deficiency. In such a case, it is acceptable to assume a primary learning disability.

Other times doctors speak about "soft signs," but this is a very controversial subject which has been accepted by some colleagues and rejected by others. Anyhow, soft signs are related to minimal brain dysfunction; and, as the reader knows, we do not feel that minimal brain dysfunction and learning disabilities are synonymous. In consequence, from a traditional medical point of view, the obtained data are very disputable.

In summary, we have outlined in this chapter why a primary learning disability is not a medical diagnosis and why the use of such a label many times induces error in medical approach, prognosis, and therapy. We also have mentioned five different conditions within the group of primary learning disabilities. These conditions need special medical examinations (for instance, computed EEGs, labyrinthine examinations, oculography, computerized tomography, and others which will be seen in Chapters IX and X), in order to provide data which will be useful (together with other psychoeducational data) in differential diagnosis and adequate orientation to the problem.

In secondary learning disabilities, traditional neuropediatric, psychiatric, or sensory examinations provide adequate medical data. Learning disabilities in these cases are the consequence of the evident central nervous system pathology, sensory impairments, psychic disturbances, socioeconomic disadvantages, cultural deprivation, ecological factors, and especially malnutrition (which corresponds with socioeconomic, ecological, cultural, and other influences).

NOTES

1. S. F. Witelson, "Abnormal Right Hemisphere Specialization in Developmental Dyslexia," in R. M. Knights and D. J. Bakker (eds.), *The Neuropsychology of Learning Disorders* (Baltimore: University Park Press, 1976): 233-255.

2. S. Kussmaul, "Disturbances of Speech," *Encyclopedia of Practical Medicine* 14:581 (1877): 875; M. Critchley, *Developmental Dyslexia* (London: Heinemann, 1964); M. Critchley, *The Dyslexic Child* (London: Heinemann, 1970).

3. W. P. Morgan, "A Case of Congenital Word-blindness," *British Medical Journal* 2 (1896): 1378; J. Kerr, "School Hygiene in its Mental, Moral and Physical Aspects," *Journal Statistics Society* 60 (1897): 613; J. Hinshelwood, "Congenital Word-blindness," *Lancet* 1 (1900): 1506; O. Wernicke, "Ceguera Verbal Congenita," *Revista de la Sociedad Medica Argentina* 11 (1903): 477; J. Hinshelwood, "Four Cases of Congenital Word-blindness Occurring in the Same Family," *British Medical Journal* 2 (1907): 1229; S. T. Orton, "Word-blindness in School Children," *Archives of Neurology and Psychiatry* 14 (1925): 581-615.

4. S. T. Orton, "Specific Reading Disability—Strephosymbolia," *Journal of the American Medical Association* 90 (1928): 1095-1099; S. T. Orton, *Reading, Writing and Speech Problems in Children* (New York: W. W. Norton, 1937).

5. H. B. Skydsgaard, *Den konstitutionelle Dyslexi* (Copenhagen: Diss, 1942); B. Hallgren, "Specific Dyslexia (Congenital Word-blindness), A Clinical and Genetic Study" (E. Odelberg, trans.), *Acta Psychiatrica et Neurologica* [Stockholm], Supplementum 65 (1950).

6. J. de Ajuriaguerra and G. Bonvalot-Soubiran, "Indications et Techniques de Reeducation Psychomotrice en Psychiatrie Infantile," *La Psychiatrie de l'Enfant* 2:2 (1959): 423-494; J. B. de Quiros, M. Della Cella, D. Carrara, and L. Allegro, *Estudios Sobre la Dislexia Infantil* (Santa Fe, Argentina: Ministerio de Educacion y Cultura, 1962).

7. S. D. Clements, *Minimal Brain Dysfunction in Children,* National Institute for Neurological Diseases and Blindness (NINDB) Monograph Number 3 (Washington, D.C.: U. S. Department of Health, Education and Welfare, 1966); S. D. Clements and R. S. Paine, *Minimal Brain Dysfunction; National Project on Learning Disabilities in Children,* Public Health Service Publications Number 2015. (Washington, D.C.: U. S. Department of Health, Education and Welfare, 1969).

8. A. A. Strauss and H. Werner, "The Mental Organization of the Brain Injured Mentally Defective Child," *American Journal of Psychiatry* 97 (1941): 1194-1202; A. A. Strauss and L. Lehtinen, *Psychopathology and Education of the Brain-Injured Child* (New York: Grune & Stratton, 1947); A. A. Strauss and N. C. Kephart, *The Brain Injured Child* (New York: Grune & Stratton, 1949); N. C. Kephart, *The Slow Learner in the Classroom* (Columbus, Ohio: C. E. Merrill, 1961); W. M. Cruickshank, F. A. Bentzen, F. H. Ratzeburg, M. T. Tannhauser, *A Teaching Method for Brain Injured and Hyperactive Children* (Syracuse, New York. Syracuse University Press, 1962).

9. R. Mac Keith and M. Bax (eds.), *Minimal Cerebral Dysfunction,* Little Club Clinics In Developmental Medicine 10 (London: National Spastics Society Medical Education and Information Unit in association with William Heinemann Medical Books, Ltd., 1963).

10. E. Kong, "Minimal Cerebral Palsy: the Importance of its Recognition," in Mac Keith and Bax (eds.), *op. cit.*; Cruickshank *et al., op cit.*

11. Mac Keith and Bax (eds.), *op. cit.*

12. B. C. L. Touwen and H. F. R. Prechtl, *The Neurological Examination of the Child with Minor Nervous Dysfunction,* Clinics in Developmental Medicine 38 (London: Heinemann, 1970); Cruickshank *et al., op. cit.*

13. S. A. Kirk, *Educating Exceptional Children* (Boston: Houghton Mifflin, 1962).

14. National Society for Crippled Children and Adults, Inc., and National Institute of Neurological Diseases and Blindness, of the National Institute of Health, *Minimal Brain Dysfunction in Children,* NINDB Monograph Number 3 (Washington, D.C.: U. S. Department of Health, Edu:ation and Welfare, 1966).

15. National Advisory Committee on Handicapped Children, First Annual Report, Special Education for Handicapped Children (Washington, D.C.: U. S. Department of Health, Education and Welfare, Office of Education, 1968).

16. Witelson, *op. cit.*

17. Morgan, *op. cit.*

18. Hinshelwood, *op. cit.*

19. Wernicke, *op. cit.*; Hinshelwood, *op. cit.*; L. G. Fildes, "A Psychological Inquiry into the Nature of the Condition known as Congenital Word-blindness," *Brain* 44 (1921): 286; E. B. Mac Cready, "Defects in the Zone of Language (Word-deafness and Word-blindness) and their Influence in Education and Behavior," *American Journal of Psychiatry* 6 (1926-27): 267.

20. P. Satz and G. K. van Nostrand, "Developmental Dyslexia: An Evaluation of a Theory," in P. Satz and J. J. Ross (eds.), *The Disabled Learner: Early Detection and Intervention* (Rotterdam: Rotterdam University Press, 1973): 121-148.

21. C. J. Thomas, "Congenital Word-blindness and Its Treatment," *Ophthalmoscope* 3 (1905): 380; J. H. Fisher, "A Case of Congenital Word-blindness (Inability to Learn to Read)," *Ophthalmological Review* 24 (1905): 315; Hinshelwood, *op. cit.*; Skydsgaard, *op. cit.*; Hallgren, *op. cit.*; T. T. S. Ingram, "Paediatric Aspects of Specific Developmental Dysphasia and Dysgraphia," *Cerebral Palsy Bulletin* 2:4 (1960): 254-277.

22. Clements, *op. cit.*

23. B. P. Rourke, "Reading Retardation in Children: Developmental Lag or Deficit? " in Knights and Bakker (eds.), *op. cit.*; 125-138.

24. P. H. Wender, "Hypothesis for a Possible Biochemical Basis of Minimal Brain Dysfunction," in Knights and Bakker (eds.), *op. cit.*: 111-124.

25. B. Bobath and K. Bobath, *Motor Development in the Different Types of Cerebral*

Palsy (London: Heinemann, 1975).

26. J. B. de Quirós, "Diagnostico Diferencial de los Sindromes Vestibulares en el Nino Pequeno y de las Mal Llamadas Afasias Infantiles," *Fonaudiologica* [Buenos Aires] 14:1 (1968): 86-102; J. B. de Quirós, "Disturbances in the Language of a Child: The Child Who Does not Speak," *Proceedings of the Children's Hospital* [Washington, D.C.] 25:7 (1969): 192-205; J. B. de Quirós, "Les Aphasies Infantiles: Un Probleme Diagnostic," *Reeducation Orthophonique* 7:44 (1969): 243-254; J. B. de Quirós, "Llamadas Afasias Infantiles y el Nino que no Habla: Sus Relaciones con las Sorderas Centrales," *Fonaudiologica* [Buenos Aires] 16:1 (1970): 83-88; O. L. Schrager, "El Concepto Actual de Afasia Infantil," *Fonaudiologica* [Buenos Aires] 16:1 (1970): 89-116.

27. J. B. de Quirós *et al.*, *Las Llamadas Afasias Infantiles,* Series del Centro Medico de Investigaciones Foniatricas y Audiologicas Number 4 (2nd ed.) (Buenos Aires: Editorial Medica Panamericana, 1975).

28. J. B. de Quirós, "Introduccion al Estudio de las Afasias," *Fonoaudiologica* [Buenos Aires] 10:1-2 (1964): 93; J. B. de Quirós, "Trastornos del Lenguaje en el Nino," *Actas del Congreso XII International de Pediatria.* (Mexico, D. F., diciembre 1968): 502-518.

29. J. Feldman, *Aritmetica en Ninos con Problemas de Lenguaje* (Buenos Aires: CEMIFA, 1977).

30. J. B. de Quirós, "Vestibular-Proprioceptive Integration: Its Influences on Learning and Speech in Children," *Proceedings of the Tenth Interamerican Congress of Psychology* (Lima, Peru, April 3-7, 1966; Mexico: Trillas, 1967): 194-202; J. B. de Quirós, "Significance of Some Therapies on Posture and Learning," *Academic Therapy* 11:3 (Spring 1976): 261-270; J. B. de Quirós, "Specific Learning Disabilities due to Vestibular Dysfunctions," in L. Tarnopol (ed.), *Reading Disabilities,* Volume 2 (Baltimore: University Park Press, in press).

NEUROPSYCHOLOGICAL FUNDAMENTALS

CHAPTER VIII

Secondary Learning Disabilities

(50) TAXONOMY OF SECONDARY LEARNING DISABILITIES

As stated in Chapter VII, secondary learning disabilities are the logical consequence of many causes which are detrimental to human beings, which disturb the biological, psychological, socioeconomic/cultural, and ecological possibilities one would expect from normal development. For instance, a mentally retarded child, an emotionally disturbed child, a chronically environmentally deprived or rejected child, or a child who continuously breaths polluted air, all have *secondary learning disabilities*. Causes, therefore, *primarily* act against the normal human development and *secondarily* against human learning acquisitions (speech, *lingua*, language, reading, and so on).

From a taxonomic point of view, secondary learning disabilities can be grouped according to principal causes and to common syndromes the medical community has internationally accepted. Secondary learning disabilities can be: (1) biological, (2) psychological, (3) socioeconomic/cultural, and (4) ecological.

Biological. We shall see in this group a variety of syndromes, some of them due to central nervous system disturbances (mental retardation, cerebral palsy and other kinds of brain damage, and seizure disorders), others being related to sensory impairments (deafness, hearing impairment, blindness, amblyopia).

Psychological. We shall comment on emotional disturbance, internalization, organic long-term diseases, and psychoses in children.

Socioeconomic/cultural. Some aspects of social and economic influences in different communities shall be reviewed. It is important to realize that socioeconomic status influences human learning abilities in quite a different manner in America than among Australian aborigines. Perhaps a tribal chief among Australoids has status in his own community *proportionally* similar to that of a successful businessman in New York City. Both of them have high socioeconomic levels compared with the standards of their own respective communities. But in New York, reading and writing are a major part of the culture, and literacy bears a significant relationship to socioeconomic level. Among Australoids literacy is not present; it has no direct relationship with the socioeconomic level because the culture does not permit such an acquisition. Cultural factors are, therefore, extremely important in order to interpret in an adequate manner the socio-economic data obtained through observations. Among socioeconomical/cultural factors malnutrition, school dropouts, and teaching errors demand special attention.

Ecological. These factors will also be mentioned and briefly analyzed. Given these criteria, we may then focus more precisely on the principal groups of secondary learning disabilities.

(51) BIOLOGICAL ABNORMALITIES AND LEARNING DISABILITIES

This kind of secondary learning disability may be traced to central nervous system disturbances or to sensory disturbances.

Central nervous system disturbances are sometimes externalized as diffuse or broad brain damage, other times as localized cerebral lesion.

Many causes can produce biological abnormalities: prenatal (inherited and intrauterine causes), perinatal (anoxia and distocic delivery), postnatal (trauma, infections, viral causes, toxic causes, vascular accidents, postnatal anoxia, postnatal endocrine disorders, and parasites, among others) being the most important ones.

These abnormalities are inherited much as are some inborn errors of metabolism, deafness, or blindness. Inheritance can act through dominant or recessive genes, or through abnormal genes, or through abnormal genetic mechanisms which are still relatively unknown. Several diseases and illnesses show these different forms of inheritance. For instance, dominant gene impact is seen in tuberous sclerosis and in neurofibromatosis; recessive gene impact is seen in Tay-Sachs disease, in gargoilism, or in phenilketonuria; abnormal gene impact is seen in divers nondifferentiated mental retardations; abnormal genetic mechanism impact is seen in some idiopathic brain damages with epilepsy and mental handicap, and so on.

Intrauterine causes are numerous: traumas, infections, toxins, and many others. The effect of rubella when it attacks the embryo or fetus during the first three months of pregnancy is well known.

Anoxia neonatorum is the principle natal cause of secondary learning disabilities. The grade (or severity) and the time period (in minutes) during which anoxia is present are extremely important for the prognosis of the resultant brain damage or sensory impairment.

Among the postnatal causes of biological secondary learning disabilities, parasitary diseases are more prevalent in some parts of the world than in others. In regard to this statement, we might do well to differentiate parasitary conditions which correspond to sporadic and direct attacks on the central nervous system or to sensory systems, from those parasitary conditions which correspond to socioeconomic/cultural causes. In many parts of South America, for instance, ascaris lumbricoide and trichocephalus trichiurus infest 100 percent of the first-grade school children, and a certain type of ancylostomiasis is also very much in evidence, in some places up to 96 to 98 percent of the population of children.[1] Ascaris and trichocephalus infest humans through the ingestion of contaminated raw vegetables and water. Simple hygienic measures can prevent or assuage these infestations (for instance, washing vegetables before eating them). Trichocephalic anemia (among other factors) can lead to secondary learning disabilities. Ancylostomiasis is produced by an intestinal parasite which generally enters the body through the skin of the feet and which may certainly produce distractibility and apathy in children when it generates organic weakness. As was previously stated in Chapter II, Section 13, when the body intervenes in higher nervous system levels, learning becomes difficult. This is also true for organic diseases which disturb higher functional levels of the central nervous system. Shoes (among other preventive measures) can prevent such illness. For these reasons they could be considered among socioeconomic/cultural causes of secondary learning disabilities. Another parasitary biological cause of this type of disability is toxoplasmosis, a protozoan disease of man caused by toxoplasma gondii. Congenital toxoplasmosis is characterized by lesions of the central nervous system, which may lead to blindness, brain defects, mental retardation, or even worse consequences, even death.

The principal goal in human rehabilitation might very well be the adjustment of handicapped children to a more regular or common environment. If this goal could be obtained, regular schools should accept these children; special teachers should reinforce their learning; and special schools should be avoided. Integration of handicapped children within the community is better achieved when (1) handicapped children are accepted by the community, and (2) it accepts normal children. We do not endorse special schools for children who can be taught or can be socially adjusted in regular schools. Mild cases of mental retardation, cerebral palsy, deafness, or blindness, improve much more with a special teacher in a regular school and social milieu than in special school programs. The future of mild cases must be to be integrated with the nonhandicapped community, and not a segregated group within the community. If they are not severely handicapped they will be able to realize that they are handicapped children. Only with their integration in the normal environment will they have a chance to be happy. *And happiness is very important. It is more important than the achievement of some elementary scholarly goals. A happy child and a happy adult are preferred over a well instructed but unhappy child or adult. Humans are social beings.* Integration is essential for happiness. Certainly, regular primary schools can provide integration through different kinds of certificates according to the academic levels reached by each child. Only regular schools can be successful in integrating slightly or mildly handicapped children. We must bear in mind that every handicapped child who can be assimilated into a regular class situation without disturbing the group must be accepted by regular schools. Benefits will be not only for the handicapped but also for the other children. A regular community will only accept the handicapped when social situations are shared from the very beginning.

Severe cases and "multiple deficiency" cases need special schools. Multiple deficiency cases are those conditions wherein different symptoms are mixed: deafness with blindness, cerebral palsy with deafness, deafness with dyslexia or with vestibular deficit, and so on.

(52) MENTAL RETARDATION AND LEARNING DISABILITIES

Mental retardation is a complex syndrome which can be traced to several causes, but which is characterized by (1) several deficits in adequate skills for one's age (intellectual deficiency); (2) learning disabilities; (3) social maladjustment; and (4) appearance of such a symptomatology during developmental ages (infancy, childhood, or adolescence).

By definition, "learning disability" can be included in the term "mental retardation." Those mentally retarded children nearer to normalcy are called "borderline." Some borderlines can be admitted by regular schools and others can be erroneously considered "dyslexics." Certainly, this is scarcely observed in well run academic institutions, but it is very frequently found in those not so well run.

Then there is the case in which borderlines and other slightly mentally retarded children are intentionally included in the regular school. If the program of inclusion is careful enough, rehabilitation for life in normal society can be attained. Social improvement is very important for the inclusion of such children in regular social environments. Early diagnosis, early therapy, and living in a normal environment may be the essential triad for rehabilitation of mildly mentally retarded children.

On the one hand, the label "mental retardation" is not really acceptable from a medical point of view. Medical diagnosis must be quite different. It must mention the clinical entity (for instance, hypothyroidism, phenilketonuria, craniostenosis, etc.), if it is feasible to make such a diagnosis. If doctors simply accept the label "mental retardation" as a medical diagnosis, they will never be able to act in time with adequate pharmacology or other medical treatments that could permit, in certain cases (like the ones just mentioned), a partial—sometimes total—recuperation of the patient. Nevertheless, doctors must sometimes accept the label "idiopathic (or essential) mental retardation" after examination and after failure to gain any significant medical orientation. "Idiopathic," or "essential," means, in common words, "I don't know what the patient has."

On the other hand, mental retardation is an acceptable psychoeducational diagnosis. It allows appropriate psychological and educational approaches.

Mentally retarded children can have associated primary learning disabilities. We disagree with the opinion that assumes that mentally retarded children cannot be dyslexics or dysphasics. Certainly, they can. They can be dyslexics, or dysphasics, or deaf, or cerebral palsied, or deprived, or anything else. The same causes that produce the syndrome of mental retardation can also determine other disturbances. So, the fact of being mentally retarded does not in the least exclude the possibility of having many other handicaps. It is therefore critical that we differentiate the secondary learning disabilities that every mentally retarded individual has (according to his own condition), from primary learning disabilities than can be present in some mentally retarded cases. The main point in this differentiation is the answer to the question: Can this learning disability be traced to the mental retardation, or not? Learning level can be obtained through various tests.[2] If the learning level is similar to the child's other abilities (for instance IQ, motor levels, and so on), it seems logical to admit that no other abnormality is added to the mental retardation itself. In cases where the learning level is lower than the child's other abilities, it could be assumed that a primary learning disability also exists.

(53) CEREBRAL PALSY, OTHER BRAIN DAMAGE, AND LEARNING DISABILITIES

Cerebral palsy is called a perinatal or infantile brain damage which always becomes manifest in motor disturbances and never grows worse.

This definition needs a few words of explanation. We speak about "perinatal" or "infantile" brain damage. The meaning of this expression is that brain damage is produced during pregnancy, during delivery, or during the first two years of postnatal life. Many authors agree with such a statement. Others do not. The important thing to remember is that walking is normally achieved during the second year of life. A child who walked and then became brain damaged and motor handicapped is quite different from a child who was brain damaged before normal maturity for walking. The former situation is not considered "cerebral palsy" but is accepted as "brain damage." In general, when brain damages are produced after the child is two years old, they are recognized only as "brain damages" and not as "cerebral palsy." This notwithstanding, some authors believe that one may speak of cerebral palsy until the child is five years old.

Cerebral palsied children constitute a group of varying syndromes. Since the pioneering descriptions of W. J. Little and of S. Freud, there has been a plethora of classifications of cerebral palsy, which can be consulted by the reader.[3] This is said in regard to the extremely close relationship between brain damage and learning disabilities. We will mention here only some of the best known levels of damage which are called cerebral palsy: (1) spastics, who have motor disturbance produced by damage at the level of the motor cerebral cortex; (2) diskinetics, who have motor disturbances due to damage at the subcortical grey nuclei level (extrapiramydal system), which includes different clinical types as chorea, athetosis, dystonia, tremors, rigidity; and (3) ataxics, who have motor disturbances produced by cerebellar damage.

As may be seen in this short review of the principal types of cerebral palsies, motor disturbance of some kind (paralysis, paresis, and in some slight cases, awkwardness) is always present. Other cerebral symptomatology can be seen, or not seen; but motor disturbance exists in all cases.

Among the different aforementioned types, choreo-athetosis is the most frequent. In choreo-athetoid children, for instance, 45 percent have a hearing impairment; and in almost all cases there is some kind of speech, *lingua,* or language disorder.

A cerebral palsied child, just like any brain damaged individual, can therefore have sensory impairments, language impairments, intellectual deficits, and so on; but one can be labeled as being cerebral palsied even without any of such disturbances. Now, if one reviews notions discussed in Chapters I and II referring to motor activities and human learning, one will realize that the former are fundamentals for the development of the latter. Consequently, secondary learning disabilities can be found in every cerebral palsied child who has received no remedial therapy. Besides, it is possible to find some symptoms relating to learning disabilities in these children, dysgraphia and deficits in attention span being the most frequent.

Finally, these conditions are very well differentiated from other progressive brain damages (a brain tumor, for instance) because the latter grow worse and many higher functions progressively deteriorate. Cerebral palsy, on the contrary, does not deteriorate. It always remains static or its symptoms diminish (mainly in regard to motor functions). This fact, then, provides a baseline for measuring the relative success of various educational and remedial approaches.

(54) EPILEPSY AND LEARNING DISABILITIES

In medical terms, "epilepsy" is defined as paroxismal transient disturbances of brain function that may be manifested as episodic impairment or loss of consciousness, abnormal motor phenomena, psychic or sensory disturbances, or a disorder of the autonomic nervous system. Symptoms result from paroxismal disturbance in the electrical activity of the brain. In other words, epileptic reactions are nonspecific pathological deviations of the processes of excitation and inhibition that usually take place in the brain. Epileptic seizures have many variables, and the distinctive characteristics are probably due to the differences of place of origin, extensiveness, and nature of the brain disturbance. Epilepsy, therefore, is a common symptom of many different syndromes. In some cases the most important facts depend on a focal cerebral lesion; in others it seems to depend on inherited predisposition; in yet others the cause remains unknown.[4]

In antiquity people used to speak about "epilepsy" or about "epileptic seizure" at any time that the individual lost his senses unexpectedly (from Greek *epilepsia,* surprise). According to H. Gastaut, the modern concept of epilepsy can be summarized as follows: (1) the epileptic seizure is now distinguished from epilepsy itself, the latter term being reserved for chronically repeated seizures; (2) the term "epileptic seizure" is presently applied only to cerebral strokes which are resultant from hypersyncronic discharge of a certain group of neurons. Epileptic seizures are therefore differentiated from those cerebral attacks which are due to the sudden depression (and not to hypersyncronic discharge) of functions of a certain group of neurons (for instance, ischemic, asphictic, anoxic, or hypoglycemic attacks), and from those which depend on activation, sometimes intentional, of cerebral neurons under the influence of psychogenic factors (histeric, anxiety attacks, and so on).[5]

Epileptic children have communication, *lingua,* language, and other learning disorders. In these cases, even when many of those disorders depend on the neuroepileptic alternation, the latter itself can imply different types of pathologies which, in variable degrees, interrupt learning processes. Some of the factors that could disturb general learning abilities in epileptic children are: (1) the coexistence of brain damage or brain dysfunction; (2) the psychological reaction of the environment and of the patient to epilepsy; and (3) the use of specific antiepileptic drugs. Let us briefly consider these factors.

Brain damage or brain dysfunction and epilepsy. According to M. Rutter, P. Graham, and W. Yule, one must keep in mind the concepts of "non-complicated epilepsy" and that of "epilepsy associated to structural brain disturbances."[6] In our own opinion, this differentiation is essential for understanding learning abilities in epileptics. In the second circumstance (i.e., epileptic children with significant associated symptomatology of brain damage or dysfunction), learning abilities will be similar to those of the clinical pictures usually described as brain injury, brain dysfunction, minimal brain dysfunction, and so on. The presence of the Strauss triad symptomatology—hyperactivity (disputed among many authors[7]), disinhibition, and perseveration—as well as perceptual handicaps, proprioceptive-kinesthetic and motor disturbances, and so on, interferes with the organization of well sequenced patterns of learning abilities, thus determining pathological patterns of cognition and, consequently, failure in human learning achievement.

Also according to Rutter, Graham, and Yule, the onset of epileptic seizures seems to be one of the variables that permit practical differentiation between the two aforementioned groups. For the cases with noncomplicated epilepsy, the mean age of onset of seizures is five to eight years of age, while in the cases of epilepsy associated with structural brain disturbances, epileptic seizures usually start during the first two years of postnatal life. These findings coincide with those of other authors.[8]

These notions allow us to conclude that secondary learning disabilities seem to be more significant in those epileptic children with an associated structural brain disturbance. In these cases onset of epileptic seizures is in early years of life, and symptomatology is rather more complex. On the other hand, in cases of noncomplicated epilepsy, specific epileptic symptomatology appears at the end of early childhood or at the beginning of childhood. By that time fundamentals of learning abilities are basically more developed, thus being less altered by the onset of epileptic symptomatology, if the latter is not very severe.

Psychological reaction and epilepsy. The effect of environmental psychological development and social and cultural pressures upon the individual's learning capacities and performance is very well known by psychiatrists, psychologists, physicians in general practice, therapists, and teachers. The way in which each member of a family faces and accepts—or refuses to accept—any deficiency in one of his relatives has been thoroughly studied by many authors.[9]

In regard to the personality of the epileptic and its influence in cognitive achievements, some authors have considered that: (1) learning disabilities in epileptics are directly related to the brain pathology which elicits seizures; (2) the epileptic personality syndrome is of constitutional origin and takes part in epilepsy as seizures do; (3) most of the disturbances of personality in epileptics are reactive to psychosocial stress; and (4) as might any patient with any other deficiency, many epileptic patients react against epilepsy as if it were a "Leitmotiv" to which everything should be subordinated.[10]

Naturally, parents also react to the deficiency, and this adds the influences of family relationships to the clinical picture, and to the formation and development of, the personality of epileptic children. It is well known that the personality of the epileptic is the final result of the family's insight into the problem and the way in which the matter is handled by the general environment.[11]

Use of drugs and learning in epilepsy. There is no doubt about the basic necessity of obtaining the remission of seizures or their equivalents, as a baseline in the medical treatment of epilepsy.

Over a long period of time, but especially during the last few years, many questions have been raised concerning antiepileptic drugs, thus opening new perspectives for research and clinical uses. One of the most important problems that remains to be solved, however, is the action of anticonvulsivants upon psychosocial behaviors and cognitive processes.[12]

From a rehabilitative point of view, to stop seizures is not sufficient. Rather, the goal is academic achievement commensurate with the personal capabilities of each student. That is, in order to avoid failures in learning abilities, how the doctor handles antiepileptic drugs is very important. The dosage level must be prescribed and the medication schedule must be carried out in such a way that, in every possible case, side effects of the drugs do not interfere in those cognitive processes related to learning abilities.[13]

Summarizing these ideas, we must emphasize that specific epileptic symptomatology must not be confused with other symptoms that can be found in some epileptic patients (hyperactivity, aggressiveness, distractibility, etc.) which depend on the basic neurological condition. In the same way, when seizures are out of control or are very strong, some cerebral deterioration may occur, thus affecting intellectual skills in epileptic children. But, epilepsy itself does not necessarily affect personality or intelligence. "Most cases of seizures in children, whether idiopathic or secondary to some identifiable disease or lesion, are not associated with any abnormalities on neurological examination."[14] So a noncomplicated, medically well cared-for epileptic child does not show features different than those of normal children; that is why he can and must be assisted to attend regular school. Learning disabilities in epileptic children are, therefore, secondary to the associated structural brain disturbances (damage, dysfunction, or mental retardation); and they depend on each case's characteristic symptomatology, on the frequency and intensity of the seizures, on social acceptance or rejection, and on the appropriate—or inappropriate—use of antiepileptic drugs. But it must be remembered that, as we mentioned in Section 53, all cases of brain damages or dysfunctions (epileptic syndromes included) can be mixed with primary learning disabilities or other handicaps. The syndrome is always worse when there are multiple handicaps present. That is why therapy of epileptic children and remediation of their learning disabilities must be based on an interdisciplinary team approach which must function closely with the family and academic environments.[15]

(55) HEARING IMPAIRMENT AND LEARNING DISABILITIES

Hearing and audition have already been differentiated in this book (see Chapter VI, Section 40). Both terms are very significant for a discussion of learning because it is through the ears that the infant first receives symbolic human communication (*lingua*). This is the main reason why some aspects of hearing impairment should be carefully considered here.

As we understand it, hypoacusis is the partial loss of the auditory sensitivity. Hypoacusis is chiefly related to auditory acuity for sound, pitch, and loudness. A person may express the difficulty by saying, "I do not hear well; repeat it a little bit louder." In a work which we published some years ago, we discussed the concepts expressed by a variety of writers about the terms "deafness" and "hypoacusis." This is not the time or place to reproduce the distinct arguments which support or oppose our ideas. We must remember, nevertheless, that for many writers, hypoacusis and deafness are established purely in terms of tones and decibels (or dB).* For example, for N. Davis and E. P. Fowler Jr., hypoacusis might be the loss of auditory sensitivity greater than 16 dB and less than 82 dB, while deafness would be a loss of more than 82 dB. Although some audiologists may rely on these figures, we do not use the latter as indicators of hypoacusis. For us, hypoacusis and deafness do not depend exclusively on an auditory loss, but imply a determined pattern of behavior and language.[16] To say it another way, a child with 65 dB of residual hearing can be considered either as deaf or as hard of hearing; it all depends on the patterns of behavior and levels of *lingua* and language attained. If behavior and *lingua* and language are comparable to normal levels for his age, the child is hard of hearing. If behavior and communication are comparable to those commonly used by nonrehabilitated deaf children, the child is deaf. Therefore, we may say that the solution to the problem of integrating of the deaf in the community, at present, is eminently an educational one. The loss of auditory sensitivity measured in decibels may be expressed as light, mild, severe, or grave "hearing impairment" or as "anacusis" (total loss of auditory sensitivity).

We understand as "dysacusis" any auditory symptom which is not related to the hearing loss or to the localization of the source of sound. A person can express the presence of dysacusis by saying, "I hear but I do not understand"; "I hear out of tune"; "I hear with noises"; etc.

Among the principal dysacusis, we must mention: (1) diplacusis, where one has a different sensation of pitch for the same sound in either ear; (2) deficient sound identification, where a sound is noted to be obscure and out of tone, distorted; (3) deficient sound discrimination, where a succession of sounds or an oral message is not discriminated or recognized, in spite of the correct tone audiometry—we emphasize—notwithstanding; (4) phonemic

---

* In practical terms, "decibel" can be defined as a psychophysic unit of measurement which represents the smaller variation of loudness that can be auditorily perceived (in 1000 Hz). In physics (acoustics), decibel is expressed as follows:

$$N \text{ (in decibels)} = 10 \log_{10} \frac{P_1}{P_2}, \text{ where } P = \text{power of intensity}$$

regression, where discrimination is deficient relative to the normal speed of speech, because these patients are capable of understanding messages given slowly; and so on. All these manifestations of auditory handicaps, quite different from hearing losses, may compromise in greater or lesser degree the social conditions of audition. They should therefore be taken into account because, if unknown, they may generate confusion and different opinions: children who do not learn with special educational methods; children and adults who refuse the use of hearing aids, or who do not benefit after using them; children who are emotionally disturbed; etc.

We understand as "auditory disorientation" a deficiency in the localization of the source of the sound. A person can express his handicap by saying, "I hear and understand that I am being called, but I do not know where from."

Some authors believe that dysacusis and auditory disorientation are produced in some cerebral damages, but others (including us) relate these symptoms to brain-stem damages.

Auditory examination procedures have developed very much during the 1960s and 1970s, and at the present time they permit us to assume different levels of auditory impairment in children.

N. F. Windle's work with monkey fetuses (during the 1960s) showed the possibility of bilateral central damage occurring in auditory pathways. This kind of damage can be also assumed in children. Anoxia (or asphyxia) neonatorum, various toxins, and other causes, can all produce central auditory damage. In these cases language is very difficult to achieve and there are grave learning disabilities in speech and *lingua.*

When deafness is only peripheral (i.e., deafness produced by any abnormality at any part of the auditory system before the entrance of the acoustic nerve to the medulla oblongata in the central nervous system), the cases must be differentiated into those which are congenital and those which are acquired before or after five years of life. As we shall discuss shortly, chances of acquisition of speech, *lingua,* and language are different in those three circumstances.

Children with congenital peripheral deafness can be taught to speak with special education techniques, but articulation is always poor. It is obviously different from normal articulation. *Lingua* is obtained and also reading and writing, but language comprehension and read/written language can only be imperfectly achieved and with much difficulty.

When peripheral deafness is acquired early in life, prognosis and learning potential are better than in the preceding case; but final results depend very much on ongoing, committed help from the teacher and family. Articulation and speech tend to remain poor.

When acquired peripheral deafness is produced after the child is five years old, the dominant hemisphere and language can help the patient very much to maintain his previous symbolic communication acquisitions. When, in addition, the student has the aid of special education, this kind of deaf child can frequently be confused with a normally-hearing child in many social situations (even in regular school classrooms).

The best results we obtain with congenitally or infancy-acquired deaf children are found with individual special teaching provided by a teacher for the deaf, placement in regular kindergarden and regular school classes, understanding and support from the family, and complete psychosocial adjustment therapy. We almost never saw such good results in such children when they were placed in special schools for the deaf. Once again, the same conclusion: Integration of a handicapped child into the normal community is the best way to help him. But the difficulty still remains in how to "integrate" the normal community with handicapped children.[17]

(56) VISUAL HANDICAPS AND LEARNING DISABILITIES

The concept of blindness refers to visual acuity of less than 20/200. The relationship "20/200" means that a person can see only at a distance of 20 feet—or less—what a normal individual can see at a distance of 200 feet. That relationship is accepted as the limit to blindness. Any less deficit in visual acuity is called "amblyopia." This term is generally used as synonymous with "visual impairment." Both terms, blindness and amblyopia (as deafness and hypoacusis), refer to only one parameter (i.e., sensory acuity). Connotation of medical terms referring to only one parameter will surely require more precise definition, because many other factors which take part in diagnosis of, for example, "deafness" or "blindness," in the near future will be included in more sophisticated examinations. Actually, blind and severely ambliopic children can have such a high degree of secondary learning disabilities that they must generally be assisted, at the beginning, by means of placement in special schools with special programs.

In cases of sensory, or perceptual, visual impairments, the small amount, deficiency, or absence of visual inputs into the vestibular-visual action-retroaction mechanisms will prevent the individual from acquiring important data for spatial notions. With the failure of visual-vestibular mechanisms, coordinated motor activities also fail; and body movements in environmental space are distorted. This not only interferes space-notion acquisition; it also alters, later on, the development of temporal notions.

It is obvious enough that, if the visual information of an object is distorted or absent, the recognition of that object and of its spatial relationships will be distorted likewise. At the very least, perceptual-sequence patterns will be different from those expected as "normal."

As we saw in Chapter II, Section 10, the relationship between proprioception, vestibular organs, and vision, is essential for correct achievement of purposeful equilibrium and for the proper development of corporal potentiality, which permits learning which is specifically human. We have also analyzed in Chapter VI, Sections 36, 37, and 38, how vestibular-visual relationships are considered to be one of the most important mechanisms for gaining sensory information. And we also know that good development of posture, knowledge of position in space, equilibrium, and movement allow the apprehension of spatial concepts. The child, then, can move his own body adequately through environmental space; and such body movements allow him to introduce new perceptual information which feeds back into his sensory-motor systems, thus increasing basic chances for learning.

In the case of congenital blindness (with no other disturbances), space-notion organization will be integrated through a pathological sequence pattern of cognition different than that of normal children. That pathological pattern will probably be similar in all similar cases. This necessarily implies extracharged and overloaded feedback information through other sensory receptors and pathways (in this case, mainly through audition and secondarily through vestibular and haptic inputs), as we discussed in Chapter VI, Section 34.

Amblyopic children have a certain amount of visual input, but it is seldom sufficient to permit a normal (or near-normal) pattern of learning. If the above considerations are related to what is expressed in the content of Chapter VI, Section 36, it will be easy to realize that delay, distortion, or absence of acquisition of visual conceptualization of objects, early visual control of movements, visual-spatial conceptualization, and so on, will generate disabilities in specifically human learning (for example, read and written language comprehension and expression), which are secondary to the main sensory or perceptual visual impairment.

Secondary learning disabilities in visual impairments, therefore, are mainly found in spatial and temporal notions and in reading and writing mechanisms, but not primarily in *lingua,* or even language. Nevertheless, language acquisition is delayed (although not particularly disturbed), due to the retention of auditory information which allows symbolic communication). Read and written language is acquired only with long and difficult training in symbolic systems (e.g., Braille) other than common handwriting.[18]

If visual handicaps are accompanied by other symptomatology, learning disabilities consequently become far more complex.

(57) PSYCHOLOGICAL DISTURBANCES AND LEARNING DISABILITIES

Psychic disturbances are very much related to human symbolization abilities, and, consequently, to secondary learning disabilities.

This subject has been closely studied all over the world; but, to date, no comprehensive international bibliography has been prepared on the subject. From a psychiatric point of view the reader can consult the *American Handbook of Psychiatry,* edited by S. Arieti (particularly Volumes I, II, IV, and VI).[19] We shall therefore review this subject here only in the most general terms.

As was previously seen, "learning disabilities" refer specifically to human achievements. These achievements are possible because biological (genetic) makeup and environmental (psychological) influences act together. Consequently, when psychological influences are disturbed, secondary learning disabilties can appear. Psychic disorders never produce isolated symbolic disturbances, but complex syndromes where *lingua,* language, reading, writing, or mathematical difficulties are only symptoms.

In Section 58 we shall speak about socioeconomic/cultural deprivations, which are closely connected with psychic disturbances. Certainly this review of the subject is artificial because all the different factors analyzed in this chapter interact with each other. It seems, however, that only with such a review some more clear orientation to the subject can be had.

A child develops speech when he feels the need to communicate with his human symbolic environment. Deaf children who have not received special education do not feel this necessity and thus do not develop speech.

Human learning abilities develop step-by-step in an adequate psychological environment. When that environment is not adequate, retardation or delay in human learning abilities always appears. For instance, behavior of institutionalized, or hospitalized, infants and children is quite different than behavior of infants and children who are with their families. On this topic, R. A. Spitz's works are now considered as classics.[20] The Hospitalism syndrome and the Institutionalization syndrome in early childhood are some of the typical conditions of social and emotional segregation that, when not correctly managed, can have a disastrous impact on children's future lives. These syndromes always produce psychic feedback: When the environment rejects the child, the child will eventually reject the environment.

Psychological studies, therefore, must approach the family environment, or the environment in which the child develops; and those studies clearly determine what kind of personality and behavior the individuals concerned with the child have. It is important to know the socioeconomic/cultural status of the environment, activities of parents (or substitute individuals), emotional rapport between them and the child, and what sort of social interaction the child has with the different members of the family. Certainly, the behavior of the child within the family, at school, on the playground, and so on, must be known.

Along these lines, it is possible to observe three main abberent behaviors: (1) reactive, (2) neurotic, and (3) psychotic.

We understand reactive behavior as that which responds to a definite environmental cause. Personality is not permanently deeply compromised, and the child's behavior improves considerably when environmental causes become basically under adequate control.

Neurotic behavior is neither very frequent nor highly structured in children. It is necessary to realize that, in order for a neurotic behavior to acquire structure, language must be well developed. With *lingua* level, or with the first stages of language, it is quite difficult to discover the structure of the neurosis.

Behavior in neurotic children is very similar to that in reactive children, but it shows a more severe degree. Anxiety neurosis is the most common syndrome among childhood neuroses. Sometimes reactive behavior develops into neurosis; and it so happens that the latter is only diagnosed when the child is near puberty, because psychosomatic or depressive symptoms (for instance) are only clearly seen by that time.

In regard to psychotic behavior, all the present definitions are extremely controversial. In 1943-44, when L. Kanner wrote in the United States about "early infantile autism," and H. Asperger in Austria about "autistic psychopathy," two main syndromes of psychosis were described. Unfortunately, that was during World War II, a time when scientific connections between the United States and Austria were nonexistant. Both, early autism and autistic psychopathy, are personality derangements in infants and young children.[21]

Early autism manifests symptomatology during the first year of postnatal life; children walk before uttering the first conditioned words. They are withdrawn; they avoid eye contact with others; and *lingua* (if acquired) never has, or it loses, its communicative goals. Both sexes can be affected. Many symptoms of mental retardation progressively appear. Obvious cognitive defects are typical of such a syndrome. The social prognosis is poor.

Autistic psychopathy is different. It begins near the third year of postnatal life, and it is commonly observed in kindergarten. *Lingua,* by this time, has been basically established. The child has a communicative goal through *lingua,* but his personal interests and his mental faculties are at best, "scatterbrained," at worst, schizoid. He avoids eye contact with others. He has a bizarre character (but never so bizarre as early autistic children). Prevalence of this syndrome is in males. Social prognosis is fair to good if professional attention is promptly and adequately provided.

If we review the preceding three different main abnormal behaviors in children (i.e., reactive, neurotic, and psychotic), we see that all of them necessarily produce secondary learning disabilities. In reactive behavior, children can fail academically but many times some appropriate orientation with parents and family environment can produce quick and complete behavior rehabilitation.

In the case of neurosis, more sophisticated psychotherapy should be provided if necessary. Certainly, symptoms are more severe; and academic maladjustment is more dramatic.

In the case of psychosis there are different syndromes which manifest some symptoms well described by H. Clancy, A. Dugdale, and J. Rendle-Short in 1969; but thus far we have only mentioned the two definite clinical syndromes described by Kanner and by Asperger in 1943-44.[22] Kanner's syndrome, or early autism, requires very sophisticated and specialized treatment. Secondary learning disabilities are already manifested by the absence of or great defect in *lingua.* These children do not seem to have much chance for placement in regular schools.

Asperger's syndrome, or autistic psychopathy, generally begins in kindergarten, but sometimes the child enters the regular school without apparent symptomatology. This condition, therefore, can be detected at regular schools (many times without the teacher identifying, at the beginning, what kind of condition it is). In these last cases, combined efforts of doctors, therapists, special workers, teachers, can help assure the reintegration of the child into the community. This last syndrome affects mainly character, and prognosis is fairly good.

(58) SOCIOECONOMIC/CULTURAL DIFFERENCES AND LEARNING DISABILITIES

The amount of research on socioeconomic/cultural deprivation connected with cognitive learning disabilities has increased very much in recent years. In the United States it developed largely because of the action of certain programs, such as Project Head Start, the Office of Economic Opportunity, the National Laboratory on Early Education of the Office of Education, and so on.[23]

School-age children who belong to socioeconomically or culturally different areas are, from an educational point of view, described with some characteristics that can be summarized as follows:

1. Having poor knowledge of their "cultural" environment.
2. Using *lingua* instead of language.
3. Maintaining objective thought instead of logical or conceptual thought.[24]
4. Having difficulties in following the rhythm of learning of reading and writing presented in regular schools.
5. Presenting potential disorders for learning to perform voluntary skilled movements.[25]
6. Showing generally very acceptable responses for "gross," "useful," or "survival" movements.[26]
7. Displaying high potential for school failure and dropping out.
8. Being present—and past—oriented, with little sense of the future, or having a "short-time perspective for planning."[27]

    "Time-without-future" refers to (1) the difficulty that these children have in answering questions about their future; and (2) the confusion they experience in using verbal tenses (present tense instead of future tense). This last observation is particularly seen in Spanish, where future tenses give a definite cast to the meaning of the verb. Latin-American regions that were very poor in their origins continue to speak Spanish without a future tense. For instance, instead of *"Iremos a comer"* ("We shall go to eat"), they say *"Vamos a ir a comer"* (something like: "We go to go to eat"). It is worth asking ourselves: Why do extremely cultivated persons in vast regions of Latin-American countries eliminate Spanish future tenses in current *lingua*—deprivations stemming from the beginning of the colonial society?*

    Perhaps when human communities are very worried during long periods about present difficulties, they do not have time to think or talk about their future. This may explain why this phenomenon occurs with certain idioms.
9. Great difficulty in establishing or in understanding perspectives.
10. Deficiency in working with representational materials (figures, imagery, etc.).

---

*The same situation occurs in English. Children of the ghetto or barrio frequently lose inflectional endings or drop ancillary verbs entirely, such as: "The man come tomorrow"; "I see you later"; "I bring it next week"; and so on. The frequency with which this occurs may rule out (1) intentional mangling of the language, and (2) sloppy modeling of proper forms of usage. Poor environmental conditions over a long period of time can make learning disabilities an epidemic in a subgroup of the general population; but the possibility also must be considered that, even given the poor conditions of life, young children are modeling accurately the *lingua* of the ghetto. Thus, the loss of such an element of language can become a linguistic-social norm. Ironically, there are some individuals (generally, entertainers) who have mastered the "dialect" sufficiently well to use it effectively (and sometimes critically) with respect to the regional or national standard dialect of English.—Ed.

The quality of childrearing and the level of language in a child's family have been shown to be extremely important for learning abilities. This is not surprising, because language itself *is* established upon *lingua*, which is a learning ability.

Cognitive handicaps, analysis-synthesis deficits, representational failures, integrative disorders, and so on, are also processes which elicit difficulties in learning symbolic communication and language.

Race and socioeconomic/cultural levels. Many times confusion exists between socioeconomic/cultural status and some ethnic groups that are considered "lower." For instance, Blacks or Indians are sometimes considered socioeconomically and culturally deprived, compared to Whites. This confusion between race and socioeconomic/cultural status can lead to erroneous conclusions. It is true that many Blacks in some countries belong to low socioeconomic/cultural levels. There are diverse historical facts that contribute to this situation. Nevertheless, it is very controversial whether Blacks perform less efficiently than Whites in tests like Kohs' *Block Designs.*[28] There are so many variables in such a study between races that no conclusion at all can be reached without many arguments.

Malnutrition and socioeconomic/cultural levels. Another increasingly studied impact of socioeconomic/cultural deprivations on learning is malnutrition. As J. W. Prescott, M. S. Read, and D. B. Coursin say, "Malnutrition is only one of many interacting variables that contribute to child development in an impoverished population. For example, infectious diseases limit a child's capability to utilize available nutrients."[29] We are in complete agreement with this statement, and we referred to some parasitarian diseases in Section 51.

According to our comments in Chapter II, Section 8, specific human achievements (for instance, *lingua* and language) develop upon biological structures and in response to environmental stimulation. Biological structures require a certain level of health in order to support the establishment of symbolic possibilities. Proper nutrition is essential for this support. Proteins, carbohydrates, vitamin B_6, and other elements, all seem to be considered extremely important for brain activity, intellectual skills, and language development.

Subjects suffering from malnutrition show definite retardation in language development, intelligence quotient (IQ), and abstract thought, explored through well known assessment instruments.[30] These symptoms are worse when malnourishment is severe during the first months of postnatal life, and in such cases remain associated with poor performances in later life.[31]

In regard to language development, J. Cravioto and E. R. De Licardie measured it (through the *Gesell Developmental Kit*) in 19 children who developed severe malnutrition; and they compared the obtained results with performances given by a group of children "never considered as severely malnourished." During the first year of postnatal life, mean language development was very similar in both groups. "As time elapsed and more children developed severe malnutrition, a difference in language performance to the matched controls became evident."[32]

Malnourished children can also have language deficiencies resulting from other factors such as poor and inadequate mother-infant interaction (for obvious reasons), or extended periods of hospitalization (for treatment).[33]

In regard to sensory integration and malnutrition, there is no agreement among various authors who correlate those parameters. While some authors believe that malnourished children perform more poorly on tests having items of sensory integration, others find no difference between well-nourished and malnourished groups.[34]

It is clear that all the deficits discussed in this section contribute to the learning disabilities of malnourished children. Unfortunately, in many parts of the world malnutrition can be considered an endemic socioeconomic disease. "If it is true that in developing countries undernutrition is the principle cause of premature deaths, the damage in the survivors is still worse."[35]

Pedagogical errors and socioeconomic/cultural levels. Among cultural deficiencies, pedagogical errors in teaching must also be considered.

In general, we believe every teacher must be concerned with:

1. The level of development and abilities of the child in accordance with every developmental age as provided by regionally standardized developmental tests.
2. The individual development, performance, and abilities of the child in daily school activities.
3. How the child's academic learning progresses at school with and without special reinforcement. Are academic performances of the child good, similar, or poor, when working alone; with special help; at school; at home?
4. What are the family or environmental demands and wished-for goals for the child?

Consequently, teachers must know the general development of the child and must observe the individual development of each child, paying attention also to the support, or rejection, and demands of the environment.

Nevertheless, some teachers who are apparently very well informed about theory are not effective from a practical point of view. Others, with a poor theoretical background in education theory are excellent teachers. Many years ago one of us divided teachers into two groups: "bony-teachers" and "maternal-teachers." The former were brilliant in giving public presentations, but the latter succeeded better with their pupils.

It is not the time to ask ourselves if the primary condition for good teaching is the personal approach of the teacher in regard to the pupil.

F. L. Ilg and L. B. Ames wrote in 1964: "In this post-Sputnik era since 1957, American education as a whole has been subjected to sharp criticism."[36] We read—and we are still reading—many books which express this concern. There are no methodologies in classrooms, there are only children. Methods are only ways of action. To know them is by all means useful, but never so important as the "gift" of being able to teach well. In Old

Spanish there was a proverb which said: *"Lo que Natura non da, Salamanca nonpresta"* (i.e., "What Nature does not give, Salamanca does not lend"). Salamanca was the most famous University in Spain in the fifteenth century. That proverb is still true: No university or course of study can provide the human sense that comes through innate and early environmental influences. We shall return to this subject in Section 59 when we discuss "ecology."

Unfortunately, all over the world, beaurocracy and politics also meddle in education. There are many papers and records to fill out, computer programs to write, computer data to evaluate, many reports to be reviewed, and so on. But there are more and more problems in the schools. Such are the rewards of "civilization."

Teacher's or pupil's absences cause the regular development of learning to deteriorate. Sometimes absences of pupils increase until they finally drop out. Certainly, there are many factors which can determine such a situation, but probably the most important one depends on socioeconomic and cultural influences. In many parts of Latin-American countries, dropping out peaks after the second- or third-grade level. In the United States the peak is at the high school level. Some countries have adopted measures to avoid regional or local school dropouts. For instance, in some regions during harvest time the whole family works and children do not go to school. In those regions, wise governments transform harvest time into school vacation time. However, the situation is usually much more complex. The higher the cultural level of community, the more complex the causes related to school dropout.

Socioeconomic/cultural causes dramatically affect opportunities for learning in school. Every government *must* realize that health and education are extremely important factors for the present and future of our species. It is not feasible to work with multidisciplinary teams arbitrarily composed of different professionals who, though working side by side, work without regard for the contributions of others, and who pay more attention to beaurocracy than to education. It is not acceptable to change frequently the subjects, programs, and purposes of the educational system without damaging the continuity and quality of teaching and learning. Every region, state, or country has its own realities; and it is simply not intelligent to imitate what such-and-such another region or country did, without a careful and cautious inspection and "tailoring." In education and learning the old Chinese proverb, "If you wish to go far you must go slowly," seems to apply.

(59) ECOLOGY AND SECONDARY LEARNING DISABILITIES

Ecology is the branch of biology which concerns relationships between organisms and their environment. During recent years ecology has received international attention mainly because of the negative effects of pollution (chiefly in urban air and water pollution) upon human beings.

Many people have been shocked by accounts of ecological disasters on television and in the newspapers—for example, Tokyo school children having to breathe oxygen during smog alerts, or the devastation of rivers and coastlines so that they are unfit for human use.

Ecological reasons lie behind the modification of school seasons in

Alaska (U.S.) or Fireland (Tierra del Fuego, Argentina): During cold weather there are school vacations. The opposite could be found in some tropical areas of the world.

All the preceding negative ecological effects have been—and are—very widely disseminated through the communicative media. Luckily, many regional or federal governments have become sensitized and have adopted—or are adopting—measures to diminish air pollution, to control sewage, to check water pollution in rivers and on sea coasts, to diminish use of tobacco, and so on. But, certainly, the importance of ecology does not end there. One of the most outstanding ecological problems we face concerns itself with how environmental stimuli are incorporated by the human species in the form of cognition or learning.

K. Lorenz insightfully discussed this subject in a book published in 1965.[37] Two traditional concepts in regard to behavior were considered: "innate" and "learned." According to Lorenz, both terms are related to the origin of the information that then elicits adaptive behavior to the environment. Information is phylogenically within organic systems (through mutation and selection-of-species evolution) or ontogenically (through reciprocal interaction between the individual and his environment). Every adaptive behavior necessarily presumes a programed mechanism from previously acquired phylogenic information. According to Lorenz, both the "innate" concept and the "learning" concept can never be defined by excluding one from the other. Innate behavior exists before any individual learning, in order for learning to take place. Species store information, coding it as chained molecules within the genome. Certainly, the more complex an adapted process is, the less probability there is that it will improve its adaptation through accidental changes. The central nervous system is a center of very complex processes; accidental changes will almost always produce central nervous disintegration.

Lorenz' work leads us to think again about the higher processes in man (i.e., symbolic processes). Secondary learning disabilities elicited by ecological factors, therefore, can appear not only as a consequence of a direct interaction between the individual and his environment, but also as a phylogenic result of the species' adaptive behavior.

Meanwhile, it must be understood that ecology also acts on learning disabilities through biological, psychological, nutritional, social, and many other influences. For instance, R. A. Spitz wrote that in overpopulation, mother-child "dyad" is absent or defective.[38] Lorenz and P. Leyhausen considered that in overpopulation the greatest danger is not exclusively (or mainly) related to difficulties of food or shelter, but instead refers to the individual limits of tolerance to the perpetual proximity of other persons.[39] In overpopulated environments secondary learning disabilities increase.

We are aware of some of the dangers of overpopulation; but we can only dimly imagine how profound will be its ramifications, if proper human educational needs and prospectives are neglected.

NOTES

1. A. J. de Oliveira, "Situacao Biologica do Aluno de Aprendizagem Lenta," in Faculdade de Educacao e Centro de Estudos e Pesquisas Educacionais, *O Aluno de Apren-*

dizagem Lenta no Ensino de 1° Grau , Volume 2 (3 vols.) (Florianopolis, Santa Catarina [Brazil] : Secretaria de Educacao, 1973-74): 246.

2. H. R. Myklebust, *Development and Disorders of Written Language; Picture Story Language Test* (New York: Grune & Stratton, 1965); H. R. Myklebust, *Development and Disorders of Written Language. Studies of Normal and Exceptional Children* (New York: Grune & Stratton, 1973); J. Feldman, "Escala de Evaluacion del Lenguaje Escrito" (doctoral dissertation; Facultad de Ciencias de la Recuperacion Humana, U.M.S.A. [Buenos Aires] , 1977; J. Feldman, *Aritmetica en Ninos con Problemas de Lenguaje* (Buenos Aires: Ares, 1977).

3. W. J. Little, "On the Influence of Abnormal Parturition, Difficult Labours, Premature Birth, and Asphyxia Neonatorum, on the Mental and Physical Condition of the Child, Specially in Relation to Deformities," *Transactions of the Obstetric Society of London* 3 (1861-62): 293 [reprinted by *Cerebral Palsy Bulletin* 1:1 (1958): 5-34] ; S. Freud, "Die Infantile Cerebral Lahmung," in Nothnagel, *Specielle Pathologie und Therapie*, Volume 9 (Wien: Holder, 1897); W. M. Phelps, "The Rehabilitation of Cerebral Palsy," *Southern Medical Journal* 34 (1941): 770; W. M. Phelps, "Cerebral Palsy," *Journal of the Iowa Medical Society* 38 (1948): 509; M. A. Perlstein, "Infantile Cerebral Palsy: Classification and Clinical Correlations," *Journal of the American Medical Association* 149 (1952): 30-34; M. A. Perlstein, "Infantile Cerebral Palsy," in *Advances in Pediatrics* 7,209 (Chicago: Year Book Publishers, Inc., 1955); C. L. Balf and R. R. S. Ingram, "Problems in the Classification of Cerebral Palsy in Childhood," *British Medical Journal* 11 (1955): 163; W. L. Minear, "A Classification of Cerebral Palsy," *Pediatrics* 18:5 (1956): 841-852; B. Crothers and R. S. Paine, *The Natural History of Cerebral Palsy* (Cambridge, Massachusetts: Harvard University Press, 1959); R. C. Mac Keith, I. C. K. Mackenzie, and P. E. Polani, "Definition of Cerebral Palsy," *Cerebral Palsy Bulletin* 2:5 (1959): 23; M. J. Mecham, M. J. Berko, and F. G. Berko, *Speech Therapy in Cerebral Palsy* (Springfield, Illinois; Charles C Thomas, 1960); J. B. de Quiros and E. E. Tormakh, "Definicion y Clasificaciones de las Paralisis Cerebrales," in J. B. de Quiros, L. Cowes, R. Gotter, O. L. Schrager, and E. E. Tormakh (eds.), *Los Grandes Problemas del Lenguaje Infantil* (Buenos Aires: CEMIFA, 1969): 265-290.

4. R. Brain, *Diseases of the Nervous System* (5th ed.) (London: Oxford University Press, 1955); R. Dreyer, "Die Behandlung der Epilepsien," in H. W. Gruhle, R. Jung, W. Mayer-Gross, and M. Muller (eds.), *Psychiatrie der Genenwart, Forschung und Praxis*, Volume 2 (Berlin: Springer, 1970): 778; H. J. Vazquez, "Convulsiones en la Infancia," *Actualizacion en Tratamientos* 31:397 (1976): 2-12.

5. H. Gastaut, *Epilepsies* (Paris: Encyclopedie Medico-Chirurgicale, 1963); H. Gastaut, H. Jasper, J. Bancaud, A. Waltregny (eds.), *The Psychopathogenesis of the Epilepsies* (Springfield, Illinois: Charles C Thomas, 1969).

6. M. Rutter, P. Graham, and W. Yule, *A Neuropsychiatric Study in Childhood* Clinics in Developmental Medicine 35/36 (London: Spastics International Medical Publications and William Heinemann Medical Books, Ltd., 1970).

7. J. J. Gallagher, "A Comparison of Brain-Injured and Non-Brain-Injured Mentally Retarded Children of Several Psychological Variables," *Monograph of the Society for Research on Child Development* 22 (1957): 2; J. L. Schulman *et al.*, *Brain Damage and Behavior: A Clinical-Experimental Study* (Springfield, Illinois: Charles Thomas, 1965); H. H. Nielsen, *A Psychological Study of Cerebral Palsied Children* (Copenhagen: Munksgaard, 1966); C. B. Ernhardt *et al.*, "Brain Injury in the Preschool Child: Some Developmental Considerations, II, Comparison of Brain-Injured and Normal Children," *Psychological Monographs* 77:11 (1963).

8. L. E. Keating, "A Review of the Literature on the Relationship of Epilepsy and Intelligence in Schoolchildren," *Journal of Mental Science* 106 (1960): 1042-1059; M. R. Chaudhry and D. A. Pond, "Mental Deterioration in Epileptic Children," *Journal of Neurology, Neurosurgery, and Psychiatry* 24 (1961): 213; J. E. Cooper, "Epilepsy in a Longitudinal Survey of 5,000 Children," *British Medical Journal* 1 (1965): 1020.

9. R. Hill, *Families Under Stress* (New York: Harper Bros., 1949); B. Farber, "Effects

of a Severely Mentally Retarded Child on Family Integration," *Monograph of the Society for Research on Child Development* 24 (1959): 2; J. Tizard and J. Grad, "The Mentally Handicapped and Their Families," *Monograph Number 7* (London: Oxford University Press, 1961); A. P. Curran *et al.*, *Handicapped Children and Their Families* (Denfermline [Carnegie]: United Kingdom Trust, 1964); J. A. Clausen, "Family Structure, Socialization and Personality," in H. L. Hoffman (ed.), *Review of Children Development Research*, Volume 2 (New York: Russel Sage Foundation, 1966); L. A. Ives, "Learning Difficulties in Children with Epilepsy," *The British Journal of Disorders of Communication* 5:1 (1970): 77-84.

10. P. W. Pruyser, "Psychological Testing in Epilepsy, II, Personality," *Epilepsia* 2 (1953): 23-26; J. Guerrant *et al.*, *Personality in Epilepsy* (Springfield, Illinois: Charles C Thomas, 1962).

11. Ives, *op. cit.*

12. A. R. A. Bengzon, "Anticonvulsivants: Historical Development, Basic Pharmacology and Future Research," *Abstracts of the Fourth International Congress of Neurologic Surgery and Ninth International Congress of Neurology* (New York, September, 1969): 4.

13. J. B. de Quirós, "Epilepsia y Lenguaje," *Fonoaudiologica* [Buenos Aires] 13:2 (1967): 84-92; O. L. Schrager, "Pautas para la Valoracion del Aprendizaje de la Lecto-Escritura en la Epilepsia," in J. B. de Quirós (ed.), *Lenguaje y Aprendizaje* (Buenos Aires: CEMIFA, 1972): 147-155; M. L. Rincon, "Aprendizaje en el Retardo Mental con Epilepsia," in J. B. de Quirós (ed.), *Lenguaje y Aprendizaje* (Buenos Aires: CEMIFA, 1972): 219-222; E. E. Tormakh, "Aprendizaje Motor y Epilepsia," in J. B. de Quirós (ed.), *Ninos con Dificultades en el Aprendizaje* (Montevideo: Instituto Interamericano del Nino [Organization of American States] and UNICEF, 1974): 189-194; J. Feldman, "Aprendizaje Escolar y Epilepsia," in J. B. de Quirós (ed.), *Ninos con Dificultades en el Aprendizaje* (Montevideo: Instituto Interamericano del Nino [Organization of American States] and UNICEF, 1974): 205-210.

14. R. S. Paine and T. E. Oppe, *Neurological Examination in Children*, Clinics in Developmental Medicine 20-21 (London: Spastics International Medical Publications and William Heinemann Medical Books, Ltd., 1968).

15. J. B. de Quiros, "Orientaciones Multidisciplinarias en la Epilepsia," in Quiros (ed.), (ed.), *Ninos con Dificultades en el Aprendizaje* (Montevideo: Instituto Interamericano del Nino [Organization of American States] and UNICEF, 1974): 215-220.

16. H. Davis and E. P. Fowler Jr., "Hearing and Deafness," in H. Davis and S. R. Silverman (eds.), *Hearing and Deafness* (New York: Holt Rinehart and Winston, 1961): 81; J. B. de Quirós, "Hipoacusias y Pseudohipoacusias en Ninos de Edad Escolar," *Fonoaudiologica* [Buenos Aires] 9:3 (1963): 197-211; N. F. Windle, "An Experimental Approach to Prevention or Reduction of Brain Damage of Birth Asphyxia," *Developmental Medicine and Child Neurology* 8:2 (1966): 129-140.

17. J. B. de Quirós, "Reflexiones sobre Distintos Diagnosticos de Sordera y Perspectivas Metodologicas de Oralizacion," in J. B. de Quirós (ed.), *Las Llamadas Afasias Infantiles* (Buenos Aires: Editorial Medica Panamericana, 1971-74): 83-94; J. B. de Quirós and N. D'Elia, *La Audiometria del Adulto y del Nino* (Buenos Aires: Editorial Paidos, 1974); O. L. Schrager, "Consideraciones Medico—Recuperativas sobre la Comunicacion-Lenguaje en el Nino Sordo," *Pedagogia Terapeutica* [Buenos Aires] 3:5 (1974): 4-23.

18. Y. Hatwell, *Privation Sensorielle et Intelligence* (Paris: Presses Universitaires de France, 1966); J. B. de Quirós, "Ceguera y Psicomotricidad," *Revista Argentina de Tiflologia* [Buenos Aires] 1:1 (1972): 34-54; O. L. Schrager, "Importancia de la Vision en la Estructuracion de la Postura y el Espacio en el Nino," *Revista Argentina de Tiflologia* [Buenos Aires] 2 (1973): 26-40; O. L. Schrager, "Vision, Sistema Postural y Aprendizaje," *Fonoaudiologica* [Buenos Aires] 20: 2-3 (1974): 67-81; J. B. de Quirós and O. L. Schrager, "Postura, Actividades Motrices y Aprendizaje," *Fonoaudiologica* [Buenos Aires] 22: 1-2 (1976): 12-21.

19. S. Arieti (ed.), *American Handbook of Psychiatry* (2nd. ed.) (New York: Basic Books, 1975).

NOTES

20. R. A. Spitz, "Hospitalism: An Inquiry into the Genesis of Psychiatric Conditions in Early Childhood," in R. A. Spitz, *The Psychoanalitic Study of the Child* (3rd. ed.) (New York: International University Press, 1958).

21. L. Kanner, "Autistic Disturbances of Affective Contact," *Nervous Child* 2 (1943): 217-250; L. Kanner, "Early Infantile Autism," *Journal of Pediatrics* 25 (1944): 211-217; H. Asperger, "Die autistischen Psychopathen im Kindesalter," *Archiv fur Psychiatrie und Nervenkrankheiten* 117 (1944): 76-136.

22. H. Clancy, A. Dugdale, and J. Rendle-Short, "The Diagnosis of Infantile Autism," *Developmental Medicine and Child Neurology* 11 (1969): 432-442.

23. United States Department of Health, Education and Welfare, *Perspectives on Human Deprivation: Biological, Psychological, and Sociological* (Washington, D.C.: National Institute of Child Health and Human Development, National Institutes of Health, Public Health Service, 1968).

24. J. Piaget, *Le Langage et la Pensee chez l'Enfant* (Neuchatel, Switzerland: Delachaux et Niestle, 1956); I. E. Sigel, "Styles of Categorization and their Intellectual and Personality Correlate in Young Children," *Human Development* 10 (1967): 1-17.

25. J. B. de Quirós, M. Della Cella, D. Carrara, and L. Allegro, *Estudies sobre la Dislexia Infantil* (Santa Fe, Argentina: Ministerio de Educacion y Cultura, 1962).

26. *Ibid.*

27. S. M. Miller, F. Riesman, and A. A. Seagull, "Poverty and Self-Indulgence: A Critique of the Non-Deferred Gratification Pattern," in L. A. German, J. L. Kornbluh, and A. Haber (eds.), *Poverty in America* (Ann Arbor: University of Michigan Press, 1965).

28. A. M. Shuey, *The Testing of Negro Intelligence* (Lynchburg, Virginia: J. P. Bell, 1958); S. C. Kohs, *Intelligence Measurement* (New York: Macmillan, 1923).

29. J. W. Prescott, M. S. Read, and D. B. Coursin (eds.), *Brain Function and Malnutrition: Neuropsychological Methods of Assessment* (New York: John Wiley & Sons, 1975).

30. J. Cravioto and B. Robles, "Evolution of Adaptive and Motor Behavior During Rehabilitation from Kwashiorkor," *American Journal of Orthopsychiatry* 35 (1965): 449-464; F. Monckeberg, "Effect of Early Marasmic Malnutrition on Subsequent Physical and Psychological Development," in N. S. Scrimshaw and J. D. Gordon (eds.), *Malnutrition, Learning and Behavior* (Cambridge, Massachussetts: M.I.T. Press, 1968); F. Monckeberg, "The Effect of Malnutrition on Physical Growth and Brain Development," in Prescott, Read, and Coursin (eds.), *op. cit.*: 15-39; G. Barrera Moncade, *Estudios sobre Alteraciones del Crecimiento y del Desarrollo Psicologico del Sindrome Pluricarencial (Kwashiorkor)* (Caracas, Venezuela: Editorial Grafos, 1963); S. Champakam, S. G. Srikantia, and C. Goplan, "Kwashiorkor and Mental Development," *American Journal of Clinical Nutrition* 21 (1968): 844-852; H. P. Chase and H. P. Martin, "Undernutrition and Child Development," *New England Journal of Medicine* 282 (1970): 933-939; J. E. McKay, A. C. McKay, and L. Sinisterra, "Behavioral Intervention Studies with Malnourished Children: A Review of Experiences," in D. J. Kallen (ed.), *Nutrition, Development and Social Behavior* D.D.E.W. Pub. No. (N.I.H.) 73-242. (Washington, D.C.: U.S. Government Printing Office, 1973); A. B. Lefevre, "Malnutrition and Language Development," in E. H. Lenneberg and E. Lenneberg (eds.), *Foundations of Language Development* (New York: Academic Press; and Paris: UNESCO Press, 1975): 279-295.

31. R. E. Klein and A. A. Adinolfi, "Measurement of the Behavioral Correlates of Malnutrition," in Prescott, Read, and Coursin (eds.), *op. cit.*

32. J. Cravioto and E. R. De Licardie, "Neurointegrative Development and Intelligence in Children Rehabilitated from Severe Malnutrition," in Prescott, Read, and Coursin (eds.), *op. cit.*: 53-72.

33. D. J. Kallen, Panel Discussion, "Neuropsychological Methods for the Assessment of Impaired Brain Function in the Malnourished Child" (cosponsored by the U.S.-Japan Cooperative Medical Science Program and the National Institute of Child Health and

Human Development), in Prescott, Read, and Coursin (eds.), *op. cit.*: 113-116.

34. Klein and Adinolfi, in Prescott, Read, and Coursin (eds.), *op. cit.*

35. Monkenberg, in Prescott, Read, and Coursin (eds.), *op. cit.*: 15-39.

36. F. L. Ilg and L. B. Ames, *School Readiness* (New York: Harper & Row, 1964).

37. K. Lorenz, *Evolution and Modification of Behavior* (Chicago: University of Chicago Press, 1965).

38. R. A. Spitz, "The Derailment of Dialogue: Stimulus Overload, Action Cycles, and the Completion Gradient," *Journal of the American Psychoanalytic Association* 12 (1964): 725-775.

39. K. Lorenz and P. Leyhausen, *Antriebe Tierischen und Menschlichen verhaltens* (Munchen: Piper and Co., 1968).

NEUROPSYCHOLOGICAL FUNDAMENTALS

CHAPTER IX

Neurological Examination

(60) NEUROLOGICAL FACTS IN ADULT READING DISABILITIES

In Chapter VII, Section 42, we reviewed some historical facts concerning alexia and dyslexia in adults. There, we mentioned "pure" alexias, pointing out that these disorders are generally included within different types of aphasia in adults. The syndrome of apractognosia in the right hemisphere (Chapter VII, Section 45), where mainly spatial relationships are disturbed, was also mentioned. In this last case, reading disabilities can be observed as a consequence of the spatial disorder.

In the case of dyslexic symptomatology, studies of adult brain damage may be useful, because "developmental dyslexia" refers to children six years old or more. From this age onward, language is regularly present (*lingua* develops into language); and hemispheric dominance can be already established. This notwithstanding, a huge difference between adults and children remains: Adults previously read.

Among "pure" alexias in adults, different types related to letters and to words can be distinguished. Alexia to sentences is also considered by some authors.

Literal alexia consists in having difficulties in recognizing letters. Words can be eventually read, but their components (syllables or letters) cannot be analyzed. Sometimes patients can understand the general meaning, or semantics, of a written word; but they change the word: When presented with the word "cream," they say "milk"; or when presented with the word "garden," they say "flower"; and so on.[1]

Names, adjectives, and adverbs, however, can be sometimes correctly read; and other times patients experience what some researchers call "visual completion" (for instance, reading "gentlemen" instead of "gentle").

Common words or "everyday-use labels" can be easily read (hotel, bar, coke, etc.).

On the other hand, "logotomes" cannot be deciphered through reading (from Greek: *logos,* word; *tome,* cut). For instance, the word "achievement" is separated in English into the syllables: "a-chieve-ment"; but in order to find logotomes we can arbitrarily divide it—for example, into "a-chie-*vem*-ent." "Vem" is an English logotome. Arbitrary combinations of a consonant, a vowel, and another consonant used in the current *lingua* constitute logotomes. In our opinion, among the most thorough studies of logotomes are those made during World War II by the United States federal government in the course of auditory clinical investigations. Since then, study of logotomes has become common in most university audiological departments. In fact, logotomes are not particularly easy to decipher or connect with the rest of the word of which they might be a part, even for the competent, experienced reader.*

If the patient is able to read or to understand (without reading aloud) simple words, he must be examined again in regard to his proficiency in reading short sentences. If he is also able to read or to understand letters, he must read more complex sentences (such as, "Put the coin between the rubber eraser and the pencil").

In literal alexia there are difficulties in recognizing numerals and figures. Copying and writing from dictation are also difficult.

Word alexia permits correct recognition of *isolated* letters. When presented with a word, however, patients try to analyze letters or syllables—but the task promptly becomes very hard and reading fails.

Categories and functional parts of speech are not recognized by these patients: Verbs are confused with nouns, adjectives, or adverbs.

Logotomes present the same difficulties as do common words. Some short and simple sentences can occasionally be read; but difficulties in reading and understanding are enormous. Sometimes the mechanics of reading can help in order for the patient to "read," but the patient cannot understand the meanings. Reading of numerals and figures, as well as writing, are possible.

Sentence alexia is accepted as a separate entity by some authors, but its differentiation from some types of aphasia seems to be very controversial, because all these conditions imply comprehension impairment.[2]

Total alexia refers to mixed forms of letter and word alexias. Reading of numerals and figures remains possible.

In general, "pure" alexias in adults allow haptic recognition of plastic letters, or kinetic recognition of the hand and arm creating a letter shape in the air, or tactile recognition when a letter is drawn on his hand. In many cases iterative and slow dictation of some words produces successful results.

---

*At least one American educator, Marnell L. Hayes, uses logotomes as part of a workshop exercise for parents and others, to give them an idea of what it is like to have a learning disability. She takes logotomes on a mimeographed sheet, which is then distributed to the audience. The task is to reconnect those "nonsense parts" into a meaningful whole. For those adults whose vocabulary is not very sophisticated, or who are not particularly good readers, the task can be an infuriating one.

"Pure" alexics have a generally intact ability to differentiate letters or numerals; they can generally recognize numerals and figures; but they cannot read letters or words. The symbolic representation of reading escapes them. On the other hand, mathematical calculation can be also disturbed in some cases; but we must be very cautious before classifying a mathematical difficulty as a computational disorder.

It seems reasonable to accept that mathematical visual recognition and reading respond to different kinds of associations. From a medical point of view mathematical visual recognition responds to occipito-parietal relationships, and reading responds to occipito-temporal relationships.

For these patients writing is possible, but they show clumsiness in copying exercises, meanwhile not understanding what they wrote through copying or writing dictation; and, many times, there are signs of dysgraphia.

N. Geschwind called attention to the fact that adult alexics have color anomia; he interpreted this symptom as a dissociation between visual areas and language areas.[3] In color anomia, patients were able to match the same colors; but they could not attach names properly to the colors they saw, nor could they point to colors when names for those colors had been provided. Visual perception could not be transferred to verbal information. This assumption was corroborated by autopsy. Visual perceptions reached the occipital lobe, but they had no direct association with the zones more related to language, because the left posterior cerebral damage also involved the corpus callosum.

We should be mindful of some of Geschwind's observations: In some patients where the posterior part of the corpus callosum was surgically sectioned, reading is possible. When written materials are presented only to the left visual hemifield (in order to send the information only to the right hemisphere), reading, or reading aloud becomes impossible.

"Pure" alexias in adults, therefore, manifest the following symptomatology:

1. Failure in reading.
2. Some difficulties in writing.
3. Recognition of numerals and figures in some cases, but frequent computational disabilities.
4. Severe difficulties in color naming.
5. Right lateral homonym hemianopsy.
6. Spatial disorientation (referring to natural and representational—or drawn—space).
7. Almost normal oral language (speech), body schema, and praxias.

Another syndrome that must be taken into consideration is that involving finger agnosia (as, for example, Gerstmann's syndrome).[4]

According to J. Gerstmann, finger agnosia is related to parietal lobe damages. Presently, doctors believe that Gerstmann's syndrome in adults only can be related to dominant parietal pathology. In many neurological examination schedules there are tests for finger agnosias. The examiner smoothly touches some of the patient's fingers (the patient having his eyes closed), and then he asks the patient to show which fingers had been touched. The examiner, seated in front of the patient, again touches some of the patient's fingers, but now demands recognition on the examiner's hand. This recognition is usually made as if being in front of a mirror, thus being called a "mirror localizing situation."

Other times, two different fingers are touched at the same time, or they are passively moved (for instance, putting one finger over another one[5]), or establishing positional relationships between two or three fingers of both hands (with the patient's eyes open). In this last case, when such a relationship is obtained, it is changed by rotating one of the hands.[6]

Many children six years old can make errors in a variety of tests, but in agnosia confusion is worse. Among dyslexics, confusion can exist between fingers, such as between the thumb and the little finger. This is a very rare confusion among normal children six years old.

Gerstmann's syndrome is characterized by finger agnosia, right-left disorientation, acalculia, and agraphia. This syndrome can be associated with a constructive apraxia. This is clearly seen when matching sets of geometric shapes are used. In such a situation, failure in directional orientation could be seen. We should say once more that dyslexia in adults does not present apraxic symptomatology. In certain cases, differentiation between dyslexia and Gerstmann's syndrome can be difficult because right-left disorientation, finger agnosia, dyscalculia, and dysgraphia can exist in both syndromes. Nevertheless, the main point is that a reading disability exists in dyslexia and is never so important in Gerstmann's syndrome. On the other hand, finger agnosia is quite infrequent in dyslexia.

Several authors (ourselves included) are still reluctant to accept the "Developmental Gerstmann Syndrome" (i.e., the Gerstmann syndrome in children) as a medical entity which could be clearly separated from other brain small lesions or dysfunctions. For A. Benton this syndrome might be the result of an artificial grouping of symptoms selected upon the baseline of biased testing. On the other hand, M. Kinsbourne and E. Warrington described the Developmental Gerstmann syndrome in 1963. This notion was later developed by Kinsbourne in 1968 and by D. F. Benson and N. Geschwind in 1970. According to Kinsbourne this syndrome would be a developmental cognitive deficit responding either to localized cerebral dysfunction or maturational lag. According to Benson and Geschwind this syndrome could have "five striking abnormalities: dyscalculia, dysgraphia, right-left disorientation, finger agnosia and constructional apraxia."[7] It is reasonable to accept that the Gerstmann syndrome—if it exists—seems to be a very rare condition in childhood.

(61) TRADITIONAL BASELINES IN NEUROLOGICAL ASSESSMENT OF THE LEARNING DISABLED

As we saw in Section 60, dyslexia can be produced by organic causes (definite brain damage related to the left posterior cerebral region). Very similar neurological symptomatology can be found, nevertheless, in school-age children with or without learning disabilities.

The main question, then, is: Can the same traditional baselines used for neurological examination in children also be practical and significant in children with learning disabilities?

We cannot forget that the medical training of a pediatrician emphasizes diagnosis of evident organic diseases. For this reason traditional examination methodologies generally used by pediatricians are not easily adaptable to other "soft" or "minor" conditions. Nevertheless, the neurological examination used for the learning disabled must first take care of organic aspects and, among those elements, must try to consider in depth all information which allows learning (auditory inputs, visual inputs, and so on). Those who have read the preceding chapters of this book are familiar with our ideas in this regard: Development of tonus, posture, and equilibrium allows the child to gain insight about surrounding space (the environment), mainly through visual and auditory information about the presence of coordinated motor activities of a certain degree of intentionality.

From our point of view, then, the criteria mentioned in the foregoing paragraph are those which should be used as a general working frame of reference for a neurologist concerned with learning-disabled children. The work should be directed to the study of physical measures (height, weight, head circumference, chest circumference, etc.), postures and positions, reflexes, movements, and to the acquisition of basic information about vision and audition. In this general list "reflexes" were placed after "postures" in order to emphasize their importance. Nevertheless, if we reconsider our definition of "posture" (see Chapter II, Section 10)—the reflex activity of the body in relation to space—it will be easy to see that no valid information can be obtained about posture without having information about reflexes. This statement recognizes the great clinical and topodiagnostic value of the externalization—or lack of externalization—of the various reflexes described by traditional neurology. But we must come back to another concept already mentioned in this book: A severely pathological reflex is not usually manifested in learning disabilities, at least in primary learning disabilities.

Therefore, a *neurological* examination of the learning disabled should include the following general items:

1. Study of physical measures: examination of physical (somatic) dimensions (height, head circumference, and so on), and how those results compare with regional—or, someday, international—standards for age and sex.

2. Study of posture and equilibrium: examination of muscular tonus and their variations in static and dynamic situations, and vestibular examination.

3. Study of motor activities: examination of body movements, locomotion, taxias, and eventually some praxias (mainly oculomotor praxias, because others may be studied within a neuropsychological examination).

4. Study of reflexes: examination of different types of reflexes (deep, superficial, etc.).

5. Study of sensory functions (when specialized people in this field do not exist).

Certainly, all these follow essential general criteria which have been established by many authors for neurological development and neurological examination in infancy and childhood.[8]

Conclusions are obtained throughout these five areas (as any other traditional examination tool does) by comparison of obtained data with "normal" standards for age and sex. It should be noted, nevertheless, that traditional neurological examinations may provide very important data about the learning disabled. For instance, it might be important to consider partial-percentage disharmonies with the obtained general physical measures: We should ask ourselves if such a disharmony might offer significant information for assuming a disturbance on the somatotrophic action of the central nervous system. It could also be useful to consider some particular characteristics of muscular tonus; careful study here may lead one to assume organic-functional failures or those depending on adaptive responses to environment. The existence of inconsistent or disorganized patterns of reflexes could be considered in the same way.

Another point to be taken into account concerns the existence of minor symptomatology, that on becoming evident in a consistent and predictable way leaves no doubt about its pathological origin.

(62) SOFT SYMPTOMS IN NEUROLOGY AND LEARNING DISABILITIES

The French were probably the first to call attention to motor "awkwardness" in learning-disabled children.[9] Soon after the appearance of the French studies, the notion of "minimal brain injury" appeared in the United States, while the French neurological school preferred to maintain use of such terms as "motor awkwardness" or "psychomotor syndromes."[10] At one time several authors of different countries used terms as "minimal brain injury," "psychomotor syndrome," "Strauss' triad," or "school dyslexia" to mean learning disabilities. Neurological examination of such clinical entities, nevertheless, has not reached the precision that has been possible when dealing with organic pathology. For organic cases, procedures for diagnosis, prognosis, and therapy are extremely clear-cut; but, for the conditions just mentioned, such procedures do not apply. In these latter conditions, where symptomatology is "diffuse" and "soft," many times the doctor with traditional training is likely to consider the obtained data as "normal." Certainly, where there is precise "lesional" symptomatology, the neuropediatrician acts with absolute efficiency. But, actually, he many times finds himself facing different situations.

Beginning in the 1940s, some neuropediatricians noticed some small or "soft" or "borderline" symptoms in children with brain dysfunctions. Those symptoms used to appear sporadically and in varying degrees.[11] According to R. S. Paine, some isolated motor signs such as awkwardness, tremor, hyperreflexia, or mild impairments in walking, may be worth attention, and may lead the physician to assume the existence of a "minor" diffuse brain syndrome. Some sensory or perceptual signs, like imperception (auditory or visual), or faulty concepts of space, were to be considered in the same way. From other points of view, a diminished attention span, difficulties in thinking abstractly, and delays in academic achievements, were characteristic features of this type of child, who sometimes also showed mild epileptic symptomatology.

It must be admitted, anyhow, that these data have a very limited *neurological* value. Elements such as delay in academic achievement, distractibility, short attention span, or imperception, can be very questionable from a strictly neurological point of view.

On making reference to neurology of learning disorders, R. J. Schain mentioned the following "borderline," "equivocal," or "soft" neurological signs in children: clumsiness in tasks requiring fine-motor coordination (for instance, tying shoe laces or fastening buttons), mild dysphasias, choreiform movements, finger agnosia, associated movements, borderline hyperreflexia and reflex asymmetries, tremor, ocular apraxia and endpoint nystagmus, dysdiadochokinesis, whirling, graphesthesias, mixed laterality and disturbances of right-left discrimination, pupilary inequalities, extinction to double simultaneous tactile stimulation, avoidance response to outstretched hands, awkward gait, unilateral winking defect.[12] As can be seen, within this enumeration of "soft," "borderline," or "equivocal" signs exist psychological, linguistic, motor, sensory, and neurological responses, in which there are variables. The validity of speaking about "minimal brain dysfunction" is therefore also controversial.

We have no doubt whatsoever that the course of action to be followed in neurological diagnosis of learning disabilities must be different than those which have been suggested by several other authors. The proper approach, we believe, must have as its main target the recognition of a neurologic and psychoneurologic symptomatology which elicits externalization, in a very precise and predictable manner, of failures of the brain systems which participate in learning abilities processes.

In Chapter I, Section 5, we spoke about "functional systems." We think that it is impossible to find any "brain dysfunctions," "minor dysfunction of the central nervous system" or any other "neurological dysfunction," "minimal brain injury," or "psychomotor syndrome," and so on, which is not more or less connected in one way or another with the environment, or which does not interact with the environment. That is why we prefer to speak about "systemic dysfunctions." And this does not mean a simple change of terminology. We are not mainly interested in changing the terms "minimal brain dysfunction" or "minor neurological dysfunction" into "systemic dysfunction." We are trying to change the concept, because that which generates a learning disability is not an assumed central nervous system dysfunction but the interaction between neurological disturbance and environmental influences.

That is why our symptomatological approach will be directed exclusively neither to neurological signs, nor to the multiple variables of the different clinical pictures. On the contrary, it will try to be very precise in the recording of signs which are elicited by neuroenvironmental interactions, thus trying to obtain profitable data which can be helpful for diagnosis and remediation of the learning disabled.

(63) PRINCIPAL STEPS IN NEUROPSYCHOLOGICAL ASSESSMENT

Among the aims of this book, there are three different principles which must be established for the neuro-symptomatological study of learning disabilities.

The first principle is based on traditionally accepted standards of neurological examination (for instance, study of tonus, reflexes, and so on).

The second principle concerns some of the innovative neuropsychological concepts which have brought their creators well deserved recognition. We feel that those concepts can be useful for gaining reliable results in some areas.

Finally, the third principle refers to some *nontraditional* psycho-neurological norms, in both symptomatology and practical neurological conclusions.

The first principle was just considered in Section 62. Nevertheless, we should remember that many neurological data are obtained through the examination and interpretation of muscular responses. That is why neuropediatrics may be defined as the vast section of pediatrics which includes diseases localized in the neuromuscular system or which have their main symptoms in that system.[13] In this book we cannot disregard those contributions of traditional neuropediatrics which can shed light upon those several syndromes recognized as "learning disabilities." We shall come back to this subject later.

The second principle refers to the inclusion of neuropsychology within the neuropediatric symptomatological approach. As is well known, clinical neuropsychology has developed very much since the 1950s. As stated in Chapter I, Section 1, neuropsychology mainly concerns itself with basic medical approaches that study relationships between cerebral functions and achievement (obtained through neurology) on the one hand, and human behavior on the other. While traditional neurology does not establish relationships between (1) brain diseases, lesions, or damage, and (2) general behavioral changes, neuropsychology does. According to A. L. Benton, neuropsychological fundamentals are: (1) clinical neurological studies, (2) experiments with animals, and (3) developmental assessments. These bases would allow us insight into relationships between brain functions and human behavior. That is why Benton considers that neuropsychology is directed (1) to behavioral syndromes associated with focal cerebral lesions; (2) to developmental aspects, both normal and abnormal, of body schema; (3) to hemispheric cerebral dominance; (4) to the problems of definitions generated by aphasic, apraxic, and agnostic disturbances; and (5) to the neurological basis that could explain the existence of dyslexia and language delays. Consequently, the appearance of behavioral maladjustments, faulty concepts of time and space, right-left disorientation, acalculia, apraxia, and so on, should be providing data of deep neurological content.[14]

A very similar concept was established by A. R. Luria when he stated that this new branch of science ". . . concerns itself with behavior changes in patients with localized cerebral lesions." According to Luria's statements, the notion emerges that neuropsychology is essential for the development of scientific psychology of man, as well as for the early and accurate diagnosis of focal cerebral lesions. Luria believes that those specifically human cerebral zones (for instance, those in relation to symbolic processes) may provide concrete and definite data for a neuropsychological examination.[15]

The third principle is related to nontraditional psychoneurological norms. This principle refers to comparative analysis of data in the different circumstances at each administration of the test.[16]

This principle is based on three main premises:

1. The comparison of the results obtained in static situations with those obtained in dynamic situations.
2. The comparison established between a function (biological, natural) and an acquisition (learned, acquired from the environment).
3. The modification of the individual's daily life and accustomed living conditions ("habitat") and the observations of how he can adapt himself to new conditions.

The comparison of the results obtained in static situations with those obtained in dynamic situations. Results obtained from the former provide data on organic or "structural" conditions. Results obtained from the latter provide data on functions or functional compensation. For example, if a static asymmetry (standing) position is observed between both legs, or at the trunk, but such an asymmetry "disappears" in a dynamic (walking) situation (i.e., no limp is observed during walking, or no scoliosis is observed during walking), it can be assumed that pathology existed in the past (past pathology) but it was functionally compensated through time. That which is functional requires time in order to be compensated. If the organic disturbances (seen at rest) maintains itself as a functional disturbance (seen during movement) it is clear that the pathology is present. Finally, if no alteration is seen in stasis, but appears during dynamic situations, a functional disturbance (dynamic) may be assumed. This past-pathology concept is of great importance in this nontraditional psychoneurological approach.

The comparison established between a function (biological, natural) and an acquisition (learned, acquired from the environment). At the end of the 1960s E. H. Lenneberg established the comparison between basic motor development and basic linguistic characteristics of the early periods of life.[17] * With this comparison it can be established that at the age of six months the child sits alone, has unilateral achievements, while he babbles—introducing some consonant sounds and performing syllabic reduplication. At a year, the child stands alone momentarily, walks sideways when holding on, has fully developed prehension (grasping ability), while he has some signs of understanding some simple words, and applies regularly some compound sounds to designate persons and objects (i.e., the first words). At 18 months, he has a propulsive, stiff gait, creeps downstairs backward, and so on, while he has a repertory of between three and fifty simple words, which are not used yet as simple phrases, sounds, and tune patterns which seems "talking," good comprehension development, etc., and so on up to 36 months, when

*From our point of view, we would prefer to compare coordinated motor activity of certain intentionality with acquisition or learning of *lingua*.

the child runs smoothly, walks stairs by alternating feet, jumps approximately twelve inches, can ride a tricycle, while he has a vocabulary of 1000 words with something like 90 percent of intelligibility, well formed sentences, using complex grammatical rules, although not perfectly.

This comparison between functions and acquisitions allows us to consider the idea of potentiality (that is, the chances that the individual has in order to improve his functional conditions or his acquired conditions). For instance, if a child has a motor activity level of three years and a *lingua* level normally expected for two years, his potentiality allows him one more year in *lingua* acquisition.

The modification of the individual's daily life and accustomed living conditions ("habitat") and the observation of how he can adapt himself to new conditions. For example, think of a child accustomed to walking on hard surfaces. If we suddenly change the hard surface into a soft one, he must adapt his tonic and balance conditions to the unusual supporting field he is on now. We call this type of test an "exigency test," and the response of the individual, "adaptive response." Difficulty in producing adequate adaptive responses to exigency tests seems to be characteristic of cerebral dysfunctions, vestibular-proprioceptive dysfunctions, and other dysfunctions.

The main goal of this approach is to obtain a clear direction with a rehabilitatory plan. That is why our course of action is at least partially different from that of traditional neurological approaches. But we must emphasize that we also use traditional neurology because all of its elements remain valid. We certainly agree with the background principles of neuropediatrics, starting with the universally accepted principle that children's pathology is completely different than that of adults', in spite of the fact that these pathologies sometimes have the same names. Obviously, adults have experiences that children can never have at their ages. In regard to learning disabilities, we should repeat once again that it is quite different to lose *lingua* rather than not reach it, to lose language than not reach it.

(64) MEDICAL TESTS OF LATERALITY AND LEARNING DISABILITIES

Many tests of laterality have been created in this century, the vast majority of them being related to handedness or to some other partial aspect of determining laterality. We have recognized already a body laterality (potentially and preferentially determined) and a cerebral laterality (dominant or symbolic hemisphere).

If lateral "specialization" is to be medically determined, then (1) common subjective procedures must be avoided and (2) more objective procedures and accurate approaches must be employed instead.

It is impossible to review in one section of this book all the medical tests of laterality. Consequently, only a few of them can be commented on here.

Cerebral dominance can be discovered through Wada's test, "dichotomous" stimulation tests, cerebral abnormalities, and surgery. Body potential laterality can be shown through electromyography and other neurological assessments related to vestibular reactions, tonus, strength, skilled and co-ordinated movements, and so on. Body preference laterality must be discovered through psychological, social, and other nonmedical tests.

Wada's test. Until now, it has always been assumed that cerebral dominance can be determined by intracarotid injection of sodium amytal. The fact is that this kind of injection depresses ipsilateral hemispheric activity for a few minutes.[18] Consequently, if transitory aphasic symptomatology appears (besides motor and somesthetic heterolateral externalizations), the cerebral hemisphere on the same side as that of the injection can be considered as the dominant one. Memory span disorders can also be manifested through this test. We might note that the hippocampus receives carotidean irrigation (through the anterior carotidean artery). According to B. Milner it is recommended that the examiner, before doing Wada's test, introduce a series of drawings (which must be named by the patient) and a few sentences (which must be repeated by the patient). Immediately after the injection the patient must recognize or recall these materials. Then, a new series of images and a new sentence are introduced. If materials presented to the patient before the injection cannot be remembered under the effects of sodium amytal, this phenomenon could be recognized as "recall trouble." If materials presented to the patient before the injection can be remembered, but materials correctly identified (and the sentence repeated) after the injection cannot be remembered later on, this phenomenon can be recognized as a problem of "registration" or "fixation" or memory span.[19]

Wada's test can help medically to determine hemispheric cerebral dominance.

Pneumo-encephalography. Very recently (1977) M. A. Dalby and E. Ratjen (in Aarhus Kommunehospital, Denmark) investigated through pneumo-encephalography 101 "language retarded" children and 100 epileptic children without speech delay. According to a personal communication and according to their paper (which presently is in press by *Acta Neurologica*, Stockholm) they found early brain asymmetry or lateralization ("lesions of atrophic nature") in "language retarded" children. These findings certainly support the genetic assumption of language, and in these cases *lingua* acquisition is delayed and language will be impaired.

"Dichotomous" stimulation tests. Also, in regard to determining cerebral dominance, "dichotomous" stimulation tests were developed. In audiology, dichotic tests refer to simultaneous and different stimuli fed to each one of the ears (for instance, through sophisticated testing equipment it is possible to receive simultaneously two different messages, one on each ear; for example: "twenty-four" in one ear and "fifty-two" in the other). The examiner then asks the person what the number or the word he heard was. This technique was created by E. E. Broadbent in 1954 and was developed mainly by Doreen Kimura. Since then, it has been discussed by many authors. In recent years it was employed in regard to developmental dyslexia.[20]

The reason for the enthusiastic reception of such a test probably was the acceptance of the fact that each hemisphere was receiving a different message (in spite of the division of the auditory pathways in both hemispheres); and, therefore, if only one message were repeated, the ear that received it was dominant and the opposite side of the brain was considered to be the dominant hemisphere. This was because *functionally* auditory pathways act as crowded pathways. In other words, Kimura and her followers believe that dichotic tests can point out the dominant (or symbolic) cerebral hemisphere. On the other hand, H. Feldmann, M. P. Bryden, and J. B. de Quiros and N. D'Elia believe that dichotic stimuli are more perceptual than linguistic, and that normal responses can be similar for both sides.[21] We believe that Kimura employed correct assessment procedures, but her interpretation of the obtained results was erroneous. An effect produced by perception of *lingua* was considered as language stimulation. *Lingua* (as a conditioned imitative process) does not need hemispheric dominance in order to be produced.

The usefulness of dichotic tests and establishment of right ear advantage in determining cerebral hemisphere dominance and the presence of learning disabilities is still relatively uncertain. At the present, it seems reasonable to believe that determining ear asymmetry with dichotic tests in dyslexics is very tenuous.[22] This statement is contrary to the original papers on this topic, which indicated that important ear asymmetries were found.[23] Our opinion is that a dichotic test cannot investigate more than basic symbolic levels (*lingua*). It cannot give any other information. Its usefulness is therefore limited.

A sort of "dichotomous" stimulation test applied to vision has been used since 1970 by a variety of authors, and has been reviewed in a recent article by P. Satz.[24] In this test the visual hemifield responses were studied. In 1970 W. F. Keever and M. D. Huling stimulated, using a four-letter noun, a visual hemifield of a small group of older children (averaging thirteen years old). At the same time the noun was presented, a fixation digit might also be recognized. Results were better when they were presented to the right visual hemifield. According to the authors, these results do not support the assumption of incomplete or delayed hemispheric speech dominance in disabled readers.[25]

More or less similar conclusions were obtained by T. Marcel, L. Katz, and M. Smith with similar procedures of assessment. Nevertheless, according to them, "relevant linguistic information is more asymmetrically stored in the good reader," because the right visual hemifield was more asymmetrical than the left one.[26]

All this notwithstanding, other authors seem to disagree with these conclusions, or at least to arrive at different results.[27] Particularly interesting in this regard were the contributions made by S. F. Witelson. She worked not only with other dichotomous stimulation tests for audition or vision (already analyzed), but also with dichotomous tactual stimulations produced by nonsense shapes and letters. Witelson wrote:

> Previous work with normal boys indicated that in contrast to left hand superiority on a dichotomous touch test with nonsense shapes, no left hand superiority was observed with letters, but rather a trend in favor to right hand. . . . This test requires participation of both hemispheres: spatial process-

ing by the right hemisphere to initially recognize the shape of the stimuli, and linguistic processing by the left hemisphere to linguistically encode the stimuli in order to name them for the response.[28]

Cerebral abnormalities and surgery. Two cerebral abnormalities in children are very important: hemispherectomies and hemiplegies. Hemispherectomy is the removal of one cerebral hemisphere, while hemiplegy is the paralysis of one body side reflecting great abnormalities in the cerebral hemisphere of the opposite side. Hemispherectomies are carried out in the presence of some malignant tumors, congenital cerebral abnormalities, or other grave cerebral lesions. Hemiplegies are produced by any pathological cause affecting the cerebral hemisphere of the opposite side (for instance: cerebral effusion or hemorrhage, trauma, tumors, hemispherectomy, and so on). Generally, hemiplegy is produced without surgical intervention, due to several organic causes like those just mentioned, When there is hemiplegy or hemispherectomy, doctors know precisely the localization of the brain abnormality. In regard to data on *lingua* and language obtained from hemispherectomized or hemiplegic children, the information is contradictory and conclusions are difficult to reach—perhaps because clinical procedures for investigation of *lingua* and language and general health conditions of the patients vary so greatly, or perhaps because cerebral plasticity also varies from one individual to another.

It seems necessary to standardize language examination procedures and to differentiate clearly *lingua* and language.

Tumors and other brain damages are still more controversial because they act not only *in situ* but also through pressures on the surrounding tissues and through many associations and connections exciting and inhibiting and changing many results into unexpected ones. One of us worked diligently with a neurosurgical team, trying to identify (before and after surgery) some of the most important neurological variables of hemispheric dominance.[29] Our conclusions were translated into English and published through the Beltone Institute for Research (1963). Nevertheless, some researchers in other countries disagreed with some of our statements, and for this reason our conclusions remain somewhat controversial. Our earlier findings, however, support many of the statements which are maintained here.

Body potential laterality. Electromyography can provide essential data in regard to body potential laterality. Also, neurological examination of the tonic component, of movement (velocity, directionality, accuracy, and strength), and vestibular and other examinations, can permit comparison of the two body sides.

Many neurological items within the general examination can provide useful data: extensiveness of muscles, studies of synkinesias, assessment of paratonias, and so on. They can show a greater potential laterality on one side. Once again we must insist that medical evaluations may or may not coincide (in regard to laterality) with psychosocial assessments. The latter concentrate not only on potential laterality but also on side preferences. Potential and preferred laterality are both important concepts and—together with cerebral dominance—constitute fundamentals for the development of learning abilities.

(65) MEDICAL APPROACH IN VESTIBULAR DISEASES

There are several diseases which stem from vestibular abnormalities, but Meniere's disease is recognized all over the world as the principle clinical entity produced by vestibular deficiency. Meniere's disease is characterized by vertigo (or dizziness), hypoacusis, and tinnitus (or ringing in the damaged ear). This entity is very difficult to discover in infants and young children. This is still more surprising because development of vestibular apparatus is already complete at the third month of pregnancy. If we accept that development of vestibular apparatus is ontogenically very old, why does Meniere's disease (or some other, similar abnormality) not appear in infants or young children? Perhaps, vestibular impairments are considered very rare in infants or young children because they do not seem to have similar symptomatology in adults. Labyrinths and proprioception act together in infancy and early childhood, thus constituting a different working system than in adults.

A very common mistake is to interpret infant or early childhood data by standards used for analyzing adult data, and then to compare the two data sets. It is indispensable to realize that neuropsychological symptoms in infants or young children are quite different. On the other hand, it is very difficult to establish the presence of vertigo in a young child: It is necessary that the child be able to manifest such a type of symptom verbally; and without language—only with *lingua*—this becomes almost impossible.

Nevertheless, in 1964 L. S. Basser described the "benign paroxysmal vertigo in childhood." He identified this disease as a variety of vestibular neuronitis. According to Basser, it would generally occur during the first four years of postnatal life. Attacks appear every four to six weeks, and last only seconds or minutes. After a few years the symptomatology spontaneously disappears. Other clinical symptoms are pallor, sweating, occasionally vomiting, and sometimes nystagmus. Caloric tests showed typical paresis of semicircular canals. Hearing was normal.[30]

According to N. S. Gordon, benign positional vertigo (of the peripheral type) can be produced through trauma or can develop spontaneously. Brief attacks (with rotatory nystagmus) could be evident when the head is moved backwards or to one side.[31]

These and other conditions also described as dizziness in children seem to us related to different causes, not connected with vestibular apparatus. We only suspected dizziness in a few young children: The youngest was around five years of age.

Vestibular abnormalities in children. From time to time it is possible to find some children with abnormal responses to caloric and/or turning tests, and/or postural and balance disturbances, symptoms of clumsiness, and delay in the appearance and development of speech (persistent dyslalias).

Since 1958 we have been very much interested in these syndromes. Perhaps the first author who mentioned such a condition was A. Precechtel in his 1925 paper, "Congenital Defect of Otolithical Apparatus." According to him, the syndrome is characterized by: (1) abnormal intrauterine position of fetus; (2) difficulties in maintaining static positions in the first year of postnatal life: delay in motor development; (3) delay in speech; and (4) lack of response to vestibular caloric tests (with or without lack of responses to turning tests).[32]

A congenital origin of fetal abnormal position is not necessary in order for this clinical syndrome to develop. Many other acquired causes can produce the same symptoms: viruses, infections, toxics, trauma. It is possible, nevertheless, to accept the existence of the syndrome described by Precechtel; but we believe that some symptoms must be corrected and others must be added to his first description: muscular hypotonia, restlessness, need of movement, frequent distractibility, and superimposed emotional disturbance are the most significant ones. The clinical picture probably can have different manifestations according to the greater or lesser involvement of vestibular centers and pathways (vestibular-oculomotor or vestibular-spinal), their irritation or destruction, and the association of other central nervous system dysfunctions. Notwithstanding, the clinical picture—in general—should be as follows:

1. Difficult pregnancy or delivery
2. Delay in motor development
3. Muscular hypotonia
4. Delay in speech acquisition and speech development
5. Lack of adequate vestibular response to caloric stimuli and torsion swing
6. Restlessness
7. Frequent imbalance
8. Distractibility
9. Superimposed emotional disturbance
10. Extraocular, neck, and trunk muscular functional disturbances.

As we stated some years ago, the "pure" syndrome of congenital defect of otolithical apparatus, described by Precechtel, is not very frequent.[33] It is much more common to find vestibular dysfunctions ("vestibular-proprioceptive dissociation" and "vestibular-oculomotor split"). Many times vestibular dysfunctions are not "pure" at all, but are combined with other central dysfunctions. It seems that the situation is similar to that already well established for deaf children: Many times they are not "purely" deaf. The principle question is to recognize the existence of vestibular impairments in some children and to differentiate them from others who have no disturbance at that level.

Vestibular impairments and learning disabilities. A primary vestibular impairment was just mentioned. Three main aspects of such a syndrome are: (1) motor activity disturbances; (2) tonus and equilibrium disturbances; (3) and extraocular, neck, and trunk muscular functional disturbances. When motor activity fails, primary learning also fails. On the other hand, it is possible to relate tonus and equilibrium disturbances to instability, restlessness, flat feet, "physiological" scoliosis, and postural modifications. In regard to the third item just listed, it could be interpreted that the modification of contraction of extraocular, neck, and trunk muscles could elicit disturbances of attention span, visual perception, and skilled movements. All these facts can provide the basis for some learning disabilities.

Certainly, a mild vestibular impairment can "appear" at school, producing confusion with "dyslexia." Some relevant symptoms of this syndrome are: (1) handicaps in skilled motor activities, which can produce dysgraphia; (2) disturbances in higher learning abilities (mental actions), which can provoke distractibility at school and restlessness; and (3) disorders in extraocular and neck muscle contraction, which can elicit reading disabilities.

(66) SPECIFIC VESTIBULAR EXAMINATIONS

Clinical testing of vestibular functioning begins with a case history and with static and dynamic examinations. Then, "specific" tests can follow.

Vestibular tests can be divided into otological and clinical categories. Otological tests are, for instance, caloric tests, rotatory tests, torsion swing tests, cupulometria, electronystagmographia, and so on. Results obtained through these tests refer to labyrinthine normalcy or labyrinthine abnormality (of peripheral or central origin).

Vestibular otological tests. Caloric (cold, warm), rotation (cupulometria, torsion swing), and linear acceleration tests are considered "specific."

Caloric tests generally are carried out with water irrigating the external ear canal. After correct irrigation, deviation of the limbs toward one side and saccadic movements of the eyes toward the opposite side (which are called "nystagmus") are observed. Actually, saccadic movements are reactive movements which oppose the "slow component" of the nystagmus. The direction of the slow component coincides with the direction of the deviation of the limbs. There are many tests for caloric stimulation in the ears, but perhaps one of the most popular ones would be Hallpike's test.

Rotatory tests are those which, for the most part, consist of turning movements. Bárány's test (which must not be confused with other Bárány's tests), for example, requires the examiner to seat the patient in a swivel (or similar) chair, and turn him around completely 10 times in the space of 20 seconds. This classical test was very much discussed during the first half of this century.[34] In order to investigate vestibular responses, this test was finally rejected by the medical community because excitations elicited by it pertain not only to the vestibular but also to many central structures (mainly localized at the brain stem). Because of this physiological fact, progressive angular accelerated and decelerated movements (instead of manual turning impulses) were employed. Cupulometria or torsion swing are more specific vestibular stimulations than manual rotation is. "Turnings" in cupulometria are electronically produced or through sophisticated mechanical equipment. Nystagmography during and after rotation permits careful later study.

Linear acceleration tests are not generally clinically investigated in adults, but can easily be produced in newborn babies.

All these procedures can provide useful information in regard to labyrinths, chiefly through the observation of nystagmus, which is not only elicited by disturbed labyrinthine functions, but also by brain dysfunctions and ocular muscle dysfunctions. Consequently, nystagmus can be defined as involuntary and rapid movement of the eyeballs elicited by disturbed functions of (1) the labyrinth, (2) some parts of the brain, or (3) the ocular muscles.

Despite the term "specific" applied to these tests, one must realize that nystagmic responses never represent the specific dysfunctions of vestibular apparatus for the following reasons:

1. They are generally produced through many "nonspecific" stimuli (for instance, caloric irrigation of the ear with cold or warm water).
2. Vestibular nystagmus is mainly related to vestibular-ocular pathways and it does not inform us "directly" about equilibrium, which is a "specific" vestibular function.
3. The nervous structures implicated in producing vestibular nystagmus are very complicated, many factors being responsible.

Vestibular clinical tests. Vestibular clinical tests are directed primarily to posture, equilibrium, and muscular tonus. In young children vestibular inputs act together with proprioception and the cerebellum. Clinical tests must therefore examine those three factors. Perhaps we should point out that, from a clinical point of view, vestibular examinations have two different purposes:

1. To look for the existence of peripheral or central lesions or damages which are able to produce conditions like vertigo, postural instability, falling, imbalance, and tonus disturbances (neurology being the fundamental basis for this examination); and
2. To observe human learning behavior modifications such as restlessness, postural disturbances, equilibrium or tonus disorders, connecting these behavior disturbances with assumed localizations in the brain (neuropsychology being the fundamental basis for this examination).

Neurology and neuropsychology are certainly very similar in some examination procedures, but are different in observation of signs and in interpretation of test results.

Several vestibular tests can be considered as clinical. Some of them are recognized as static and others as dynamic. Among traditional static tests we can mention Romberg's test, Mann's test, the one-leg test, and the sitting test. Among traditional dynamic tests are Wartenberg's test, tonus tests, the past-pointing test, and cerebellar tests (synergic, eumetric, diadochokinetic tests, rebound test).

It is impossible to describe here each one of these traditional tests. We can, however, comment briefly on some of them, and refer the interested reader to the proper sources of information.[35]

Romberg's test and Mann's test. Romberg's test examines static equilibrium in the standing position, with both feet together, both upper limbs freely hanging at the sides of the body, and both eyes voluntarily closed. The tendency to fall or the direction of falling is then carefully observed. Peripheral vestibular disturbances are able to elicit such reactions toward the damaged side and according to the head position. In central vestibular damages falling is not influenced by the position of the head. Other signs which must be registered are the following:

1. Separation between both feet. This is seen as cerebellar disturbances or "immaturity" in children (vestibular-cerebellar pathway damage).
2. Oscillations in standing position (equilibrium instability). This is seen as lack of adequate proprioceptive information.
3. Greater abduction of one arm (i.e., withdrawal from the axes of the body) than of the other. This is seen as vestibular reinforcement of tonic-neck reflexes in Romberg's, Mann's, the one-leg, and other tests.
4. Associated movements (opening of the mouth, contractions of the tongue, movements of the hands and/or fingers, grimaces) outline the inefficiency in the maintenance of Romberg's position. In order to maintain equilibrium, some children use other simultaneous actions which escape voluntary control of the position. Higher cortical functions in such children are not completely controlling equilibrium.

Mann's test, or the "tandem" test, or the "toe-heel" test, is a sensitized version of Romberg's test: The toe of one foot is behind the heel of the other, both feet being on an imaginary straight line. Interpretation is also similar to that of Romberg's test, but more clear because balance exigency is greater in this position.

The gait test. This test is extremely important, not only to observe if the head or the trunk sways, or if a hemisyndrome exists,[36] but also to compare symmetries or asymmetries of both parts of the body, statically and dynamically (or kinetically). Many signs can provide useful data: the movement of the arms in regard to the movements of the legs, the separation between the feet, the regular or variable width of the gait, the ability to walk with the heels, with the sides of the feet, with the tiptoes, forward and backward, slowly or with increasing speed, following a straight line, the ability to make sudden stops and turns, the comparison of the results obtained with eyes opened and closed. It is important to qualify the character of the gait: smooth, rigid, staggering, reeling, and so on. Deviations to one side generally are according to cerebellar damages or dysfunctions affecting the same side.

Bárány's past-pointing test. This is carried out with the patient seated in front of the examiner (who is standing). The examiner asks the patient to extend his arm and to stretch out his index finger. Then the patient must raise his finger from his knee until it touches the examiner's finger held in a horizontal plane. At the beginning the patient does that with opened eyes, then with closed eyes. The movement is repeated several times. The examiner observes any *deviation* or *deflection* of the patient's finger. Any abduction (or separation) of the finger and arm from the body axis is called "deviation." The erroneous distance in the vertical movement of the finger and the arm is called "deflection" (i.e., the patient's finger movement does not attain the plane of the examiner's finger). In unilateral vestibular disturbances there is past-pointing deviation of both arms toward the affected side. In unilateral cerebellar disturbances only the ipsilateral arm (of the affected side) shows past-pointing with both deviation and deflection.

(67) REVIEW OF SOME EXPERIMENTS RELATED TO VESTIBULAR-PROPRIOCEPTIVE DISTURBANCES IN CHILDREN

It was difficult to arrive at the concept of "disintegration" or dissociation between vestibular apparatus and the proprioceptive system. We started out in 1958 studying what happens when vestibular-proprioceptive integration fails. In newborn babies vestibular and proprioceptive inputs act together. Neurolabyrinthine, caloric, rotatory, and other specific tests were carried out in infants and young children. The first series of experiments was performed in the Children's Hospital of Buenos Aires; the second, at the Centenario Hospital (Rosario City); the third, at several schools for both normal and exceptional children, as well as at an "experimental" school; the fourth series is under way in our own medical center in Buenos Aires. The total number of examined children is 1,902 so far, with different age distributions and diagnoses for each series, according to the aim of the particular study.

The goal of the first series of experiments was to obtain a research methodology for the study of vestibular-proprioceptive disturbances of newborn babies. We studied infants from one day old to two years old, using various examination procedures.[37] Neurological and labyrinthine data of our research were submitted to statistical methodology and computation. Table 2 shows the neurolabyrinthine responses in infants and young children through neurological assessments which were carried out from 1958 to 1961. Table 3 shows the data for the neurolabyrinthine assessment of newborn infants (first month after birth) and the general evaluation scale. Table 4 shows the data for the caloric-rotatory assessment in newborn infants and the general evaluation scale. Table 5 shows normal caloric and rotatory reactions during the first week of life. Table 6 shows computation from scatter diagram obtained with neurolabyrinthine (x) and caloric-rotatory (y) scores in newborn children. Table 7 shows a summary of steps in computation of the regression formula from neurolabyrinthine (x) and caloric-rotatory (y) scores. All tables appear on pages 160-164.

If the existence of other variables (vision, cerebellum, etc.) which also participate in posture and equilibrium control is considered, the presented results are very acceptable.

The second series of experiments was carried out between 1961 and 1963. A minimum of 900 neurological tests, 800 caloric tests, and 154 turning tests were carried out on a total number of 77 slow learners. This group was compared with a similar group of "normal" learners. We had erroneously believed at that time that among slow learners we should find a greater number of "vestibular impairments." This study, led by us, was presented as a thesis for professorship by M. Alba, MD, in 1962.[38] The first conclusion in this thesis stated: "Children with learning disabilities give responses to the vestibular caloric test which may be comparable to normal ones." We recall

TABLE 2
Neurolabyrinthine Responses in the Young Child

Responses / Month of life	Placing response and stepping movements (proprio-exteroceptive and labyrinthine)	Labyrinthine righting reflexes	TONIC NECK REFLEXES (with secondary labyrinthine participation)		
			Neck righting reflexes (by rotation of the head)	Asymmetric	Symmetric
Premature	+	−	−	+	−
At birth	+	±	−	+	−
1	+	+	−	+	−
2	+	+	−	+	−
3	±	+	+?	+?	+?
4	−	+	+	−	+
5	−	+	+	−	+
6	−	+	+	−	±
7	−	+	+	−	−
8	−	+	+	−	−
9	−	+	±?	−	−
10	−	+	+	−	−
11	−	+	±	−	−
12	−	+	−	−	−
24	−	+	−	−	−
36	−	+	−	−	−

+   Response is produced.
−   Response is not produced.
±   Response is sometimes produced (fluctuant, iterative).
+? Response is produced in some cases and not in others.
(+) Response is produced with eyes closed.

From J. B. de Quiros, L. Coriat, and L. Benasayag,
Fonoaudiologica [Buenos Aires] 7:1 (1961): 27-55.

TABLE 2, Continued
Neurolabyrinthine Responses in the Young Child

Tonic labyrinthine reflexes (otolithic-proprioceptive) Landau	LINEAR ACCELERATION (otolithic or from canals; vision)		COMPENSATING EYE POSITIONS (labyrinthine-optic)		Tilting table (labyrinthine-proprio-exteroceptive)
	Moro's reflex	Parachutism	Opposite deviation (doll's-eye reflex)	Counter-rolling	
−	+	−	+	−	−
−	+	−	+	−	−
−	+	−	(+)	±	Lying position ±
−	+	−	(+)	+	+
−	+?	−	(+)	+	+
−	±?	−	(+)	+	+
−	−	−	(+)	+	+
+?	−	±	(+)	+	Sitting position ±
+	−	+	(+)	+	+
+	−	+	(+)	+	+
+	−	+	(+)	+	+
+	−	+	(+)	+	+
+	−	+	(+)	+	+
+	−	+	(+)	+	Standing position ±
+	−	+	(+)	+	+
±	−	+	(+)	+	+

TABLE 3

Assessment of Neurolabyrinthine Responses in Newborn Infants
(First Month of Life)

TEST ITEMS

1. Pregnancy
2. Delivery
3. Post-delivery
4. Tonus
5. Labyrinthine righting reflexes (normal is 0 to 0.5)
6. Leg straightening
7. Walking reactions
8. Linear acceleration–Moro's reflex
9. Asymmetric tonic-neck reflex (normal when produced by rotation of the head)
10. Opposite deviation of the head (doll's-eye reflex)
11. Tilting table (normal is 0 to 0.5)
12. Postural reactions (crying, congestion, "opposition" to the test)

GENERAL EVALUATION

Bad. 0
Poor or abnormal (or exaggerated) 0.5
Normal (or good) 1
Total (Normal) 9-12

TABLE 4

Assessment of Caloric-Rotatory Tests in Newborn Infants
(First Month of Life)

TEST ITEMS

1. Water-filling (Frenzel) 20°C Right Ear
2. Water-filling (Frenzel) 20°C Left Ear
3. Water-filling (Frenzel) 44°C Right Ear
4. Water-filling (Frenzel) 44°C Left Ear
5. Water-filling (Frenzel) 4°C Right Ear
6. Water-filling (Frenzel) 4°C Left Ear
7. $20°C/10$ cm^3/10 sec. Right Ear
8. $20°C/10$ cm^3/10 sec. Left Ear
9. Rotatory test, clockwise
10. Rotatory test, counterclockwise

GENERAL EVALUATION

According to Pattern of Response	According to Duration and Amplitude of Response
No response 0	Normal time or amplitude. . . same value
Abnormal deviation or	Less time or amplitude. . . . discount 0.5
Abnormal nystagmus 0.5	Greater time or amplitude. . .increase 0.5
Nystagmus in correct direction. 1	Time and amplitude dim. . . . .discount 1
Normal deviation or	Greater time and amplitude. . . increase 1
Deviation and jerking. 1.5	Time diminished and amplitude
Exaggerated deviation 2	increased (or vice-versa) . . . . same value

TABLE 5

Normal Caloric-Rotatory Test Responses in Newborn Infants
(First Week of Life)

Test Items	Average Duration of Deviation (sometimes with jerking)	Nystagmus	Extreme Values	Period of Clearest Phenomenon
Water-filling (Frenzel) 20°C	Ipsilateral 32 sec.	—	15-60 sec.	25-45 sec.
Water-filling (Frenzel) 44°C	Heterolateral 26 sec.	—	15-45 sec.	15-27 sec.
Water-filling (Frenzel) 4°C	Ipsilateral 34 sec.	Possibly	25-55 sec.	30-45 sec.
20°C/10cm^3/10 sec	Ipsilateral 42 sec.	—	25-57 sec.	34-45 sec.
Rotatory test	31 sec.	—	15-60 sec.	20-45 sec.

TABLE 6

Computation from a Scatter Diagram

fy	y^1	fyy^1	$fy(y^1)^2$	x^1	$y^1 \quad x^1$
8	8	64	512	52	416
5	7	35	245	30	210
21	6	126	756	101	606
9	5	45	225	36	180
4	4	16	64	13	52
11	3	33	99	31	93
7	2	14	28	21	42
2	1	2	2	1	1
1	0	0	0	2	0
68		335	1931	287	1600

fx	x^1	fxx^1	$fx(x^1)^2$	y^1	$x^1 \quad y^1$
1	0	0	0	1	0
1	1	1	1	1	1
8	2	16	32	18	36
11	3	33	99	39	117
17	4	68	272	77	308
16	5	80	400	94	470
9	66	54	324	67	402
5	7	35	245	38	266
68		287	1373	335	1600

Obtained with neurolabyrinthine (x) and caloric-rotatory (y) scores in newborn children.

TABLE 7

Summary of Steps in Computation of the Regression Formula From Neurolabyrinthine (x) and Caloric-Rotatory (y) Test Scores

$\Sigma x = 5,660$ $\qquad\qquad$ $\Sigma y = 6.285$ $\qquad\qquad$ $\Sigma xy = 563,575$
$\Sigma x^2 = 505,400$ $\qquad\qquad$ $\Sigma y^2 = 644,925$

$$\overline{X} = \frac{5,660}{68} = 83,23 \qquad\qquad \overline{y} = \frac{6,285}{68} = 92,42$$

$N\Sigma x^2 - (\Sigma x)^2 =$ $\qquad$ $N\Sigma y^2 - (\Sigma y)^2 =$ $\qquad$ $N\Sigma xy - (\Sigma x)(\Sigma y) =$
$= 68(505,400) - (5,660)^2 =$ $\quad$ $= 68(644,925) - (6,285)^2$ $\quad$ $= 68(563,575) -$
$= 2,331,600$ $\qquad\qquad$ $= 4,353,675$ $\qquad\qquad$ $(5,660)(6,285) =$
$\qquad\qquad\qquad\qquad\qquad\qquad\qquad\qquad\qquad\qquad$ $= 2,750,000$

$$S_x^2 = \frac{2,331,600}{68(67)} = 511.76 \qquad S_y^2 = \frac{4,353,675}{68(67)} = 959.59$$

$$S_x = \sqrt{511.76} = 22.61 \qquad S_y = \sqrt{959.59} = 30.90$$

$$b = \frac{N\Sigma xy - (\Sigma x)(\Sigma y)}{N\Sigma x^2 - (\Sigma x)^2} = \frac{68(563,575) - (5,660)(6,285)}{68(505,400) - (5,660)^2} = \frac{2,750,000}{2,331,600} = 1.17$$

$$a = \overline{y} - b\overline{x} = 92.42 - (1.17)(83.23) = -4.96$$

$$\widetilde{y} = -4.96 + 1.17x$$

$$\Sigma(y - \widetilde{y})^2 = \frac{1}{N}\left(N\Sigma y^2 - (\Sigma y)^2 - \frac{[N\Sigma xy - (\Sigma x)(\Sigma y)]^2}{N\Sigma x^2 - (\Sigma x)^2}\right) =$$

$$= \frac{1}{68}\left(4.353.675 - \frac{(2,750,000)^2}{2,331,600}\right) = 16,326.39$$

$$S_{y \cdot x}^2 = \frac{\Sigma(y - \widetilde{y})^2}{N - 2} = \frac{16,326.39}{66} = 247.36$$

$$S_{y \cdot x} = \sqrt{247.36} = 15.72$$

that, more or less simultaneously, a very similar experiment was being carried out independently by H. McHugh, who arrived at the same conclusion.[39] Our error was the type of children studied. From 1963 onward, we recommenced the investigation of the syndromes of vestibular-proprioceptive abnormalities in young children. The choice of children was then made on the basis of another criterion: the difficulty in learning *without apparently justifiable cause.* This study brought us some satisfaction: Out of 63 cases, fully tested, 52 did not have normal vestibular responses with caloric stimuli. In the other cases it was possible to suspect finally the presence of other factors as possible causes of the disturbances.[40] Conclusions related to the third and fourth series of experiments will be reviewed in Section 68; but it is necessary to emphasize that, after the second series, Quirós already began to accept two learning abnormalities or "syndromes"—both connected with vestibular-proprioceptive dissociation. At present, we are also considering a third syndrome related to vestibular-oculomotor split.

(68) A SHORT REVIEW OF THE LITERATURE RELATED TO VESTIBULAR-PROPRIOCEPTIVE EXAMINATION

In 1965, the two of us, along with E. E. Tormakh and other collaborators, began a third series of experiments. Not only a thorough review of the international literature was carried out; we also assumed inheritance of some vestibular impairments; and the bases for neuropsychological examination were established.[41]

By 1965 we had seen considerable relevant medical literature on this topic; but among the many writings we can only recall here the outstanding experimental investigations carried out, chronologically, by Bárány (1906), de Kleijn (1923), Landau (1925), Magnus (1924, 1926), Magnus and de Kleijn (1924), Lorente de No (1926), Di Giorgio and Castelli-Borgiotti (1938).[42]

It is also important to mention here the relevant clinical contributions chronologically carried out by Schaltenbrand (1925), Rademaker (1926, 1935), Zador (1938), Lawrence and Feind (1953), Bieber (1954), Andre-Thomas (1955).[43]

By that time we already realized some important facts:

1. Vestibular-proprioceptive dissociation only produces learning disabilities when damages or dysfunctions exist in infancy and early childhood.

2. Failure to obtain control of eye movements can interfere with learning abilities in infancy, early childhood, and school age.

3. When vestibular impairment appears after five years of age, Meniere's disease (or another similar syndrome) is clinically evident. In such cases difficulties in academic learning were probably compensated by the cerebellum and other central nervous structures. (For instance, we have already called attention to the fact that, according to P. I. Yakovlev and A. R. Lecours, ponto-cerebellar pathways myelinate at the fourth postnatal year).[44]

4. Psychotic children have other causes responsible for their behavior disturbances and vestibular dysreflexia. E. M. Ornitz and G. Harris, among others, are producing new research in this area.[45]

5. We assume that vestibular organs somehow influence prevalent laterality, mainly through vestibular-spinal pathways, acting upon muscular tonus, as noted in Chapter III, Sections 17 and 18. In the same chapter, Section 64, we mentioned some clinical procedures that can be used in order to determine precisely muscular tonus on each body side. It might be also interesting to recall here some vestibular asymmetries in right- and left-handed people, reported by B. Milojevic and J. L. Watson in 1965.[46] This investigation is directly concerned with our assumption that vestibular organs influence body potential laterality. Milojevic and Watson consider that handedness can influence vestibular-spinal and vestibular-ocular reflexes, showing different vestibular test results in right- and left-handed people, vestibular responses being greater on the same side as handedness.

Traditional examinations of vestibular organs are very useful for the diagnosis of vestibular impairment, but they provide poor information in regard to vestibular dysfunctions. Neuropsychological approaches add other points of view that can help our comprehension of these clinical conditions.[47]

Given the background of all neurological data which have been considered in this book so far (particularly those summarized in this chapter), neuropsychological examination directed to gaining useful information related to learning disabilities will be attempted in the next chapter.

NOTES

1. H. M. Schuell, "Review of the Month: Speech and Brain Mechanisms," *Rehabilitatory Literature* 21 (1960): 181-184; H. M. Schuell, *Aphasia Theory and Therapy* (Selected Lectures and Papers) edited and with an introduction by L. F. Sies (Baltimore: University Park Press, 1974); J. J. Jenkins, E. Jimenez-Pabon, R. E. Shaw, and J. W. Sefer, *Schuell's Aphasia in Adults* (2nd ed.) (New York: Harper & Row, 1975).

2. H. Hecaen, *Introduction a la Neuropsychologie* (Paris: Larousse, 1972); J. Buttet and G. Assal, "Clinique et Neuropsychologie des Alexies. Etudes Neuropsychologiques (Premier Partie)," *Bulletin d'Audiophonologie* 5:1 (1975): 27-54.

3. D. F. Benson and N. Geschwind, "The Alexias," in P. J. Vinken and G. W. Bruyn (eds.), *Handbook of Clinical Neurology* (Amsterdam: North-Holland Publishing Co., 1969): 112-140; N. Geschwind, *Selected Papers on Language and the Brain* (Amsterdam: Reidel Publishing Co., 1974): N. Geschwind, "The Anatomical Basis of Hemispheric Differentiation," in S. J. Dimond and J. G. Beaumont (eds.), *Hemisphere Function in the Human Brain* (London: Elek Science, 1974): 7-24.

4. J. Gerstmann, "Fingeragnosie: Eine umschriebne Storung der Orientierung am eigenen Korper," *Wiener Clinische Wochenschrift* 37 (1924): 1010.

5. A. R. Luria, *Higher Cortical Functions in Man* (London: Tavistock, 1966).

NEUROPSYCHOLOGICAL FUNDAMENTALS

6. J. B. de Quirós, "Una Orientacion Clinica Respecto a la Adquisicion del Lenguaje Lectoescrito," in J. B. de Quirós *et al., El Lenguaje Lectoscrito y sus Problemas* (Buenos Aires: Editorial Medica Panamericana, 1975).

7. R. Olea and H. Sicilia, "Acerca de las Bases Neurologicas de la Dislexia de Evolucion," *Fonoaudiologica* [Buenos Aires] 8:1 (1962): 11-25; A. Benton, "The Fiction of the Gerstmann Syndrome," *Journal of Neurology, Neurosurgery and Psychiatry* 24 (1961): 176; M. Kinsbourne and E. Warrington, "The Developmental Gerstmann Syndrome," *Archives of Neurology* [Chicago] 8 (1963): 490; M. Kinsbourne, "Developmental Gerstmann Syndrome," *The Pediatric Clinics of North America* 15 (1968): 771; D. F. Benson and N. Geschwind, "Developmental Gerstmann Syndrome," *Neurology* 20 (1970): 293.

8. M. B. McGraw, *The Neuromuscular Maturation of the Human Infant.* (New York: Hafner, 1943); A. Gesell and C. S. Amatruda, *Developmental Diagnosis* (New York: Harper & Row, 1947); A. F. B. Lefevre, *Contribuicao a Padronisacao do Exame Neurologico do Recem Nascido Normal* (Sao Paulo, Brasil: Facultade de Medicina da Universadade de Sao Paulo, 1950); Andre-Thomas and S. Saint Anne Dargassies, *Etudes Neurologiques sur le Nouveau-Ne et le Jeune Nourrison* (Paris: Masson, 1952); R. Griffiths, *The Abilities of Babies* (London: University of London Press, 1954); G. Koupernik, *Developpement Psycho-Moteur du Premier Age* (Paris: Presses Universitaires de France, 1956); A. Dekaban, *Neurology of Infancy* (London: Bailliere, Tindall and Co., 1959); R. S. Paine, "Neurological Examination of Infants and Children," *Pediatrics Clincs of North America* 7 (1960): 471; H. F. R. Prechtl, "Die neurologische Untersuchung des Neugeborenen," *Wiener Medizinische Wochenschrift* 110 (1960): 1035; A. Peiper, *Die Eigenart der kindlichen Hirntatigkeit* (3rd ed.) (Leipzig: Georg Thieme, 1961; English edition, London: Pitman, 1963); H. F. R. Prechtl and D. J. Beintema, *The Neurological Examination of Fullterm Newborn Infant,* Clinics in Developmental Medicine 12 (London: Spastics International Medical Publications with W. Heinemann, 1964); R. S. Paine and T. Oppe, *The Neurological Examination of Children,* Clinics in Developmental Medicine 20-21 (London: Spastics International Medical Publications with W. Heinemann, 1966); R. S. Illingworth, *The Development of Infant and Young Children, Normal and Abnormal* (3rd ed.) (Edinburgh: Livingstone, 1966): J. H. DiLeo, *"Developmental Evolution of Very Young Infants,"* in J. Hellmuth (ed.), *The Exceptional Infant,* Volume I, The Normal Infant (Seattle: Special Child Publications, 1967): 121; L. T. Taft and H. J. Cohen, "Neonatal and Infant Reflexology," in Hellmuth (ed.), *op. cit.:* 79; B. C. L. Touwen, "The Neurological Development of the Human Infant," in J. A. Davis and J. Dobbing (eds.), *Scientific Foundations of Pediatrics* (London: W. Heinemann, 1974); S. Saint Anne Dargassies, *Le Developpement Neurologique du Nouveau-Ne a Terme et Premature* (Paris: Masson, 1974); M. Le Metayer, "Bilan Neuromoteur du Nourrison Normal et Pathologique," *Cahier du Centre du Developpement Infantile* [Paris] 15:65 (1975): 35; B. C. L. Touwen, *Neurological Development in Infancy,* Clinics in Developmental Medicine 58 (London: Spastics International Medical Publications with W. Heinemann, 1976).

9. E. Dupre, "Debilite Motrice," in E. Dupre, *Pathologie de l'Imagination et de l'Emotivite* (Paris: Payot, 1925).

10. J. de Ajuriaguerra and G. Bonvalot-Soubiran, "Indications et Techniques de Reeducation Psychomotrice en Psychiatrie Infantile," *La Psychiatrie de l'Enfant* [Paris] 2:2 (1959): 423-493.

11. Andre-Thomas, *Equilibre et Equilibration* (Paris: Masson et Cie., 1940); Andre-Thomas and Saint Anne Dargassies, *op. cit.;* L. Bender, "Clinical Study of One Hundred Schizophrenic Children," *American Journal of Orthopsychiatry* 17 (1947): 40-46; L. Bender, "The Brain and the Child Behavior," *A.M.A. Archives of General Psychiatry* 4 (1961): 531-547; R. S. Paine, "Minimal Chronic Brain Symptoms in Children," *Developmental Medicine and Child Neurology* 4 (1962): 21-27; Paine and Oppe, *op. cit.*

12. R. J. Schain, *Neurology of Childhood Learning Disorders* (Baltimore: Williams and Wilkins, 1972).

13. I. Gamstorp, *Pediatric Neurology* (New York: Appleton-Century-Crofts, Educational Division, Meredith Co., 1970).

14. A. L. Benton, *Introduccion a la Neuropsycologia* (J. Sanchez de Vega, trans.) (Barcelona: Edit. Fontanella, 1971).

15. A. R. Luria, Foreword to the Spanish edition, *El Cerebro en Accion* (C. Ballas, trans.) (Barcelona: Edit. Fontanella, 1974).

16. J. B. de Quirós, "Exclusions in Learning Disabled Children" (Keynote Address, Tenth International Conference of the Association for Children with Learning Disabilities, Program Staff, Center for Effecting Educational Change, Fairfax County Public Schools, March 1973); J. B. de Quiros, "Diagnosis of Developmental Language Disorders," *Folia Phoniatrica* [Basel] 26 (1974): 13-32; J. B. de Quirós, "Diagnosis of Vestibular Disorders in the Learning Disabled," *Journal of Learning Disabilities* 9:1 (1976): 39-47; J. B. de Quirós, "Significance of Some Therapies on Posture and Learning," *Academic Therapy* 11:3 (Spring 1976): 261-270; J. B. de Quirós and O. L. Schrager, "Postural System, Corporal Potentiality and Language," in E. H. Lenneberg and E. Lenneberg (eds.), *Foundations of Language Development*, Volume 2 (New York: Academic Press; and Paris: UNESCO, 1975); 297-307; J. B. de Quirós and O. L. Schrager, "Posturas, Actividades Motrices y Aprendizajes," *Fonoaudiologica* [Buenos Aires] 22:1-2 (1976).

17. E. H. Lenneberg, "The Natural History of Language," in *The Genesis of Language* (Boston: M.I.T. Press, 1968): 219-249; J. Wada, "A New Method for the Determination of the Side of Cerebral Speech Dominance: A Preliminary Report on the Intracarotid Injection of Sodium Amytal in Man," *Medical Biology* 14 (1949): 221.

18. J. Wada and T. Rasmussen, "Intracarotid Injection of Sodium Amytal for the Lateralization of Cerebral Speech Dominance, Experimental and Clinical Observations," *Journal of Neurosurgery* 17 (1960): 266-282; J. A. Wada, R. Clarke, and A. Hamm, "Cerebral Hemispheric Asymmetry in Humans: Cortical Speech Zones in 100 Adult and 100 Infant Brains," *Archives of Neurology* 32 (1975): 239-246.

19. B. Milner, "Memory and the Medial Temporal Region of the Brain," in K. H. Pribram and E. E. Broadbent (eds.), *Biology of Memory* (New York: Academic Press, 1970): 29-50.

20. E. E. Broadbent, "The Role of Auditory Localization in Attention and Memory Span," *Journal of Experimental Psychology* 47 (1954): 191-196; D. Kimura, "Some Effects of Temporal-lobe Damage on Auditory Perception," *Canadian Journal of Psychology* 15 (1961): 156-165; D. Kimura, "A Note on Cerebral Dominance in Learning," *Acta Otolaryngologica* [Stockholm] 56:5 (1963): 617; D. Kimura, "Speech Lateralization in Young Children as Determined by an Auditory Test," *Cortex* 56 (1963): 899-902; D. Kimura, "Effect of Focal Cerebral Lesions on Perspective and Movement Reversals," *Journal of Nervous and Mental Diseases* 2 (1967): 144; D. Kimura and M. Durnford, "Normal Studies on the Functions of the Right Hemisphere in Vision," in Dimond and Beaumont (eds.) *op. cit.*: 25-47; C. Calearo and R. Antonelli, "Cortical Hearing Tests and Cerebral Dominance," *Acta Otolaryngologica* [Stockholm] 56:1 (1963): 17-26; D. Dirks, "Perception of Dichotic and Monoaural Verbal Material and Cerebral Dominance for Speech," *Acta Otolaryngologica* [Stockholm] 58:1 (1964): 73-80; J. Inglis, "Dichotic Listening and Cerebral Dominance," *Acta Otolaryngologica* [Stockholm] 60:2 (1965): 230-238; H. Feldmann, "Untersuchungen zur Diskrimination differente Schallbilder bei simultaner, monauraler und binauraler Darbietung," *Archives Ohren-Heilk* 1765 (1960): 600-605; H. Feldmann, "Diaural Hearing Test," *International Audiology* 1:2 (1962): 222; H. Feldmann, "Die Bedeutung des biauralen Horens fur die Sprachlicke Verstandigung unter Larmeinwirkung," *Acta Otolaryngologica* [Stockholm] 59:2-4 (1965): 133-139; M. P. Bryden, "An Evaluation of Some Models of Laterality Effects in Dichotic Listening," *Acta Otolaryngologica* [Stockholm] 63:3 (1967): 599-604; M. P. Bryden, "Laterality Effects in Dichotic Listening: Relations with Handedness and Reading Ability in Children," *Neuropsychologia* 8 (1970): 443-450; A. L. Benton, "Developmental Dyslexia: Neurological Aspects," in W. J. Friedlander (ed.), *Advances in Neurology*, Volume 7 (New York: Raven Press, 1975): 1-47.

21. Feldmann, "Diaural Hearing Test," *loc. cit.*; Feldmann, "Die Bedeutung . . .," *loc. cit.*; Bryden, "An Evaluation . . .," *loc. cit.*; Bryden, "Laterality Effects . . .," *loc. cit.*; J. B. de Quirós and N. D'Elia, *La Audiometria del Adulto y del Nino* (Buenos Aires: Edit. Paidos, 1974).

22. Benton, "Developmental Dyslexia . . .," *loc. cit.*

23. Kimura, "Effect of Focal Cerebral Lesions . . .," *loc. cit.*; E. F. Zurif, and G. Carson, "Dyslexia in Relation to Cerebral Dominance and Temporal Analysis," *Neuropsychologia* 8 (1970): 351-361.

24. P. Satz, "Cerebral Dominance and Reading Disability: An Old Problem Revisited," in R. M. Knights and D. J. Bakker (eds.), *The Neuropsychology of Learning Disorders* (Baltimore: University Park Press, 1976): 273-294.

25. W. F. McKeever and M. D. Huling, "Lateral Dominance in Tachistoscopic Word Recognitions of Children at Two Levels of Ability," *Journal of Experimental Psychology* 22 (1970): 600-604.

26. T. Marcel, L. Katz, and M. Smith, "Laterality and Reading Proficiency," *Neuropsychologia* 12 (1974): 131-139.

27. G. H. Yemi-Komshian, S. Isenberg, and H. Goldberg, "Central dominance and Reading Disability: Left-visual Field Deficit in Poor Readers," *Neuropsychologia* 13 (1975): 83-94.

28. S. F. Witelson, "Abnormal Right Hemisphere Specialization in Developmental Dyslexia," in Knights and Bakker (eds.) *op. cit.*

29. J. B. de Quirós, "Remarques Phoniatriques Faites sur des Sujets Ayant des Lesions du Systeme Nerveux Central," *Revue de Oto-Neuro-Ophtalmologie* [Strasbourg] 31:2 (1959): 79; J. B. de Quirós and G. Ruiz Moreno, "Bases Neurologicas de la Foniatria," *Revista de la Asociacion Medica Argentina* [Buenos Aires] 71:4 (1957): 101-108.

30. L. S. Basser, "Benign Paroxysmal Vertigo of Childhood (a Variety of Vestibular Neuronitis)," *Brain* 87 (1964): 141.

31. N. S. Gordon, "Post-traumatic Vertigo with Special Reference to Positional Nystagmus," *Lancet* 1 (1954): 1216; N. S. Gordon, "Dizziness in Children," *Developmental Medicine and Child Neurology*, 6:4 (1964): 416.

32. A Precechtel, "Contribution a l'Etude de la Fonction Statique dans la Periode de la Vie Extrauterine; Syndrome Typique du Defaut Congenital de l'Appareil Otolithique," *Acta Otolaryngologica* [Stockholm] 7 (1925): 206-226.

33. J. B. de Quirós, "Diagnostico Diferencial de los Sindromes Vestibulares en el Nino Pequeno," *Fonoaudiologica* [Buenos Aires] 17 (1968): 86-102; J. B. de Quirós, "Disturbances in the Language of a Child: The Child Who does not Speak," *Clinical Proceedings of the Children's Hospital* [Washington, D.C.] 25 (1969): 192-205; J. B. de Quirós, "Les Aphasies Infantiles: un Probleme Diagnostic," *Reeducation Orthophonique* [Paris] 7 (1969): 243-254.

34. R. Barany, "Ueber die vom Ohrlabyrinth ausgeloste gegenrollung der Augen bei Normalhorenden, Ohrenkranken und Taubstummen," *Archiv fur Klinische und Experimentelle Ohren-,Nasen und Kehlh Kopfheilkunde* 68 (1906): 1-30; R. Barany, "Ueber einige Augen und Halsmus kehlreflexe bei Neugeborenen," *Acta Otolaryngologica* [Stockholm] 1:1 (1918): 97.

35. J. J. Fischer, *The Labyrinth* (New York: Grune & Stratton, 1956).

36. B. C. L. Touwen and H. F. R. Prechtl, *The Neurological Examination of the Child with Minor Nervous Dysfunction*, Clinics in Developmental Medicine 38 (London: Spastics International Medical Publications with W. Heinemann, 1970).

37. Quirós (1967, 1976), *loc. cit.;* Quirós and Schrager (1975), *loc. cit.*

38. M. Alba, *Las Respuestas Vestibulares en Ninos con Problemas de Audicion y de Lenguaje.* (thesis, directed by J. B. de Quirós; Rosario, Argentina: Facultad de Medicina del Litoral, 1962).

39. H. McHugh, "Auditory and Vestibular Disorders in Children," *Laryngoscope* 72 (1962): 555-565.

40. J. B. de Quirós, "Vestibular-Proprioceptive Integration: Its Influence in Learning and Speech in Children." *Proceedings of Tenth International Congress of Psychology* (April 3-7, Lima Peru: Mexico: Trillas, 1967): 194-202.

41. Quirós (1967, 1974, 1976), *loc. cit.;* J. B. de Quirós, O. L. Schrager, and E. E. Tormakh, "Learning and Language Therapies" *Proceedings of the Fifteenth International Congress of Logopedics and Phoniatrics* (Buenos Aires, August 14-19, 1971): 763-782; O. L. Schrager, "El Sistema Postural y sus Relaciones con las Llamadas Afasias Infantiles," in J. B. de Quirós *et al., Las Llamadas Afasias Infantiles* (Buenos Aires: CEMIFA, 1971): 46-60; O. L. Schrager, "El Sistema Postural y las Basas del Aprendizaje," in J. B. de Quirós, *et al., Lenguaje y Aprendizaje* (Buenos Aires: CEMIFA, 1972): 35-49; O. L. Schrager, "La Importancia de la Vision en la Estructuracion de la Postura y el Espacio en el Nino," *Revista Argentina de Tiflologia* [Buenos Aires] 2 (1973): 26-40; O. L. Schrager, "Vision, Sistema Postural y Aprendizajes," *Fonoaudiologica* [Buenos Aires] 20 (1974): 67-81; O. L. Schrager and L. Cowes, "Exploracion Vestibular en el Nino Pequeno," *Fonoaudiologica* [Buenos Aires] 14 (1968): 51-70; O. L. Schrager and J. L. Braier, "Perturbaciones en los Procesos de Aprendizaje y en la Motricidad, Determinados por Aberraciones Cromosomicas y Enfermedades Geneticas," in J. B. de Quirós *et al., Lenguaje y Aprendizaje* (Buenos Aires: CEMIFA, 1972); E. E. Tormakh, "La Influencia del Sistema Gamma Sobre el Movimiento y la Postura," *Fonoaudiologica* [Buenos Aires] 12 (1966): 25-10; E. E. Tormakh, "Examen Neurologico, Vestibular en el Nino: Su Fundamentacion," *Fonoaudiologica* [Buenos Aires] 16 (1970): 123-126; J. L. Braier and O. L. Schrager, "Genetopatia Vestibular: Hipotesis de su Existencia como Causa de Trastornos de Aprendizaje," *Proceedings of the Fifteenth International Congress of Pediatrics,* Volume 10 (Buenos Aires, July 1974): 142-144.

42. Barany, "Ueber die vom Ohrlabyrinth . . .," *loc. cit.;* A. de Kleijn, "Experimental Physiology of the Labyrinth," *Journal of Laryngology and Otology* 36 (1923): 646: A. Landau, "Ueber motorische Besonderheiten des zweiten Lebehnshalbjahres, *Monatschrift fur Kinderheilhunde* 29 (1925); 555; R. Magnus, "Some Results in the Study of the Physiology of Posture," *Lancet* 212 (1926): 531-536, 585-588; R. Magnus and A. de Kleijn, "Experimentelle Physiologie des Vestibularapparates," *Handbuch der Neurologie des Ohres* 1 (1924); 465; R. Lorente de No, "On The Tonic Labyrinth Reflexes of the Eyes," *Acta Otolaryngologica* [Stockholm] 9 (1926): 162-176; A. M. Di Giorgio and C. Castelli-Borgioti, "Sul Graduale Instaurarsi nel 'Uomo della Corrispondenza fra il Piano dell'Orbita in cui si Manifesta il Nistagmo Ocular da Eccitamento Rotatorio," *Archivio de Fisiologia* [Torino] 38 (1938): 117-185.

43. G. Schaltenbrand, "Normale Bewegungs, und Haltungs–und Lagereaktionen bei Kindern," *Deutsche Zeitschrift fur Nervenheilkunde* 37 (1925): 29-59; G.. G. J. Rademaker, *Reaction Labyrinthique et Equilibre* (Paris: Masson, 1935); J. Zador, *Les Reactions d'Equilibre chez l'Homme* (Paris: Masson, 1935); J. Zador, *Les Reactions d'Equilibre chez l'Homme* (Paris: Masson, 1938); M. M. Lawrence and C. R. Feind, "Vestibular Responses to Rotation in Newborn Infants," *American Medical Association Pediatrics* 12:3 (1953): 300-306; G.. Bieber, "Ricerche sul Determinismo del Reflesso di Aggrappamento nel Neonato," *Rivista di Clinica Pediatrica* [Milano] 54 (1954): 401-419; Andre-Thomas, "L'Equilibre et la Fonction Labyrinthique chez le Nouveau-Ne et le Nourrison," *L'Encephale* 44:2 (1955): 97-137.

44. P. I. Yakovlev and A. R. Lecours, "The Myelogenetic Cycles of Regional Maturation of the Brain," in A. Minkowski (ed.), *Regional Development of the Brain in Early life* (Oxford and Edinburgh: Blackwell Scientific Publications, 1967): 3-70.

45. E. M. Ornitz, "Vestibular Dysfunction in Schizophrenia in Childhood," *Comprehensive Psychiatry* 11 (1970): 159-173; E. M. Ornitz, "Childhood Autism—A Review of the Clinical and Experimental Literature (Medical Progress)," *California Medicine* 118 (1973): 21-47; L. C. Erway, "Otolith Formation and Trace Elements: A Theory of Schizophrenic Behavior," *Journal of Orthomolecular Psychiatry* 4:1 (1973):

16-26; G. Harris, "Influences of Vestibular-Gravity System in Human Behavior" (unpublished paper and personal communication, 1976).

46. B. Milojevic, and J. L. Watson, "Vestibular Asymmetries in Right- and Left-Handed People," *Acta Otolaryngologica* [Stockholm] 60 (1965): 322-329.

47. Luria, *Higher Cortical Functions . . ., loc. cit.*; Luria, *El Cerebro . . ., loc. cit.*; A. J. Ayres, *Sensory Integration and Learning Disorders* (Los Angeles: Western Psychological Services, 1973).

NEUROPSYCHOLOGICAL FUNDAMENTALS

CHAPTER X

Neuropsychological Examination

(69) A WELL-KNOWN TYPE OF NEUROPSYCHOLOGICAL EXAMINATION

In Section 1 of this book, and again in Chapter IX, a definition of neuropsychology was discussed. We said that neuropsychology is a new branch of health sciences which deals with the study of relationships between cerebral functions (and achievements) and human behavior. We also said that, in adults, neuropsychology is mainly related to localized cerebral lesions and, in children, it refers mainly to specifically human achievements and disorders (learning disabilities).

Principal authorities in neuropsychology use psychological tests (or items from psychological tests) in order to obtain data concerning different localized brain lesions or suspected dysfunctions. We are not at all convinced of the benefits of neurological use of psychological materials for reaching such a goal. We believe that every specialty has its own field of action and that neurologists can have their own specific diagnostic procedures. Certainly, psychiatrists, psychologists, and other professional people can make positive contributions to reaching a diagnosis through a variety of clinical procedures. Neurologists can obtain useful data on localization of brain damages or dysfunctions and on postural impairments or dysfunctions by using specific neurologic evaluation techniques. Perhaps, it is necessary to change some of the environmental conditions and to observe whether the same reflexes, reactions, or responses (previously obtained through traditional neurological procedures) change or are modified in such circumstances.

A short review of A. R. Luria's excellent neuropsychological examination can help us to understand many aspects of this topic.[1]

Besides the preliminary conversation with the patient (or relatives) and the observation of the principal complaints, Luria investigates motor functions, acoustico-motor coordination, higher cutaneous and kinesthetic functions, higher visual functions, receptive speech, expressive speech, writing, reading, arithmetical skill, mnestic (i.e., memory) processes, and intellectual processes.

According to Luria, some conclusions in regard to brain localization can be reached. We shall try to summarize these conclusions according to our personal interpretations, reviewing the following parts: frontal syndromes; temporal syndromes; occipital syndromes; parietal syndromes; diffuse damages; signs in corpus callosum damages; signs in pseudobulbar syndromes and basal ganglia lesions; signs related to kinesthesia and kinesis; signs related to simple movements of the hands.

Frontal syndromes. Patients manifest echopraxia, mirror image reversal of movements, motor disturbance of speech, inertia of motor acts, and perseveration.

1. Echopraxia refers to the imitation of the movement pattern given by the examiner. For instance, mirror image *reversal of movements* is an echopraxia. (The patient, sitting face to face with the investigator, "extends the little finger of his right hand when he should extend the index finger.")

2. Inertia refers to "difficulties of inhibition of a movement once initiated, like perseveratory movements." "The examiner places one of the patient's hands in a certain pose and requests that he reproduce the pose with the other hand while keeping his eyes shut." The examiner shows how he "plays piano" with some series of fingers (I-II-III, or I-II-V). Patients with inertia follow with all the fingers, using I-II-III-IV-V.

3. Perseveration means to continue performing the same movement or action in spite of the new command received from the examiner.

In severe frontal syndromes patients perseverate in copying the first drawn figure they saw, in spite of the presentation of new figures.

In premotor and postcentral hemispheric syndromes the contralateral hand follows the movement of the other hand. For instance, Luria uses the assessment with reciprocal coordination first suggested by Oseretsky in 1930.[2] "In this test the patient is requested to place both hands in front of him, one with the fist clenched and the other with the fingers outstretched. He is then asked to simultaneously change the positions of both hands, stretching the first and clenching the other."

In premotor syndromes, awkwardness can be seen in doing alternately two taps with one's right hand and one tap with the left hand, "changing smoothly from one hand to the other." Confusion also can be seen with the "fist-ring test" and with the "test of the dynamic coordination of movement." Patients must make a fist when the arm is extended and must "do a ring" (with thumb and index fingertips; the OK sign) when the arm is flexed. In a similar item patients must also stretch out the hand when the arm is extended and must make a fist when the arm is flexed, and so on. In premotor syndromes all these movements are imitated with clumsiness, confusion, and perseveration.

In bilateral sensorimotor syndromes, the patient's phonation is severely handicapped. In inferior premotor areas it seems to be vocal-motor perseveration for singing.

According to Luria, echopraxia and inertia are outstanding symptoms in frontal syndromes. An example of echopraxia in Luria's tests can be found in "simple inflective constructions," belonging to "understanding of logical grammatical structures." Luria shows a pencil, a key, and a comb. After the patient has recognized these three objects, he asks the patient: (1) to point with the key toward the pencil, (2) with the pencil toward the key, and finally (3) to point to the pencil with the comb and to the key with the pencil.

The echopraxic tendency is to jumble the order of the words in the sentence; and patients, instead of pointing to the key with the pencil, for instance, point to the pencil with the key.

On the other hand, when they initially can solve a similar echopraxic problem and they draw, for instance, a cross beneath a circle, if we change the order into another, patients who have inertial stereotypes continue doing the same drawing: a circle with a cross beneath it.

Temporal syndromes. According to Luria, in these syndromes vocal reproduction is poor and acoustic analysis synthesis is faulty.

There are always difficulties (mainly on the left side) in making or reproducing rhythmic structures. Higher temporal divisions of the left hemisphere are dedicated to speech-sound analysis and synthesis. They work closely with associative fibers and projections with cerebral divisions responsible for speech articulation. Disturbance in phonemic audition produces a secondary disturbance in speech articulation and in expressive speech. Disturbance in articulatory processes and in inner speech can also inevitably alter receptive processes (as, for example, speech-sound perception) and comprehension of oral language. Luria uses perception and reproduction of pitch relationships and of rhythmic structures, series of different sounds, words, and simple sentences. In the left fronto-temporal syndrome they repeat series of sounds.

Patients having fronto-temporal syndromes understand the meaning of isolated words, but they have difficulties when other words are spoken. Inertia for the meaning (when successive words are heard) is also found in extensive frontal lesions.

In temporal lesions and acoustic or sensory aphasia, patients have great difficulties in language comprehension and expression. Their difficulties in symbolization are severe: They are unable to create logical grammatical structures, and they present receptive agrammatism. The same example that was used in regard to frontal syndromes (i.e., the circle and the cross) is not understood by these patients and therefore is not produced.

When cortical endings of the auditory analyzer are damaged, patients cannot perceive the sentence as a whole; and they react only to isolated words within the message. Sensory or acoustic aphasia shows a rapid extinction of words' meanings and difficulties in perceiving the words.

Occipital syndromes. In severe occipital syndromes, simple objects or realistic figures are not recognized. Patients with less severe problems have difficulty in recognizing a reversed figure. Still less severe syndromes are found in individuals who have some difficulties with complex figures. Slight cases have difficulties only with "silhouettes" (i.e., unfinished drawings or confused photos) or with superimposed figures.

Parietal and parieto-occipital syndromes. In inferoparietal syndromes there are failures in optic-spatial organization. Luria's studies on visual perception were mainly made by using different items belonging to several well-known tests (as for instance, Poppelreuter's, Raven's, and others are). Tests demanding recognition of superimposed figures or analysis and synthesis are employed. Then, figures that show different spatial orientation or that demand intellectual spatial operations are presented.

In parietal syndromes some abnormalities in "cutaneous sensation" are also found. Luria investigates cutaneous sensation through classical examinations (for instance, such as produced by the point or head of a pin touching the skin or the recognition of a letter or a number written on the skin with a wooden stick).

Patients having inferoparietal syndromes without kinesthetic disturbances fail in optic-spatial organization. In postcentral and inferoparietal syndromes reception of cutaneous and kinesthetic information is erroneous.

Postcentral or posterior parietal syndromes maintain identification of direction of the cutaneous passive movement of an object touching the skin and also of numbers or letters drawn on the skin.

Left (or bilateral) occipitoparietal lesions fail in establishing ocular spatial relationships. For instance, patients see a sign—the most outstanding one—but fail to relate it with other signs, or they are able to point out objects when the names of those objects are given, but they do not find any relationship between them. Lack of synthesis and spatial orientation are characteristics of such a syndrome. Comprehension of words having space meanings is very difficult for patients having parieto-occipital lesions, semantic aphasia, or diffuse brain damages.

Individuals with lesions in the postero-superior left-cortical region show great difficulty in differentiating distinct phonemes from one another ($b = p$, $t = d$).

Diffuse damages. Many of the symptoms already seen in different localized cerebral regions are also found in diffuse brain damages. Their value, therefore, can be great, when there are other medical symptoms which corroborate such a diagnosis. Let us review some of the most common symptoms that are mentioned by Luria as belonging to diffuse cerebral damage: difficulties related to spatial meanings of the words or of the message; impulsive responses related to parts of the sentences; and great difficulties in performing some tests, for instance, (1) successfully performing series of movements with both hands, such as "fist-edge-palm," (2) doing successfully the previously mentioned "piano" sequence, (3) performing adequately the third item of the "key-pencil-comb" test already mentioned.

Patients with diffuse brain damage can solve simple logical grammatical structures; and, consequently, they can correctly perform the two first items of these tests; but they cannot solve the third one.

Signs in corpus callosum damages. We are speaking here only about Luria's approach in neuropsychology. Nevertheless, we should remember that in Chapter IX, Section 60, we referred to Geschwind's investigations in regard to some patients in whom the posterior part of the corpus callosum was surgically sectioned (or cut).

According to Luria, Oseretsky's reciprocal coordination test, previously mentioned, fails in patients having lesions or disturbances in the anterior divisions of the corpus callosum. In parasagital lesions (which involve the anterior divisions) reciprocal coordination becomes impossible.

Signs in pseudobulbar syndromes and basal ganglia lesions. As is well known, in pseudobulbar syndromes and basal ganglia lesions, voice problems can appear (sometimes voice tremors, sometimes out of register, and so on). Luria mentions "intermittent" vocal utterances, and he also points out that patients cannot modulate smoothly and have difficulties in reproducing simple melodies.

Signs related to kinesthesia and kinesis. Movements with hands, imitations of imposed hand movements with the other hand (the patient with eyes closed), and others are investigated in order to see whether the kinesthetic basis of movements is disturbed.

If there are disturbances in the kinesthetic component of speech, patients may show defects in differentiating utterances of p and b or t and d, even if they can be auditorily distinguished. Patients always show difficulties in discriminating sounds which are acoustically different but which have similar articulations, for example, b and m or d and n.

In afferent (kinesthetic) motor aphasia there is neither word extinction nor difficulty in obtaining meaning, but patients have difficulties in understanding words when they themselves utter them aloud.

In efferent (kinetic) motor aphasia, patients understand word meanings, but pathological inertia does not allow patient's speech, because it interferes with the flexibility of transferring comprehension from one verbal utterance to another.

Signs related to simple movements of the hands. Luria mentions the following as the main symptoms: paresis, lack of accuracy, pathological dystonic movement, ataxia, differences in fatigue of both hands, and kinesthesic failures (imitation without visual help).

All of the foregoing signs and symptoms, obtained through various neuropsychological tests, may lead to better understanding of the cerebral region affected or damaged; but certainly they do not allow a definite and precise topological diagnosis, at least in brain dysfunctions and learning disabilities.

(70) NEUROPSYCHOLOGICAL EXAMINATION OF DYSPHASIA, DYSLEXIA, APRACTOGNOSIA, AND DISCRIMINATION DISORDERS

From a medical point of view, examination of higher symbolic levels in human beings is a very difficult task, because such levels involve mainly the use of language, reading, and writing, which require assessment procedures which are not specifically medical. Only a few pediatricians have some background in these nonmedical areas.

On the one hand, doctors who are well trained with items from Benton's, Luria's, Hécaen's neuropsychological batteries, can use them with accurate results.[3]

On the other hand, if doctors consider traditional neuropediatrics as an acceptable method of examination, in some cases they probably will arrive at the diagnosis of minimal brain dysfunction and in other cases they will not obtain any diagnosis.

In consequence, when faced with dysphasia, dyslexia, apractognosia, or discrimination disorders, doctors generally have three different approaches:

1. Using special tests focusing upon symbolic abilities (language, reading, writing, spatial relationships, and so on). In some cases sophisticated mechanical and electronic equipment is used.
2. Accepting the existence of different "soft" signs and arriving at the general diagnosis of "minimal brain dysfunction." With such an approach doctors identify all the conditions listed in item 1 within a wide heterogeneous group of "minimal brain dysfunctions." We shall not refer specifically to this second approach because it is already so well known in the medical profession.
3. Looking for classical neurological abnormalities and denying the existence of "labels" such as "dyslexia" or "minimal brain dysfunction." We shall not specifically refer to this third approach because it also is well known in medical circles.

These three approaches are controversial; no single approach is universally agreed upon. We, ourselves, follow a different medical approach, mainly directed to rehabilitatory purposes. We use many principles (also maintained by proponents of each of the three other medical positions); but we consider that every child's nervous system has the "plasticity" to recover quite well in some circumstances. If in the past there were certain abnormalities which were subsequently compensated, this situation can provide the necessary information for explaining present abnormalities (such as dyslexia, dysphasia, apractognosia, or discrimination disorders) in children. If past abnormalities were compensated, present neurological examinations can only show some "soft" signs in some cases and no abnormalities in others.

The concept of past pathology described in Chapter IX, Section 63, can help us to understand why some neurological disorders may be found to have caused these learning disabilities.

It could be necessary, however, to develop our knowledge of this subject sufficiently to obtain more accurate and significant results. It might be worth our while to remember that (from a traditional point of view) neurological symptomatology is only "slightly" or "minimally" manifested in primary learning disabilities, symbolic human acquisitions being the more disturbed ones.

The past-pathology concept, when comparing differences between static and dynamic situations, permits the acquisition of other data that can be useful for a final medical diagnosis.

(71) TESTS OF SYMBOLIC ABILITIES

These tests are widely used by doctors and nonmedical professionals in learning disabilities. They intend to obtain the following goals:

1. Differentiating hemispheric disturbances (dominant or nondominant)
2. Locating dysfunctions (or slight damages) in certain brain regions
3. Connecting the obtained findings with some specific symptoms directly indicating the presence of primary learning disabilities

In regard to item 1, many tests are used, but mainly *lingua*-language tests, space tests, and body awareness tests.

In the United States, Templin's, Wepman's, and Buktenica's are the most widely used *lingua*-language tests.[4]

The *Templin-Darley Screening and Diagnostic Tests of Articulation* is a short test of sound discrimination. Examiners give successively two speech sounds, and patients must recognize when both sounds are the same or different. According to Charles Van Riper, a child who at least has ten or more errors over the normal result average for his age shows a clear impairment in phonetic discrimination.[5]

Wepman's *Auditory Discrimination Test* is also directed to auditory discrimination in regard to verbal materials that pupils recognize as "same" or "different." Wepman relates his test with speech and reading.

Buktenica's TENVAD is a nonverbal auditory discrimination test. It uses recognition of pitch, loudness, rhythm, direction, and timbre. In this test "the pupils' responses are a mix of 'same' and 'different' and 'same' and 'not the same.'" It was standardized on middle-class White children, lower-class White children, and lower-class Black children. Results seem to be related neither to socioeconomic status nor to race. Different items are registered in a record in order to provide constant and similar stimulations.

Many other tests have been created to assess language handicaps, mainly for aphasia in adults, and more recently for learning-disabled children.[6]

J. J. McCarthy and S. A. Kirk developed the *Illinois Test of Psycholinguistic Abilities* (ITPA), which is widely used in many countries. From a pedagogical and vocabulary-conceptual point of view, it can be useful; but its use from a medical point of view is controversial. Certainly, the test was devised in order to explore psycholinguistic abilities, rather than to obtain medical data.

Perhaps it could be interesting from a medical point of view to identify if the child is still using *lingua* or if he is using language. Differentiation between concepts of speech, *lingua,* and language was outlined in Chapter II, Section 8. Now it is important to review briefly some of the principal clinical indicators of (1) the existence of language, or (2) the existence of *lingua* developing into language.[7] According to the criteria followed by Quirós, three main characteristics can be considered: (1) *lingua*-thought identification; (2) hemispheric symbolization; and (3) linguistic formulation. Let us summarize these three characteristics.

Lingua-thought identification. It is necessary to observe some of the following phenomena:

1. The child is talking when playing.
2. The child establishes logical temporal sequences.
3. The child "discovers" irregular terms used idiomatically.
4. The child begins to use syntactic patterns to talk. This observation includes temporal notions (today, yesterday, tomorrow), coherent or rational conversation, ability to tell stories, smooth and easy use of verbal tenses, articles, prepositions, conjunctions, and agreement of number (plural, singular) and gender.
5. The child can repeat a story without using the same words previously said by the examiner, but telling substantially the same things.
6. The child can explain verbal absurdities and jokes (if appropriate for his age).

Hemispheric symbolization. Observe the following phenomena:

1. The child recognizes (without seeing) "right" and "left."
2. The child can classify items according to perceptual cues *and nonperceptual cues* (symbolic concepts).
3. The child begins to obey language commands; he also acts according to his own language, in spite of motor and perceptual stimuli.

   For example, we use several tests in order to explore this leadership function of language. The procedure is almost always the same. We give a command to the child while at the same time we are perceptually or motorically stimulating him. For instance, we give to the child two similar toys, each of different color (a blue car and a red car). The child amuses himself with the cars. Then, we ask him to "give me the red car" (the child gives it). We give the red car back to the child, telling him to take the red car (the child takes it). The same commands are given in regard to the blue car. Twice more we successively repeat the same commands; but then we abruptly change the command; and we ask for the blue car when the child is expecting to be asked for the red one. If the child gives the red car, we interpret that rhythmic movement was able to create perseveration, and it was therefore stronger than the symbolic message. If the child gives the blue car, we interpret this to mean that he is obeying a linguistic command.

   Another test consists, for example, in asking the child to point to his eye at the same time the examiner is pointing to his ear. The examiner asks the child to point to his nose and at the same time he is pointing to his mouth, etc.

　　　　　　　　　　　　　NEUROPSYCHOLOGICAL FUNDAMENTALS

4. The child reveals interest for letters and numerals as representations of sounds and words.
5. The child can be amused by pure linguistic tasks such as riddles, absurdities, and so on.

Linguistic formulation. One should observe these phenomena:

1. The child can think according to others' thoughts. (For instance, he can accept game rules, such as football rules, domino game rules, etc.)
2. The child can "invent" adequate answers when faced with new situations.

    For instance, the child is drawing with a pencil, and the point of the pencil breaks. If the child has language, he will verbally ask for a solution; he spontaneously will ask for another pencil, or will ask for something to sharpen the end of the pencil, or will ask the teacher to do so, etc. If the child has only *lingua,* he will not ask (verbally and spontaneously) for new and adequate solutions.
3. The child can learn to reason mathematical calculations without confusion in regard to the presentation of the words. Consider this problem:

    "Do you know that in South America, as in Africa, there are ostriches? But South-American ostriches have three toes on each foot, *one more than* African ostriches. How many toes on each foot have African ostriches?"

    If the words "one more than" are operatively interpreted, the answer will be correct (two toes on each foot). When interpretation is not in operative terms (nor reversible), the child adds "one more" toe and he answers "four."

    "Reversible thought" is a term coined at the beginning of this century. When a child is able to reason that, if $3 + 2 = 5$, then $5 - 2 = 3$, psychoeducationalists speak about reversible thought. The child needs reversible thought in order to solve the problem of ostriches.

    Another test we use is based on an original test of Luria's already discussed: "Draw a ball beneath a square." We see whether the child follows the sequence of the words, or the inner sense of the command.
4. The child begins to use speech of his peer group (his classmates, his friends, etc.).
5. The child is ready to adopt new systems of symbolic communication (reading and writing). When writing about a picture representing a child doing something, he is able not only to enumerate "statically" the objects he is seeing, but also to introduce *action* in his description.

The nondominant hemisphere mainly concerns itself with space and body awareness. Space is generally tested through visual tests. Space tests and body awareness tests can be very useful. Many aspects of these tests were already discussed in Chapter VI, Section 36. The *Marianne Frostig Developmental Test of Visual Perception* and the Benton *Visual Retention Test* are particularly important procedures of evaluation.[8]

See Figures 7, 8, and 9 for examples of stimulus items.

(72) LOCATIONS OF BRAIN DYSFUNCTIONS AND FINDINGS RELATED TO PRIMARY LEARNING DISABILITIES

In regard to the location of dysfunctions or slight damages in certain brain regions, modern advances in audiometry provide useful investigation procedures. Certainly, these tests require more sophisticated evaluation

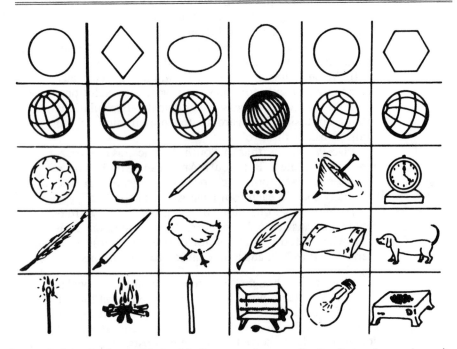

Figure 7. Stimulus Items (I). In this figure can be seen (in the first and second rows) traditional perceptual items mainly based on shapes and details. In the third row items based on a concept (a toy) are represented, which can only be matched by using symbolic abilities. In the fourth row items are represented which can be matched in different ways: (a) the child matches the feather with the penholder or the leaf—the child acts *perceptually*; (b) the child matches the feather with the pillow—the child acts according to the *use* that feathers can have; (c) the child matches the feather with the chicken—the child acts according to his *knowledge* of the origin of feathers; or (d) the child selects the dog only— uncomprehension and/or thought dissociation. In the lowest row the inflamed match can be associated with the pencil—perceptual shape; with the bonfire (first level); with kitchen (second level)—the "fire" concept; with the stove (second level)—the "heat" concept. In order to be more easily handled, these and other materials can also be used as cards.

procedures than the ones we discussed in Chapter IX. One of us studied carefully such tests, recognizing them within the general name of "sensitized tests." "Sensitization" refers to the modifications of the normal arrival of sound or speech stimuli. The latter can be modified through electronic procedures. It is possible to distort messages through filters, through changes in message speed (see Figure 10), through modification of the word or sentence, codes, sentence structure, and so on.

Some school children—for instance, stutterers, or symbolic handicapped, or learning-disabled—can fail this kind of test.[9]

All the procedures recognized as sensitized audiometry can provide useful supplementary data in identifying brain dysfunctions or damages, and particularly dominant hemisphere dysfunctions or damage.

With this same purpose other kinds of auditory tests (such as the dichotic ones) can also be of practical value; the same can be said about dichotomous tests, visual or tactual (see Chapter IX, Section 64).

It is open to discussion whether symbolic abilities are also related to localization of sound sources. It seems clear enough, however, that directional audition can help the symbolic development processes. On the other hand, the establishment of a dominant or symbolic hemisphere coincides with the rapid increase of directional auditory abilities.

Figure 8. Stimulus Items (II). Every one of these drawings can be selected in order to observe with which other drawing of the same figure a child matches the selected drawing. If he selects shapes, he works perceptually; if he selects concepts, he works linguistically.

SYMBOLIC FORMULATION AND LANGUAGE (7.5 years old)

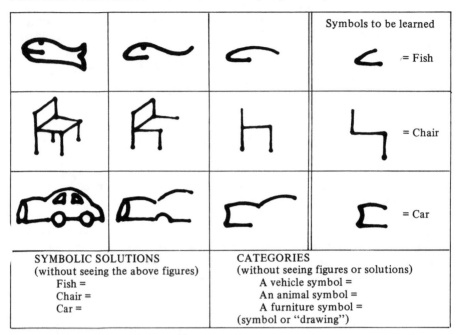

Figure 9. Stimulus Items (III). In order to examine symbolic communication abilities, we draw new rough symbols on the blackboard while the child is seeing our work. We say: "You saw how I obtained this final drawing. This drawing means "fish" (or "chair," or "car"). Now I'll erase the blackboard and you must draw the same final drawings I did for each word." After doing this task: "Well, now you must repeat the same drawings (symbolic solutions); but pay attention; you must think, to which row does each drawing correspond?" (categories).

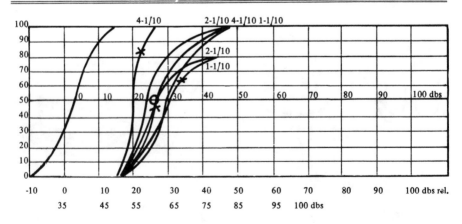

Figure 10. Modifications of Speech Audiometry in Central Dysfunctions. Circles represent the right ear. Crosses represent the left ear. Numbers represent differences of speed of sentence-stimulations.

NEUROPSYCHOLOGICAL FUNDAMENTALS

Directional audiometry provides information about the brain stem and particularly the level of the third auditory pathway neuron (superior olivary nucleus).[10] It seems that "binaural interaction," as some researchers have called it, takes place at that level. As a matter of fact, directional audition is directly connected with the ability to establish time and loudness differences between the sound stimulation of both ears (a phenomenon which is directly related to "binaural interaction").[11] Failures in directional audition, therefore, can suggest the existence of a brain dysfunction or damage.

Young children (those under five years of age) can differentiate only sound sources which are placed on both sides or in front of them, always in the same plane as their ears. Between six and seven years of age, directional audition allows the localization of all the sound sources placed at the level of the child's ears (in front, both sides, and behind). Normal adults can recognize not only sound sources which are placed at ear level, but also sound stimuli coming from higher and lower sources.[12]

Specially designed acoustic chambers can be used to determine a child's ability to recognize sources of sound. But here, the conditions are clinical; and the sounds to be recognized are, generally, pure tones. In daily life, there are ample opportunities to assess, informally, directional handicaps to noises and complex sounds. It is important, therefore, to pay attention to parents' observations, such as, "When I call him from the kitchen he goes to the bedroom."

Directional dysacusis can interfere with school children's learning abilities.

Many other tests using symbolization and concerning brain localization can be used by doctors, but the ones just discussed seem to be the most important ones.

The linguistic formulation mentioned in Section 71 is related to the acquisition of data directly connected with some primary learning disabilities. An excellent example of this approach is E. Boder's diagnostic screening procedure for developmental dyslexia.[13] The main contribution of this author was a qualitative evaluation of a child's ability to read and spell.

Boder uses a reading test, a spelling test, and supplementary tasks.

The reading test consists in word recognition of lists of twenty words each, presented in two ways: "flash," in order to determine the child's immediate recognition of whole word configurations; and "untimed," in order to determine the child's ability to analyze unfamiliar words phonetically. Comparison between the number of correctly read words in "flash" and "untimed" presentations, indicates how the child is reading (predominantly through whole-word Gestalt, or through phonetic analysis, or both). The reading test "taps the central visual and auditory processes necessary for reading."

The spelling test has two sections, and it is presented in two columns: "known words" (i.e., sight vocabulary) and "unknown words" (i.e., words not in the sight vocabulary). First a dictation of 10 "known" words (at his reading level or below) are made. With this test the author investigates the child's ability to "revisualize" words in his sight vocabulary (known words) and to spell phonetically words not in his sight vocabulary (unknown words). The spelling test "taps the central auditory and visual processes necessary for spelling."

Supplementary tasks can give additional data in regard to the severity of the child's reading spelling ability but they are not essential to the diagnostic screening procedure. Among these tasks are: reciting and writing the alphabet, reading a paragraph, syllabicating of phonetic words, writing phonetic equivalents with help in oral syllabicating.

According to this test, Boder classifies dyslexia in dysphonetic (deficit in symbol-sound integration), dyseidetic (deficit in visual Gestalten), and mixed dysphonetic-dyseidetic (deficit in both these reading and spelling patterns).

All the tests mentioned above are useful for medical diagnostic purposes. When learning disabilities respond to a postural tonic vestibular-cerebellar dysfunction or slight damage, doctors have at their disposal many more neurological assessment procedures in order to establish a correct diagnosis.

Aside from posture and tonus examinations, asymmetric tonic-neck reflexes require special discussion, which follows in Section 73.

(73) ASYMMETRIC TONIC-NECK REFLEXES AND THE ONE-LEG POSITION

Tonic-neck reflexes are seen in newborn babies, infants, and children. They consist in extension of the "facial" limbs and flexion of the occipital limbs, when the head is rotated to one or the other side of the body. They also can be seen in abnormal cases who are brain damaged.

As was reviewed in Chapter V, Section 32, Gesell's statement that he observed tonic-neck reflexes in newborn babies in the supine position is controversial. In that section we recognized other positions that could elicit such a reflex in children, particularly the quadruped position and one-leg position.

The quadruped position consists in supporting the body on both hands and knees. If in such a body position the child's head is passively rotated to 90 degrees to one or the other side, it is feasible to see that the arms adopt the asymmetric reflexes in regard to the occipital and facial sides of the head.

Our present knowledge of tonic-neck reflexes can be briefly summarized as follows:

1. Magnus described asymmetric tonic-neck reflexes in decerebrated and labyrinthectomized animals.[14] (See Chapter V, Section 29.)
2. Gesell considered the asymmetric tonic-neck reflex as normal during the first three months of postnatal life. The reflex was always elicited in supine position by passive rotation of the head. This statement was not accepted by other authors.[15] (See Chapter V, Section 32.)
3. R. Tokizane, M. Murao, T. Ogata, and T. Kondo stated that electromyography showed greater increased activity

of muscles involved in asymmetric tonic-neck reflexes by rotation of the head when the person was in the sitting position.[16]

4. T. Fukuda stated the well-developed use of asymmetric tonic-neck reflexes in efficient sportsmen.[17]

5. F. A. Hellebrandt, M. Shade, and M. L. Carns called attention to the existence of asymmetric tonic-neck reflexes in normal subjects (both children and adults). They used the quadruped position created by Lord Brain. Probably, they used an exaggerated rotation of the head (more than 90 degrees), which produced a biomechanical response in adults. The asymmetric tonic-neck reflex can be elicited in children (between three and eight years of age) by passive rotation of the head in the quadruped position.[18]

6. C. Parr, D. K. Routh, M. T. Byrd, and J. McMillan studied the development of the asymmetric tonic-neck reflex in 84 children between three and nine years of age, and considered this type of response as normal between those ages.[19]

7. There are some other authors who have written remarkably cogent papers on the same or allied subjects: G. P. McCouch, I. D. Deering, and T. H. Ling; M. Bridge Denkla; and Eviatar, Eviatar, and Naray.[20]

In order to examine tonic-neck reflexes, we use traditional tests, other tests (such as the quadruped position), the one-leg position, sunshine position, and changing-consistency boards. We obtain useful data on proprioception and vestibular influences and on central damages or dysfunctions. We shall describe the following tests:

1. The one-leg position
2. The one-leg position with eyes closed (or blindfolded)
3. The changing-consistency board
4. The weights on one side of the body
5. The sunshine position

In this section we shall only examine the first test.

A general principle for this examination was provided by the present knowledge on the role of vestibular system in the control of posture and movement in man. As Purdom Martin stated in 1967:

The postural reflexes that are active when an individual is standing or sitting on a firm base and blindfolded are excited by somatic proprioception, and so, under conditions of stability, proprioception is dominant and the vestibular reactions are suppressed; under conditions of instability the vestibular influence predominates and proprioceptive reactions are relatively in abeyance.[21]

In Figures 11, 12, and 13, following, it is possible to see normal reactions in the one-leg position. This test can be exaggerated by closing the eyes or by changing the consistency of the floor.

Figure 11. A Normal Boy (19 years old). It is possible to see the tonic-neck reflex on the right arm. There is a slight deviation of the head toward the right side.

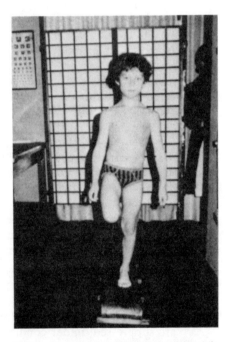

Figure 12. A Normal Child (7 years old). He is walking with eyes closed. Movement of the arms are typical tonic-neck reflexes elicited by the "one-leg alternating position."

Figure 13. A Normal Child (5 years old). The (left) one-leg position on the soft portion of the changing-consistency board elicits a clear tonic-neck reflex on the left side.

When a child or an adult is standing on one foot, all the weight of the body determines the exaggeration of the muscular stretch reflexes on that leg. This exaggeration is regulated by other low-level reflexes (Laporte and Lloyd's reflexes). But the modification of the body gravity determines neck (and head) compensatory movements. Consequently, some tonic-neck and vestibular-spinal reflexes are elicited. These reflexes deal with the compensation of body equilibrium. Neck and vestibular stimulation generates an asymmetric tonic-neck reflex (sometimes with slight head rotation), this reflex in some cases being voluntarily inhibited by the cortex. The reflex consists in greater extension and abduction in the arm which is ipsilateral to the leg which maintains the weight of the body. This normal asymmetric tonic-neck reflex can be exaggerated by closing the subject's eyes, or by maintaining balance on a soft surface. Sometimes it is possible to observe a clear head sway to the same side as the leg maintaining the weight of the body. The limbs of the opposite side do not lean upon the body.

(74) NEUROPSYCHOLOGICAL EXAMINATION OF VESTIBULAR-PROPRIOCEPTIVE DISSOCIATIONS. THE CHANGING-CONSISTENCY BOARD

We speak about vestibular-proprioceptive dissociation when proprioception dominates on one side of the body and vestibular action on the other. When proprioception is dominant in vestibular-proprioceptive dissociation, the one-leg position determines the total sway of the trunk toward the same side of the leg which supports the weight of the body. In order to maintain equilibrium, sometimes deviation of the trunk to the opposite side (for short periods of time) is seen. Generally, the head remains in the upright position. This situation is exaggerated when the subject's eyes are closed (or blindfolded), or when balance must be achieved on soft surfaces. The upper limb—which corresponds to the leg which supports the body—sometimes is close to the body and other times it can be separated (abducted). The limbs of the opposite side are firmly lean upon the body, producing a proprioceptive and tactual feedback that can help equilibrium. Sometimes the hands also feedback as fists. (See Figures 14 and 15, next page.)

In order to examine vestibular-proprioceptive dissociation with dominant vestibular action, we use a changing-consistency board with the patient's eyes opened or closed (or blindfolded). A changing-consistency board looks like a wooden board, but its consistency is abruptly changed from hard to soft (wood/nylon).[22] Its standard size is 6.5 feet long, 1 foot wide, and 3 inches high. The entire board is wrapped by a simulated-wood plastic cover; and at the middle of the board the hard consistency is changed to soft (nylon or polyurethane plastic). It must be clarified that the patient's vision cannot provide him with any information about this change of consistency, because of the wood-like plastic sheet. When a person starts walking on the changing-consistency board, he disregards visual information about it because he has seen and felt it as wood. Then his eyes are directed to the persons calling him from the other end of the board. In this situation, when the child suddenly steps on the soft part of the board, he must employ chiefly vestibular reflexes but also all his available systems of postural compensation (proprioception, kinesthesis, sense of touch, and—last—vision) in order to maintain equilibrium. Normal responses of asymmetric tonic-neck reflexes are obtained when vestibular responses are adequate. The opposite reaction can be seen when vestibular impairment does not elicit correct responses: The greatest extension and abduction of an arm corresponds to the opposite side of the leg which supports the weight of the body. This is more clearly seen with the patient's eyes closed.

For instance, when a child has left vestibular-spinal impairment, proprioception of the left side tends to compensate this handicap. Patellar (knee) and deep reflexes can be more definite and clear also on the left side. If these reflexes are inhibited, voluntary semi-extension of the legs (in the sitting position) allows the examiner to see the different responses of both sides. On the other hand, traditional vestibular tests show hypereflexia *on the right side.* This is a characteristic of vestibular-proprioceptive dissociation with dominant right vestibular action.

Vestibular-proprioceptive dissociation in early childhood always means there will be a learning disability. In childhood clear signs of cerebellar interconnections are widely established. (See Chapter II, Section 12 and Chapter V, Sections 30 and 31.) We differentiated these symptoms from developmental dyslexia in successive papers and books.[23] Other authors

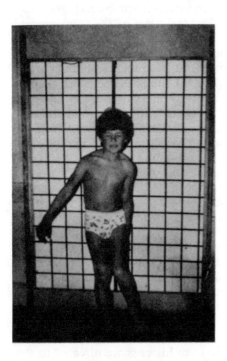

Figure 14. A Boy (13 years old). He shows vestibular-proprioceptive dissociation with proprioceptive preponderance.

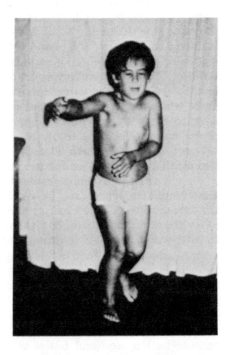

Figure 15. A Child (5 years old). He shows vestibular-proprioceptive dissociation with proprioceptive preponderance.

NEUROPSYCHOLOGICAL FUNDAMENTALS

prefer to consider these syndromes within the general term "dyslexia."[24] (See Figures 16 and 17.)

(75) SYMMETRIC TONIC-NECK RESPONSES AND THE SUNSHINE POSITION

In some cases it is possible to see symmetric tonic-neck responses in the one-leg position and on the changing-consistency board. In the one-leg position both arms are flexed and raised, and occasionally the leg which supports the weight of the body becomes slightly flexed. This reaction is more evident on the changing-consistency board. It is clear enough that symmetric tonic-neck responses generally follow the movement of the patient's head in order to see the ground. Vision and symmetric tonic-neck reflexes seem to be very near each other. At the beginning of the third postnatal month the infant introduces symmetric tonic-neck reflexes as a consequence of the possibility of visual fixation, accommodation, and convergence. Then, some eye-head-hand modalities are almost always established. These essential modalities are maintained in different brain injuries and dysfunctions. When normal young children begin to stand on one leg, the appearance of symmetric tonic-neck responses is quite common.

When we see symmetric tonic-neck responses in static and dynamic situations we suspect brain injury; when we see symmetric tonic-neck re-

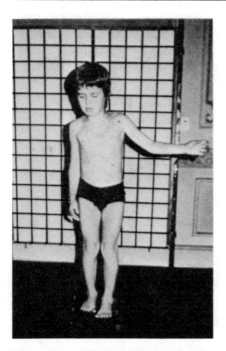

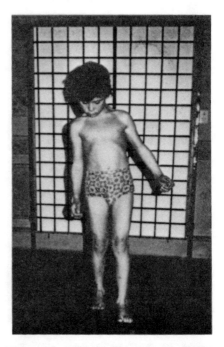

Figure 16. A Child (6 years old). Vestibular-proprioceptive dissociation (with dominant vestibular action) is elicited on the changing-consistency board.

Figure 17. A Child (8 years old). Vestibular-proprioceptive dissociation (with dominant vestibular action) is elicited on the changing-consistency board.

flexes only in dynamic situations we suspect at least mild brain dysfunctions. (See Figure 18.) The weights on one side of the body (hand) elicit clearer asymmetric tonic neck reflexes on the opposite side. (See Figure 19.)

The sunshine position is the same position which is used to take sun at the beach (supporting the trunk backwards with both hands and the head held in hyperextension). In this position we rotate the head passively to right and left, looking for asymmetric tonic-neck reflexes. When they appear, we may assume brain damage.

(76) NEUROPSYCHOLOGICAL EXAMINATION OF VESTIBULAR-OCULOMOTOR SPLIT

Through various kinds of vestibular stimulations it is feasible to elicit a saccadic movement of the eyes which is called nystagmus (see Chapter IX, Section 66). Vestibular nystagmus has a slow component and a rapid component. Its direction is recognized according to the direction of the rapid component and can be assumed in normal persons. For instance, when a doctor stimulates a labyrinth through caloric, turning, galvanic, or other tests, he assumes the characteristics that nystagmus and other responses can have. When, through different vestibular tests, ocular responses are also different, we speak about a vestibular-oculomotor split. An example of a vestibular-

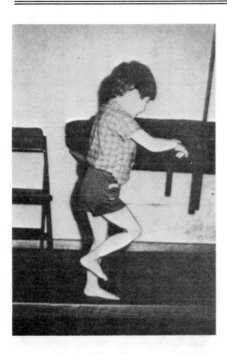

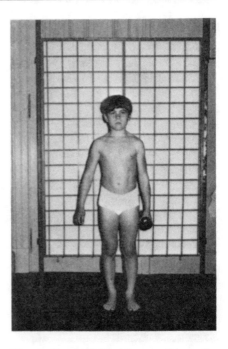

Figure 18. A Child (3 years old). The symmetric tonic-neck response appears as he is walking on the changing-consistency board.

Figure 19. A Child (6 years 8 months old). The effort response is determined by applying a weight on one side of the body (hand).

　　　　　　　　　NEUROPSYCHOLOGICAL FUNDAMENTALS

oculomotor split can be seen, for instance, when caloric tests determine nystagmus and rotatory tests elicit only the slow movement of the eyes.

It is indispensable to differentiate between vestibular-oculomotor split and "vestibular disharmony." Traditionally, vestibular disharmony refers to the discordant result obtained between nystagmic responses on the one hand, and body responses on the other.

Three different conditions of vestibular disharmony are classically recognized: (1) ascending disharmony, which suggests vestibular-oculomotor damage or disturbance; (2) descending disharmony, which suggests vestibular-spinal damage or disturbance; and (3) total disharmony, which suggests extensive vestibular damage or disturbance.

In ascending disharmony vestibular clinical tests (see Romberg's, gait, and past-pointing tests described in Chapter IX, Section 66) give performances which are in accordance with each other; but nystagmus is produced in an unexpected direction.

In descending disharmony nystagmus agrees with our clinical assumptions in regard to direction, but vestibular clinical tests give performances which are not coincident with the signs traditionally expected.

In total disharmony all performances and nystagmus do not match the clinical assumptions and signs previously expected.

As can be seen, in ascending disharmony Romberg's, gait, and past-pointing results are in accord, but nystagmus is produced in an unexpected direction. This is also connected with the possibility of making normal ocular movements. Certainly, ocular movements are influenced by many brain structures; but, from a practical point of view, they can be divided into vestibular, regard, pursuit, and command movements.[25] Vestibular movements are elicited by vestibular-oculomotor actions. Regard movements are those elicited by certain external objects. Pursuit or optokinetic movements are those elicited by a moving object; they are following movements. Command movements are those elicited through commands.

Vestibular-oculomotor movements classically refer to head movements (rotation, linear acceleration, etc.). In rotatory tests, acceleration produces the eyes' deviation to the opposite side of the direction of the movement of the head, and deceleration produces the eyes' deviation to the same side of the direction of the movement of the head. Otolithic influences in reading, therefore, cannot be doubted. (See the discussion of "otoliths" in Chapter V, Section 30.) When reading, many head movements (mainly, turning movements) are produced. These movements can easily stimulate otoliths, and consequently can modify static tonus and horizontal or vertical eye movements. In normal children, visual stimuli and voluntary movements of the eyes can mask otolithic oculomotor influences; but, in vestibular-oculomotor split, otoliths cannot contribute in order to obtain skilled smooth movement of the eyes.

If we review some developmental concepts related to vestibular physiology, we shall be able to understand the clinical interpretation of the example of the vestibular-oculomotor split just mentioned.

It is well known that in normal newborn babies vestibular maturation is already complete. Nevertheless, and according to our own experiments, when normal newborns are rotated about a vertical axis, they show (at least during the first three weeks after birth) a phase of slow deviation of the eyes instead of a jerking nystagmus.[26] According to our experiments with caloric and rotatory tests, premature babies always show a vestibulogenic jerking nystagmus (similar to adult nystagmus); but full-term infants—with similar stimulation—have only slow movement of the eyes. These results are obtained only if many variables of pregnancy and delivery are carefully controlled. We relate those different responses to different stages of myelination and to inhibitory actions of the thalamus. As a hypothesis, in premature babies, vestibular centers at the medulla can act freely; in normal newborn babies medullar centers are inhibited by thalamic centers; in babies (after the first three weeks after birth— thalamic centers are also inhibited by cortical centers and medullar centers become again "free."

When neonates' ocular deviation is maintained during infancy, it seems that rotatory tests only determine the slow component of the nystagmus, because reactive fast movements are not elicited. Only voluntary movements and visual stimuli could eventually modify visual information. But it is necessary to realize that voluntary movements and the phase of the component of vestibular nystagmus, both seem to use the same neural arc.

The preceding example of vestibular-oculomotor split is probably similar—in some children—to what has sometimes been called "congenital oculomotor apraxia." On the other hand, it seems to be different from "defective dissociation of accommodation and convergence."[27] Perhaps, in some learning-disabled children (including vestibular ones), the latter symptoms can appear.

A reading disability can be the consequence of the failure in obtaining head-vestibular-ocular coordination. We reiterate that voluntary skilled movements are strongly related to some vestibular reactions (the fast component of the nystagmus).

A writing disability can be the consequence of the failure in eye-head-hand coordination. When both coordinations are disturbed, reading and writing disabilities are produced.

If ascending disharmony is found, it is critical that the examiner look for the type of nystagmus elicited through various procedures. According to the results obtained, it would be feasible to assume the existence of vestibular-oculomotor split.

(77) A GENERAL NEUROPSYCHOLOGICAL APPROACH IN LEARNING DISABILITIES

When doctors are to examine a learning-disabled child, they must direct their examinations according to results obtained from screening tests conducted earlier.

First, doctors must determine whether the learning-disabled child is a primary or secondary case. Through the case history, behavior, and traditional medical examinations, they can admit or dismiss the existence of secondary factors of learning disabilities.

When the patient is considered as being primary learning disabled, doctors must establish, in the first place, the coexistence or nonexistence of "minimal brain dysfunction" and of "vestibular-proprioceptive dysfunctions." Principal examinations related to both dysfunctions can be seen in this chapter, as well as in Chapter IX. Both dysfunctions are "systemic" (see Chapter I, Section 5) because both interfere with the correct higher cortical functions of human beings.

Neuropsychological examinations of systemic dysfunctions (which also include vestibular dysfunctions) may be established on several criteria, remnant signs, extracharges, overloaded systems, asymmetries, potential capacities, and nonadaptive responses being the principal ones.

Although we have already discussed these concepts in this book, let us review them here, and provide some additional information which was inappropriate to bring up before.

Remnant signs. We call remnant signs the continued presence of postural or sensory responses at an age by which "normally" they should be modified or changed. For instance, the presence of asymmetric postures in a baby during the third, fourth, or fifth month after birth is a remnant sign. The importance of remnant signs is related to diagnostic assumptions. In the case just mentioned, we must ask ourselves if we are examining a blind baby, where vision elicits symmetric postures during the second quarter of the first year of postnatal life. If symmetric postures were not established, what happens to vision?

Remnant signs must be differentiated from "primitive signs." For instance, when asymmetric tonic-neck reflexes are elicited through rotation of a baby's head (in supine position), after six months of postnatal life, such reflexes can be interpreted in neuropediatrics as primitive signs; and they permit the assumption of the existence of brain damage. Nevertheless, we believe that it is indispensable to check any "primitive" reflex by adding other appropriate stimuli to the medical maneuver. For example, we must know whether or not vision is able to modify asymmetric tonic-neck reflexes into symmetric ones. When visual stimuli modify a baby's responses through similar medical maneuvers, primitive signs probably exist. When in such a case visual stimuli do not modify baby's responses, remnant signs probably exist. On the other hand, remnant signs can be produced through modifications in habitat. For instance, asymmetric tonic-neck reflexes can be examined in the quadrupedic posture until the child is nine years of age, and examined on changing-consistency boards in teen-agers or adults.

Similar questions exist concerning equilibrium and vestibular dysfunction. For instance, after the age of five years, the cerebellum also intervenes when vestibular proprioceptive dissociation is set up. What happens with Romberg's position, with the one-leg position, with some cerebellar tests? Did not the cerebellum intervene in such a dissociation? Are there remnant signs present? Why? Perhaps because cerebellar functions are not yet "mature"? Perhaps for another reason? Through careful examination important answers to these and other questions can be given.

Extracharges and overloads. We discussed these subjects in detail in Chapter VI, Section 34. When some organs or body parts must fulfill not only their specific functions but also some nonspecific functions, we say that they have extracharges. We recall that, in equilibrium or balance tests, the exaggerated use of proprioceptive, kinesthetic, or haptic information (plus visual survey) can reveal a vestibular disturbance, because deep sensitivity and the skin are providing an extracharge for equilibrium.

The overload notion, on the other hand, refers to an organ or part which receives multiple stimuli simultaneously. Brain-injured children or those with "minimal brain dysfunction" continuously receive multiple stimuli. They are overloaded, and this situation interferes with learning abilities.

Asymmetries. In speaking about the principal steps in neuropsychological assessments (Chapter IX, Section 63), we introduced the notion of past pathology. Let us now consider past pathology with respect to symmetries and asymmetries.

In order to study asymmetries, one must compare the obtained results in static positions (prone, supine, sitting, etc.) with those in dynamic position (walking, jumping, hopping, etc.).

When static asymmetries are also evident during dynamic situations, we assume present organic damage.

When static asymmetries disappear during dynamic situations, we suspect past pathology.

When static apparent symmetries are transformed into asymmetries during dynamic situations, we believe dysfunctions exist.

Potential capacities. Also in Chapter IX, Section 63, we spoke about this notion. In order to study potentiality, a comparison is made between the developmental level in major functional areas and the acquisitional level in related areas.

The difference between actual acquisiton performance and assumed levels of functional potential give the potential capacity. For example, if the neuromotor assessment yielded a developmental age of eight years five months, but the psychoeducational assessment showed an achievement quotient of six years two months, the difference of two years three months would represent the "potential capacity" for improvement with appropriate psychoeducation intervention.

Nonadaptive responses. This subject is also discussed in various places in this book (and mainly in Chapter IX, Section 63). In order to study adaptation, comparison is made between the responses obtained in the same patient through several tests made in two different environments: (1) of daily living ("habitat"); and (2) of unusual living conditions ("nonhabitat").

The child with normal "adaptive exigency responses" can quickly adapt and function in spite of changes in his environment. Many learning-disabled children have difficulty in adapting to changes in the environment of daily living. The changing-consistency board was made to detect non-adaptive responses.

From a practical point of view, some items that can orient doctors in regard to the way that must be taken are the following:

1. Present or past pathology of one cerebral hemisphere
2. Language, *lingua,* or symbolization disturbance
3. Vestibular proprioceptive or cerebellar abnormalities

Other rapid nonmedical screening tests that can help doctors to arrive at a diagnosis are the following:

1. Thought (objective, logical)
2. Auditory discrimination

3. Visual symbolic recognition
4. Spatial relationships
5. Body awareness
6. Temporal relationships
7. Laterality (body potential, body preferences, and hemispheric symbolization)
8. Comprehension (verbal absurdities)
9. Speech
10. Perceptual integration

According to these data, doctors can provide useful medical guidelines for learning-disabled children and for their therapists and teachers.

NOTES

1. A. R. Luria, *Higher Cortical Functions in Man* (B. Haigh, trans.) (London: Tavistock Publications, 1966); A. L. Christensen, *Luria's Neuropsychological Investigation* (Copenhagen: Munksgaard, 1975).

2. N. I. Oseretsky, "Technique of Investigating Motor Functions," in M. Gurevich and N. Oseretsky, *Psychomotor Functions* (Moscow: Medgiz, 1930).

3. H. Hecaen, *Introduction a la Neuropsycholgie* (Paris: Larousse, 1972); A. L. Benton, "Developmental Dyslexia: Neurological Aspect," in W. J. Friedlander (ed.), *Advances in Neurology* (New York: Raven Press, 1975); A. R. Luria, *El Cerebro en Accion* (M. Torres, trans.) (Barcelona: Ed. Fontanella, 1974).

4. M. C. Templin, *Certain Language Skills in Children*, Institute of Child Welfare, Monograph Number 26 (Minneapolis: University of Minnesota Press, 1957); J. M. Wepman, *Auditory Discrimination Test* (Chicago: author, 1958); N. A. Buktenica, *Test of Nonverbal Auditory Discrimination (TENVAD)* (Chicago: Follett Publishing Company, 1975).

5. C. Van Riper, *Speech Correction Principles and Methods* (Englewood Cliffs, New Jersey: Prentice-Hall, 1954).

6. J. Eisenson, *Examining for Aphasia* (New York: The Psychological Corporation, 1954); J. M. Wepman and L. V. Jones, *The Language Modalities Test for Aphasia* (Chicago: The Industrial Relations Center, University of Chicago, 1961); H. Schuell, *Differential Diagnosis of Aphasia with the Minnesota Test* (Minneapolis: University of Minnesota Press, 1965); H. Goodglass and E. Kaplan, *The Assessment of Aphasia and Related Disorders* (Philadelphia: Lea & Febiger, 1972); J. J. McCarthey and S. A. Kirk, *Illinois Test of Psycholinguistic Abilities* (rev. ed.) (Urbana: University of Illinois Press, 1968); S. A. Kirk, *"Illinois Test of Psycholinguistic Abilities:* Its Origin and Implications," in J. Hellmuth (ed.), *Learning Disorders*, Volume 3 (Seattle: Special Child Publications, 1968).

7. J. B. de Quirós, "Lengua y Lenguaje," *Fonoaudiologica* [Buenos Aires] 21:3 (1975) 4-20.

8. M. Frostig, W. Lefever, and J. R. B. Whittlesey, *Administration and Scoring Manual for the Marianne Frostig Developmental Test of Visual Perception* (Palo Alto: Consulting Psychologists Press, 1960); A. L. Benton, *The Revised Visual Retention Test* (3rd ed.) (Iowa City, Iowa: The State University of Iowa; New York: The Psychological Corporation, 1963).

9. J. B. de Quirós, *Accelerated Speech Audiometry, An Examination of Test Results*, Translations of the Beltone Institute for Hearing Research, Number 17 (Chicago: Beltone, 1964); J. M. Tato and J. B. de Quirós, "Die Sensibilisierte Sprachaudiometrie," *Acta Otolaryngologica* [Stockholm] 51:6 (1960): 593-614; J. B. de Quirós, "La Logoaudiometria Sensibilizada: Su Estado Actual," *Actas del Decimo Congreso Argentino de Otorinolaringologia* (Buenos Aires: Edit. Artes y Ciencias, 1968): 496-518.

10. A. A. Azzi, "Clinical Application of Binaural Audiometry," *International Audiology* [Leyden] 32 (1964): 197-205; E. Bocca, G. P. Teatini, and R. Antonelli, "Binaural Hearing," *International Audiology* [Leyden] 3:2 (1964): 193-196; N. D'Elia, "Aporte del Examen de la Audicion Hacia la Diferenciacion de Algunos Sindromes," *Fonoaudiologica* [Buenos Aires] 16 (1970): 133-136; T. C. Greene, "The Ability to Localize Sound (A Study of Binaural Hearing in Patients with Tumor of the Brain)," *Archives of Surgery* 18:2 (1929): 18-25; J. J. Groen, "Binaural Hearing: Introduction," *International Audiology* [Leyden] 3:2 (1964): 167-169; J. P. A. Lochner and F. J. Burger, "The Binaural Summation of Speech Signals," *Acustica* 11 (1961): 313-317; J. B. de Quiro's, "Importancia Diagnostica de la Audicion Direccional," *Grupo de Acusticos Latino-Americanos* [Cordoba, Argentina] 1:3 (1968): 44-48; G. A. Sedee, "The Volume of Coherence Necessary in Directional Hearing," *International Audiology* 5:2 (1966): 127-132; F. M. Tonning, "Directional Audiometry," *Acta Otolaryngologica* [Stockholm] 69 (1970): 388; *idem*, 72 (1971a): 352; *idem*, 72 (1971b): 404; *idem*, 73 (1972a): 44; *idem*, 74 (1972b): 37; *idem*, 74 (1972c): 206.

11. Quiro's, "Importancia Diagnostica . . .," *loc. cit.*

12. J. B. de Quiro's and N. D'Elia, *La Audiometria del Adulto y del Nino* (Buenos Aires: Ed. Paidos, 1974).

13. E. Boder, "Developmental Dyslexia: A Diagnostic Approach Based on Three Atypical Reading-Spelling Patterns," *Developmental Medicine and Child Neurology* 15:5 (1973): 663-687; E. Boder, "Developmental Dyslexia: A Diagnostic Screening Procedure Based on Three Characteristic Patterns of Reading and Spelling," in B. D. Bateman (ed.), *Learning Disorders*, Volume 4 (Seattle: Special Child Publications, 1971).

14. R. Magnus, *Korperstellung* (Berlin: Springer, 1924).

15. A. Gesell, "The Tonic-neck Reflex in the Human Infant," *Journal of Pediatrics* 13 (1938): 455; R. S. Paine and T. E. Oppe, *Neurological Examination of Children*, Clinics in Developmental Medicine 20-21 (London: Spastics Society with W. Heinemann, 1966).

16. R. Tokizane, M. Murao, T. Ogata, and T. Kondo, "Electromyographic Studies on Tonic-neck, Lumbar and Labyrinthine Reflexes in Normal Persons," *Japanese Journal of Physiology* 2 (1951): 130.

17. T. Fukuda, "Studies on Dynamic Postures from the Viewpoint of Postural Reflexes," *Acta Otolaryngologica* [Stockholm] Supplement 161.

18. F. A. Hellebrandt, M. Schade, and M. L. Carns, "Methods of Evoking the Tonic-neck Reflexes in Normal Human Subjects," *American Journal of Physical Medicine* 41 (1962): 90.

19. C. Parr, D. K. Routh, M. T. Byrd, and J. McMillan, "A Developmental Study of the Asymmetrical Tonic-neck Reflex," *Developmental Medicine and Child Neurology* 16 (1974): 329-335.

20. G. P. McCouch, I. D. Deering, and T. H. Ling, "Location of Receptors for Tonic-neck Reflexes," *Journal of Neurophysiology* 14 (1951): 191; M. Bridge Denckla, "Development in Speed Repetitive and Successive Finger Movements in Normal Children," *Developmental Medicine and Child Neurology* 15 (1973) 5: 635-645; L. Eviatar, A. Eviatar, and I. Naray, "Maturation of Neurovestibular Responses in Infants," *Developmental Medicine and Child Neurology* 16 (1974): 435-446.

21. J. Purdon Martin, "Role of the Vestibular System in the Control of Posture and Movement in Man," in A. V. S. de Reuck and J. Knight (eds), The *CIBA* Foundation, *Myotatic, Kinesthetic and Vestibular Mechanisms* (London: J. & A. Churchill Ltd., 1967): 92-96.

22. J. B. de Quiro's, "Diagnosis of Developmental Language Disorders," *Folia Phoniatrica* [Basel] 26 (1974): 13-32; J. B. de Quiro's, "Diagnosis of Vestibular Disorders in the Learning Disabled," *Journal of Learning Disabilities* 9:1 (1976): 39-47.

23. J. B. de Quiro's and M. Della Cella, "La Dislexia como Sintoma y como Sindrome," *Acta Neuropsiquiatrica Argentina* 5:2 (1959): 178-193; J. B. de Quiro's, M. Della

Cella, D. Carrara, and L. Allegro, *Estudios Sobre la Dislexia Infantil* (Santa Fe, Argentina: Ministerio de Educacion y Cultura, 1962); J. B. de Quiros, "Dysphasic Symptoms in School Children as Manifestation of Central Deafness," *International Audiology* [Leyden] 1 (1962): 95-104; J. B. de Quiros, "Dysphasia and Dyslexia in School Children," *Folia Phoniatrica* [Basel] 16:3 (1964): 201-222; J. B. de Quiros and M. Della Cella, *La Dislexia en la Ninez* (Buenos Aires: Ed. Paidos, 1965); J. B. de Quiros, "Vestibular-proprioceptive Integration: Its Influence on Learning and Speech in Children," in *Proceedings of the Tenth International Congress of Psychology* (April 3-7, 1966, Lima, Peru; Mexico: Trillas, 1967): 194-202.

24.   J. Frank and H. N. Levinson, "Dysmetric Dyslexia and Dyspraxia–Hypothesis and Study," *The Journal of the American Academy of Child Psychiatry* 12 (1973): 690-701; J. Frank and H. N. Levinson, "Dysmetric Dyslexia and Dyspraxia. Synopsis of a Continuing Research Project," *Academic Therapy* 11:2 (Winter 1975-76): 133-143.

25   D. G. Cogan and J. B. Wurster, "Normal and Abnormal Ocular Movements," in F. A. Young and D. B. Lindsley (eds.), *Early Experience and Visual Information Processing in Perceptual and Reading Disorders* (Washington, D.C.: National Academy of Sciences, 1970).

26.   J. B. de Quiros, "Vestibular-propriorecptive Integration . . .," *loc. cit.*

27.   E. Hammerberg and M. S. Norn, "Defective Dissociation or Accommodation and Convergence in Dyslectic Children," *Acta Ophtalmologica* [Stockholm] 50 (1972): 651-654.

NEUROPSYCHOLOGICAL FUNDAMENTALS

CHAPTER XI

Postural-Motor Training in Vestibular Learning Disorders

(78) REVIEW OF VESTIBULAR ANATOMO-FUNCTIONAL RELATIONSHIPS
(79) VESTIBULAR APPARATUS AND BEHAVIOR
(80) VESTIBULAR APPARATUS, SPEECH,
AND LEARNING DISABILITIES
(81) VESTIBULAR TRAINING FOR
VESTIBULAR HANDICAPPED ADULTS AND CHILDREN
(82) GENERAL APPROACH OF REMEDIATION/
SEQUENCING POSTURAL-MOTOR TRAINING
(83) REMEDIAL PRINCIPLES FOR VESTIBULAR DYSFUNCTIONS
AND OTHER LEARNING DISABILITIES
(84) THERAPY IN VESTIBULAR HANDICAPPED SCHOOL CHILDREN
(85) BODY AWARENESS TRAINING
(86) BALANCE AND LATERALITY
(87) VISION, POSTURE, EQUILIBRIUM, AND SPACE

(78) REVIEW OF VESTIBULAR ANATOMO-FUNCTIONAL RELATIONSHIPS

So that we may present the main subject of this chapter as accurately and clearly as possible, it seems worthwhile to review here and in section 80 some of the vestibular anatomo-functional relationships discussed in earlier pages.

The inner ear in humans has auditory and nonauditory organs. The cochlea is the auditory organ dedicated to hearing, while the vestibular apparatus (also called the labyrinth) is the nonauditory organ dedicated to posture, equilibrium, muscular tonus, and spatial orientation. We should remember that the word "vestibule" in human anatomy means only a part of the vestibular apparatus or labyrinth: It is formed by the saccule and the utricle. The vestibular apparatus also controls the movements of the eyes (through the vestibular-oculomotor pathways) and many other functions connected with intentional and coordinated movements. (The term "intentional movements" connotes purposeful movements, consciously or unconsciously made by the individual: They are not always voluntary!) The vestibular apparatus specifically responds to gravitational forces and accelerated or decelerated movements. Any movement (and chiefly linear and rotatory movements), and spatial modification of head position, any bone vibration of the head, can stimulate the vestibular receptors. These stimulations create inputs which have consequences primarily in posture and equilib-

This chapter originated as a lecture belonging to a symposium by Julio B. de Quiros, presented by the University of Michigan, Institute for the Study of Mental Retardation and Related Disabilities, in conjunction with the Office of Continuing Medical Education, Towsley Center (University of Michigan), Ann Arbor, February 27-28, 1978.

rium, muscular tonus, skilled movements of the eyes and, secondarily, eye-hand coordination.

Posture and equilibrium both depend on three principal actions: vestibular input, vision, and proprioception. Throughout infancy and childhood, these three actions are increasingly coordinated by the cerebellum. Consequently, remedial treatment oriented toward posture and equilibrium must include visual, haptic, and coordination exercises. (The term "haptic," we recall, means kinesthesis plus tactual input.)

Muscular tonus, skilled movements of the eyes, and complex eye-hand coordination are extremely important for the complex process of human learning. If early vestibular abnormalities exist, they can prevent the development of learning achievements (speech, *lingua*, reading, and writing). Everybody knows that speech and writing require movement. Some of the disorders of speech and writing, therefore, can be easily explained through vestibular disturbances. Reading ability absolutely requires skilled movements of the eyes: Without this, it is very difficult for one to learn to read normally.

The vestibular apparatus, mainly through descending vestibular-spinal fibers and through vestibular-cerebellar interconnections, can produce stabilization of the whole body—stabilization that human symbolic learning requires. When vestibular-cerebellar and/or vestibular-spinal controls have failed, symbolic learning can be developed therapeutically to increase stability of the whole body.

(79) VESTIBULAR APPARATUS AND BEHAVIOR

In 1933, P. Schilder stated his assumption that there are vestibular influences on human behavior.[1] He provided a theory in order to relate vestibular disorders to neurosis and psychosis (schizophrenia). He suggested that many behavioral symptoms could be explained by vestibular impairment. Schilder's theoretical approach to the role of the otoliths (which take part in vestibular reception) is no longer considered as a primary factor in schizophrenia. None of the symptoms associated with vestibular impairments in adults are found here: ataxia, falling, spontaneous nystagmus, nausea, etc. On the other hand, in adult schizophrenia a wide variety of unusual vestibular responses (marginally normal or abnormal) is found.

In 1958, M. Pollack and H. P. Krieger observed schizophrenics during caloric, rotatory, and optokinetic stimulation.[2] These authors have found that schizophrenics cannot dissociate head and eye movements with optokinetic stimuli and that they may also exhibit defective righting reflexes.

The reader can consult the review of some experiments related to vestibular-proprioceptive disturbances in children in Chapter IX, Section 67.

In 1959, the team of G. Colbert, R. R. Koegler, and C. H. Markham described vestibular impairment in childhood schizophrenia.[3] According to these authors, among all children having vestibular dysfunction, 98 percent were probably schizophrenics. Shortly thereafter, in 1960, those results were discussed by B. Rosenblut, R. Goldstein, and W. M. Landau, because they found similar results among "aphasic" children.[4] During the 1950s many people spoke about "infantile aphasia." Even now, some people still maintain this label. But "aphasia" means loss of language, and it is not possible to lose something you never had. Infants don't have language. They cannot, therefore, lose it. Most authors have used such a label to mean "a child who does not talk due to some neurological cause."

Other authors, at about the same time, began to find vestibular impairments in different cases, such as those with secondary learning and language disabilities. For instance, N. Torok and M. A. Perlstein (1962) found vestibular disorders among 34 percent of cerebral palsied children.[5]

There are other studies which confirmed (directly or indirectly) the existence of vestibular deficits in schizophrenic children: For example, the decreased muscle tone and rotation of the body following gentle rotation of the head suggested childhood schizophrenia for A. A. Silver and H. P. Gabriel.[6] In recent years E. M. Ornitz has also made important contributions to our knowledge of vestibular dysfunction in childhood schizophrenia.[7]

As can be seen, the vestibular apparatus, which is functionally related mainly to posture and equilibrium, seems to be impaired in a high percentage of individuals with learning disabilities—in particular, those dysfunctions related to symbolic communication.

(80) VESTIBULAR APPARATUS, SPEECH, AND LEARNING DISABILITIES

Researchers are becoming increasingly interested in the relationship between motor activity and learning. We should remember that the vestibular apparatus has a strong connection with motor activity. Vestibular input establishes the necessary muscular tonus that every movement requires. Perhaps the pioneering research for these relationships was established by H. Wallon, N. C. Kephart, and G. N. Getman.[8] Other leading authors who are developing significant new clinical criteria on posture and action related to learning are R. H. Barsch, A. J. Ayres, J. Frank and H. N. Levinson, L. C. Erway, and G. Harris.[9] Our own work can be consulted, likewise, in several publications.[10]

Perhaps the first author to mention vestibular influences on speech was A. Precechtel (from Prague) in his 1925 article, "Congenital Defect of Otolithic Apparatus."[11] According to him, congenital defect was characterized by: (1) abnormal intrauterine position of the fetus; (2) difficulties in maintaining static positions in the first year of postnatal life; (3) delay of speech; and (4) lack of responses to vestibular caloric tests (whether or not there are responses to rotatory tests). Precechtel's work is open to criticism. The principal criticism against Precechtel's work is that Precechtel described only few cases with a lack of otoliths. The lack of such organs is very rare in infants. Another argument against Precechtel's syndrome is that fetuses with otolithic disturbances many times have normal intrauterine postures. The syndromes which show abnormal vestibular responses are much more frequent than Precechtel's one. Other causes can produce the same symptoms: viruses, infections, toxic substances, trauma, and so on. It is possible, therefore, to accept the existence of the syndrome described by Precechtel; but some of the symptoms he specifies must be revised and others must be added to his first description: Muscular hypotonia, restlessness, the drive to be in motion, frequent distractibility, and superimposed emotional disturbances are the most significant ones.

It is necessary to bear in mind that vestibular abnormalities can be "pure," or combined with other central dysfunctions. It seems that the situation is similar to that of deaf children: Many times they are not totally deaf. The principal point to recognize is the existence of vestibular impairments in some children and to differentiate them from others who have no disturbance at that level. In 1962 our own research group was very confused by the vestibular results obtained in a group of slow learners and normal learners: They were comparable in both groups. Similar experiments with the same conclusions were made independently by H. McHugh in Canada.[12] We shall repeat here some data already mentioned earlier in this book. From 1963 on, we recommenced the investigation of vestibular dysfunctions in young children. The choice of children was then made using another criterion: learning difficulty without apparently justifiable cause. This study brought some satisfaction: Out of 63 cases, fully tested, 52 did not have normal vestibular responses with caloric stimuli.[13]

(81) VESTIBULAR TRAINING FOR VESTIBULAR HANDICAPPED ADULTS AND CHILDREN

Several authors, such as T. Cawthorne, D. F. McCabe, and H. P. Voisin and J. Boussens, have written about labyrinthine exercises for vestibular handicapped individuals.[14] McCabe looks for improvement such as disappearance of the handicaps in posture, muscular tonus, and equilibrium, so that free, voluntary movements may finally be obtained. Exercises include many explanations and suggestions to the patient, for instance, this encouraging advice: "Essentially, seek out that which is hardest for you to do. Practice it, bear it, master it!" Voisin and Boussens advocate rehabilitation of balance in vestibular disorders, in central disorders of the vestibular pathways, and in certain neurological disorders (with or without vestibular involvement). They use three approaches: proprioceptive, visuomotor, and auditory (stereophonic awareness). According to them, "For complete rehabilitation, static balance is tackled first, followed by balance while walking."[15]

There are not many training programs for adults having vestibular diseases; moreover, relationships between therapists and adults are quite different than relationships between therapists and children. It is very easy to introduce strict commands for an adult, but it is very difficult to do the same thing with a child. In general, when the therapist is working with adults it is not necessary to introduce toys or incentives. With children this could be indispensable for success (e.g., "Do you know how the snake moves? It moves like this . . ."). This kind of explanation is simply idiotic when a therapist is working with an adult. It is worthwhile to remember that many adults suffering vestibular damage are not helped at all by the use of these exercises. Only some cases can be improved through these measures, especially when they are treated when the onset and the acute period of the condition are overcome. Motor exercises are strictly forbidden when dizziness is still present.

Therapists have to work very much with vestibular damaged adults in training relaxation. Therapists working with vestibular impaired children, on the contrary, have much to do with development of the cerebellum and other allied mechanisms related to balance and muscular tonus. Consequently, therapists of vestibular impaired children must use movements and actions in a well-structured program which must emphasize posture, muscular tonus, and equilibrium as well as development or remediation in all perceptual modalities.

(82) GENERAL APPROACH OF REMEDIATION/ SEQUENCING POSTURAL-MOTOR TRAINING

Therapy of primary learning disabilities must be programed according to the specific diagnosis obtained in each case. It is obvious that therapeutic approaches will demand several criteria according to the following assumed conditions:

1. Vestibular dysfunctions
   a. vestibular-proprioceptive dissociation
   b. vestibular-oculomotor split
2. Discrimination handicaps
3. Cerebral dysfunctions
   a. dyslexia
   b. dysphasia
   c. apractognosia

Certainly, remediation must emphasize three different paths: (1) vestibular-proprioceptive and vestibular-oculomotor integrations, (2) perceptual modalities, and (3) symbolic thought. It is worth remembering that primary integration of the postural system is obtained at the third year of age. Some externalizations of this phenomenon are the ability to perform Romberg's test without difficulty and the ability to avoid synkinesis when the thumb of one hand successively touches the tips of the other four fingers. Romberg's test indicates clearly that, without vision and with only proprioception and vestibular inputs, balance can be controlled. This is a tremendous step in the development of equilibrium, posture, tonus, and therefore intentional and coordinated motor activities which are basic for human learning processes. The other test (the oppositional finger test) also shows the ability of each side of the body to act independently, prior to the establishment of laterality. Training directed to the division of the body into two halves and then to the establishment of prevalent preferred laterality can be very useful. It is important to recall that vestibular-proprioceptive integration takes part in laterality. When proprioceptive action increases on one side of the body, vestibular reaction also increases on the same side, and vice versa. Vestibular-proprioceptive dissociation disrupts this kind of integration.

This shall be one of our premises in the following sections of this chapter. Many other thoughts about remediation of each of the primary learning disabilities can be found in different parts of Chapter XII.

Before continuing with the discussion of the subject of this section, it is worth our while to recall that the sequence or order of exercises in postural-motor training must be programed by the therapist. Often, such a sequence is established according to the developmental stages in normal children. Therapists, nevertheless, must realize that development is the result of evolution, maturation, and learning. Development depends, therefore, on many variables, the most important being biological (or neuromuscular) and environmental. When these variables change (and in abnormal children they do change!), development also changes. In abnormal children some achievements are delayed (that is, there is an abnormal developmental pattern). What is most essential, is for the therapist to recognize the needs of each child and to understand fully the basis or principles which underlie his therapy. Then, the necessary modifications can be made to meet the needs of each patient, in accord with accepted therapeutic principles, resources, and sequences.

Another criterion of postural-motor training is the neuropsychological. The neuropsychological approach must consider the relationships existing between (1) the spine and muscular tonus; (2) the brain stem and the cerebellum, and equilibrium, coordination of movements, and sensory discrimination; and (3) the cerebrum, and perceptions, symbolization, language, and human learning abilities. Any central nervous system structure or pathway related to vestibular apparatus takes a specific part in posture and equilibrium. Study of posture and equilibrium, therefore, permit program modifications in the general training of vestibular handicaps.

A third criterion of postural-motor training is concerned mainly with four areas: (1) body awareness, (2) motor action, (3) perceptual modalities, and (4) motor verbalizations. In each of these four areas, specific exercises can improve postures and motor abilities.

Our approach to vestibular therapy employs the three criteria just mentioned, but also employs the knowledge of relevant world literature on sensory-motor, psychomotor, motor development, and sensory integration. Let us cite alphabetically some few writers of several books in English: A. J. Ayres, R. H. Barsch, B. J. Cratty, M. Frostig, G. N. Getman, B. Holle, and N. C. Kephart.[16]

A general therapeutic approach to vestibular disorders might primarily include posture training, balance training, and visual training. Of course, these three divisions are empirically based on the fact that posture, balance, and vision interact with one another. On the other hand exercises also must train auditory and tactile modalities.

(83) REMEDIAL PRINCIPLES FOR VESTIBULAR DYSFUNCTIONS AND OTHER LEARNING DISABILITIES

It is impossible to speak about remediation of vestibular dysfunctions without speaking first about the important contributions of many authors on sensory-motor, psychomotor, motor development, and sensory integration approaches. For instance, many of Jean Ayres' approaches are ideal for this purpose. We cannot mention here all the outstanding world literature on this topic; but certainly we can cite (alphabetically) some few relevant books in English and French: Ajuriaguerra (1970); Ajuriaguerra and Bonvalot-Soubiran (1959); Ayres (1973); Barsch (1965, 1967-1968); Benos (1972); Cratty (1974); Defontaine (1976); Frostig (1970); Frostig and Maslow (1973); Getman (1967); Kephart (1960); Le Boulch (1966); Maigre and

Destrooper (1976); and Wallon (1949).[17] The interested reader can find further information in these sources.

In general, traditional remediation techniques related to motor skills have been established on a developmental basis. We do not believe that "normal" developmental approaches are sufficient. We also believe in "abnormal motor patterns" and in pathological ones.

B. Bobath and K. Bobath defined "abnormal motor patterns" as those not seen at any stage of a normal full-term baby's development. We accept, of course, this definition; but we accept also a wider term such as "pathological motor pattern." We can define "pathological motor pattern" as: (1) any abnormal motor pattern; (2) any delay in motor patterns; and (3) any deviation or distortion in normal motor patterns.[18]

Similarly, we can define "pathological developmental pattern" as: (1) any abnormal developmental pattern; (2) any delay in developmental patterns; and (3) any deviation or distortion in normal developmental patterns. According to these criteria in learning-disabled children, there are pathological developmental patterns. The same occurs in cerebral palsy, mental retardation, deafness or blindness, epilepsy, etc.

For these reasons, individual approaches are needed for remedial actions with disabled children. In spite of this, there is only one reasonable technique which provides remedial therapies for groups of learning-disabled children and particularly for vestibular dysfunctions. This technique consists of training of the different factors which make up the neuropsychological fundamentals of learning. It is therefore necessary to train the following levels:

1. The spine
   a. tonus
2. The brain stem and cerebellum
   a. equilibrium
   b. coordination of movements
   c. sensory discrimination
3. The cerebrum
   a. perceptions
   b. symbolization
   c. *lingua* and language
   d. human learning abilities

As can be seen, the second and third levels mainly correspond to sensory discrimination and *lingua* and language.

We cannot divide these three levels precisely because there are so many and different various nervous pathways. The therapist, therefore, can check how learning abilities are developing in each child; and, according to the results obtained, he can program individual or group remediation.

When the therapist knows the relationship between functions and anatomical pathways, he is much better prepared to act than he would be otherwise. With these criteria it might be convenient to recall here some well-known tracts and their functional connections. If some specific functions are disturbed, therapists must act to combine work procedures, methods, and systems specifically directed to compensate or to improve the principal "lag" observed. Every tract refers to different skills, but also various tracts serve only one skill. This knowledge allows the therapist to introduce several "allied" activities and abilities in order to ameliorate certain dysfunctions. Thus, vestibular dysfunctions can be very much improved.

Let us review some of the more important tracts related to vestibular functions. The descriptions which follow are very skeletal, and must be "fleshed out" by employing many exercises that can be found in the books mentioned earlier in this section. In these descriptions only some general instructions are given.

Fasciculus gracilis and fasciculus cuneatus (Goll's tract and Burdach's tract). Phylogenetically speaking, they are recent. These tracts are the principal pathways for discriminatory (or "epicritic") sensitivity. These fasciculi are strongly connected with proprioception (posture and movement), space-skin discriminations, vibrations (i.e., time-skin discrimination). Kinesthetic and tactile stimuli travel through these pathways ("haptic" information). For remediation, use skin cognition; skin stimulation; proprioceptive stimuli; kinesthetic (haptic) stimuli; vibration; body emphasis.

Spino-thalamic and spino-tectal tracts (anterior, dorsal, and ventral). These different tracts are related to somesthesis, pressure, pain, temperature, and to their affective or emotional characteristics. Through these tracts the information related to "corporal space" is structured. For remediation, try exercises with slight stimulation of large muscles; applying pressure; localized stimulation with heat and cold.

Spino-cerebellar tracts (dorsal or Flechsig's tract; crossed or Gowers' tract). Proprioceptive information arrives at the cerebellum through these. Voluntary action is tonically and synergically controlled. For remediation, employ synergic movements; skilled synergic movements; coordinated movements.

Spino-olivar and spino-spinal tracts. These are proprioceptive reciprocal pathways. They govern reciprocal movements. For remediation, use reciprocal exercises; diadokokinesis; imitation of deep postures without visual feedback.

Spino-reticular and spino-cortical tracts. Use exteroceptive approaches.

Cortico-spinal, extra-pyramidal, and reticular-spinal tracts. Facilitating or inhibiting impulses are transmitted from the brain stem to the anterior horns of the spine (motoneurons). Their main function is in regulating muscular together with vestibular-spinal tonus. For remediation, use voluntary movements; blocks (for instance, walking upon or between blocks); fine-motor movements (for instance, finger movements).

External and medial vestibular-spinal tracts. These control balance positions: dynamic postures and equilibrium in soft surfaces. For remediation, use balance exercises (upon toes, heels, edges of feet, backwards, forewards, upon different boards and runways); jumping; hopping; etc.; actions with movements of the head; free positions in activities.

Rubro-spinal tracts. These have to do with postural regulation and cerebellar participation. For remediation, use bilateral alternating kinesis.

Tecto-spinal and tecto-medullar tracts. These control reflex activities as a response to auditory and visual stimuli. For remediation, use auditory and visual stimuli which provoke motor activities.

Medial longitudinal fasciculus and short-spine fasciculi. They connect segmentary interrelations and tonus, posture, and equilibrium. For remediation, use partial and segmentary contraction and relaxation.

Sequence of exercises. In regard to vestibular-oculomotor exercises, it must be pointed out that they belong to a sequence which always follows the following steps:

I. Visuo-haptic-motor
II. Audio-haptic-motor
III. Visuo-motor
IV. Audio-motor
V. Vision
VI. Audition
VII. Audio-visuo-motor

This sequence must be followed according to the several procedures that can be found in many series of exercises introduced in this same chapter. It is important also to review the books already mentioned in this section because they contain many relevant suggestions and pertinent observations.

If some theoretical concepts about vestibular-oculomotor split are new, empirical remediation has been well known from antiquity.

In relation to discrimination handicaps and cerebral dysfunctions, many of the traditional approaches, summarized in Sections 80, 81, and 82, can be useful. Also, examination procedures can help in order to suggest new courses of action and better remediation techniques.

(84) THERAPY IN VESTIBULAR HANDICAPPED SCHOOL CHILDREN

In order to carry out vestibular exercises, one must have a large room which can be darkened, since in many circumstances it might be appropriate to work without using visual information.

Relationships between the therapist and the child must be psychologically viable. If necessary, supplementary psychotherapy should be provided.

Some tools which allow for the desired vestibular therapy are the following: hard surfaces, soft surfaces, stairs, barrier-stairs, incline-boards, changing-consistency boards, movable boards (hemicylinders), bricks, balls, large balls, trampolines, spring boards, scooterboards, hammocks, a torsion-swing chair (manual rotatory chairs are avoided), portable mirrors, and a platform scale.

With such equipment in mind, let us use the next several pages to review the following principles and exercises:

A. Posture and position
B. Kinesthesis and proprioception
C. Body awareness training
D. Body recognition and body verbalization
E. Body action
F. Vibration (or palesthesis)
G. Body and postural imitation

H. Body representation
I. Haptic exercises
J. Exercising different modalities together
K. Body division
L. Preferent and prevalent body laterality
M. Balance and postural integration
N. Corporal potentiality
O. Effort exercises
P. Exigency exercises
Q. Acceleration and deceleration exercises
R. Vision, posture, equilibrium, and space
S. Visual and eye-hand exercises

In the course of this chapter we will describe these items as they are advocated for use with six- to seven-year-old school children.

A. *Posture and position.* Posture is the reflex activity of the body in relation to space (i.e., flexed [bent], or extended [stretched] tonic postures). Posture is based on muscular tonus: It is chiefly related to the body. Posture (like equilibrium) is established upon vestibular, proprioceptive, and visual influences coordinated by the cerebellum. Position concerns the typical postures of a species (e.g., sitting in cats is different than sitting in humans).

1. Therapists must exercise the child in different positions: supine, prone, quadruped, sitting, standing, tandem walking (toe-heel), standing on one leg, and so on.

2. It is important to determine whether, with passive or active turning of the head (i.e., the therapist manually imposes the head movement, or verbally directs the patient to perform the voluntary movement), primitive or remnant reflexes (such as asymmetric tonic neck reflexes) are elicited. For instance, after six months of age (in the supine position), the asymmetric tonic neck reflex is abnormal; the presence of such a reflex is considered "primitive." Exercises to reduce primitive reflexes must follow developmental patterns.

3. At the same time, the asymmetric tonic neck reflex (upon passive turning of the head) could be normal until eight years of age in the quadruped position. Thus, exercise to reduce this reflex action is not indicated. As a matter of fact, any "primitive" reflex can reappear when the patient's positions, and neuromuscular or environmental conditions, are changed: This reflex is no longer called "primitive," but "remnant." Differentiation between primitive and remnant reflexes is very important. Primitive reflexes need special treatment; remnant reflexes generally do not.

4. Introduce relaxation, contraction, flexion, extension.

5. Instruct the child to maintain an erect position when standing on tiptoes, on both sides of the feet, and the heels.

NEUROPSYCHOLOGICAL FUNDAMENTALS

6. If postures or positions are abnormal, corrective exercises must then be instituted to counteract them.

B. Kinesthesis and proprioception. Proprioception is the sensitivity provided by proprioceptors (i.e., by receptors in muscles, tendons, and joints). Muscular movements produce a sensitivity recognized as kinesthesis. Only through kinesthesis can a person adopt specific postures and positions of the species; this enables him to control his own body and the position of his own head in order to learn. It is a fundamental sensitivity for mankind. Kinesthesis and proprioception act together with vestibular and visual inputs on the one hand, and according to gravitational forces on the other, to produce the necessary postural equilibrium throughout movement. The term "haptic" includes simultaneous sensory information arising from kinesthetic and tactual (or skin) input.

7. Exercises using walking, jumping, kicking, hopping, and so on, can help very much in kinesthetic development.
8. Activities entailing forward, backward, upward, downward, sideward motions are used.
9. Use of various supports attached to the child's shoes is recommended for walking and other motor exercises.
10. Use various kinds of surfaces or platforms: wide-narrow, low-high, hard-soft.
11. Have the child walk laterally, walk laterally with feet crossed, walk with abrupt stops, tandem-walk (toe-heel).

The therapist must differentiate voluntary movements from dynamic equilibrium situations. In voluntary movements the first impulse is given by motor activity itself (information of such a movement given by kinesthesis). In dynamic equilibrium situations, the action of kinesthesis (plus vestibular and visual inputs) is produced against gravitational forces: In this case the first impulse is kinesthetic (plus vestibular and visual); and the result is the maintenance of equilibrium at any moment of any dynamic situation. Consequently this type of exercise must be complemented by balance exercises (see Section 86).

(85) BODY AWARENESS TRAINING

C. Body awareness training. The notion of body awareness is internationally well known. It includes body schema, body image, body insight, and body concept. Body schema is the reception, registration, and memory at the higher cerebral levels, mainly of neuromuscular and haptic action resulting from all the deep parts and tissues which contribute to maintain a position in a static or dynamic situation. Body schema is quite different from kinesthesis and proprioception. While the latter two are related to sensitivity (i.e., to information from the body), the former, body schema (with H. Head's approach), is more connected with cortical reception, registration, and the formation of traces (or engrams) at the higher cortical levels.[19] Body image is a notion referring to the feelings, information, or experiences given by the body itself (haptic and sensory inputs, emotional reactions, and social influences). According to P. Schilder, the image of the human body means the picture of our own body which we form in our mind.[20] Finally, body insight is the nonverbal knowledge of the body, which is the beginning of body concept (i.e., the verbalized knowledge that a person has about his own body). Many writers (ourselves included) have developed body awareness exercises. Recognition of the parts and functions of one's own body seem to be fascinating to children. Independently of data obtained through the case history of the child's development, it is important to remember that normal children, between five and six years of age, are able to recognize the parts of their bodies and the bodies of other persons. (They can imitate attitudes in a mirror-like situation.) Exercises correspond to items D through J in our alphabetical list in Section 84.

D. Body recognition and body verbalization. As is well known, body awareness has four main levels, which can be consulted in Chapter II, Section 11 (and also in the Glossary): body schema, body image, body insight, and body concept. The following exercises correspond chiefly to the last two notions.

12. Through gestures and mimicry, the child recognizes parts of the body in the mother, in a doll, in himself, in a drawing, and so on.
13. With verbal commands alone the child identifies parts of the body in the therapist, in himself, in a drawing. Practice this exercise using the following body parts: "Show me your (my, his) . . . ."
    a. Face, eye, eyes, mouth, nose, ear, ears, hair, teeth, tongue, lip, cheek, chin, forehead, eyebrows, eyelids, eyelashes.
    b. Neck, nape.
    c. Chest, stomach, hip, back.
    d. Hand, elbow, finger, shoulder, wrist, upper arm, forearm, palm.
    e. Foot, knee, toes, hip, ankle, calf.
14. "Move your . . . ," using the same body parts just listed.

E. Body action. Movements of the head particularly stimulate the vestibular organs, and therefore the vestibular apparatus. Movements can be made voluntarily or compensatorily.

15. Voluntary head movements: move the patient's to one side, to the other side; up, down; neck circumgiration; head lateralization.
16. Compensatory head movements: push or pull the patient's body (mainly when he is standing upon sand or soft surfaces). Observe the compensatory movements of his head.
17. Initiate passive movements of relaxed parts of the child's body.
18. Initiate passive movements (against the child's voluntary resistance) of parts of his body. The child is told to per-

form first with eyes open, then closed. The child must then repeat the movement alone.

19. Movement correlated with verbal language: The therapist moves his own hand, for instance, and says at the same time, "I move my ... ," waiting for the child to supply the appropriate name for the body part. Then the child must say, as he performs the action, "I move my ...."

20. Verbal action: The therapist says, "I take the spoon, keeping my elbow bent." ("Do it; tell me what happens.") "I pick up the spoon like this." ("Do it; tell me what happens.") Similar exercises can be developed.

21. Rhythm: The therapist says, "Take this pencil. You must try to tap out the same regular beat with it as I do." It is necessary to correct any modification or irregularity in speed, strength, etc. Then, the exercise should be repeated with the other hand.

22. Rhythm: The therapist says to the child (who is seated in a chair), "Tap regular beats with one foot against the floor .... Now, with the other foot .... Now, with both feet together .... Now, by clapping hands." If necessary, the therapist should correct the child. The correction should be made verbally, by repeating the exercise, or manually upon the child, depending on the child's level of comprehension.

23. Rhythm: The therapist says, "Tap with the pencil very fast .... Now without seeing ... fast ... faster, stop! Now, tap a slow beat; don't stop until I tell you to ... now fast ... slow ... fast ... ," and so on.

24. Repeat similar exercises with the feet.

F. Vibration (or palesthesis). Vibration is an important stimulus for vestibular organs. The lack of vibratory sensitivity in a person is called "apalesthesis," and distortion is called "dyspalesthesis." When this is found, a vibratory stimulus must be employed in exercises. Various instruments can be used: Special tuning forks and commercial vibrators are the most practical ones. These instruments must be applied on the body over certain bony prominences. Some exercises might also be suggested with the child's vision occluded.

25. Both hands are open on the table. Vision is excluded. "Excluded" refers not only to blindfolding the eyes, but much more frequently to interfering with vision by putting a book, a screen, or other object between the child's eyes and his own hands on the table. The child must identify the finger *touched*; then, identify the finger *vibrated.*

26. The therapist may ask the child to identify different places on the body through cutaneous and vibratory stimuli (both sides of the face, both sides of the trunk, both arms, both legs).

27. The therapist may use two different stimuli together, for instance, skin stimulus on the cheek of one face side, vibratory on the cheek and cutaneous on the knee.

The child must differentiate vibration from cutaneous stimuli and point out correctly the two places where each of these stimuli was applied. Does the child have difficulty in recognizing vibration, or cutaneous stimuli, or both? A gross handicap in identification of these stimuli indicates the need for major emphasis in that specific area.

28. Two similar stimuli may be used together, for instance, two tuning forks (one under hearing level [or very grave] and another of 60 Hz) are used in order to vibrate equivalent points of each side of the body. Has the child preference for clear sounds (i.e., a sound modality), or a vibration modality, or both?

G. Body and postural imitation. In physiology, reciprocal movements are very much related to the contraction of some muscular groups at the same time that the relaxation of other opposite muscular group is produced. For instance, in order to kick a ball, or in order to bend the arm, some muscular groups contract and some others relax. Reciprocal movements are synergistic, that is, the faculty by which movements are adjusted according to the needed performances (and also, generally, to the required goals). From a practical point of view it is possible to exercise reciprocal movements by imposing a certain action in a hand or limb and asking at the same time an opposite action on the other hand or limb. Certainly this kind of exercise does not *directly* correspond with reciprocal movements in the same limb or hand, but it is the only way to train these complex abilities easily. When opposite movements are performed with both hands or both limbs, actions must refer to both cerebral hemispheres. In other words, it is indispensable to have sufficient maturity of the central nervous system in order to be able to do this type of task.

29. In reciprocal imitation, one hand is open at the same time the other is closed, and vice versa. This exercise is performed first in the air, then on the table. Various responses will be observed, such as:
    a. The child can imitate the reciprocal movement and the rhythm imposed by the therapist.
    b. The child can imitate the reciprocal movement, but he cannot imitate the rhythm. His movement is not simultaneous. One hand moves first, then the other.
    c. At the beginning the child can imitate reciprocal movements; but he rapidly becomes confused with his own movements; and he cannot follow the movement sequence (both hands act together).
    d. The child cannot imitate the movement or rhythm.

In Chapter X the reader can find some interpretations of these various results. When the child is unable to duplicate the therapist's actions,

NEUROPSYCHOLOGICAL FUNDAMENTALS

then corrective exercises involving movement and rhythm, such as the following, are recommended. The therapist takes the child's hands and imposes rhythmic movements on them. The child must then reproduce those movements. Repeat same rhythms with feet.

30. Tap out a rhythm with a pencil, or with the knuckles of the fist, or with the foot, for the child to imitate.
31. The same as before, but the example is given only through hearing. (Gradually use more complex rhythms.)
32. The same as before, but the example is given only visually.
33. The same as before, but the example is given through cards marked with clearly spaced dots and dashes. This exercise is also "representational" (i.e., it requires visual symbolic recognition), but for didactic reasons it is introduced here.
34. The child must imitate, with his eyes closed, postures and attitudes imposed on him with his eyes open.
35. The child is asked to close his eyes while the therapist stands behind him and positions, for instance, one of his arms horizontally, the other vertically, for a period of several seconds. The child is then asked to open his eyes and demonstrate these positions. The therapist, with a similar technique, can ask for the duplication of many other positions.
36. The child is asked, with his eyes closed, to place his hands in a neutral position on the table. The therapist then passively imposes a different attitude (position) for each hand; after two seconds, the hands are returned to the neutral position. With his eyes open, the child must reproduce the attitudes previously imposed on his hands. Similar exercises should also be applied to the child's feet.
37. Similar exercises can be performed with fingers, and so on.
38. The therapist presents the child with a doll whose posture and limbs are adjustable. The child must then imitate various postures and attitudes of the doll.
39. Pictures illustrating children in various postures and attitudes are presented for the child to imitate.
40. The child is asked to move in the opposite direction from that which the therapist demonstrates: up, down; in front of, behind; and so forth.
41. The child is asked to imitate, with one side of his body, those movements imposed by the therapist on the other side of his body.
42. In a similar manner, the child must now imitate in reverse, with one side of the body, those movements imposed by the therapist on the other side of his body. For instance, if one arm (and the corresponding leg) is bent, the limbs on the other side of the body must be stretched, and vice versa. If the child is not able to recognize "right"

or "left," the therapist must say "with this arm" or "with this leg."

H. Body representation. Imitations, drawings, plays, and language are all representations. When representations are more primitive, they are more individualized. As representations become more developed, they become more socialized or standardized. To explain this further, pay attention to the drawings of a young child, of a child, and of a youngster: As drawings become more developed they can be progressively more readily identified. If a child five years old is drawing a car, he generally must explain to an adult what kind of object he is drawing. Little by little, through development of representations, he will later be able to draw a car which others will recognize as a car.

43. Some tests (such as the *Draw-a-Person*) are extremely important for assessing body awareness.
44. Other representational exercises of special interest are those concerning identification of shapes, signs, or symbols drawn by the therapist's index finger on the skin of the child's forearm while his eyes are closed.
45. Another exercise consists of tracing in the air, with the child's hand, movements which correspond to shapes, signs, or symbols.
46. When the child is not able to recognize the shapes (with eyes shut), the therapist asks him to open his eyes and follow the movement.
47. Puzzles that, when put together, form a picture of a person's head, face, body, etc., can be very useful.

Disturbances in body representation influence children adversely, to produce feelings of insecurity; this is often manifested through negative behavior. The child needs assistance and emotional support in helping him to develop body awareness. The child's lack of adequate body awareness may be demonstrated by exaggerated tenderness, caresses, and need to handle everything in his surroundings, and we refer to this as "affectivity"; a contrasting behavior which also suggests poor body awareness is "aggressivity," in which there is pushing, fighting, and on occasion, temper tantrums.

I. Haptic exercises. The term "haptic," as we have said before, refers to simultaneous kinesthetic and skin sensitivity (cutaneous and subcutaneous inputs); it is impossible to make a movement without also receiving tactual information, and vice versa. It is very difficult to obtain responses from the skin alone without performing any movement.

48. When we put a common object on the palm of a blindfolded adult's hand, only some features are recognized (cold, warm, large, small, hard, soft); if we passively flex the person's fingers, he is not able to recognize the object, but he can recognize other physical characteristics (for instance: "It seems to be a box ... but I don't know what kind ..."). If we leave the person free to move his fingers, he can recognize the nature and the name of the

NEUROPSYCHOLOGICAL FUNDAMENTALS

object (i.e., stereognosis is achieved: "It's a matchbox").

49. The child has his hands on the table. The therapist touches one finger; and the child (without seeing) must move it. The therapist touches two fingers simultaneously (for instance I-III or II-IV or III-V or I-IV or II-V) and the child must move them.

J. Exercising different modalities together. Perhaps one of the most interesting aspects of training consists of working with different modalities together, particularly the kinetic, perceptual, and verbal modalities.

50. The therapist says to a child, "Point to your nose." If the child is able to do that, the therapist repeats the same command while pointing to the therapist's own *ear.* During the second command a conflict is created between auditory/verbal (nose) and visual/gestural (ear) information received. How will the child answer? Which stimulus is more (or less) powerful for the child? In normal young children, up to three years of age, nonverbal perception governs their responses. Between three and four years of age, language begins to govern their responses. It is possible to show them incorrect, nonverbal perceptual stimuli without danger of confusing them in their understanding of verbal commands. The child who is able to exclude actions and perceptions, is also able to identify language with thought, and thus can use a verbal modality (essential for learning ability).

51. Alternate two different commands. After repeating these commands three or four times, modify the sequence. For instance, with the child in front of the therapist:
a. "Take the blue pencil" (in the child's left hand).
b. "Take the red pencil" (in the child's right hand).
c. "Give me the blue pencil" (in the therapist's right hand).
d. "Give me the red pencil" (in the therapist's left hand).
After repeating the same sequence three times, the therapist asks for the red pencil while he opens his right hand. The child has the red pencil in his right hand and must "cross" his body midline with his arm in order to follow the instruction. Some children prefer to give the therapist the blue pencil in spite of understanding the command. Others show perseveration and respond to perceptual cues (the therapist's open hand). It is important to overcome perceptual or perseveration stages.

The ability to adapt rapidly to new situations must be trained in all types of exercises.

52. If the child is walking, he is asked to stop, to follow, to vary his speed, to change direction, and so on.

53. Use different sources for sound localization. The child must continue to walk in the direction of the sound as the source of the sound is changed.

54. The child must walk only on bricks, which are spaced at varying distances from each other. Bricks can be disposed linearly or follow arbitrary shapes, such as an *L* shape, a *4* shape, and so on.
55. The child must walk only between the bricks and/or avoid obstacles.
56. Different paths or itineraries can be commanded by the therapist in order to avoid bricks and obstacles.
57. The same distance must be walked in three steps, in four, in five, in six.
58. The chalkboard is assigned the number one, the chair is number two, the desk is number three. Instruct the child to run from two to three and from three to one. Repeat two-three-one several times. Abruptly change: three-two-one or one-two-three, and so on.

(86) BALANCE AND LATERALITY

K. Body division. When the child can move a hand or can make skilled movements with a hand, without any kind of imitation, contraction, or reaction in the motor activities of the other hand, one can speak about body division (see Chapter II, Section 12, and Chapter III, Section 17). This phenomenon normally takes place between three and five years of age. The body is divided into two halves before the establishment of laterality.

59. Instruct the child to touch the tips of the other four fingers on the same hand with the tip of his thumb. Observe whether or not there are movements or contractions in the other hand. Practice and train similar exercises.
60. If there are synkinetic movements on the other hand, exercises must be performed simultaneously with both hands.

It might be worthwhile to recall here that the purpose of these exercises is the achievement of body division (i.e., of the functional independence of both sides of the body). This is obtained not only through the increasing abilities of the dominant body side, but also through the development of the abilities of the opposite body side. This is one of the reasons why similar exercises must be trained with both hands at the same time, and with each hand independently.

61. Reverse the direction of the finger tips touched by the thumb tip.
62. Vary the sequence of the fingers touched by the thumb: first in one direction (II-III-IV; II-III-V; II-IV-V; III-IV-V); then in the opposite direction (V-IV-III; V-IV-II; V-III-II; IV-III-II); finally in both directions with all possible combinations.
63. Same exercises, but varying the speed of performance.
64. Combine changes of speed with different finger sequences.
65. Same exercises with different rhythms of performance.

66. Combine changes of rhythms with different speeds and sequences.

Diadochokinesis is the motor function which permits subsequent opposite skilled movements (like forearm movements of successive pronation and supination). When, for instance, the normal six-year-old child is asked to produce this kind of movement in one arm, one may observe (on the other arm) a muscular contraction, or reaction, or movement imitation, that is, synkinesis. After development of body division has been achieved, there may still be a few indications of synkinesis in normal children. Special exercises can be used, however, to help the child overcome any remnant reflexes which are excessive.

L. Preferent and prevalent body laterality. In general, laterality refers to motoric prevalences and preferences of one side of the body. Prevalences are imposed by genetic (neuromuscular) codes, and preferences are acquired by environmental (psycho-socio-cultural) influences. Motoric lateralization often coincides with both sensory predominance of the same side of the body and the greater ability for symbolic representation on the opposite cerebral hemisphere. Almost all current tests of laterality measure control of the preferred side, as influenced by the environment, rather than the genetic prevalence of a child. The principal factor in developing body laterality, nevertheless, is through development of motor ability. This factor is strongly connected with (1) sensory inputs, (2) vestibular-proprioceptive inputs, and (3) cerebral hemispheric specialization. It is important for the therapist to know how the child's preferences and prevalences are disposed before labeling him as either left- or right-sided. If the child has reached the stage of body division, ambilaterality—or ambidexterity—will probably be found. If prevalence (which is neuromuscularly determined) predominates on one side of the body, and preference (which is environmentally determined through psycho-socio-cultural influences) predominates on the other side, the result is commonly recognized in what we refer to as mixed, or crossed, laterality (e.g., right-hand with left-eye and left-foot dominance, or vice versa). If testing for laterality is comprised solely of psycho-socio-cultural batteries, then one must recognize in these results the disregard for genetic, biological, neuromuscular aspects of laterality. In spite of the presence of "mixed" laterality, spontaneous preferences of hand, eye, and foot selection do not elicit the disturbances which are commonly described. These disturbances arise when the process of a natural selection is interfered with, by determining for the child which hand to write with before his own selection can be developed.

In order to recognize how important an influence preferences exert, let us consider this example: Right-sided children, who spontaneously stand on the right leg when they were asked "to stand on one leg," later changed to a preferred left leg for standing, after being trained in English football (that is, American soccer). The only explanation is that they were unconsciously accustomed to having their right leg free to kick the ball.

67. The therapist may ask the child to stand on one leg and to move the other leg freely (as if kicking). Alternate both legs.

68. The therapist must respect spontaneous preferences and must reinforce natural prevalences before training right and left.

M. Balance and postural integration. Primary integration of the postural system is obtained between three and four years of age. Postural integration means that vestibular inputs, proprioceptive inputs, and visual inputs act together and are coordinated by the cerebellum.

69. One of the indicators that postural integration has been obtained is the ability of the child to maintain an erect posture with eyes closed, feet together, and both arms hanging normally at the sides of the body (Romberg's test). Only with adequate proprioception and vestibular inputs can the child control his balance.
70. Another indicator is the ability of the child to maintain balance briefly on one leg. (At first this is accompanied by an excitation or appearance of the symmetric, and later asymmetric, tonic-neck reflexes.)
71. The therapist must devise exercises which establish equilibrium, both with and without visual assistance. For full integration of the postural system, various exercises must be used to develop eye control, head balance, body balance, crawling (on one's stomach, and on all fours), falling, bearlike walking (or "lumbering"), elephant-walking, standing on one leg, walking. If sufficient development has been attained, these exercises could also include hopping, kicking, and so on.

N. Corporal potentiality. We advocate that efforts to develop cognitive learning in humans should be integrated with motoric development. There is a relatively direct relationship between "symbolic specialization" and "body exclusion." At the same time as symbolic specialization increases in a cerebral hemisphere, the ability to "exclude" body information also develops in the same hemisphere. Corporal potentiality precisely refers to the ability to exclude body information in a cerebral hemisphere in order to allow symbolic specialization. Between the ages of four and six years, language begins to take precedence over and control motor activity, and symbolic thought begins to dominate the left cerebral hemisphere.

72. Exercise standing on one foot.
73. Exercise the toe-heel position (tandem position or Mann's test).
74. Therapists must use language (not *lingua*) as the determinant of any exercise. Training must include simultaneous action and/or perceptual stimuli.

O. Effort exercises. Posture and equilibrium can also be trained by adding weights (proper for each stage of development) to certain exercises. For instance, the child stands on one leg, meanwhile holding a weight of two kilograms (4.4 lb.) in one hand, and so on. (A 5-lb. weight would likewise suffice.) Repeat previous balance exercises with the addition of different weights.

P. *Exigency exercises.* Posture and equilibrium can also be trained through changing-consistency boards. The use of soft surfaces serves to challenge the child's posture and equilibrium responses.

75. Do similar exercises adding different weights to the children's hands.

Q. *Acceleration and deceleration exercises.* The use of scooterboards and hammocks exposes the child to accelerated and decelerated movements and the resulting body reactions which they elicit. Rolling down an inclined platform on the scooterboard provides suitable stimulation and exercise, while at the same time being a pleasurable experience for the child.

76. Vestibular stimulation through manual rotation (or turning) exercises are *not* recommended; the torsion swing is preferred for this.

(87) VISION, POSTURE, EQUILIBRIUM, AND SPACE

R. *Vision, posture, equilibrium, and space.* It is well known that movements of the eyes, from vestibular origin, are already registered in the fetus. They occur during the fifth gestational month.[21] The first ocular movements in newborn babies are of vestibular origin. In infancy, eye movements rapidly increase with the stimulation produced by light, and through the development of new postural reflexes as well as auditory-tactile reflexes. Some important points to keep in mind are the following:

First, confluence in the primary visual cerebral cortex of vestibular and retinal inputs strongly facilitates sensory integration.[22]

Second, spatial stability is dynamically maintained by retino-cortical and vestibular-cortical projections.[23]

Third, almost all visual cortical neurons are activated by labyrinthine inputs.[24]

Fourth, neck proprioceptors (located in vertebral joints and muscles) act not only upon body balance but also upon the regulation of eye movements.[25]

Fifth, labyrinthine, oculomotor inputs, and neck proprioceptive input continuously interact in order to obtain, to develop, and to control body postures and positions, equilibrium, and spatial stabilization.[26]

Sixth, the cerebellum does not seem to exert direct control on eye movements, but it acts indirectly in modifying and influencing them.[27]

R. Held emphasizes the importance of active and normal body movements in the development of perceptual skills and in the ability to compensate for distorted visual or auditory perceptions.[28] Haptic inputs are integrated through information coming from the eyes and ears, which is processed in the sensory parts of the central nervous system in order to obtain perceptual adaptation to the environment. Consequently, muscles are included in this adaptive process.

Visual and eye-hand exercises. As we have said before, eye-hand movements constitute one of the first human synergies; they are also essential

for many early learning processes. Eye-hand coordination is therefore fundamental for academic learning, and it is obvious that only through proper
development of such a synergy can regular handwriting and reading be properly achieved. Exercises directed to this coordination must be introduced in
all training programs for the learning disabled.

77. Standing erect, with feet together and head held still, the
therapist may have the child practice moving the eyes:
from side to side, up and down, midline, circular movements, and so on.

78. Similar exercises, pursuing a small light (small lantern)
moved by the therapist in a semidark room.

79. Similar exercises, pursuing an object (finger, pencil, etc.),
moved by the therapist in a luminous room.

80. The child is asked to look at a picture (or figure) on the
opposite wall. Crossing the room with eyes open and then
with eyes closed, he must point out the picture or a certain part of the picture. Games such as "Pin the Tail on
the Donkey" can also be useful.

81. After adding obstacles to the room, which the child can
see, the therapist then asks the child to close his eyes
(that is, to use visual memory) and find his way through
them, to point out the picture which is hanging on the
opposite wall.

82. The child should walk, fixing his eyes on an object.

83. Walk, with the eyes fixed on an object kept in the child's
hand.

84. Walk, with the eyes fixed on an object attached to the
child's clothes.

85. Walk, fixing his eyes on a moving object.

86. Walk, moving the head and having eyes fixed on an object.

87. Walk, opening and closing his eyes.

88. Walk, while covering one eye (alternating right and left).

89. The child must visually follow a moving light or object
from the lateral visual borders to the midline of his face,
from right to left and from left to right, from up to down
and from down to up, etc. It is important to train recognition of various kinds of visual stimuli, such as colors
and shapes, from different directions and varying depths.

90. Movements of the head are associated with the previous
exercises.

91. Use several postures and positions for reading and writing.

92. Use visual exercises such as showing the reader one word
at a time, covering the other words with a cardboard
template.[29]

93. The child should visually track the movement of a ball
as it is tossed from one hand to the other by the child
himself, by the therapist, or by another person; track
the movement of the ball in playing ping-pong, tennis, etc.

NEUROPSYCHOLOGICAL FUNDAMENTALS

94. Practice reading and writing readiness exercises; many of these are also practical vestibular-oculomotor and eye-hand training procedures.

Many other exercises for vestibular learning disorders could also be suggested; but the fundamentals and exercises mentioned here permit adequate vestibular approaches and correct development of new exercises.

NOTES

1. P. Schilder, "The Vestibular Apparatus in Neurosis and Psychosis," *Journal of Nervous and Mental Diseases* 78 (1933): 1-23, 137-164.

2. M. Pollack and H. P. Krieger, "Oculomotor and Postural Patterns in Schizophrenic Children," *Archives of Neurology and Psychiatry* 79 (1958): 720-726.

3. G. Colbert, R. R. Koegler, and C. H. Markham, "Vestibular Dysfunction in Childhood Schizophrenia," *A.M.A. Archives of General Psychiatry* 62 (1959): 600-617.

4. B. Rosenblut, R. Goldstein, and W. M. Landau, "Vestibular Responses of Some Deaf and Aphasic Children," *Annals of Otology, Rhinology, and Laryngology* [St. Louis] 69 (1960): 747-755.

5. N. Torok and M. A. Pearlstein, "Vestibular Findings in Cerebral Palsy," *Annals of Otology, Rhinology, and Laryngology* [St. Louis] 71 (1962): 51-58.

6. A. A. Silver and H. P. Gabriel, "The Association of Schizophrenia in Childhood with Primitive Postural Responses and Decreased Muscle Tone," *Developmental Medicine and Child Neurology* 6 (1964): 495-497.

7. E. M. Ornitz, "Vestibular Dysfunction in Schizophrenia in Childhood," *Comprehensive Psychiatry* 11 (1970): 159-173; E. M. Ornitz, "Childhood Autism: A Review of the Clinical and Experimental Literature," *California Medicine* 118 (1973): 21-47.

8. H. Wallon, *Les Origines du Caractere chez l'Enfant* (Paris: Presses Universitaires de France, 1949); N. C. Kephart, *The Slow Learner in the Classroom* (Columbus, Ohio: Charles E. Merrill, 1960); G. N. Getman, *How to Develop Your Child's Intelligence* (Irvine, California: Research Publications, 1967).

9. R. H. Barsch, *Achieving Perceptual-Motor Efficiency*, Volumes 1 and 2 (Seattle: Special Child Publications, 1967-68); A. J. Ayres, *Sensory Integration and Learning Disorders* (Los Angeles: Western Psychological Services, 1973); J. Frank and H. N. Levinson, "Dysmetric Dyslexia and Dyspraxia—Hypothesis and Study," *Journal of the American Academy of Child Psychiatry* 12 (1973): 690-701; L. C. Erway, "Otolith Formation and Trace Elements: A Theory of Schizophrenic Behavior," *Journal of Orthomolecular Psychiatry* 4 (1973): 16-26; G. Harris, "Influences of Vestibular-Gravity System in Human Behavior" (unpublished).

10. O. L. Schrager, "Vision, sistema postural y aprendizaje," *Fonoaudiologica* [Buenos Aires] 20 (1974): 67-81; J. B. de Quirós, "Vestibular-proprioceptive Integration: Its Influences on Learning and Speech in Children," *Proceedings of the Tenth Interamerican Congress of Psychology* (Lima, Peru, April 3-7, 1966; Mexico: Trillas, 1967): 194-202; J. B. de Quirós, "Disturbances in the Language of a Child: The Child Who Does not Speak," *Clinical Proceedings of the Children's Hospital* [Washington, D.C.] 25:7 (1969): 195-205; J. B. de Quiros, "Exclusion in Learning-Disabled Children" (keynote address, presented before the Tenth International Conference of the Association for Children with Learning Disabilities; reproduced by the learning disabilities program staff, Center for Effecting Educational Change, Fairfax County Public Schools, March, 1973); J. B. de Quirós, "Diagnosis of Developmental Language Disorders," *Folia Phoniatrica* [Basel] 26 (1974): 13-32; J. B. de Quirós, "Diagnosis of Vestibular Disorders in the Learning Disabled," *Journal of Learning Disabilities* 9:1 (1976): 39-47; J. B. de Quirós, "Significance of Some Therapies on Posture and Learning," *Academic Therapy* 11:3 (Spring 1976): 261-270; J. B. de Quirós and O. L. Schrager, "Postural System, Corporal Potentiality, and Language," in E. H. Lenneberg and E. Lenneberg (eds.), *Foundations of Language Development,*

Volume 2 (New York: Academic Press; and Paris: UNESCO, 1975): 297-307; J. B. de Quirós and O. L. Schrager, *Neuropsychological Fundamentals in Learning Disabilities* (1st ed.) (San Rafael, California: Academic Therapy Publications, 1978).

11. A. Precechtel, "Contribution a l'Etude de la Fonction Statique dans la Periode de la Vie Extrauterine: Syndrome Typique du Defaut Congenital de l'Appareil Otolithique," *Acta Otolaryngologica* [Stockholm] 7 (1925): 206-226.

12. H. McHugh, "Auditory and Vestibular Disorders in Children," *The Laryngoscope* 72 (1962): 555-565.

13. Quirós, "Vestibular-proprioceptive Integration . . . ," *loc. cit.*

14. T. Cawthorne, "The Physiological Basis for Head Exercises," *Journal of the Charter Society of Physiotherapists* (1944): 106-107 (cited in McCabe); B. F. McCabe, "Labrynthine Exercises in the Treatment of Diseases Characterized by Vertigo: Their Physiologic Basis and Methodology," *The Laryngoscope* 80 (1970): 1429-1433; H. P. Voisin and J. Boussens, "Reeducation de l'Equilibration," *Revue de Laryngologie, Otologie et Rhinologie* [Bordeaux] 98 (1977): 443-447.

15. Voisin and Boussens, *op. cit.*

16. Ayres, *op. cit.*; R. H. Barsch, *A Movigenic Curriculum*, Bulletin Number 25 (Madison, Wisconsin: Department of Public Instruction, Bureau for the Handicapped, 1965); Barsch, *Achieving . . . , loc. cit.*; B. J. Cratty, *Motor Activity and the Education of Retardates* (2nd ed.) (Philadelphia: Lea and Febiger, 1974); M. Frostig, *Movement Education Theory and Practice* (Chicago: Follett, 1970); Getman, *op. cit.*; B. Holle, *Motor Development in Children* (Oxford: Blackwell Scientific Publications, 1976); Kephart, *op. cit.*

17. J. de Ajuriaguerra, *Manuel de Psychiatrie de l'Enfant* (Paris: Masson et Cie., 1970); Ayres, *op. cit.*; Barsch, *A Movigenic Curriculum, loc. cit.*; Barsch, *Achieving . . . , loc. cit.*; J. Benos, *L'Enfance Inadaptee et l'Education Psychomotrice* (Paris: Maloine S. A., 1972). Cratty, *Motor Activity . . . op. cit.*; J. Defontaine, *Manuel de Reeducation Psychomotrice* (Paris, Maloine S. A., 1976); Frostig, *Movement Education . . . , op. cit.*; M. Frostig and P. Maslow, *Learning Problems in the Classroom* (New York: Grune & Stratton, 1973); Getman, *op. cit.*; Kephart, *op. cit.*; J. Le Boulch, *L'Education par le Movement: la Psychocinetique* (Paris: Ed. Sociales Francaises, 1966); A. Maigre and J. Destrooper, *L'Education Psychomotrice* (Paris: Presses Universitaires de France, 1975); R. G. Roach and N. C. Kephart, *The Purdue Perceptual-Motor Survey* (Columbus, Ohio: Charles E. Merrill, 1966); G. Rossel, *Manuel d'Education Psychomotrice* (Paris: Masson et Cie., 1967); G. B. Soubiran and P. Mazo, *La Readaptation Scolaire* (Paris: Doin, 1965); M. Stambak, *Tonus et Psychomotricite* (Neuchatel, Switzerland: Delachaux et Niestle, 1963); P. Vayer, *L'Enfant Face au Monde* (Paris, Doin, 1972); P. Vayer and J. Destrooper, *La Dynamique de l'Action Educative* (Paris: Doin, 1976); Wallon, *op. cit.*

18. B. Bobath and K. Bobath, *Motor Development in the Different Types of Cerebral Palsy* (London: William Heineman, 1975).

19. H. Head, *Aphasia and Kindred Disorders* (Cambridge: Cambridge University Press, 1926 [reprint, 1963]).

20. P. Schilder, *Image and Appearance of the Human Body* (New York: International University Press, 1951).

21. M. Minkowski, "Sull'evoluzione la Localizzazione delle Funzione Nervose, Sopratutto dei Movimenti e dei Riflessi nel Feto e nel Neonato," *Atti del Convenio Italo-Swizzero* (Bologna: Editoriale Capelli, 1948).

22. R. Jung, "Coordination of Specific and Non-specific Afferent Impulses at Single Neurons of the Visual Cortex," in H. H. Jasper (ed.), *Reticular Formation of the Brain* (Boston: Little, Brown, 1958): 423-434; O. J. Grusser and U. Grusser-Cornehls, "Mikroelektrodenuntersuchungen zur Konvergenz vestibularer und retinaler Afferenzen an einzelnen Neuronen des optischen Cortex der Katze," *Pflugers Archiv Gesant Physiologie* 270 (1960): 227-238.

23. R. Jung and H. H. Kornhuber (eds.), *Neurophysiologie und Psychophysic des Visuallen Systems* (Berlin: Springer, 1961); H. H. Kornhuber, "Vestibular Influences on the Vestibular and the Somatosensory Cortex," in A. Brodal and O. Pompeiano

(eds.), *Basic Aspects of Central Vestibular Mechanisms* (Amsterdam: Elsevier, 1972): 567-572.

24. Grusser and Grusser-Cornehls, "Mikroelektrodenuntersuchungen . . . ," *loc. cit.*; O. J. Grusser and U. Grusser-Cornehls, "Interaction of Vestibular and Visual Inputs in the Visual System," in Brodal and Pompeiano (eds.), *op. cit.*: 573-583.

25. O. Pompeiano, "Spinovestibular Relations: Anatomical and Physiological Aspects," in Brodal and Pompeiano (eds.), *op. cit.*: 263-296.

26. A. Brodal, "Anatomy of Commisural Connections," in Brodal and Pompeiano (eds.), *op. cit.*: 167-176; P. Bach-Y-Rita, "Structural and Functional Aspects of Extra-ocular Muscles in Relation to Vestibulo-ocular Function," in Brodal and Pompeiano (eds.), *op. cit.*

27. R. S. Dow and F. Manni, "The Relationship of the Cerebellum to Extraocular Movements," in M. B. Bender (ed.), *The Oculomotor System* (New York: Hoeber [div. of Harper & Row], 1964): 37-48.

28. R. Held, "Plasticity in Sensory Motor Systems," *Scientific American* 213:5 (1965): 84-88; R. Held and J. Bossom, "Neonatal Deprivation and Adult Rearrangement: Complementary Techniques for Analyzing Afferent Sensori-motor Coordination," *The Journal of Compared Physiology and Psychology* 54 (1961): 33-37.

29. A. Rey, *Psychologie Clinique et Neurologie* (Neuchatel, Switzerland: Delachaux et Niestle, 1969).

NEUROPSYCHOLOGICAL FUNDAMENTALS

CHAPTER XII

Bases for Therapy

(88) A BRIEF REVIEW OF DRUGS AND LEARNING DISABILITIES

There are three main sets of criteria in medical or pharmacological use of drugs in learning disabilities: (1) general criteria, (2) special criteria, (3) specific criteria.

General criteria are based upon physiopathological fundamentals. For instance, the use of essential amino acids, potassium, phosphates, gamma amino butiric acid (G.A.B.A.), the inhibitors of the monoamino oxidase (M.A.O.), the now-obsolete glutamic acid, and other stimulators of brain cell oxidation, vitamin B_6, and so on, can be included in this group.[1]

Particularly noteworthy is the importance that ribonucleic acid synthesis could have for learning abilities. Several studies related to chemical analysis of learning consistently found leucine (a purine forming nucleotides, which are the units for nucleic acids). Nevertheless, ribonucleic acid (RNA) and desoxiribonucleic acid (DNA) do not influence learning as much as they were thought to at the beginning of the 1960s, according to H. Hyden's studies. Consequently, the pharmacology used for learning disabilities changed in regard to the different findings and principles established little by little during the last several years. The use of glutamic acid, of acetylcholine, of strychnine, of amino acids, of RNA and DNA, are in agreement with successive biochemical investigations of learning and memory.[2]

If it is true that learning seems to be controlled by different biochemical substances within the central nervous system, it is also true that it is yet unknown how specific synthesis of RNA or proteins can be facilitated in the brain of man, or how macromolecular synthesis can be disrupted without producing other simultaneous effects. Even so, other substances acting upon cognitive processes also seem to be peripheral to learning.

Special criteria are directed toward symptomatology which is concomitant to the learning disability (*lingua,* language, reading, writing, mathematical calculation, and so on). Special criteria are extremely important because they focus upon hyperactivity, restlessness, minimal brain dysfunction, and other coexisting symptomatology of many learning disabilities. We shall return to this subject later on.

Specific criteria act upon well-determined causes, and their action tends to ameliorate the main disturbance, thus compensating and diminishing secondary learning disabilities. For instance, a young child who has a secondary learning disability due to hypothyroidism can be very much improved or cured through the adequate administration of thyroid hormones. Specific therapeutic action can be obtained not only through hormones or drug administration, but also through many other clinical and surgical measures, for instance: a phenilalanine-restricted diet in phenilketonuric infants, the installation of a valve in noncompensated hydrocephaly, the repair of an abnormal vascular ductus, the early surgical separation of skull bones in craniostenosis, etc.

Perhaps the most controversial point related to learning disabilities is connected with the use of drugs in hyperactivity, restlessness, and "minimal brain dysfunction." As was just stated, these therapies employ special criteria.

One of the most extended drugs against hyperactivity was diphenhydramine.[3] In 1937 C. Bradley and E. Green used Benzedrine for behavior disorders in children. The use of amphetamine sulphate, or Benzedrine, was used to alleviate various symptoms: fear, depression, sexual tension, hyperkinesis. Disagreement among different authors emerges when they want to establish how much this drug improves mental abilities or diminishes learning disabilities.[4]

Benzedrine was then replaced by dextroamphetamine, or Dexedrine. It has been widely used in the United States and has been much discussed in regard to its effective action in hyperkinesis and learning disabilities.[5]

During the 1950s methylphenidate, or Ritalin, obtained general medical approval as the medication of choice in cases of hyperactivity. In 1960 Quiros wrote: "Lytton and Knobel (1959) have observed that hyperkinetic children respond to Ritalin with movement reduction, better movement coordination, more adequated and adapted general behavior, greater attention span, and better tolerance to frustration." It was insisted that these treatments be combined with psychotherapy.[6]

Many colleagues even now consider that amphetamines and methylphenidate, both, stabilize brain irritability, reduce hyperkinesis, and improve learning. We, on the contrary, scarcely use these drugs. When a child is classified as "hyperkinetic," we try to differentiate him as having "hyperactivity" or "restlessness" (see Chapter VII, Section 47). Hyperactivity seems to be related to brain dysfunction, and *prima facie* it can be improved by amphetamines or methylphenidate. This notwithstanding, when the condition is already neurologically compensated, these drugs seem to produce a greatly excited state in the patient. How can it be supposed that neurological compensation occurs? Perhaps through signs revealing the existence of past pathology (see Chapter IX, Section 63, and Chapter X, Section

77). Consequently, when a child shows dynamic correction of asymmetries, introduction of such drugs can produce cortical excitation. In those circumstances we prefer to use general criteria for treatment instead of amphetamines or methylphenidate.

On the other hand, when restlessness exists with a vestibular disorder, cynarizine (R. 5106, cynamil 4 diphenilmethyl-piperazone) has a peculiar depressive action upon vestibules, at the same time that it improves peripheral and brain-stem circulation and exerts antihistamine effects.

Another special criterion in regard to use of drugs is the administration of antiepileptic drugs. We must recall that in Chapter VIII, Section 54, we dealt with some effects produced by anticonvulsivants. This is not the time or the place to speak about specific drugs; however, some general approaches can be discussed.

1. Doctors must determine whether a learning disability in a child is associated with epilepsy or anticonvulsive drugs. Many times the causes of such a learning disability have other origins.

2. If anticonvulsives produce drowsiness or a learning disability, but if they are effective against seizures, doctors must wait at least 15 days before considering any change of medication, because it frequently takes that long for the body to accustom itself to the drug, before such things as drowsiness—and the learning disability—diminish. In the meantime, doctors can help brain actions through other drugs in order to diminish the negative side effects of the anticonvulsives.

3. When a learning-disabled child is found to have any abnormalities in an EEG record, anticonvulsive drugs will in general not act to ameliorate the learning disability. Only when seizures or epilepsy can be clinically determined, some specific drugs can improve learning disabilities.

Unfortunately, medical treatment of epilepsy is still mostly based on a trial-and-error approach. Ignorance in this field is still very great.

(89) DRUGS, THE HIPPOCAMPUS, THE CHOLINERGIC SYSTEM, AND LEARNING

According to several research projects, scientific criteria now support the assumption that the hippocampus may have two different but related modes of functioning. One consists of a gross, nonspecific inhibition of general emotional reactivity, this mode of hippocampal functioning being present in infancy and at times in adulthood. The other mode corresponds to a specific inhibition of an emotional reaction to a particular stimulus or set of stimuli, it being therefore called "stimulus-specific inhibition."[8]

It has been pointed out many times that the hippocampal and cholinergic systems appear to be very closely related. Because acetylcholine has frequently been assumed to be the transmitter within the central nervous system, cholinergic drugs (like di-isopropyl-fluorophosphate [DEP] or like physostigmine) were said to increase learning by prolonging the effect of acetylcholine if injected into the hippocampus of rats, while anticholinergic drugs (like scopolamine) had an opposite effect.[9] The exact relationship between the effects of hippocampal lesions and anticholinergic drugs are said to be not at all coincident, but it suggests to researchers that the hippocampus may function "in series" within the cholinergic system.

The control of attention is considered to be dependent on two systems which act in eliciting opposite effects. The first involves the cerebral amigdala and the monoaminergic system, and it has an excitatory effect which directs attention toward the stimulus. The second involves the hippocampus and the cholinergic system, having an inhibitory effect, thus directing attention away from stimuli as a consequence of nonreinforcement and other factors. According to these assumptions, poor learning performance might depend on a simultaneous interference of both of these systems, while a simultaneous enhancement of them might improve learning ability.

In 1972 D. Douglas postulated that the maturation of adult hippocampal function was a necessary but insufficient prerequisite for Piaget's stage of concrete operation.[10] Some results of other research projects, especially those of R. J. Douglas, tentatively support the assumption that conservation and alternation are based largely on the same brain mechanisms. "Alternation" is considered to be one of the many ways of measuring behaviors depending of hippocampal functions. According to some recent studies, human behaviors considered to be dependent on hippocampal functions consistently improve between one and a half to six years of age, with four and one third years being a critical age in this maturational behavioral change.[11]

R. J. Douglas, whose work we have just cited, says:

> Spontaneous alternation is usually studied by giving a small animal two consecutive unrewarded trials in a T-shaped maze. The subject is placed in a start-box at the "bottom" of the main stem and allowed to approach the choice point or intersection and enter one of the two side alleys. The animal is confined to the chosen alley for 30 seconds or so and is then removed and replaced in the start-box for a second, identical trial. If the choices on the two trials were independent, then the animal would enter opposite alleys or alternate about 50 percent of the time by chance.

Behaviors related to hippocampal functions, such as spontaneous alternation, are attributable to vestibular cues, while others depend on olfactory or other stimuli but also with the usual dominion of vestibular cues. This leads us to assume that the influence of vestibular-proprioceptive integration in order to facilitate human learning (for example, "corporal potentiality"), might be mediated through correct hippocampal functional maturation.

According to all previous considerations, it is clear enough that the administration of cholinergic drugs might be significant in treating some learning disabilities; however, further research in this field seems in order.

(90) REMEDIATION BASED ON DATA FURNISHED BY EXAMINATION (SUMMARY OF RESEARCH PUBLISHED 1962, 1965)

As a general principle, in order to undertake remediation of learning disabilities, it must be first realized that even though this therapy is basically aimed at reading and writing mechanisms (as mechanics and as language), it must necessarily be started by paying attention to other fundamentals of human learning abilities.

This principle was delineated in 1962, when Quiros and colleagues published a book on dyslexia in childhood, which included several chapters about rehabilitation of dyslexics.[12]

Let us summarize in this section and the following two sections the main thoughts we had on the subject at that time. We will try to give a general view rather than detailed instructions for remediation, since our research in the intervening fifteen years has rendered several of those details obsolete.

Data resulting from the case history, which may suggest norms of treatment. The case history, from the point of view of treatment, is highly enlightening, since it informs us about the existence of different factors which may determine various therapeutic approaches. Among these factors we shall mention some of the most important ones.

In the first place, the case history orients us toward a presumptive cause of the case of the learning disability under study, and also provides us with very important data in connection with the environment and the psychological reactions of the child.

When the case history indicates principally the presence of psycho-neurological factors, work with the child has high probability of success, but all too frequently the mistake is made of believing that the child who has acquired the mechanics of reading and writing has already overcome his greatest deficiency in dyslexia. Of course this is not so, since through these mechanics comes interpretation, and *then* a stage of personal comprehension is reached. It is unnecessary to stress again here that dysphasia and dyslexia are language syndromes. Once reading and writing as a mechanism have been remediated, it does not necessarily follow that the child has free use of reading and writing as a symbolic communication or language system. But on the other hand, when the problems involved in acquisition of reading and writing are purely psychological or pedagogical, once the initial stage of mechanics is overcome, the child may develop all his linguistic faculties, since only the latter are involved.

In fact, developmental-motor, perceptual, or linguistic disturbances suggest a plan of rehabilitation based on the developmental abnormalities that they might point to. It should be noted that not only the developmental delay is of interest, but also the appearance of an apparent "jump" between stages of development (a pathological developmental pattern). A general principle that we must accept is that any omission in an early stage of development is later translated into deficiencies in the acquisition of learning; naturally, the developmental stages should be reexamined and the different stages within the proposed rehabilitation plan should be readapted.

Finally, the case history also gives us elements which might suggest the existence of a primary deficiency in the ability to visualize or to auditorize, this giving us efficient leads on methodologies of audiovisual or visuoauditory teaching—that is, systems which offer their heaviest support in audition or vision.

Bases for postural and psychomotor therapy in dyslexia. The first experience and learning of the human being is one's need to "connect with oneself" and with the world around him. The information for the purpose of "connecting with oneself" arises first from the impressions received through inner sensitivity (visceroceptivity and proprioception), and then through exteroceptivity (see Chapters I through V).

From this standpoint we must insist that, to work on body schema, body image, body insight, body concept, and so on, is to work on posture, movement, hemispheric dominance, body laterality, and concepts of right and left, spatial orientation, and exteroceptivity, for all these are factors the disturbance of which determine or are the result of a disturbance of the body schema. That is why, if remediation of reading and writing of a dyslexic child is only attempted without paying attention to those other components of his condition, failure in learning may follow, even though the person undertaking the task may be a widely experienced teacher.

Postural development normally allows, as we have said, the connection and communication of the child with himself and with the world around him. *But to possess "language" in its widest sense is to perceive the existence of things and direct oneself toward them; it is to experience them, to comprehend them in their objectivity and/or function, and to react mimically and gesturally.* Then the misnamed "inner language" will come: the adaptation to standardized systems of speech (*lingua*). But the experience of the child, prior to speech comprehension and utterance, has been very rich and has been based fundamentally on postural and perceptual development: During the first three months of infancy, vestibular-proprioceptive and exteroceptive reflexes were set into motion, which determine the predominance of the asymmetric tonic-neck reflexes, and which culminate in control of the head. From the third to the sixth month after birth, the child begins his body training (hands, in the symmetric tonic-neck posture), and orientation in relation to his own body. Later on the child will sit (sixth month), crawl and stand (ninth month), and walk (twelfth month). Each one of these stages allows the child a greater connection with his own self and with his environment: Control of the head, for example, allows the three-month-old child to hold it in the attitude demanded by his external surroundings, this being translated into orientation movements toward acoustic and visual stimuli. It is undeniable that all postural or motor delay disturbs the acquisition of adequate connections with the environment and hence, with the acquisition of *lingua* and language. After body knowledge comes knowledge of the world around him and, later still, symbolic communication. To miss any of these stages is to fall into defective systems of connection and communication (abnormal patterns); so for example, imitative speech follows postural, motor, and exteroceptive training; but this training refers not only to the body but also to phonoarticulatory organs (through crying, wailing, or "autogenetic" gurgling) which involve, in the course of the first months, different utterances.

Naturally, postural development in the young preschool child has passed through stages of neurological integration very different from those presented by the school-age child. For this reason we cannot think of imposing postures and making the child move as if he were a baby, since this would not agree with his actual degree of development. Such maneuvers would only be justified with a brain-damaged child, in whom we try (through several exercises) to inhibit certain reflexes in order to activate other more effective and better ones.[13] But in the child with language organization deficiency, what we shall try to attain is greater body knowledge, better information from body postures, and better motor realization—all of which permit improved performances in reading, in graphisms (drawing, writing, and all graphic communicative productions), and eventually, better articulation in speaking. The remedial plan, therefore, will be designed according to whether postural and motor development are normal or abnormal. It is through better body schema, and better basic neuromuscular and body knowledge, that it will be possible for the child to develop control of the complex neuromuscular systems on which reading, writing, and speech depend.

This is why with the school-age child we shall carry out a series of exercises based on primitive postures and—depending on whether the developmental pattern is normal or abnormal—adapt the majority of them to the existence of a cerebro-cortical predominance. This should be done without imposing postures according to the development of reflexes in infancy, a criterion which would not be acceptable at this age.

Each set of exercises is based on the three fundamental positions of static and motor development: lying on the back, sitting, and standing. In each of these positions static exercises (modifications of tonus with variations of speed in the tonic muscular modification) and dynamic exercises (movements, body swinging, marching, and jumping) are carried out. Both the static and dynamic series of exercises provide some items based on equilibrium. Also, both combine coordinated movements (starting, moving, stopping) with respect to the indications and commands given. Our publications (1962, 1965) describe these exercises in detail.

These exercises are to be carried out with small groups of children, except when the defects presented by the child are too great, in which case individual training is to be preferred, with later incorporation into the working group.

We consider of great interest the pioneer approach of J. de Ajuriaguerra and G. Bonvalot-Soubiran for children with "psychomotor disturbances." This approach can be used profitably with the type of child we are dealing with.[14]

Sensoriperceptive remediation. As various authors—and especially Piaget—have pointed out, the child before reaching school age has passed through two fundamental stages: (1) the stage of sensorimotor knowledge, and (2) the stage of symbolic objective representations. While the first leads the child in search of objects and to acquisition of experience with these, the second leads him to interiorize those experiences and identify them with thought. Even though every age is relative, it may be accepted that the first stage culminates at around eighteen months, and the second continues from eighteen months to six years.[15]

The examination of these different stages will increase understanding of, and ability to deal properly with, the perceptual problems that may be presented by the learning disabled. Every preschool child must have established his symbolic representations and must be capable of arriving at analogical deductions and of establishing incorrect preconceptions or generalizations. (For instance, just as a very young child may call a dog a "cat" or a "horse," a preschool boy cannot identify newborn or small flies with adult flies; he believes they are two different "animals," and so on.) It is fundamental to establish the perceptual stage reached by the child before attempting to undertake treatment from the point of view of sensoriperceptive therapy. It is useful to bear in mind, however, that the treatment should not be established on the basis of the so-called "intelligence quotients" (IQs) or "maturational ages." The main issue is this: W. Stern created IQs by comparing chronological age with mental age, and he believed that IQs gave practical, definite, and permanent values. But what does "mental age" mean?—certain abilities to perform "this" or "that." Can we accept that abilities cannot change by the action of special education procedures? Can we accept that we cannot improve abilities in a handicapped child? If we are able to improve certain abilities to a great extent, IQs *immediately* change. This is seen all over the world. Now: What is the practical value of IQs?

On dealing with the examination of the perceptions, several tests can be mentioned, mostly those based on psychometric tests, which could be used in this connection. These investigations strongly suggest a number of rehabilitating contributions for the perceptual deficiencies previously determined. Thus, for example, we can mention the series of O. Decroly and S. Monchamp dealing with the jug and the chair: The theme could be varied by using different motivations that could awaken the child's interest. In Argentina the series might be connected with our popular little *hornero** and his curious nest; in the United States with the sprightly squirrel and the branch of a tree, etc. Using similar resources one can achieve a great number of combinations with which to drill the child without tiring him. In the same way, other archetypal tests can be used. One of the *Sabadell Test* series, for instance, may be changed into series of balloons and trees, or circles and triangles, or any other variety of combinations.[16]

There is obviously an enormous quantity of exercises that can be derived from different exploratory tests; we could not possibly list them all; but we can, in the following paragraphs, offer a few general suggestions.

*In English, "oven-bird." "Oven" is *horno* in Spanish and in Argentina this bird is called *hornero* because its name refers to an oven, or *horno*. The *hornero* is a favorite bird of children because it constructs its nest with mud; and when it dries it becomes a "clay house" (which shape reminds one of an Eskimo's igloo) between two branches of a tree. A primitive oven, in Argentina, has a very similar shape and is made with the same materials. That is the origin of this bird's name. It is a very industrious bird, very friendly with humans, but very independent in its habits (like squirrels in the United States). It "marries" only once. It is also popular because it eats insects and, of course, it respects cultivated fields. A children's song says: *"La casita del hornero / tiene sala y tiene alcoba, / y aunque en ella no hay escoba / limpia esta contodo esmero."* ("The oven-bird's little house has a livingroom and bedroom, and even when there is no broom in it, it is carefully cleaned.") The *hornero* has been used in folktales and in children's literature by many writers. There are tests which currently employ this bird and its nest.

Procedures for visual and visuo-manual development may be started by seeking differentiation of different colors of objects. Later the shape is associated with the color; and finally each shape is presented in series of different colors and the child must group accoarding to color, then according to shape. Also, visuomotor coordination may be achieved in many ways.

Procedures for auditory and audiotemporal training is based on the previously mentioned fact that a dyslexic individual may have shown a major deficiency in the ability to auditorize. Reference has also been made to the principal auditory confusions of phonemes and words which many learning disabled may reveal (see Chapter VII, Sections 45 and 46). Independently of the great number of exercises that can be used for these purposes, it might be interesting to note that, from the point of view of music therapy, the method created by Karl Orff may be very useful.[17] Other authors have also used music, rhythm, and melody to develop ideas of space (up, down, beside, in front of, and so on), arranging a set of exercises of body movements which fit in with simple lyrics to musical accompaniment. Using the same procedure, number concepts can be also introduced.[18]

Exercises for gnosic and tactile perception (exercising for hand, finger, and body gonsias) should be carried out at the slightest exploratory verification of deficiencies in this sense and should proceed gradually, always starting from visual association exercises. This training, that in some learning disabilities is not so important as the auditory and visual drilling (for instance, with dyslexics) can be carried out in a variety of ways; and all the tests indicated for investigation (motor screening tests, etc.) may serve as a basis for the planning of remedial exercises.

Other senses, such as olfactory and gustatory, can be exercised as a complement of the fundamental remediation practice, although it is generally accepted that this is only recommended when the other pathways of *lingua* and language acquisition are very poor.

Correction of articulatory defects of speech. From the statements of this book it should be plain that primary learning disabilities always manifest deficiencies in *lingua* and language acquisition and organization and that, as a result, primary·learning disabilities may have as their antecedent the delay in the acquisition of speech or persistent dyslalias. This leads to the deduction that articulatory disturbance of speech may present itself in two ways: (1) within the same syndromes of primary learning disabilities, and (2) as an independent element which complicates such syndromes. Secondary learning disabilities may—or may not—also have articulatory disturbances of speech due to several causes. The fact that articulatory disturbances are present does not allow the supposition that they necessarily form part of a learning disability syndrome.

When articulatory defects are found within primary disability or some secondary disability syndromes, they generally derive from disturbance of a proprioceptive nature, that is, a deficient representation of the phono-articulatory body scheme; and the gnosic deficiencies of the patient must be placed in evidence. Primary learning-disabled children (dysphasics, dyslexics, and so on) may also present within one's own particular syndrome audiogenic dyslalias (that is, of auditory origin, without peripheral organic involvement). But to verify this fact it is advisable to carry out the investigation using sensitized procedures of speech audiometry (see Chapter X, Section 72). Finally, in the learning-disabled child, developmental immaturity may also give the impression of dyslalias, dyspraxias, etc. On the other hand, when it can be established that the determining causes of the articulatory defects of speech are psychogenic or organic (the latter resulting from disturbances of the peripheral phonoarticulatory organs) the participation of the articulatory defect must of course be discounted in the learning disability syndrome of primary origin. Thus, it should be considered as an independent element which complicates such a syndrome.

The techniques which allow correction of articulatory defects come within the province of general speech therapy, and it is not our aim in this book to go into detail about principles of treatment of this type. It is enough to mention that, when the process is independent of the learning disability syndrome, it may be treated at any period of development, if the schemes of speech and language are basically correct for articulation.

It is another matter to consider articulatory defects which form part of primary—and some secondary—learning disability syndromes. Some authors advise dealing from the beginning with the correction of these disturbances and simultaneously carrying out treatment of the reading defects. Our opinion is that it is often inconvenient to attempt articulatory correction at the outset, because there is the danger of this helping to create a phobia for language and especially for speech. We have seen some dyslexic children develop a stutter after having begun orthophonic or speech correction of their articulatory deficiencies.

The most suitable thing to do in these cases is to define the proprioceptogenic or audiogenic characteristics of the articulatory defects, and proceed to reinforce and modify the patterns which are found to be weakened and distorted.

(91) BASIC PSYCHOEDUCATIONAL REMEDIATION (SUMMARY OF RESEARCH PUBLISHED 1962, 1965)

To continue with the review of the approach (published in 1962, 1965), in this section we will summarize some basic psychoeducational remediation criteria stated in the mentioned books.

The psychoeducational orientation to be followed will vary according to the particular characteristics of each case; and, although the approach we gave in 1962 and 1965 was imperfect (as every outline is), it was at that time considered to be useful and practical.

First, the so-called "specific" or primary learning disability syndrome must be differentiated from the secondary learning disability syndrome in which the diagnosis can be upheld of slight or mild (but always evident) brain damage or other causes.

Second, the child who has already had learning failures associated with psychological problems must be differentiated from the child detected before school age and who was treated in a suitable manner.

Third, it must be verified before the beginning of any treatment, whether the syndrome has revealed a predominant deficiency in the ability to visualize, or in the ability to auditorize, or in any other of the fundamentals of learning.

Finally, the basic characteristics of speech must be established: *lingua* and language organization which allow a learning-disabled child to embark on reading and writing mechanisms, processes, and read/written language (this last constituting a higher stage in the development of language).

It could be important for the psychoeducational specialist to know if the learning-disabled child does or does not present a demonstrable brain lesion or other detectable organic causes: If he has brain damage or other organic causes, special individualized teaching (with few environmental stimuli) must be provided. Individualized classes must reinforce regular classes. When the child's behavior does not permit his socialization, only individualized teaching should be provided. Rather than going into other considerations regarding the measures which may be undertaken with a child suffering slight brain damage, we refer the reader to other publications we cited in our works in 1962 and 1965 for further information.[19]

The psychological situation of the learning disabled becomes more serious when the student is confronted with the difficulties of learning to read. It is natural, therefore, that school life may lead to considerable stress, the child's problem being worsened even more by distressing situations and feelings of failure. In this case, the rejection of reading and writing acquisition tends to be as great as, or greater than, the difficulties of learning.

In connection with the teaching of the first letters (the sounds and shapes of letters which can be combined as a short word: *m-a-n, man; c-a-t, cat;* and so on), the therapist should proceed carefully, selecting material which is completely within the perceptual and comprehensive abilities of the child who, when he realizes the ability to carry out these tasks successfully, will begin to accept them and can then be led on, slowly and gradually, to the acquisition of reading and writing. From the psychoeducational viewpoint, the fundamental precept which should guide us is that the learning-disabled child with learning failure must feel sure of himself when he again begins schoolwork; he should therefore be placed at a somewhat lower level than the one at which he would have been put on the strength of the examination. (It should be remembered that, if the examiner has been warm and kind, the child is likely to perform better during the examination than he would otherwise.) Added to this, the child has worked alone with the examiner; and it is natural in these circumstances that his performance should be rather better than it would be if he were within a school group. Now, when we say that it is appropriate to place these children at a lower level than what the examination would have indicated, we do not mean to imply that the work material should be more "childish" than that corresponding to the child's intelligence and chronological age. If this were done, the risk of disturbing the psychological and intellectual development proper to the child's age would be very high indeed.

The first therapeutic measures for the child who has failed in learning are conditioned for the most part by the examination cautiously carried out: An error in evaluation of his various aptitudes may lead to a new placement of the child (in a different school, grade, or class), with considerable damage to his future. This is one of the reasons why we urge that attention must be paid to the specialized teamwork which, when properly carried out, resolves these problems.

From the standpoint of the greatest deficiency in learning disability (for instance, the ability to visualize or the ability to auditorize), all therapeutic efforts should be oriented toward simultaneous audio-visual work, choosing as the principal point of departure the ability which is most intact; that is, if the deficiency is visual, fundamentally the auditory pathway should be chosen to establish the audio-visual associations, and vice versa.

The demands of comprehensive and expressive *lingua* and language level, as well as "inner language" development which should be attained during the preschool years, have been analyzed by several authors with various aims, the writings on this theme by J. Piaget, A. Gesell, and L. S. Vygotzky being especially noteworthy by the time of our 1965 publication.[20] With measureable objectives (motor performances, manual abilities, elementary knowledge, attention span, and so on), the classical treatise writers of psychometry, such as A. Binet and his followers, have also worked on this subject.[21] At the beginning of the 1960s a series of tests had appeared to assess maturity levels for school entry and readiness for reading.[22]

Therapy from the standpoint of language should be carried out in accordance with a developmental program (corresponding to normal or to abnormal patterns). Of course, *everything* referring to the body, perceptual and motor deficiencies, should be handled according to normal or abnormal developmental patterns. Evaluation of understanding, expression, and internalization of language permits the therapist (according to such a process) to program his specific plan. Therapeutic work should be made attractive and frequently take the form of play.

Should the teaching of reading to the learning disabled be carried out simultaneously with the teaching of writing, or before, or after it? There are arguments for and against each one of these postulates, even in the case of the normal child.

Those who uphold the developmental principles of word function (such as H. Myklebust[23]) maintained by 1965 the belief that comprehension of the written word (or reading) precedes the expression of the written word (or writing). Therefore, audio-visual associations should be directed toward reading at the outset.

But, on the other hand, if one bears in mind the difficulties that the learning-disabled child experiences in the visuo-auditory or audio-visual recognition of written symbols, we must agree that perhaps the introduction of "writing" prior to reading (through drawing and through the reproduction of letters perceived stereognostically and autotopognostically) could be a help in the subsequent visuo-auditory perceptual integration of those written symbols.

Last, the simultaneous teaching of written symbols through vision, audition, touch, kinesthesia, stereognosia, and so on, could help the child to acquire and to retain these symbols more easily. Frequently, special education teachers fall into the error of using the "shotgun approach" and incorporate the teaching of reading and writing to the learning-disabled child with the usual teaching of mentally deficient children—that is, a multisensory approach, in which all resources would *seem* to be appropriate. In the case of the mentally handicapped, the final educational aim in view will be, at most, the attainment of the primary grades; with the learning disabled, higher degrees of education may be aspired to. It is a serious mistake with this latter child not to develop written language primarily through visuo-auditory associations. We are in agreement, of course, with Orton's approaches, that is, on starting with the recognition and interpretation of the initial sounds of such drawings (*b* from *ball, i* from *ink,* and so on). These sounds are representative of basic sounds of the *lingua.* Then, it is possible to follow with the correspondence between sounds of drawings and letters. Finally, syllables and units having linguistic significance are understood and employed. It would seem that visuo-auditory comprehension should always come before any type of symbolic performance.

The preparations for remediation in order to introduce reading and writing should be based on the relative severity of the difficulties presented by the child. A number of interviews with the parent of the child and with the child himself will simplify the organization and direction the work will take.

Psychomotor exercises may be useful for developing body awareness and adequate spatial knowledge. Consequently they may serve as preparation for the learning of reading and writing. Other exercises which have also been described by various writers are based on free and rhythmatized movements, metronomic or not, or based on stereognostic or kinesthetic stimuli.[24] Also graphic lines, zigzags, curves, waves, longer and shorter, heavier or lighter, can be made with verbal commands and with rapid and rhythmic performance.[25]

There are also procedures such as the audio-visual method of Thea Bugnet (which was called *"Le Bon Depart"* by the authoress), which effects general psychomotor education while at the same time improves the coordination and flexibility of the hands. They are a series of motor and gestural exercises of arm, wrist, hand, and finger, using (1) rhythm and melodies, (2) visualization and graphic reproductions, and (3) total motor activities. The method includes a series of 26 simple geometric figures (vertical and horizontal lines, squares, circles, and broken lines). The teacher shows one of the figures to the pupils, and she also reproduces the shape of the figure with a gesture. The pupils must repeat with the gesture of the teacher with an ample movement. Then they must progressively reduce the movements, always maintaining the same shape. When the child is participating in the movement with the whole body, he also manifests his own personality through the movement. Each figure corresponds to a different melody, which everybody sings. First the melodies use rhythms of two beats, then of four beats, and finally of three beats, in order to integrate the children into the concepts of *strong* beats and *weak* beats (which should correspond to muscular contraction and muscular relaxation respectively). Gestures are initially made only with one arm; then one leg is included in the movement; and finally the movement is made by the whole body and limbs.

The teacher commands pupils to shut their eyes and to repeat the movements in order to memorize motor activities. The 26 figures demand successively greater complexity in motor functions.

After doing these exercises, the teacher establishes the reproduction of such movements against *resistance* (for instance, *vertical* movements with hands moving around the surface of a wall, then of a blackboard; *horizontal* movements on the surface of a table or on the floor; using hands, fingers, paint brushes, chalks, and so on, until pencils, papers, and other school materials can be employed).[26]

Mme. S. Borel-Maisonny holds that writing should begin only when the pupil is capable of orienting himself spatially and can distinguish and reproduce forms. Then he can associate auditory orders referring to directions, establishing the changes of direction on the basis of differences of color.[27] In the same way that M. Montessori has associated form with relief and the stereognostic sense (letters in sandpaper),[28] Borel-Maisonny associates it with movement and color.

The remedial plan, therefore, should be aimed primarily toward spatial orientation and elementary directions, according to the techniques specified by many psychomotor methods. Then it will continue with orientation in writing, especially the letters p, q, b, and d. Then guidance will follow in the formation of letters, establishing orally the changes of direction or associating them visually with different colors. Later, rhythm would be imposed, writing large letters and associating them with rhythmic melodic forms and silences which will mark pauses. To all this would be added gestures, associated with simple melodies, the movement of the fingers or the hand and special postures, and positions which help the child gain an awareness of his articulation and of the functions of these.

There are many traditional approaches in the United States that deal with special therapy for learning disabilities. Some of them are those of M. Stanger and E. Donohue; G. Fernald; A. Gillingham and B. Stillman; J. L. Cooper; T. Hegge, A. Thorleif, S. Kirk, and W. Kirk; M. A. McGinnis, F. Kleffner, and R. Goldstein; and others.[29]

(92) TEACHING OF READING AND WRITING (SUMMARY OF RESEARCH PUBLISHED 1962, 1965)

To continue the review of a previous approach published in 1962-1965, some concepts about the teaching of reading and writing will be summarized in this section.

Methods of teaching reading. In the book on the teaching of reading and writing which William S. Gray wrote for UNESCO in 1957, this author came up against the difficulties involved in the use of the terms "analytic" and "synthetic" for the classification of the different methods.[30] We will rely on the definitions that have been internationally accepted on the subject, without entering into discussion of the correctness of these terms.

The synthetic methods. These lead toward synthesis, starting with the simple elements of *lingua* (letters, sonorities, or syllables), to arrive at the word, the phrase, and the sentence. Of the present methods of teaching Western Indo-European languages, they are the oldest, for they were used in ancient times. These methods are called "classical" or "traditional," and in some ordinary school circles they are still designated as "analytical." Both labels ("analytic" and "synthetic") have gained currency in the academic world and are applied to languages worldwide; despite that, according to some linguistic scholars, no language is wholly "synthetic" or "analytic."

One of the synthetic methods is the "alphabetical" (ABC), which consists first in recognizing the letters by name and later spelling and pronouncing two-letter syllables, passing on finally to combinations of letters.

The method called "phonic" is based on the teaching of sonorities which form the word, trying to identify as far as possible each sonority with a symbol (letter). This method has probably been in use from antiquity, and remains popular, because the results of teaching are generally good in accordance with the phonetic-graphic relationships.

There remains to be considered the "syllabic" method, which has the advantage of presenting all the sonorities resulting from the combination of the same consonant with different vowels. But although this is convenient for the teacher, the demands made on the pupil's memory are greater. Because the demands on the pupil's memory increase geometrically with complexity in a given idiom's syllabic structure, the teaching method becomes increasingly awkward.

The analytic methods. These are aimed at analysis, starting with the gestaltic, or global, units of *lingua* and language (words, phrases, and sentences) to arrive later at the recognition of the simpler elements which constitute these. These methods in some ordinary school circles are still designated as being "synthetic."

The method termed "word method" has frequently been attributed—according to W. S. Gray—to Comenius, who sustained the belief that, when words are presented with drawings, it is not necessary to revert to "painful spelling" for them to be quickly learned. John Amos Komensky (i.e., Comenius, 1592-1670) was born in Moravia. He spoke Czeck, German, Dutch, and—of course—Latin. His book *Pansophiae Prodromus* (1639) brought much attention in England, and elicited an invitation to visit that country. Two scholarly (or academic) handbooks, *Janua Linguarum Reserata* (1631) and *Orbis Sensualium Pictus* (Written in 1650 and published in 1657), were translated into almost all European languages and also into Arabian and Perse. In the *Orbis,* Comenius introduced many words and phrases accompanied by drawings. Certainly, spelling in the seventeenth century was still very difficult because there was no standard for how to spell any language. We must bear in mind that, for that time, some principles of grammar already existed, but hardly standards of spelling or orthography. To teach Latin or English, therefore, by the "whole word" method was *linguistically* unacceptable in Comenius' era. The "global" method has had perhaps its greatest modern upholder in O. Decroly, who considered that the reader's attention is directed mainly to understanding the content and that, if we teach the reading of words (or "short phrases") as a whole, and only then begin to deal with the constituent elements, we are acting in accord with the logical development of the visual developmental dispositions.[31] Decroly's "global" methodology has been criticized by various writers.

Other analytical methods are the "phrasal," the "sentence," and the "story" methods. They aim at the creation of "linguistic units" of greater interest, leading to better comprehension of the semantic meaning.

The global methods have ardent defenders and no less enthusiastic detractors.

The analytic-synthetic methods. According to these methods, very popular in the 1960s, the learning of reading cannot be purely analytic or synthetic. There are not methods, there are children; methods must be adapted to children's individual characteristics. It is easier to change methods than to change children's abilities to learn. Consequently, it is necessary to revert continually to different analytic and synthetic procedures in order to teach real children's necessities. According to many authors, these methods allow the attainment of wider objectives in the teaching of reading than do the highly specialized methods.

Methods of teaching writing. We shall try to fit the concepts referring to the systems of teaching writing, to the previously discussed concepts of the teaching of reading.

The synthetic methods. The synthetic methods are based on visual practice and on the art of letter imitation. With the achievement of letter formation, syllables, words, phrases, and sentences follow. Some writers start with the copying of drawings "without meaning" in which parts of letters are represented, and manual movements are trained. During the 1960s there was a growing tendency to abandon this type of learning and begin right away with letters.[32]

As we shall see, writing emerged from drawing; and all methods, whether analytic or synthetic, tend to arrive at writing through drawing (such as meaningless, symbolic, concrete drawings, etc.)

The analytic methods. The analytical methods are based on the search for meaning in material, that is, that the writing shall have a meaning for the pupil and awake his interest and his desire for communication. The first question which arises is whether writing should come simultaneously with reading, follow it, or precede it. Decroly started with reading and then, through drawing, arrived at writing. Writing was learned by copying, using the visual concept. The basic difference between the notions of Decroly and those of J. E. Segers is that the former believed in free copying while the latter arranged copying in a useful order.[33]

For many defenders of the global methods, writing is a language and a means of expression. Hence, what is important is not calligraphic imitation of the letters but the possibility of obtaining legible, ordinary writing, using means suitable for the particular age, mental aptitude, and motor ability of the child.[34] C. Freinet relies on the "natural development of graphisms" for the acquisition of writing, starting with the first scribbled graphisms (at two or three years of age) and allowing or suggesting the interpretation of meaning in the strokes.[35] In this way, expressive intention is gradually achieved from the scribbled strokes. The authoress first worked with her daughter Bal, establishing that the principles for writing are similar to those for reading, drawing, doing mathematical calculations, and so on. Understanding of what is written is prior to learning writing mechanics and rules. Consequently, writing can be learned "according to a general and natural process of trial-and-error experience (*experience tatonnee*), and certainly it does not follow the steps given by adult logic." Freinet's method is based on the "helping environment" (*milieu aidant*); and it does not follow a preestablished technique. It is through imitation (and not through copying) that children learn to write letters and words. At around three years of age the child will differentiate some of his scribbles as writing. Later, this differentiation will be accentuated; and little by little the child will manage to learn some letters and "intuitive" learning. Every child must develop his own technique of writing. According to Freinet, after six years of age the child *discovers* correspondences between sounds and letters, with many orthographic errors, and then he will be able to write correctly. Freinet's method is the most analytic or "global" method known in Europe; it is more analytic than Comenius' or Decroly's approaches; and it seems, therefore, to follow the same wrong track, but at a brisker rate.

Method and type of letter-style suitable for teaching of reading and writing. To attempt to homogenize the learning characteristics of reading and writing for all learning-disabled children, would be to make a grave mistake: It is not a matter of a learning disability but of a learning-disabled person, with special circumstances for each case. We cannot say that we should always begin with this or that step, or adopt this or that measure in the teaching of reading and writing; but we can accept postulates and learn pedagogic methods. In our opinion the opportunity to use them might or might not arise. It all depends on the individual and environmental characteristics of each case.

Suppose we know that the learning-disabled child tends to have analytic-synthetic difficulties, and from this we infer that the most advisable methodology will be found within the synthetic or "classic" group of teaching methods—that is, those supporting the teaching by units, these units being graphic or phonetic.

Now, if the speech therapist or the special education teacher in charge of the case considers that the child is able to advance toward more globalization, of course a mixed, analytic-synthetic method will be adopted. The fact that in general it is advisable, in Spanish, to start with phonetic procedures does not exclude the use of other resources or methods in special cases. See Figure 20.

In the same way, the type of writing with which one should commence the teaching should be based on clear simple strokes, which are easy to read, in common use, and capable of being formed with a crayon or piece of chalk, or (later) a pencil. Of course, italic script could facilitate learning this during the early school years, but it has the disadvantage of making it difficult to join the letters and the categorizing of the groups of letters into words. We also know that a defect which is apt to appear in dyslexic children is a lack of understanding of these categories, revealed in the changes of structure in a sentence, in the mixing of syllables of one word with the word which follows, or in the contraction or distortion of some words. For this reason, in some cases it might be more convenient to utilize another type of letter which allows a better union and bond between the constituent elements of the word. But if the learning-disabled child reveals a certain manual clumsiness it would be better, at first, to sacrifice graphic unity in the word (that is, union of all the letters that make up the word) to a clear reproduction of the letters, with the consequent difference in the choice of suitable letter type. It may be that with the same child for whom we have chosen script letters for the teaching of writing, we decide on the simultaneous teaching of printed letters and cursive letters for reading purposes. This could happen when the principal handicap is to be found in auditorizing being associated with certain graphic disturbances. As may be seen, the norms are variable; and what is important is to rely on a rational criterion for each case.

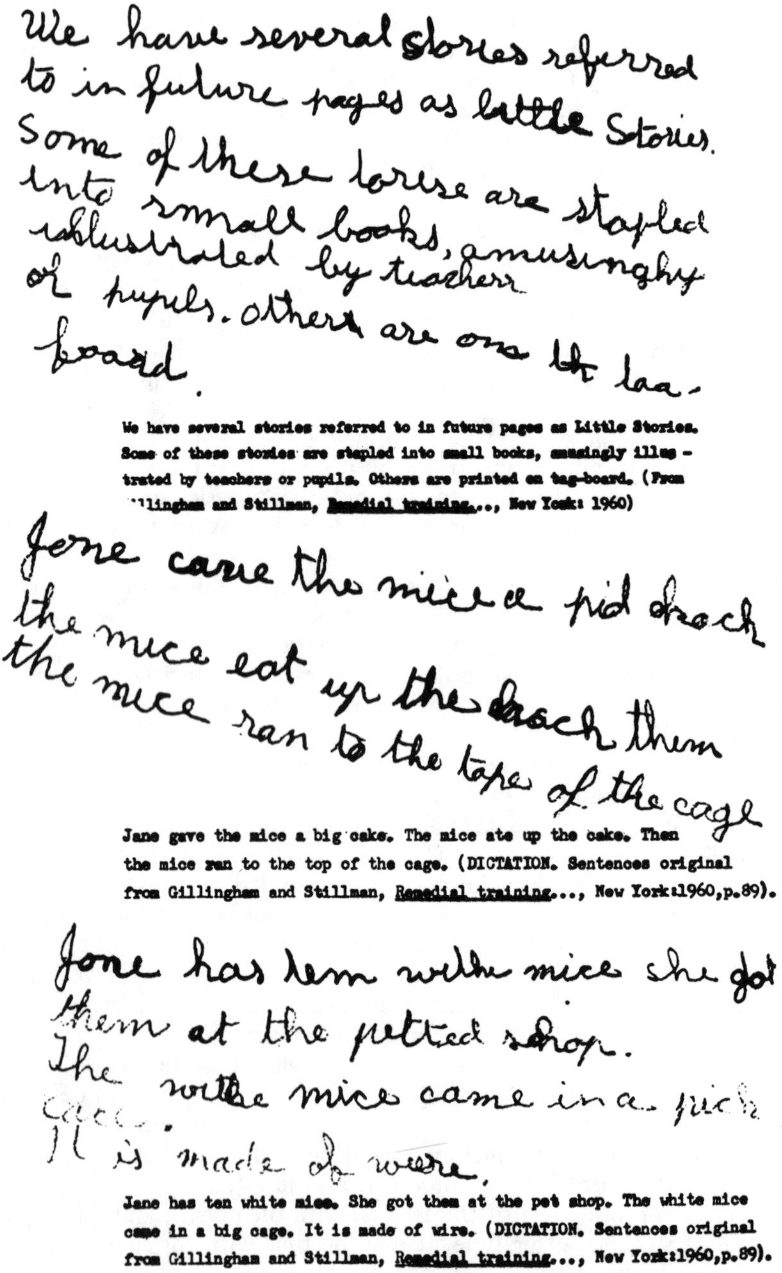

We have several stories referred to in future pages as little Stories. Some of these torese are stapled into small books, amusingly illustrated by teachers or pupils. Others are one the laa.

We have several stories referred to in future pages as Little Stories. Some of these stories are stapled into small books, amusingly illus- trated by teachers or pupils. Others are printed on tag-board. (From "illingham and Stillman, Remedial training..., New York: 1960)

Jone cave the miee a pid krach the muce eat up the krach them the mice ran to the tape of the cage

Jane gave the mice a big cake. The mice ate up the cake. Then the mice ran to the top of the cage. (DICTATION. Sentences original from Gillingham and Stillman, Remedial training..., New York:1960,p.89).

Jone has lem with mice she got them at the petted shop. The withe mice came in a pick cace. It is made of wire.

Jane has ten white mice. She got them at the pet shop. The white mice came in a big cage. It is made of wire. (DICTATION. Sentences original from Gillingham and Stillman, Remedial training..., New York:1960,p.89).

Figure 20. Dictation to a dyslexic American child in Buenos Aires. Some significant mistakes are: *torese* instead of *stories, cave* instead of *gave, pid* and *pick* instead of *big, kack* instead of *cake,* unfinished "Ts," lack of maintenance of horizontal lines during writing, and so on. Nevertheless, these Orton's twisted symbols (strephosymbolia) are many times found in nondyslexic children. (Research 1962-1965).

General plan for the teaching of reading and writing to the dyslexic child. It is not our intention here to refer in detail to all the steps necessary for the teaching of reading and writing to dyslexic children; it is beyond our present scope, and is already being done by many other authors. Here we shall try to take a general look at the specific treatment for difficulties in reading and writing, going on in subsequent paragraphs to examine some special aspects of these problems and some methods of interest.

It is customary to divide the treatment of reading and writing into three parts: developmental therapy, corrective therapy, and remedial therapy.[36]

Developmental therapy. This is aimed at obtaining the levels of intelligence, attention and memory, *lingua* and language, socialization, and general capacity and abilities which are considered indispensable for the learning of reading and writing.

Corrective therapy looks into the organic or functional causes which disturb the possibilities of learning and which consequently hinder the acquisition of reading and writing. It is important not to confuse these conditions with dyslexia. Here we are treating secondary learning disabilities (see Chapter VIII).

Remedial therapy. Such therapy concerns itself with the problems of reading and writing in children who reveal sufficient capacity to acquire these processes but who present eifficulties in acquiring them through ordinary teaching procedures. It also applies to children who present dyslexia combined with any of the problems mentioned in connection with developmental and corrective therapies, once these problems have been suitably overcome.

Remedial therapy adopts different procedures according to the characteristics of the patient. Hence, we are able to speak of slightly different therapeutic plans depending on the results obtained in the case hisotyr and results from the various examinations previously carried out. The studies we published in 1962 and 1965 permit classification of the following characteristics deserving special attention in the teaching of reading and writing:

1. Therapy of reading and writing mechanisms for the severe dyslexic child.
2. Therapy of reading and writing according to the level of learning attained by the dyslexic child.
3. Therapy of reading and writing according to the level of language of the dyslexic child.
4. Therapy according to the type of dyslexia being treated.

If the child is not found to be at the maturational stage of reading and writing, we may begin by teaching some mechanisms of written language, such as shapes of letters or fragments of letters, and also by conditioning him to the sound or the name (in nonphonetic *linguae*), without these exercises being interpreted as formal teaching, but as therapeutic play. All the exercises referring to body schema, laterality, perceptual training, and so on (preschool training), may be continued if the therapist considers that the child has not yet quite overcome any of these stages. If the therapist considers that all or some of these stages have been completed, however, he should not insist on drill, since in these circumstances it is unnecessary. Logically, each stage will be considered as overcome when the correct responses are consistent and unstable reactions tend to disappear.

If the child needs to bridge a gap in communication (as is the case with a deaf child), the preceding general rule may be changed without much danger because in this kind of child the early chances for learning to read and write are well established.

Therapy of reading and writing mechanisms for the severe dyslexic child. The more severe the dyslexia (that is, the greater number of dysphasic symptoms present), the greater should be the care taken in the measures for teaching reading and writing. The pace should be very slow, providing one element at a time and with plenty of repetition to help the child to retain it. Teaching in the case of severe dyslexia should combine many of the conditions mentioned in connection with teaching a child with minimal brain dysfunction. This teaching must be as individualized as possible, be carried out in suitable surroundings, the teacher introducing associations of graphisms' size with shape and color, etc. The elements presented at first should be large, should always be introduced one at a time, and should be impressed on the child thoroughly and frequently enough for him to retain them.

At the outset, each element will be presented in isolation from the others, but the aim should not be lost sight of: that it is preferable for the child to grasp the mechanics of reading and not that he should have to remember many discrete elements. Therefore, the first elements taught should allow the reading of some short words and even some phrases. Later there will be time to go on with new elements, but meanwhile the child will have the encouraging feeling of being able to "read." Once the first group of letters is taught, and words and eventually phrases built up, the child may go on to the second group of letters, and so on in turn. At the same time, exercises such as the game of "statues" may be very useful and will allow the child to try to hold the pencil or crayon correctly, attempting to control those movements which might involuntarily occur.[37] It would seem very convincing to him if he were shown some statue or drawing of one of the famous men of his country in the act of writing; when he is asked to imitate the statue, he would enjoy trying to keep absolutely still, this effort being encouraged meanwhile by suitable comments. Immobility of the hand can also be achieved with other suitable positions, representing other "statues."

There are other activities which may be helpful in achieving correct muscular control; for example, ask the child to close his eyes and take up again some position which he had held first with his eyes open.[38] In the case of dysgraphic movement, it may be found of positive help to use accessory guidelines and even to outline the letter faintly for the child to trace over it, keeping to the original lines. At first the guidelines or the faint outline of the letters will be made to allow large strokes. Later the guidelines will be made narrower or the faint lines smaller. If his writing is too hasty, the child's hand may be guided (this may also be done with other ends in view); and a chosen rhythm of knocks may be used to guide the child in the speed of his writing, or the command "go...go...go...," may be given as described by D. Johnson.[39] Also we have the child say this word while he writes the letter, as suggested by E. Garde.[40] Another thing which may be done with this end in view is to change the color for each one of the strokes that make up a letter. The child should write his first words as soon as he has been taught the first group of letters with which he can begin to work. If necessary, various exercises can be used to make sure the child can write letters that are already recognized. So, for example, if he has been taught capital A, he can be given the lines that go to make up the A, separately, and be asked to reconstruct the letter. If he is given the parts of A on different blocks, he must go about it as if it were a puzzle; if the A lines are pictures on the chalkboard or in his copybook, the child must "imagine" what would result form the union of these lines and write down the result of his thought. In this type of exercise it is better, especially at first, to place the parts of the letters in the same order in which they should be joined up, for example, $/ - \backslash$ = A. Only later, when the child's control is greater and he has completely overcome his problems of laterality and spatial orientation, will it be possible to present the letter elements in a disordered way, for example, $- / \diagup$ = A, solution of which requires sufficient thinking abilities. When the child has mastered the first words, however short they may be, the child should perceive each whole word as a unit. We must remark, however, that in certain cases the teaching of italic-script writing may be convenient, although—as we said earlier—italic script cannot be written as quickly as English cursive; nor does it give the sense of unity to each word (as cursive does). Whenever the notion of unity of a word is difficult to grasp, it may be convenient to write the word (by copying or from dictation) and draw its general shape or Gestalt, by outlining all the edges of the word as a whole.

Therapy of reading and writing according to the level of learning attained by the dyslexic child. As reading and writing skills advance, increasingly complex exercises can be utilized. We shall not discuss them at any length here except to mention a few helpful and interesting aspects. In words which have no separation between one another, for example, *booktablehandtomatocatcreampencil,* which the child must separate by pencil strokes. Also of interest might be the reading of disconnected words, in which the strokes have been interrupted in the middle of the letters, the upper and lower strokes remaining intact. On the chalkboard it is very easy to write several words in a row and then erase only the central part of the letters, for example:

child book

The two foregoing exercises have been inspired by different tests called reading comprehension tests (tests of separation and of lacunar words)[41] and may be found in various descriptions by European writers.

The degree of reading and writing attained, as well as other deficiencies in the child, will determine the complexity of the exercises. In this way one can use written commands dealing with the carrying out of body or spatial or temporal actions, or dealing with the right-left sense (potential or preferences and hemispheric dominance, according to Chapter IV, Section 21, and Chapter X, Section 71). The child may be given nonsense phrases in writing, which will allow a concept to be formed on the child's degree of comprehension of written language. It may be that the child will read perfectly well and even be able to repeat what he has read, but that he does not understand the fact of the absurdity of the phrase; and yet prove to be capable of interpreting similar phrases well enough when they are given to him orally. At other times it happens that the child is not able even to repeat what he has read, although he has apparently read sensitively. Here, without doubt, the child is practicing the mechanics of reading without advancing any further. In these cases it would be advisable to study the possible causes which have led to this result. Sometimes there are coexistent psychological phenomena which inhibit or retard progress toward reading comprehension. At other times it is a case of pedagogic or organic phenomena. Reading practice at different speeds may be useful: At first the speed may be given by means of Rey's procedure.[42]

According to Rey, in dyslexic children there evidently exists insufficient perceptive anticipation of the "elocutionary" act, which results in anomalies in the division or splitting of visual forms. Rey described a procedure to study this functional disturbance. In a card 6" by 6" he cuts out a gap, 2 and ¾" long by ½" deep, in one of the edges. Placing the card so that the gap lies on the line which is to be read, it may then be moved along toward the right, uncovering the words as the reader needs them.

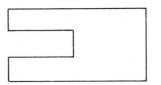

Only the first word of the text will be revealed through the gap at the start. In the normal reader it is observed that the movement of the card anticipates the utterances of the words and that the uncovered words constitute a perceptive whole. In the dyslexic child there is no such perceptive anticipation in the reading exercises and there is an arbitrary division of word form.

If the child's development allows, instead of commencing with this procedure, he can begin reading at standard rhythm, to speed reading, and to slow reading, observing the defects which occur at the various speeds. If the difficulty occurs in the recognition of words, a drill may be used which is based on the *Word-Recognition Flash Test*.[43] This exercise is carried out with cards bearing one word only (on one side, printed, and on the other in longhand), each of which is held up for the child to see for one second; he is asked to read each word aloud. If he makes a mistake, the card is held up for as long as the child wants, and he is helped eventually to recognize the word. Such a warm, encouraging atmosphere as this (even making a game out of the exercises, if necessary) will greatly enhance remedial progress.

Similarly, for writing, exercises may be carried out involving interpretation, speed, spelling, and handwriting. The first series deals with exercises consisting of a story or a brief passage which must then be written.

Orthographic and calligraphic disturbances may result as much from pedagogic faults as from the child's personal difficulties. In this book, however, it is not our purpose to deal with the pedagogic system which would lead to the acquisition of correct orthography and clear handwriting in the normal child.

We have said that, whenever a learning disability is accompanied by disturbances of body image and of temporo-spatial orientation, we should attempt to improve those deficits; and, if the child's level of language permits it, reading exercises may be begun, even though those disturbances have not been totally overcome. Once adequate levels have been obtained with respect to eye-hand coordination, attention, and sensory and motor training, we may proceed with remediation, depending on the type of learning disability under treatment. In this work the therapist or teacher should always have at his disposal plenty of multimedia items, including objects, slides, and film projector, attracting the child's attention by means of audio-visual or visuo-auditory associations, as required by the type of learning disability being dealth with. Also, special care must be taken to see that the length of each session is appropriate for the child: Fatigue and boredom may hinder progress. The length of sessions will vary according to the type and severity of the child's disability; but, as a general rule, the sessions should at first last a short time, ten or fifteen minutes, the rest of the time being filled with different amusements or games. Later, as the child responds, the work period can be gradually lengthened until, if the child is able, the instructional period can last for 45 minutes with a few minutes left for recreation.

Therapy of reading and writing according to the level of language of the dyslexic child. The importance of language organization in the acquisition of reading and writing mechanisms, reading and writing processes, and read/written language, has been stated in several places in this book. In fact, the normal child entering first grade already possesses a wide vocabulary and is capable of transforming *lingua* (symbolic communication) into language (symbolic communication plus formulation; see Chapter II, Section 8). One might well ask how much more difficult it must be for the dyslexic child. In the case of the latter there are basic difficulties for the acquisition of reading and writing, and difficulties in establishing the relationships existing between the auditory images and the visual images of the constituent elements of speech. For this reason we must insist on the characteristics differentiating language from *lingua* and use all the procedures we can to establish the correct associations to allow acceptable acquisition of reading and writing. The teaching of the words in a short written sentence should present one aspect which is purely automatic and another which is reasoned. Automatic and reasoned aspects depend on many variables, but they also depend on the different *lingua* taught.

Also, the teaching of grammatical usage to the dyslexic child is obviously important, since—as has been emphasized in this book—dyslexia constitutes a language disturbance, and as such it can be ameliorated by a basic knowledge of grammar. It is true that, in many dyslexics, it is very common to find difficulties in the acquisition of reading and writing mechanics, and in others to find disturbances in the achievement of proper understanding of written language and adequate development of comprehension skills. Teaching of proper grammatical usage will help the child to achieve a satisfactory grasp of the meaning of written sentences; and so, we must remember both the importance of correct presentation of the elements constituting the language, and the importance of using precise methodology in teaching language at school. The fostering and gradual, correct development of oral language will greatly simplify the child's task of learning to read and to write, for it will help the child to assimilate the teaching more easily and more meaningfully. The therapist must never forget this precept, passing it on as well to the teacher and to the persons closest to the child. A coordinated effort aimed at constantly developing each stage of oral language, in harmony with the characteristics of the language (*lingua,* idioms) spoken by the child, will then be a useful and positive force in the education of the dyslexic child.

As we have remarked, teaching of reading and writing is seen to be influenced by the development of oral language. Now, since this development in the dyslexic child may be affected by the simultaneous use of two or more languages, the child's parents should be urged to use one language only, which will be (with some peculiar exceptions) the language spoken in the family's neighborhood. We must not forget the influence of the environment on the child's *lingua* and language, since his daily life is in contact with that environment.

Exercises can be initiated by using items dealing with the individual sounds or the names of the letters, meaningless syllables, or short words with meaning, then going on to oral exercises of syllable reversal (for example, we say "am" and the child must say "ma"); and finally, we provide the elements separately (sounds or letters), and the child must make a word with them. Exercises should progressively become more difficult. From the standpoing of reading and writing, the use of syllables given for recognition, as suggested by J. Dubosson, can be of value.[44] The child is given a page on which syllables have been written in pairs:

ar-ra	fo-of
ro-or	chi-ich
il-li	vu-uv
is-si	ab-ba
ac-ca	de-ed

He is then given a board on which are written only ten syllables (one of each pair); and he must place the other corresponding ten (given in the form of little cards) on top of the ones written on the board. With monosyllabic words in direct and inverse order, similar exercises may be carried out. In writing, too, series of exercises may be used which are quite similar to those mentioned for reading: Given the constituent letters of a word (in order of sequence or jumbled), write the word, or separate a word into its letters, or put into order the words that have been mixed up, so as to construct a phrease correcting the elements of nonsense that it contains; or copy a word or phrase presented through a mirror, etc.

It is the therapist's ability as well as his imagination and his experience that will identify the suitable exercises for each student at the opportune moment, and with clear pedagogic sense.

Therapy according to the type of dyslexia being treated. As we already stated, in 1962 and 1965 special emphasis was given to some procedures useful for developing auditorizing or visualizing in children.[45] Difficulty in visualizing needs element-by-element audio-visual reinforcement. If the difficulty lies predominantly in auditorizing, the teaching was directed in particular toward visuo-auditory reinforcement, beginning with the general stage of language maturation. At that time we called attention to the fact that, when there are auditorizing disorders, language disturbances are present and different degrees between dysphasia and dyslexia can be found.

In the case of visualizing disorders, teaching can begin with differentiation of shapes. Always, materials which could be seen and grasped (shape, size) were used before materials which could only be seen (colors). Initially, the important sequence is the perceptual one; then concepts must be introduced. Many popular series in the United States, such as the *Primary Mental Abilities* or Dolch *Picture-Word Cards,* can be used in this regard. Since the child principally presents difficulties in visualizing, one should try to avoid confusion between two or more words by next introducing a completely new word, such as "p–i–n." Through adequate therapy the child will be capable of recognizing word families visually (for instance, *cat, rat, bat, mat, fat, hat,* etc.).

Little by little, and while he is simultaneously developing oral language, he will be asked to recognize some verbs of action, prepositions, adverbs, adjectives, etc. Different exercises may be performed with the word family groups, in which the child is asked to differentiate visually, for example, the words ending in *at* from among a group of cards having different words printed on them. Another exercise is the "discovery" of small words within other bigger ones, such as *all* within *wall,* or *in* within *pin,* or *it* within *bit.* If the child's reading acquisition level allows, he can tackle exercises containing much more complex words, such as *spire* within *transpire.* The child is given the complete word, and he is shown that inside it there is another word with a different meaning. This requires careful visual observation in an attempt to seek out the "hidden" word. Other procedures based on visual, stereognostic, and kinesthetic reinforcement can be also used. For this purpose we begin first by associating the element with a gesture of the hand, as suggested by Borel-Maisonny, among others.[46]

Of course the therapist can choose other signs if necessary to facilitate the child's comparison, and can similarly add to the audio-visual association, the tactile and proprioceptive recognition of the letter contour or shape (letter molds or letters made in modeling clay, or in relief, using sandpaper or other types of paper, outlining the letter shapes in the air or on the skin, and so on). But it should never be forgotten that the fundamental aid for the dyslexic with a predominating deficiency in visualization lies in the reinforcement through hearing the elements which have been taught visually. Nor should it be forgotten that the most important work is achieved through the frequency and thoroughness with which the elements are given, with which the process of analysis and synthesis is elicited, with which meaningful units are introduced, and with which the child is spared all boredom, frustration, and fatigue. The amount of language utilized for the teaching of reading and writing should be limited; and, whether the material is presented or requested, it should be well spaced and large. Many other suggestions in regard to dysphasia, dyslexia, and apractognosia are offered in different parts of this book.

In the case of common dyslexia when the predominate difficulty is in auditorizing, the teaching will be principally visuo-auditory and will also introduce one element at a time. In these cases one should always begin with supports and then use different expedients to facilitate auditorizing of the elements which are being presented. The expedients can consist, for instance, of playing with cards which show various drawings and monosyllabic words: If the teacher wants the recognition of the letter and sound correspondences to p, the child must, for example, differentiate if the "*peg*" corresponds to the drawing of the "peg" or of the "leg"; or if "*pad*" corresponds to the drawing of "pad" or of "mad" or of "sad"; and so on. When the child gives right answers, he is rewarded; when he is wrong, the reward is given to a toy or a doll. Then the toy or the doll participates in the exercise. (The teacher says: "He [she, or it] says . . . .") The child must determine whether the answer given by the toy or the doll is right or wrong. Emphasis is, in this example, on the letter p, which is written in a bright color (so that it is easily differentiated through vision); and it is also strongly pronounced by the teacher. Sometimes it is better to begin with a given vowel or consonant which can be prolonged or sustained (as "*s*un," "*f*un," and so on).

Therapy of dyslexia when the predominate difficulty is in the ability to auditorize may be supported also by methods inspired by language examination tests. Other procedures may be used, associating the heard sound or word with various activities (which the child enjoys), or conditionings (both operant and Pavlovian), or prizes when they are properly performed or repeated, and so on.

It is beyond our present scope to list specific methods and procedures; but before ending, we should point out that such therapeutic techniques as we have been discussing frequently do not apply, where difficulties in visualizing and auditorizing appear together—in which case, the therapist must employ a wide range of resources. In any case, it is up to the therapist to use the right technique at any given time.[47]

(93) REMEDIATION OF LEARNING DISABILITIES AND LEVEL OF INTELLIGENCE

The measurement of intelligence in its different aspects has considerable importance in the remediation of learning disabilities. It is well known that delay in reading may be caused by different factors; among them, perhaps the most important are mental retardation, learning disabilities, "immaturity" for reading (which some Americans call "late blooming"), and psychological problems (mainly, emotional disturbances). The first two factors are particularly significant because it is not unlikely (at least in our environment) that some teachers, psychologists, and doctors consider the learning disabled as being slightly mentally retarded; and that others, in these professions, with "better" instruction, consider some mentally retarded children as being learning disabled.

It is obvious that, given a similar degree of "dyslexic" severity, the chances of learning to read of a dyslexic child with (for instance) an IQ of 120 are much greater than the chances of a dyslexic child with an IQ of 90. On the other hand, were the intellectual potential lower (of IQ between 70 and 80), the difficulties in learning to read would be much greater than they would be with a slight or mild degree of dyslexia in a gifted child. Consequently, remediation should be established: (1) with reference to the co-existence of learning disabilities with a slight deficiency in mental abilities; (2) with reference to a learning-disabled child with normal IQ; (3) with reference to the learning-disabled child who is mentally gifted. In this work we cannot enter into the details concerning remediation of the child who is intellectually sub- or supernormal, since this subject is a matter of specialization and would require a treatise devoted exclusively to it.

Among the children who reveal a normal intellectual level, there may be spurious learning disabilities or simple delays in reading achievement. According to a variety of authors, there would seem to be a lapse of two or three years (from six to eight years of age, or from six to nine years of age) which could be considered as a period of normal variation in the acquisition of reading skills. We have to be especially careful not to confuse a reading delay with a learning disability. In a reading delay *lingua* and language, body image, perception, etc., tend to be normal; and it is only severe psychological problems which can appear as coexisting with the reading difficulty— problems which are more marked when the child has not been discovered or diagnosed at an early age.

Two of the most disagreeable consequences of a learning disability are, perhaps, (1) the resistance which the children feel toward intellectual exercise through reading, and (2) the great difficulties they have in enriching their store of knowledge through written language. These characteristics produce a progressive decline in their intellectual progress in comparison with other normal children of the same age. This can lead, after the age of nine, to results which, if they are assessed by means of the so-called "intelligence" tests, might be interpreted as subnormal. This is why we may read in the works of several authors who consider that, after nine years of age, dyslexia (or another learning disability) has repercussions on intellectual development. We, however, believe less and less in "intelligence" assessments.

Today nobody disputes the fact that children who are brought up far from the influence of books and of other manifestations of civilization may—upon "scientific" evaluation—be labeled as mentally retarded, even if at birth they were apparently "normal." It is precisely in the case of the learning-disabled child that he is in danger of finding himself limited in his development through the lack of stimulation, mental exercise, and information that the other children receive through reading and writing. Therapy oriented to stimulate mental abilities in the learning-disabled child, therefore, will be connected principally with language; but it will also be aimed at increasing the child's sensitivity to other artistic and cultural manifestations. Mental alertness may be encouraged in a practical way through a great variety of exercises: oral reproductions of heard or read narratives; inferring morals or conclusions from given stories; thinking up narratives on the basis of plots, descriptions of characters, vocabulary words, and the like given by the therapist; telling a story suggested by a certain picture; and so on. This sort of exercise not only tends to increase the child's vocabulary, but will also help him to use phrases which are similar to those he would use if he were expressing himself in writing.

We have emphasized that inner language, spoken language, and written language utilize—partially—different structures. While pure inner language is contracted and allows very fast semi-verbal thought, spoken language is slower (since it seldom allows phrasal contraction), and it is manifested by poor usage, repetitions, interruptions, and omissions complemented or replaced by gestures; and written language, the slowest of all, requires deep study of grammar (which involves verbal reorganization of inner language), allowing clarity of meaning to be obtained on the basis only of the text. In accordance with these facts, the therapist should proceed through various exercises to reorganize verbally *lingua* and inner language in order to obtain grammatically correct forms in the child's speech (*lingua* and language). At the outset, the therapist will remember that the patterns of expression must be formulated by him through *lingua*, since the child will tend unconsciously to imitate him. After some time, a second stage is reached, at which point conversation takes place. The therapist must not forget that all conversation has the goal of influencing the language of the other party (in this case the child). When two adults talk together, there are always words, expressions, and phrases which are unconsciously reproduced by the other party; this can be noticed even more clearly when a person is learning a foreign language and constantly tends, without even noticing, to reproduce phrases or words spoken by the professor during a conversation. Something similar is apt to happen during conversations on given subjects between the therapist and the learning-disabled child. At a third stage, progress may be made toward complete perceptual "instruction": When the therapist speaks to him (for instance) about colors, he can be led to an appreciation of the distribution of colors in nature, and then the value of pictoral art in human culture can be explained. This kind of training can produce an excellent intellectual stimulus and can permit some very good practice in grammatically correct spoken language (in order to be "transferred" to written language). Like these, many other perceptual (visual, auditory, tactile, etc.) stimuli can contribute greatly to mental activation and be a powerful aid to the child's chances of catching up with his classmates.

(94) NEUROPSYCHOLOGICAL PRINCIPLES AT HOME AND AT SCHOOL

We have repeatedly mentioned the emotional disturbance which occurs so frequently in learning-disabled children. The cause of this emotional disturbance, derived from the condition itself, is to be found in the frequent lack of understanding of his family and school environment, as well as in the child's own feeling of inferiority, frustration, and guilt.[48] In some cases, these aspects increase greatly in complexity as a result of other abetting factors; and the child requires individual neuropsychological treatment.

On the other hand, when the emotional problem is connected only with the reading difficulty, a general neuropsychological approach may be adopted. The norms to be adopted are aimed: (1) at the family environment; (2) at the school environment; (3) at the child's relationship with the teacher and the therapist.

Let us first see what measures are advisable from the point of view of the family.

Once the correct diagnosis is established, to have an interview with the parents is recommended, to explain to them the nature of the condition and to request their understanding and cooperation. Depending on the socio-economic status, as well as on the degree of culture attained and the existing family relations, the examiner may arrange for the visit of the social worker and the incorporation of the parents into a group for the interchange of ideas and discussion; or he may decide on the immediate participation of a neuropsychiatrist to obtain better adjustment in an individual case; or he can recommend perceptual, or psychomotor training (and he must explain why he is recommending such a measure). The most frequent resolution is to arrange for the parents to join in a group with other parents of learning-disabled children or of children with problems (according to the resources of the school district). In this way, simultaneous with the remedial treatment of the child, the parents should periodically attend meetings which are organized and led at first by the therapist himself. The neuropsychologist and the therapist who deals with these children should always be present in the meetings and be ready to take part if necessary. The results obtained through the formation of these groups, in which there should pervade a friendly, disciplined, and calm atmosphere, are usually very satisfactory, since the parents meet others with the same problems, exchange ideas, discuss family procedures of childrearing, and how to deal with problems they encounter. Through these parents' meetings they find a proper outlet for their worries and anxieties. Hence, the formation of family groups should be interpreted as an integral part of the general plan of rehabilitation of the center, or the school, or the individual therapist who is in charge of the case.

Along general lines, the first aim in the formation of groups is to establish a proper relationship among the participants, trying to make them accept an objective attitude. Then, encourage the recounting of each particular case history. Also, invite one or all of the members of the group to write down what they consider of interest about their children, noting their observations and doubts. Next, there is discussion about each case and the reading and discussion of what has been written, and later a discussion of measures to be adopted in trying to form a plan that is coordinated with the management of the child (from the other points of view: academic, remedial, and neuropsychological). It is important to recall the general approach of remediation (see Chapter XI, Section 82) in order to explain what vestibular dysfunctions, discrimination handicaps, or cerebral dysfunctions mean.

Psychotherapy, when it is needed, is beyond the scope of this book; but we would emphasize that perhaps the best psychotherapy for these cases would be prophylaxis—that is, early diagnosis and adequate remedial treatment from the outset.

Both in the school environment and in the child's relations with the therapist, extreme care should be taken to avoid creating any negative feeling in the child. Naturally, this will also be dependent on correct placement of the learning-disabled child in a suitable school group.

If the child is sufficiently able, the therapist will proceed to reinforce the teaching already received, in a small school group of children with reading difficulties, functioning in an ordinary school. If the characteristics of the child's learning disability do not allow his incorporation into a group functioning in a regular school, he should be treated on a one-to-one basis by the specialized therapist. When the teacher and the therapist work simultaneously, there should be coordination between them; and they will have to agree not only on the steps to be taken in teaching, but also on the way the child is to be treated. Both teacher and therapist should proceed with caution in the introduction of reading and writing. They must not forget that, when there is cordial and affectionate treatment, far better results can be obtained than those produced by severe requirements for work. It will be much more important at first to establish bonds of reciprocal empathy and not to attempt to advance too quickly in the knowledge of the first letters to be learned. With this aim in view the precaution should be taken of making clear to the parents (to avoid possible unpleasant misunderstandings) that, at the outset, teaching of academic subjects will not be fully embarked upon. An understanding and stimulating attitude will not, on the other hand, exclude the firmness necessary to guide the child in the progressive effort his learning will require. It will be found indispensable to form centers of interest and of motivation sufficient for an unconscious orientation toward reading. In almost all cases, motor activities through play must be introduced.

In dealing with placement of the learning-disabled child at school, we must bear in mind that the criterion to be followed is different according to whether this kind of child has been detected early, or after repeated school failures.

In the first of these two situations, his placement can be planned according to the degree of severity of the disability. Children with merely a delay in reading acquisition can attend a normal class with slow progress in learning to read, and receive remedial classes from a specialized speech therapist and suitable sessions with a neuropsychologist.

In the case of a severely learning-disabled child who is detected early, it is advised that the child should be placed in a small group of children with difficulties similar to those of the patient. This group may exist within the normal school or in a reading center, but never in a school for subnormal children with other types of problems. The need for individual work will be greater with this type of child than when the disability is less severe.

As the child improves, he can take his place in different groups until he reaches the point where he receives all his teaching in one work group; and, when the time is right for it, he goes into a normal grade. Whenever a learning-disabled child is to be placed in a normal grade, we should remember that the assessment made for his placement has generally been formed under the best examining conditions and that—as a result—his performance in school surroundings is generally below the results obtained experimentally. Hence, his placement should be considered in terms of a level slightly lower than the one indicated by such results. Added to this, the child will at first feel psychologically surer of himself about school requirements, which will give rise to self-confidence.

A serious problem of school placement is presented by the child with prior failures in learning. Here, too, we must consider the different degrees of the learning disability. Generally, with a mild degree of learning disability, when there is failure in a school grade, the child should be taken out of school for the time being, placed under proper remedial teaching and psychological help, and reintegrated later at the level advised by the specialized team, in another ordinary school, so that the child will not suffer from a feeling of inferiority at having to see his last year's classmates in a higher grade. Simultaneously with his re-entry into the regular school, he should continue with the remedial help until he is sure of his abilities and is self-confident. In some cases, perhaps the school failure, taken in time, can be compensated by the remedial teaching. In these cases the specialized team will decide if the child should or should not repeat the grade, even when he has been promoted to the next grade. When the failures occur in severe cases, the prognosis is more reserved. It is evident that the child should be taken out of the regular school and placed in accordance with the plan established for severely learning-disabled children without failures; but here, much greater neuropsychological support should be obtained and much more intense remedial work carried out. It is in these cases, especially, where one has "to get down to rock bottom" and work individually and very intensively. Once the stages of adaptation have been overcome, the plan outlined above can be followed.

(95) FINAL WORDS

When in 1959 we published our first research on dyslexia in childhood, we were sure about the social importance of dysfunctions in human learning; but, we were also unfortunately confusing a wide variety of conditions within a single, general label.[49] More than twenty years later we are recognizing many primary learning disabilities, but we are still taking only our first steps in a very complex research field.

There are many outstanding contributions all over the world that are clarifying our ideas more and more in this regard. These contributions come from various origins, several specialties, and different approaches. We agree that, many times, to understand vocabularies and terminologies which are not familiar to the educational community becomes very difficult. Knowledge about learning disabilities, however, demands new concepts and approaches as well as new terms and vocabulary. In this book many of these new ideas have been reviewed, and we have presented some of our own conclusions about learning disabilities.

Our criteria from 1959 recede in the distance; and we are still learning new things, and changing our minds accordingly, about learning disabilities. Perhaps some of the most important realizations we have had are (1) that dyslexia is only one of the many conditions labeled within the general term of "primary learning disabilities," and (2) that many other conditions within this group can be identified.

Some steps have already been provided, but many others must be added, in order to identify so many and diverse cases of learning disabilities.

We promise to be prompt in changing our position if new evidence shows us that our ideas have been wrong. At this writing our ideas seem to be useful, but it is desirable that in the near future they can be superseded.

All this notwithstanding, children with learning disabilities exist. They are *there*. They deserve our best efforts because tomorrow they will be adults. Our civilization will remain only if we preserve and develop what has been so difficult and what has taken so long to obtain: our human language.

NOTES

1. N. Weil Malherbe, "Studies on Brain Metabolism of Glutamic Acid in Brain," *Biochemical Journal* 30 (1936): 665; J. B. de Quirós, "Le Potassium," *Revue de Laryngologie* [Bordeaux] 79:12 (1958): 81-92; J. B. de Quirós, "El Potasio en Laringologia," *Revista de la Asociacion Medica Argentina* [Buenos Aires] 72:2 (1958): 68-73; J. B. de Quirós *et al.*, *Terapeutica Clinica en Oto-Laringologia* (mimeographed; Buenos Aires: Ares, 1960); J. B. de Quirós, "Enfoque Terapeutico de los Trastornos Del Lenguaje," *Actas del Segundo Congreso Latinoamericano de Neuropediatria* (Mexico, D.F., August 29-September 1, 1973; Direccion General de los Servicios Medicos del Departamento del Distrito Federal): 50-70; B. Schepartz, "Oxidation of L-aminoacid in Homogenates of Immature Brain," *Biochemistry and Biophysics Acta* 53 (1961): 602; J. Delay and P. Deniker, *Methodes Chimiotherapiques en Psychiatrie* (Paris: Masson, 1961); R. Schain and D. Freedman, "Studies on 5-Hydroxindole Metabolism in Autistic and other Mentally Retarded Children," *Journal of Pediatrics* 58:3 (1961): 315-320; D. Boullin, M. Coleman, and R. A. O'Brien, "Abnormalities in Platelet 5-Hydroxitryptamine (Serotonin) Efflux in Patients with Infantile Autism," *Nature* 226 (1970): 3717.

2. J. R. Hughes, "Biochemical and Electroencephalic Correlates of Learning Disabilities," in R. M. Knights and D. J. Bakker (eds.), *The Neuropsychology of Learning Disorders* (Baltimore: University Park Press, 1976): 53-70; H. Hyden, "Biochemical Aspects in Brain Activity," in S. Farber and S. Wilson (eds.), *Control of the Mind* (New York: McGraw-Hill, 1961); H. Hyden and E. Egyhazi, "Changes in RNA Content and Base Composition in Cortical Neurons of Rats in a Learning Experiment Involving Transfer of Handedness," *Proceedings of the National Academy of Sciences* [U.S.A.] 52 (1964): 2040-2046; H. Hyden and P. W. Langhe, "Protein Synthesis in the Hippocampal Pyramidal Cells of Rats during a Behavioral Test," *Science* 159 (1970): 1370-1373; J. Gaito, "A Biochemical Approach to Learning and Memory," *Psychology Review* 68 (1961): 288-292; W. B. Essman and S. Nakajima, *Current Biochemical Approaches to Learning and Memory* (New York: Wiley and Sons, 1973).

3. A. S. Effron and A. M. Freedman, "The Treatment of Behavior Disorders in Children with Benadryl," *Journal of Pediatrics* 42 (1953): 261-266; A. M. Freedman, A. S. Effron, and L. Bender, "Pharmacotherapy in Children with Psychiatric Illness," *Journal of Nervous and Mental Diseases* 122 (1955): 479-486.

4. C. Bradley and E. Green, "Psychometric Performance of Children Receiving Amphetamine Sulphate (Benzedrine)," *American Journal of Psychiatry* 97 (1940): 388-384; M. Cuttler, J. W. Little, and A. A. Strauss, "Effect of Benzedrine on Mentally Deficient Children," *American Journal of Mental Deficiency* 45 (1940): 59-65; H. Moskowitz, "Benzedrine Therapy for the Mentally Handicapped," *American Journal of Mental Deficiency* 65 (1961): 540-543; L. Bender and F. Cottington, "The Use of Amphetamine Sulphate (Benzedrine) in Child Psychiatry," *American Journal of Psychiatry* 99 (1942-1943): 116-121.

5. C. Bradley, "Benzedrine and Dexedrine in the Treatment of Children's Behavior Disorders," *Pediatrics* 5:1 (1950): 24-37; C. K. Conners, L. Eisenberg, and A. Barcai, "Effect of Dextramphetamine on Children: Studies on Subjects with Learning Disabilities and School Behavior Problems," *Archives of General Psychiatry* 17:4 (1967): 478-485.

6. G. J. Lytton and M. Knobel, "Diagnosis and Treatment of Behavior Disorders in Children," *Diseases of the Nervous System* 20 (1959): 334-340; Quiros *et al.*, *Terapeu-*

tica Clinica . . . , loc. cit.; M. Knobel, "Diagnosis and Treatment of Psychiatric Problems in Children," *Journal of Neuropsychiatry* 1 (1959): 82-91; M. Knobel, "Tratamiento de la Conducta Hiperkinetica," *La Semana Medica* [Buenos Aires] 117:29 (1960): 1129; M. Knobel, "Psychopharmacology for the Hyperkinetic Child," *Archives of General Psychiatry* 6 (1962): 198-202.

7. L. Oettinger, "Learning Disorders, Hyperkinesis and the Use of Drugs in Children," *Rehabilitation Literature* 32:6 (1971): 162-167.

8. R. J. Douglas, "The Development of Hippocampal Function: Implication for Theory and for Therapy," in R. L. Isaacson and K. L. Pribram (eds.), *The Hippocampus*, Volume 2 (New York and London: Plenum Press, 1975): 327-361.

9. Hughes, *op. cit.*

10. R. J. Douglas, K. Packouz, and D. Douglas, "The Development of Inhibition in Man," *Proceedings of the American Psychological Association* (1972): 121-122 (cited by Douglas, *op. cit.*).

11. *Ibid.*

12. J. B. de Quirós, M. Della Cella, D. Carrara, and L. Allegro, *Estudios sobre la Dislexia Infantil* (Santa Fe, Argentina: Ministerio de Educacion y Cultura, 1962); J. B. de Quirós and M. Della Cella, *La Dislexia en la Ninez* (Buenos Aires: Paidos, 1965).

13. B. Bobath, "A New Treatment of Lesions of the Upper Motor Neurons," *British Journal of Physical Medicine* 2 (1948): 26-29.

14. J. de Ajuriaguerra and G. Bonvalot-Soubiran, "Indications et Techniques de Reeducation Psychomotrice en Psychiatrie Infantile," *La Psychiatrie de l'Enfant* [Paris] 2:2 (1959): 423-493.

15. J. Piaget, *La Construction du Reel chez l'Engant* (Neuchatel, Switzerland: Delachaux et Niestle, 1950); J. Piaget, *Le Langage et la Pensee chez l'Enfant* (Neuchatel, Switzerland: Delachaux et Niestle, 1956).

16. O. Decroly and S. Monchamp, *L'Initiation a l'Activite Intellectuelle et Motrice par les Jeux Educatifs* (4th ed.) (Neuchatel, Switzerland: Delachaux et Niestle, 1932); F. de Olmo, "Test Sabadell," in B. Szekely, *Los Tests,* Volume II (3rd ed.) (Buenos Aires: Kapelusz, 1953): 27.

17. K. Orff, *Metodologia Musical* (G. Graetzer, trans.) (Buenos Aires: Barry y Cia., 1960).

18. S. Borel-Maisonny, *Langage Oral et Ecrit* (in 2 vols.) (Neuchatel, Switzerland: Delachaux et Niestle, 1960).

19. A. A. Strauss and L. Lehtinen, *Psychopathology and Education of the Brain Injured Child* (New York: Grune & Stratton, 1947); W. M. Cruickshank, F. A. Bentzen, F. H. Ratzenburg, and M. T. Tannhauser, *A Teaching Method for Brain Injured and Hyperactive Children* (New York: Syracuse University Press, 1961); L. Bender et al., *Psychopathology of Children with Organic Brain Disorders* (Springfield, Illinois: Charles C Thomas, 1956); L. Bender, "Cerebral Sequelae and Behavior Disorders Following Byogenic Meningoencephalitis in Children," *Archives of Pediatrics* 59 (1942): 772-783; K. Cameron, "Is there a Syndrome of Brain Damage in Children?" *Cerebral Palsy Bulletin* [Edinburgh] 3:1 (1961): 74-75; I. Lesny, "Minimal Cerebral Palsy," *Cerebral Palsy Bulletin* [Edinburgh] 3:6 (1961): 615; R. S. Paine, "Minimal Chronic Brain Syndromes in Children," *Developmental Medicine and Child Neurology* 4:1 (1962): 21-27; D. Pond, "Is There a Syndrome of 'Brain Damage' in Children?" *Cerebral Palsy Bulletin* [Edinburgh] 2:4 (1960): 296; J. B. de Quirós, "Remarques Phoniatriques Faites sur des Sujets ayant des Lesions du Systeme Nerveux Central," *Revue d'Oto-Neuro-Ophtalmologie* [Strasbourg] 31:2 (1959): 79; A. A. Silver, "Diagnosis and Prognosis of Behavior Disorder Associated with Organic Brain Disease in Children," *Journal of Insurance Medicine* 6 (1951): 38; H. Werner, "Perceptual Behavior of Brain-Injured, Mentally Defective Children: An Experimental Study by Means of the Rorschach Technique," *Genetic Psychology Monographs* 31 (1945): 51-110; H. Werner and A. A. Strauss, "Pathology of Figure-Ground Relations in the Child," *Journal of Abnormal and Social Psychology* 36 (1941): 236-248; J. N. Walton, "Minimal Cerebral Palsy," *Cerebral Palsy Bulletin* [Edinburgh] 3:4 (1961): 391; R. Wigglesworth, "Minimal Cerebral Palsy," *Cerebral Palsy Bulletin* [Edinburgh] 3:3 (1961): 293.

20. Piaget, *La Construction* . . . , *loc. cit.*; Piaget, *Le Langage* . . . , *loc. cit.*, J. Piaget, *Le Jugement et le Rasonnement chez l'Enfant* (Neuchatel, Switzerland: Delachaux et Niestle, 1956); A. Gesell and C. Amatruda, *Developmental Diagnosis, Normal and Abnormal* (New York: Hoeber, 1971); A. Gesell and F. L. Ilg, *The Child from Five to Ten* (New York: Harper and Bros., 1946); L. S. Vygotsky, *Thought and Language* (E. Hanfmann and G. Vakar, trans.) (Cambridge, Massachusetts: M.I.T. Press, 1962).

21. A. Binet and T. Simon, *Les Enfants Anormaux* (Paris: A. Colin, 1907); A. Binet and T. Simon, "Le Developpement de l'Intelligence chez les Enfants," *L'Annee Psychologique* 14 (1908): 2-95; A. M. Terman and M. Merrill, *Measuring Intelligence: A Guide to the Administration of the New Revised Stanford-Binet Tests of Intelligence* (Boston: Houghton Mifflin Co., 1938).

22. B. Lourenco Filho, *Test ABC de Verificacion de la Madurez Necesaria para el Aprendizaje de la Lectura y la Escritura* (5th ed.); (Buenos Aires: Kapelusz, 1944); A. L. Gates, *Gates Primary Reading Tests* (New York: Bureau of Publications, Teachers College, Columbia University, 1958); E. E. Doll, *The Measurement of Social Competence* (Minneapolis: Educational Test Bureau, 1953); K. Banham, *Maturity for School Entrance and Reading Readiness* (Minneapolis: Educational Test Bureau, 1959); M. J. Mecham, *Verbal Language Development Scale* (Minneapolis: Educational Test Bureau, 1958).

23. H. R. Myklebust, *The Psychology of Deafness* (New York and London: Grune & Stratton, 1960).

24. H. B. MacLean, *The MacLean Method of Writing: Teacher's Complete Manual and Books I-VIII* (Toronto: W. J. Cage and Co., 1921); A. N. Palmer, *The Palmer Method of Business Writing* (New York: The A. N. Palmer Co., 1944).

25. M. Richardson, *Writing and Writing Patterns: Teacher's Book and Books I-V* (London: University of London Press, 1948).

26. T. Bugnet van der Voort, "Une Experience de Reeducation du Geste chez l'Enfant," *Revue de Culture Humaine* [Paris] 12:7 (1950): 403.

27. Borel-Maisonny, *op. cit.*

28. M. Montessori, *Pedagogie Scientifique* (G. Bernard, trans.) (Paris: Desclee de Brower, 1952): 149-202; L. L. Gitter, *The Montessori Approach to Special Education* (rotaprinted, with a Monessori bibliography in English) (Johnstown, Pennsylvania: Mafex Associates, 1971).

29. M. Stanger and E. Donohue, *Prediction and Prevention of Reading Difficulties* (New York: Oxford University Press, 1937); G. Fernald, *Remedial Techniques in the Basic School Subjects* (New York: McGraw-Hill, 1943); A. Gillingham and B. Stillman, *Remedial Training for Children with Specific Disability in Reading, Spelling, and Penmanship* (New York: A. Gillingham, 1946, 1960); J. L. Cooper, "A Procedure for Teacihing Non-Readers," *Education* 67 (1947): 494; T. Hegge, A. Thorleif, S. Kirk, and W. Kirk, *Remedial Reading Drills* (Ann Arbor, Michigan: George Wahr Publishing Co., 1955); M. A. McGinnis, F. Kleffner, and R. Goldstein, *Teaching Aphasic Children* (New York: The Volta Bureau, 1963).

30. W. S. Gray, *La Ensenanza de la Lectura y de la Escritura* (Paris: UNESCO, 1957); W. S. Gray, "Reading," in Chester W. Harris (ed.), *Encyclopedia of Educational Research* (New York: Macmillan 1960): 1086-1135.

31. O. Decroly, "Le Role du Phenomene de Globalisation dans l'Enseignement," *Bulletin Annuel de la Societe Royal des Sciences Medicales et Naturelles* [Bruxelles] (1927): 65-79; O. Decroly, *La Fonction de Globalisation et l'Enseignement* (Bruxelles Lamartin, 1929).

32. Hulliger, "Aprentissage de l'Ecriture et du Dessin," *Congres International de l'Enseignement Primaire et de l'Education Populaire* (Paris, 1937): 233-239.

33. J. E. Segers, "Quelques Fondements de la Methode d'Ecriture Globale," *Archives Belges de Sciences de l'Education* 4 (1937): 269-274; J. E. Segers, "La Fonction de la Globalisation et l'Enseignement de l'Ecriture," *Archives Belges de Sciences de l'Education* 1 (1935): 5-15.

34. R. Dottrens, *L'Enseignement de l'Ecriture Nouvelles Methodes* (Neuchatel, Switzerland: Delachaux et Niestle, 1931); R. Dottrens, *L'Ecriture Script* (Neuchatel, Switzerland: Delachaux et Niestle, 1943); R. Dottrens and F. Kuhn, *De l'Ecriture Script a l'Ecriture Lise* (Neuchatel, Switzerland: Delachaux et Niestle, 1952).

35. C. Freinet, "Pour une Methode Naturelle d'Ecriture," *L'Educateur* [Paris] 8 (1956): 29; C. Freinet, *Les Methodes Naturelles dans la Pedagogie Moderne* (Paris: Bourrelier, 1956).

36. J. Money, *Reading Disability: Progress and Research Needs in Dyslexia* (Baltimore: The Johns Hopkins Press, 1962).

37. M. Rassekh Ardjomand, *L'Enfant Probleme et sa Reeducation* (Neuchatel, Switzerland: Delachaux et Niestle, 1962); P. Bascou, "La Reeducation Psycho-Motrice," *Sauvegarde* [Paris] 5:6 (1953): 558.

38. Bascou, *op. cit.*

39. D. Johnson, personal communication, 1962.

40. E. J. Garde, "Fisiopatologia y Terpeutica de las Tartamudeces," *Fonoaudiologica* [Buenos Aires] 3:2 (1957): 64-79.

41. J. Dubosson, *Le Probleme de l'Orientation Scolaire* (Neuchatel, Switzerland: Delachaux et Niestle, 1957).

42. A. Rey, *Monographies de Psychologie Clinique.* (Neuchatel, Switzerland: Delachaux et Niestle, 1952): 269-279.

43. G. Schiffman, "Dyslexia as an Educational Phenomenon: Its Recognition and Treatment," in Money, *op. cit.*

44. Dubosson, *op. cit.*

45. Quirós, Della Cella, Carrara, and Allegro, *op. cit.*; Quirós and Della Cella, *op. cit.*

46. Borel-Maisonny, *op. cit.*

47. Quirós, Della Cella, Carrara, and Allegro, *op. cit.*

48. R. D. Rabinovitch, "Dyslexia: Psychiatric Considerations," in Money, *op. cit.*

49. J. B. de Quirós and M. Della Cella, "La Dislexia como Sintoma y como Sindrome," *Acta Neuropsiqyiatrica Argentina* [Buenos Aires] 5:2 (1959): 178-193.

NEUROPSYCHOLOGICAL FUNDAMENTALS

Glossary

Acalculia: see dyscalculia.

Accommodation: the adjustment of the eye according to various distances (see Chapter VI, Section 35).

Afferent: nervous inputs to the central nervous system (see Chapter II, Section 13).

Afferential synthesis: the synthesis of all the sensory inputs processed at the central nervous system (see Chapter VI, Section 34).

Agnosia: the impaired ability or lack of ability to attach meaning to sensory inputs. Generally, it is a symptom of brain damage (see Chapter IX, Section 60).

Alexia: the inability to understand written or printed symbols (see Chapter VII, Section 42). Generally, alexia is related to adult aphasic patients (see Chapter IX, Section 60).

Alpha fibers: the nervous fibers starting from spinal motoneurons (after receiving pyramidal, vestibular and other outputs), going to skeletal muscles, and taking part in the modification of myotatic reflex. (The word *myotatic* is also explained in Chapter IV, Section 22.)

Ambilaterality (or ambidexterity): the use of one or the other hand for all the actions that need a dominant hand. It is the use of both the prevalent (or potential) and preferent hand indistinctly.

Amblyopia: any deficit in visual acuity (see Chapter VIII, Section 56).

Ancylostomiasis: a condition produced by Ancylostoma duodenal or Necator americanus, nematode worms.

Anomia: the inability to recall names, generally due to aphasia. *Color anomia:* the inability to recall names of colors (see Chapter IX, Section 60).

Anticholinergic: the substances which can inhibit the actions of acetylcholine (principal agent for transmission of impulses within the central nervous system).

Aphasia: the partial or complete loss of the ability to use language due to cerebral damage or dysfunction.

Apractognosia: the partial or complete loss of the ability to recognize body schema and spatial relationships, due to cerebral damage or dysfunction. See *developmental apractognosia.*

Apraxia: the impaired ability or lack of ability to perform a series of purposeful movements (for instance, striking a match) (see Chapter IX, Section 60).

Ascaris lumbricoide: a worm of the superfamily Ascharidoidea, found in the small intestine, causing colicky pains and diarrhea, generally in children.

Ascending or *reticular activating system:* see *reticular formation.*

Asymmetries: the differences between both sides of the body obtained through the comparison of performances in static and dynamic situations during neuropsychological examination, allowing the assumption of actual central nervous system damage, dysfunction, or past pathology.

Ataxia: the impaired ability/inability to perform coordinated movements (see Chapter VIII, Section 53; Chapter IX, Section 60).

Athetosis: the involuntary, slow, sinuous, and recurrent movements, especially severe in the hands, which occurs in some cerebral damage, mainly subcortical.

Attitude: the reaction of some intentionality, related to reflexes, that leads to the return to the species-specific position (see Chapter II, Section 10).

Audition: auditory discrimination, especially for *lingua.* Formerly considered the sense of hearing.

Auditorization: a process by which auditory cognition permits proper acquisition and development of speech, *lingua,* and language and, later on, reading and writing.

Auditory disorders of discrimination: a group of primary learning disabilities related to problems in auditory cognitive processes which are prior to language integration.

Auditory disorientation: a deficiency in the localization of the source of the sound (see Chapter VIII, Section 55).

Balance: see *equilibrium.*

Behaviorism: a psychological theory maintaining that behavior is the subject matter of psychology, without connection to consciousness or mentalistic criteria.

Binaural interaction: an afferential auditory synthesis mainly produced at the brain stem (particularly the level of the third neuron of the auditory pathway), concerning itself with time and loudness differences between the sound stimulation of both ears (see Chapter X, Section 72).

Blindness: the lack or loss of the ability to see (see Chapter VIII, Section 56).

Body awareness: a complex notion including body image, body schema, and body concept (see Chapter II, Section 11).

Body concept: the verbalized knowledge that a person has about his own body.

Body exclusion: the inhibition of body information, motor actions, and perceptions at awareness level, in order to obtain symbolic learning. Body exclusion permits "deictic function" of language (see Chapter IV, Section 21). See *deictic.*

Body image: a notion referring to the feelings, information, or experiences given by the body itself (haptic, emotional and sensory inputs, social influences). According to Paul Schilder, the image of the human body means the picture of our own body which we form in our mind (see Chapter II, Section 11). See *body schema.*

Body insight: the nonverbal knowledge of the body (which is the beginning of body concept).

Body laterality: the greater abilities in performing motor activities and in sensory potential on one side of the body than on the other.

Body potential laterality: the body laterality established by better anatomo-functional structures and abilities on one side of the body than on the other (see Chapter IX, Section 64).

Body schema: the reception, registration, and memory at the higher cerebral levels, mainly of neuromuscular and haptic (functional) action resulting from all the deep parts and tissues which contribute to maintain a position in a static or dynamic situation. See *body image.*

Borderline: the level of intelligence which is near the dividing line between normalcy and deficiency. This term is used also in several medical specialties to mean values which are near to any normal standard.

Brain (or encephalon): the part of the central nervous system within the cranium including the cerebrum, cerebellum, pons, and medulla oblongata.

Bulbar: a term referring to the medulla oblongata.

Caloric tests: vestibular stimulation through warm or cold water in the auditory external canal (see Chapter IX, Section 66). See *vestibular tests.*

Cerebral dominance: the achievement of symbolic abilities in one cerebral hemisphere (see Chapter II, Section 12).

Cerebral dysfunction: the slight or mild types of pathology whose signs do not allow the clinical diagnosis of damage or specific lesion at the central nervous system (see Chapter I, Section 4).

Cerebral palsy: a perinatal or infantile brain damage which always presents motor disturbances and never grows worse (see Chapter VIII, Section 53).

Chorea: the involuntary motor jerks and spasmodic movements, due to some brain damage.

Choreiform: resembling chorea. *Choreiform movements:* ample, irregular, jerky movements (see Chapter IX, Section 62).

Command movements of the eyes: see *ocular movements.*

Communication: the ability to understand what another individual wants "to say" (or "to mean") and the ability to have one's meaning understood by another individual (see Chapter II, Section 9).

Conditioning: Pavlov's discovery, in which an originally neutral or indifferent stimulus, repeatedly paired with a reinforcer, comes to elicit a response.

Conflicting laterality: the imposition of the nonpotential hand (against the potential one) in order to perform skilled, coordinated, or forceful movements, thus developing a stress situation (see Chapter III, Section 19).

Congenital word blindness: a term coined at the end of the nineteenth century to designate an early deficiency in the acquisition of reading and writing (see Chapter VII, Section 42). See *word blindness.*

Connection: an expression understandable for an observer: cries, movements, gestures, mimicries, and so on (see Chapter II, Section 9).

Conservation: J. Piaget's term referring to the ability to act upon objects with reversible thought. See *reversible thought.*

Convergence: the coordinated movement of the two eyeballs toward a common near point of fixation.

Corporal hemisphere: see *postural cerebral hemisphere.*

Corporal potentiality: the possibility that human beings have of excluding the body in order to obtain higher learning processes (see Chapter II, Section 12; Chapter IV, Section 21).

Corpus callosum: a major nervous body constituted by white fibers connecting the two cerebral hemispheres.

Craniostenosis: a deformity of the skull resulting from a premature fusion of the cranial sutures, thus provoking the consequent cessation of growth of the skull and nervous tissues within it.

Creativity: a term referring to inventiveness and discoveries. *Symbolic creativity* concerns inventiveness, discoveries, fantasy, or originality in language, including innovation (see Chapter II, Section 8).

Crossed (or *mixed*) *laterality:* the use of the nonprevalent (i.e., the preferred) hand for almost all actions that need a dominant hand.

Cupulometria: the registration of the deflection of the cupullae during special rotatory tests (see Chapter IX, Section 66). See *vestibular tests.*

Cybernetics: the science of control mechanisms and their associated information systems (see Chapter II, Section 10; Chapter IV, Section 23).

Deafness: hearing impairment worse than a loss of 82 decibels with a nonadapted behavior to the normal (oral) environment (see Chapter VIII, Section 55).

"Deficit" notion: the concept concerning the assumption of some "cerebral dysfunction" in the basis of reading retardation (see Chapter VII, Section 43).

Deictic: the leadership function of speech in human behavior, in regard to interferences from motor activity and perceptions (see Chapter III, Section 16; Chapter IV, Section 26).

Development: the continuous changes which occur from conception to death or, in diseases, to degeneration of tissues (see Chapter I, Section 2).

Developmental apractognosia: a primary learning disability in infants and children due to a compensated damage or dysfunction of the equivalent to Wernicke's zone in the right cerebral hemisphere, mainly concerned with body schema and spatial concept disturbances.

Developmental dyslexia: see *dyslexia.*

Developmental dysphasia: a primary learning disability in infants and children due to a compensated damage or lesion at Wernicke's zone in the left cerebral hemisphere, mainly concerned with *lingua* and language disturbances (see Chapter VII, Section 45).

Developmental lag: a theory which considers reading retardation to be produced by a lag in brain maturation (mainly, in the left cerebral hemisphere) (see Chapter VII, Section 43).

Diadochokinesis: the motor function which permits subsequent opposite skilled movements.

Dichotic tests: the simultaneous and different stimuli fed through special electronic equipment into each one of the ears (see Chapter IX, Section 64).

Dichotomous tests: the simultaneous and different stimuli fed through special techniques to each one of the eyes or each one of the hands. Dichotomous tests, for some authors, also include dichotic tests (see Chapter IX, Section 64).

Diencephalon: the posterior part of the prosencephalon, including mainly the thalamus, the hypothalamus, the subthalamus, among other nervous structures.

Diffused brain syndrome: the symptoms produced by not-definitely-localized brain damages or lesions.

Diplacusis: the different sensation of pitch for the same sound in each one of the ears.

Directional audiometry: a sophisticated audiometric test investigating the ability to localize sound sources.

Dominance: see *cerebral dominance.*

Dominant hemisphere (or *symbolic hemisphere*): the cerebral hemisphere (generally the left) which from 4.5 to 6.5 years of age starts concerning itself with symbolic processes of communication, thought, and formulation (see Chapter IV, Section 21).

Dynamic reactions: the reactions which are considered to be the fundamentals of movements (see Chapter V, Section 29).

Dysacusis: an abnormal auditory reception (for instance, distorted audition) which is not related to the hearing loss or to the localization of the source of the sound.

Dyscalculia: a symptom related to impaired ability or inability to recognize numbers or to perform mathematical calculations (see Chapter VII, Section 46; Chapter IX, Section 60).

Dysdiadochokinesis: a disorder in the function of diadochokinesis.

Dysfunction: the disturbance of a function.

Dysgraphia: a disorder consisting in incorrectly tracing shapes, sizes, directions, and pressures in writing, independent of symbolic or perceptual disabilities (see Chapter I, Section 6; Chapter VII, Section 46).

Dyskinesis: the disturbance in the ability of performing voluntary movements.

Dyslalia: an articulatory disorder of speech which is not due to central nervous system damage or lesion. It must be differentiated from dysarthria, which is an articulatory disorder of speech produced by a central nervous system damage or lesion.

Dysleria: a syndrome very closely related to primary learning disabilities, consisting in the delay of maturation for reading and writing.

Dyslexia: a term which originally was used to replace the term "word blindness." From the very beginning, both terms were related to aphasia in adults. When dyslexia is produced by a well established cerebral damage, it is usually called "alexia." For some authors "developmental dyslexia," "school dyslexia," and "learning disabilities" are synonymous. For others, developmental dyslexia is only a type of learning disabilities, mainly consisting in a visual-cognitive handicap (see Chapter VII, Sections 42 and 46).

Dysmetria: the improper voluntary movement when it must be adapted to a distance toward an object or a point.

Dysphasia: see *developmental dysphasia.*

Dystonia: a disordered tonicity in a muscle.

Echopraxia: the imitation of a movement demonstrated by another person (see Chapter X, Section 69).

Ecology: the branch of biology which concerns itself with relationships between organisms and the environment in which they live (see Chapter VIII, Section 59).

Efferent theory: the outputs from the central nervous system.

Electronystagmography: the electrical registration of nystagmus elicited by any type of vestibular or ocular stimulation. See *vestibular tests.*

Epilepsy: Paroxismal disturbances of the electrical activity of the brain which are mainly manifested by either focal or generalized convulsions, episodic impairment or loss of consciousness, abnormal motor phenomena, psychic or sensory disturbances, or disorder of the autonomic nervous system (see Chapter VII, Section 54).

Epileptic seizure: the cerebral strokes which are resultant of a hypersynchronic discharge of a certain group of neurons.

Epistemology: the branch of philosophy related to origin, nature, and validity of knowledge. *Genetic epistemology:* a term used by J. Piaget and his followers to describe the development of knowledge in an ideal child.

Equilibrium: the interplay between various forces, particularly gravity, and the motor power of the skeletal muscles (see Chapter IX, Section 60; Chapter II, Section 10). *Purposeful equilibrium:* the position that allows the processes of "natural learning" (i.e., those skills necessary for the survival of the species).

Eumetry: the proper movement in regard to space and distance adaptation. *Dysmetric:* the movement that takes place before or after the expected point (see Chapter IV, Section 22).

Evolution: the biological development of inherited behaviors (see Chapter I, Section 2).

Expression: a term meaning all external manifestations and utterances in human or other living creatures (see Chapter II, Section 9).

Exteroception: the sensoriality which provides information from outside environment (see Chapter II, Section 11; Chapter V, Section 29).

Extracharge: the information entering the central nervous system through a perceptual modality which generally is not used for such an information (for example, in blind people, information about space entering through audition) (see Chapter VI, Section 34; Chapter X, Section 77).

Feedback: the arrival at the central nervous system of the information from any action performed by the individual or produced within the individual (see Chapter IV, Section 23).

Fixation: the ability to direct the center of the retina (i.e., the point of clearest vision and most visual acuity) to the object seen (see Chapter VI, Section 35).

Formulation: the ability to generate symbolic creativity and innovation. Language formulation, for some authors, is synonymous to "inner speech."

Function: the special, normal, or proper action of any part or organ (*Dorland's Medical Dictionary*).

Functional system: the function that becomes evident only through human environmental help (see Chapter I, Section 5).

Gamma fibers: the fibers going toward muscles spindles in order to compensate, or to help, the myotatic reflex action.

Geniculate body (medial) (corpus geniculatum mediale): an eminence, just lateral to the superior colliculus, which corresponds to the fourth synapse of the auditory pathway.

Gerstmann's syndrome: the syndrome which consists of right-left disorientation, finger agnosia, acalculia, and agraphia (see Chapter IX, Section 60). Developmental Gerstmann's syndrome can be consulted in the same Section.

Golgi tendon organs: the sensitive organs pertaining to the proprioceptive system, which are found at the end of tendons, when they attach to muscles, thus being stimulated by muscles' stretching.

Graphesthesia: the recognition of figures or numbers drawn on the skin (see Chapter IX, Section 62).

Gyrus angularis: a posterior convolution of the inferior parietal cerebral lobe which is continuous with the middle temporal gyrus.

Habitat: the environmental daily life and accustomed conditions of an individual (see Chapter IX, Section 62).

Haptic: the information referring to simultaneous kinesthetic and skin sensitivity (i.e., motor activities, movements, cutaneous and subcutaneous inputs) (see Chapter III, Section 18).

Hearing: auditory function related to auditory acuity (see Chapter VI, Section 40; Chapter VIII, Section 55).

Hemianopsia: the loss of vision in a half of the visual field.

Hemiplegy: the lack of movement in the side of the body opposite to the damaged cerebral hemisphere.

Hemispherectomy: the removal of one cerebral hemisphere.

Heschl's convolution: the primary auditory area at the temporal lobe cerebral cortex.

Hippocampus: an anatomical structure on the floor of the middle horn of the lateral ventricle.

Hyperactivity: excess movement in children depending on a great amount of motor disinhibition elicited by external stimuli. It mainly concerns itself with minimal brain dysfunction or brain damage (see Chapter VII, Section 47).

Hyperkinesis: a term used to designate the excess of movement in children.

Hypoactivity: a term used to mean less motor activity than the standards observed for the same age and sex.

Hypoacusis: the hearing impairment between 16 decibels and 82 decibels, with adaptive behavior to the regular (oral) environment (see Chapter VIII, Section 55).

Hypothyroidism: a deficiency of thyroid activity. In infants, severe hypothyroidism leads to cretinism.

Inertia: a difficulty in inhibiting a movement sequence, once initiated (see Chapter X, Section 69).

Innovation: the introduction of new expressions to the familiar *lingua* (see Chapter I, Section 3; Chapter II, Section 8).

Insight, in learning: a sudden or novel solution—with high understanding—of any problem which previously was not understood.

Interoceptive: the sensitivity which provides information coming from nervous endings localized at the visceral level.

Kinesis: the motion, the movement.

Kinesthesis: the perception of movement, weight, position. The sense of position and movement of the body. It belongs to somesthesis. Practically, it refers mainly to body information provided by motor activities and movements.

Kinetic: the action produced by movement.

Labyrinth: see *vestibular apparatus.*

Language: symbolic communication plus formulation (i.e., with creativity and innovation), representing individual personality. It is a symbolic communication identified with thought and developed through formulation (see Chapter I, Sections 1 and 8; Chapter IV, Section 25).

Langue: the store of conventional expressions used by a community (for instance, wordlike signs or fixed phrases) (see Chapter II, Section 8).

Laporte and Lloyd's reflex: a reflex opposite to the myotatic reflex, which enters into action after a certain level of muscular contraction has been reached.

Laterality: see *body laterality.*

Learning: the development of acquired behaviors which depend on environmental influences (see Chapter I, Section 2).

Learning disabilities: disturbances in human skills, such as symbolic communication, language, reading, writing, or mathematical calculations (see Chapter VII, Sections 43, 49).

Lingua: The symbolic communication belonging to a human community. In the beginning it is a conditioned acquisition and then becomes a learned process (see Chapter I, Section 1; Chapter II, Section 8).

Locomotion: the movement of a live body from one place to another.

Logotome: the arbitrary combination of a consonant, a vowel, and another consonant, or other arbitrary combinations (see Chapter IX, Section 60).

Maturation: the developmental signs which can be seen (see Chapter I, Section 2).

Ménière's disease: a disease of the inner ear characterized by vertigo, hypoacusis, and tinnitus (or ringing) in the damaged ear. This entity is usually seen after six years of age. See *vertigo* and *hypoacusis.*

Mental action: the use of mental capabilities in order to avoid the necessity of performing motor activities while learning (see Chapter IV, Section 27).

Mental retardation: a complex syndrome which responds to various causes but which is characterized by intellectual deficiency, learning disability, social maladjustment, such a symptomatology occurring during developmental ages (infancy, childhood, or adolescence) (see Chapter VIII, Section 52).

Minimal brain injury: see *minimal cerebral dysfunction* (see Chapter IX, Section 62).

Minimal cerebral dysfunction: a poorly defined syndrome which usually includes hyperactivity, distractibility, perseveration, perceptual handicaps, body image disturbances, and laterality disorders. Frequently it also manifests difficulties in symbolization (in learning, *lingua,* or in developing language) (see Chapter I, Section 4; Chapter VII, Sections 42 and 43).

Mirror-image movement: the movement made with the reverse side of the segment used as sample given to the patient (see Chapter X, Section 69).

Motor outflow theory: see *efferent theory of movements* (see also Chapter IV, Section 24).

Muscle spindle: the muscle endings, receptors, constituted by spirals and flower sprays, that when stretched elicit a myotatic reflex (see Chapter IV, Section 22). See *myotatic reflex.*

Myelogeny: the evolution of the myelin sheaths of nerve fibers in the development of the central nervous system (see Chapter V, Section 28).

Myotatic reflex: a stretch reflex (also called Sherrington's reflex or the monosynaptic reflex) starting from muscle endings, making a synapse in the ventral horn of the spine, and then going to the skeletal muscle fibers. It controls muscular tonus (see Chapter IV, Section 22).

Neuropsychology: the branch of health sciences which generally deals with basic medical approaches which study interrelationships between cerebral functions (and achievements) and human behavior (see Chapter I, Section 1).

Nonadaptive responses: the neuropsychological responses which are normal in the usual habitat and abnormal in an unusual habitat (see Chapter X, Section 77). See *habitat.*

Nystagmus: the involuntary, saccadic, and rapid movements of the eyeballs, elicited by disturbed functions of (1) the labyrinth, (2) some parts of the brain, or (3) the ocular muscles (see Chapter IX, Section 66).

Ocular movements: the movements of the eye, which from a clinical viewpoint are: (1) vestibular, (2) regard, (3) pursuit, and (4) command. Vestibular movements are elicited by vestibular-oculomotor outputs. Regard movements are those elicited by objects placed in the external parts of the visual field. Pursuit or optokinetic movements are those elicited by a moving object. Command movements are those elicited through commands.

Ontogeny: the complete developmental history of the individual organism.

Optokinetic movements: also called pursuit movements. See *ocular movements.*

Otoconia: see *otoliths.*

Otoliths: the prisms of calcium carbonate within the gelatinous substance covering the maculae in the inner ear. They have an important role in vestibular functions.

Overload: a large volume of diverse information entering to the central nervous system through the same perceptual modality, thus inhibiting the chances of its proper function (see Chapter VI, Section 34; Chapter X, Section 77).

Paralysis: the impaired ability or lack of ability to perform motor activities with the limbs, body, or head; caused by a neural or muscular disorder or damage (see Chapter VIII, Section 53).

Paratonias: the difficulties in changing muscular contraction into muscular relaxation.

Paresis: slight or incomplete paralysis.

Past pathology: the neurological abnormalities which existed in neonatal life but then, with development, were compensated. They can be shown through neuropsychological examinations (see Chapter VII, Section 43; Chapter IX, Section 63).

Perceptual handicaps: a group of primary learning disabilities mainly resulting from auditory and visual disorders of discrimination prior to language integration (see Chapter VII, Section 45). See *auditorization* and *visualization.*

Perceptual modality: the preferred sensory channel in order to learn and in order to receive information (see Chapter III, Section 20).

Perseveration: continued performance of the same movements in spite of receiving new commands from the examiner (see Chapter X, Section 69).

Phenylketonuria: an inborn error of metabolism produced by a lack of phenylalanine hydroxylase. The syndrome manifests itself in mental retardation and other neurological symptoms. Early treatment with a diet low in phenylalanine can avoid these symptoms, and patients can develop in a normal way.

Phonemic regression: deficient auditory discrimination related to the normal speed of speech.

Phylogeny: the complete developmental history of a race or group of animals (see Chapter III, Section 16).

Position: the characteristic posture of a species (see Chapter II, Section 1Q).

Postcentral: a term which means "located behind the center." Postcentral hemispheric syndromes refer to damages or lesions situated behind the fissure of Rolando.

Postural hemisphere: the nondominant hemisphere, which is mainly related to body information and its relationships with environmental space (see Chapter IV, Section 21).

Postural system: the integration of posture and equilibrium (see Chapter II, Section 12).

Posture: the reflex activity of the body in relation to space (e.g., flexed or extended tonic postures) (see Chapter II, Section 10; Chapter IX, Section 60).

Potential capacities: the comparison between the developmental level in major *functional* areas and the *acquisitional* level in related areas permits the examiner to know if impaired areas are functional or acquisitional (see Chapter X, Section 77).

Potentiality: the possibilities that an individual has to improve his functional conditions or his acquired conditions.

Praxia: the ability to perform a series of purposeful movements (for instance tying shoe laces).

Precentral fissure: the fissure parallel and anterior to the fissure of Rolando.

Preference: the laterality which depends on psycho-socio-cultural influences (see Chapter III, Section 14).

Premotor: the zone of the frontal cerebral lobe which is in front of the motor cerebral zone.

Prevalence (or *potential*): the laterality which depends on biological innate conditions (see Chapter III, Section 14).

Primary learning disabilities: the exclusive (or almost exclusive) disturbances of symbolic learning, specific to humans, such as in *lingua* or language (see Chapter VII, Section 43).

Proprioception: the sensitivity which provides information coming from nervous endings (or *proprioceptors*) localized in muscles, tendons, and joints (related to movements and body positions) (see Chapter V, Section 29).

Pseudobulbar: the syndromes which seem to be produced by bulbar lesions, but which are really produced by other central lesions.

Psycholinguistics: the study of *lingua* or language as related to persons who use *lingua* or language (see Chapter II, Section 10).

Psychomotor syndrome: see *minimal cerebral dysfunction.*

Pursuit movements: see *ocular movements.*

Reactive behavior: a behavior which responds to clear and definite environmental causes (see Chapter VIII, Section 57).

Reading and writing grammar: ability to respect rules of spelling, syntax, and so on. It is not only symbolic communication through written words, but *correct* use of rules, that govern combination of words within phrases or sentences in every idiom.

Reading and writing mechanics: psychophysiological skills to associate sounds with letters (symbols) and vice versa.

Reading and writing mechanisms: physical abilities to hold a pencil properly, form letters correctly, and the like.

Reading and writing (read/written) language: linguistic ability to communicate through written symbols; to understand when one is reading; to be understood when one has written a message for others.

Reflex: the unlearned stimulus-response sequence which is common to all members of a species and usually unmodifiable by outside factors. Its neurological unit (reflex arc) involves a receptor neuron and an effector neuron. *Conditioned reflex:* a reflex elicited by regular associations between physiological functions and unrelated events (sound, light, etc.). *Deep reflex:* the reflex elicited by irritating a deep structure (tendons, muscles, etc.).

Regard movements: see *ocular movements.*

Relais: synapse.

Remnant signs: the existence of postural or sensory responses at an age by which "normally" they should be modified or changed (see Chapter X, Section 77).

Residual hearing: the hearing in hypoacusis (see Chapter VI, Section 40).

Restlessness: the excess of movement in children depending on a great amount of postural disinhibition elicited by poor body information (or internal stimuli). It mainly relates to vestibular-proprioceptive dissociations (see Chapter VII, Section 47).

Reticular formation, reticular substance, or *reticular activating system:* a non-precise network of cells extending from the upper part of the spinal cord to the brain stem. At higher levels it constitutes the reticular activating system, which is considered as a structure eliciting attention, alertness, selectivity of perception, and being inhibited during sleep.

Retroaction: the specific inner information related to kinetic action. Retroaction is connected to the action itself (kinetic-kinesthetic circuits) (see Chapter IV, Section 23).

Reversible thought: the ability to obtain reverse, logical conclusions from a previous statement (for instance, if 2 + 1 = 3, then 3 - 1 = 2).

Rigidity: stiffness or inflexibility, chiefly that which is abnormal (usually elicited in the limbs and neck through cortical or subcortical cerebral damage).

Rotatory or turning tests: the vestibular stimulation through progressive angular acceleration and deceleration (see Chapter IX, Section 66). See *vestibular tests.*

Sarcoplasm: the interfibrillary matter of the striated or skeletal muscles.

Scoliosis: the lateral deviation of the vertebral column.

Secondary learning disabilities: learning disabilities in which nonspecifically human achievements are primarily disturbed. They respond to many causes which damage or disturb human beings (biological, psychological, socioeconomic-cultural, and ecological) (see Chapters VII, VIII; Sections 43 and 50).

Sensitized audiometry: the audiometric tests in which the normal arrival of sound or speech is modified through highly sophisticated electronic equipment (see Chapter X, Section 72).

Sensorimotor syndromes: the symptoms representing damages or lesions situated in both zones, before and behind the fissure of Rolando.

Soft signs: very slight, equivocal, minor, or fine signs registered in some patients during careful neurological examinations (see Chapter IX, Sections 61, 62).

Somatic: a term meaning "pertaining to the body." It is opposed to *psychic.*

Somatotrophic: the factors which stimulate body nutrition and growth.

Somesthesis: a term referring to cutaneous, subcutaneous, kinesthetic, and internal or organic sensitivities (see Chapter III, Section 18).

Space and body: the *facing space* is the space in front of the baby's face (first half of the first year of postnatal life); *surrounding space* is the space all around the baby's body (second half of the first year of postnatal life); *limiting space* is the space immediate to the infant's body, which limits his movements (i.e., gravity and obstacles, during the second year of postnatal life); *environmental space* is the space mediate to the young child's body (third and fourth year of postnatal life) (see Chapter VI, Section 33).

Spasticity: a state of hypertonicity (i.e., increase of tonus), with heightened deep reflexes (see Chapter VIII, Section 52). See *tonus* and *deep reflexes.*

Specific learning disabilities: see *primary learning disabilities.*

Speech: the oral *lingua* or the oral language. For traditional linguists, speech is the individual part of language (see Chapter I, Section 1; Chapter II, Section 8).

Static reactions: the reactions observed when partial or total support is given to the body. They are *local, segmentary,* or *general.* Local static reactions involve only a part of the body (for instance, a limb); segmentary static reactions involve a great segment of the body (for instance, two or three limbs); general static reactions involve the whole body (see Chapter V, Section 29).

Strauss syndrome: a group of symptoms (described by A. A. Strauss) in the spheres of movements, perception, thinking, and behavior, which can be found in brain-injured children (see Chapter 9, Section 62).

Strauss triad: the three main symptoms of Strauss syndrome: hyperactivity, disinhibition, and perseveration.

Strephosymbolia: a term coined by S. T. Orton meaning "twisted symbols" and referring to some writing difficulties as characteristics of dyslexic children (see Chapter VII, Section 42).

Stretch reflex: a reflex contraction of a muscle in response to passive longitudinal stretching (see Chapter IV, Section 22). See *myotatic reflex.*

Structural maturation: the development of some organs and tissues which are related to the acquisition of certain functions which are fundamental for specific human achievements (see Chapter IV, Section 26).

Symbolic hemisphere: the dominant hemisphere; the major hemisphere; the cerebral hemisphere which is able to develop symbolic processes (see Chapter IV, Section 21).

Synapse: the connection between the endings of two or more neurons.

Synergy: the faculty by which movements are properly grouped for the performance of acts requiring special adjustments.

Synkinesis: an unintentional imitative movement or tonic movement made by one side of the body when a voluntary movement is made by the other side.

Systemic dysfunctions: the function disturbances related to environmental influences (see Chapter I, Section 5).

Taxia: a movement with muscular coordination.

Timing: a term used by proponents of the motor outflow theory for the control of movements, meaning the certain temporal sequence of outputs ("order") from the central nervous system, which are considered essential for obtaining a pattern of skilled movements (see Chapter IV, Section 24).

Tonus: the normal degree of slight and continuous contraction of muscles (see Chapter IX, Section 61).

Torsion swing test: vestibular stimulation through progressive partially angular acceleration and deceleration (see Chapter IX, Section 66).

Toxoplasmosis: a protozoan disease of man and other mammals. It is caused by toxoplasma gondii.

Tract: the group or bundle of nerve fibers which originate and end in the same regions and which have the same function.

Tremor: an involuntary trembling or shaking of the arms, of the limbs, or of the entire body.

Trichocephalus-trichiurus: the former name of a genus of nematode, now called (when infesting man's intestines) trichiuris trichiura.

Vertigo: a sensation of being revolved in space, or of space being revolved around oneself.

Vestibular apparatus: the nonauditory organ of the inner ear dedicated to posture, equilibrium, muscular tonus, and orientation in environmental space. It is also called *labyrinth* (see Chapter V, Section 30).

Vestibular disharmony: the lack of concordance among results obtained through various vestibular tests. Usually, this kind of abnormal results indicates the existence of vestibular central damage (see Chapter X, Section 77).

Vestibular-ocular movements: see *ocular movements.*

Vestibular-oculomotor split: a primary learning disability belonging to the group of postural disorders, resulting from damage or dysfunction in the vestibular-oculomotor pathways, mainly concerned with the lack of appropriate vestibular-oculomotor coordination (see Chapter VII, Section 46).

Vestibular-proprioceptive dissociation: a primary learning disability belonging to the group of postural disorders, resulting from damage to or dysfunction of the vestibular-proprioceptive system. In this condition proprioception predominates on one side of the body and vestibular influences on the other side (see Chapter VIII, Section 46).

Vestibular tests: the vestibular organs, pathways, and centers can be medically assessed by several tests: for instance, through caloric tests, rotatory tests, torsion swing tests, cupulometria, electronystagmography, and so on (see Chapter IX, Section 66).

Visual disorders of discrimination: a group of primary learning disabilities belonging to perceptual handicaps and referring to visual-cognitive processes which are prior to that of language integration (see Chapter VII, Section 45). See *Visualization.*

Visualization: the necessary visual cognition in order to elicit reading and writing.

Wada's test: the cerebral dominance can be determined by intracarotid injection of sodium amytal. According to Wada's test, transitory aphasic symptomatology appears on the same side as the injection when that cerebral hemisphere is dominant (see Chapter IX, Section 64).

Word blindness: a term coined by Kussmaul in 1877 in order to describe reading difficulties in some aphasic adult patients. Since then, it has become synonymous with *dyslexia* (see Chapter VII, Section 42). See *congenital word blindness.*

Index

A

Abercrombie, M. L. T.: 79
Acalculia: *see* dyscalculia
Accommodation: 83, 263. *See also* vision
Adaptive responses: 150
Afferent inputs: 24, 27, 263
Afferential synthesis: 88-89, 263
Affolter, F.: 44, 45
Agnosia: 241; finger agnosia, 143-144
Ajuriaguerra, J. de: 37, 206, 233
Alba, M.: 159
Alexia: 78, 141-143, 263
Alpha fibers: 53, 55, 73, 263
Alternation: 230
Ambidexterity: *see* ambilaterality
Ambilaterality: 42-43, 263
Amblyopia: 127-128, 263
American Handbook of Psychiatry: 128
Ames, L. B.: 133
Ancylostomiasis: 119, 263
Andre-Thomas: 165

Angelergues, R.: 37, 101
Anomia: 264; color anomia, 143, 264
Anoxia: 118, 126
Anticholinergic drugs: 230, 264
Antiepileptic drugs: 229
Apalesthesis: *see* vibration
Aphasia: 29, 37, 98, 104, 202, 203, 264. *See also* developmental aphasia
Apractognosia: 178, 264. *See also* developmental apractognosia
Apraxia: 144, 264
Area 39: *see* angular gyrus, and Wernicke's zone
Area 41: *see* Heschel's convolution
Arieti, S.: 128
Ascaris lumbricoide: 119, 264
Ascending or reticular activating system: *see* reticular formation
Asperger, H.: 129, 130
Asperger's syndrome: *see* autism
Asymmetries: 196, 264
Ataxia: 121, 264
Athetosis: 72, 264; choreo-athetosis, 121

NEUROPSYCHOLOGICAL FUNDAMENTALS

Perceptual modality: 44-46, 77-82, 251, 273.
Perlstein, M. A.: 203
Perella, P. N.: 58
Perseveration: 60, 174, 273
Phenylketonuria: 118, 273-274
Phonemic regression: 126-127, 274
Phylogeny: 36, 274
Piaget, Jean: 24, 39, 63, 233, 238
Placing response: 55
Pneumo-encephalography: 151
Pollack, M.: 202
Ponto-cerebellar pathways: 28, 37, 71-72
Poppelreuter's test: 176
Position: 23, 210, 274
Positivism: 65
Postcentral syndromes: 174. *See also* frontal syndromes
Postural and psychomotor therapy: 205
Postural hemisphere: 50, 59, 274
Postural model: 25
Postural system: 17, 27-28, 30, 51-55, 59, 68, 78, 88, 205, 274; integration, 220
Posture: 23, 27, 29, 59, 63, 72-74, 78, 80-81, 88, 107, 145, 202; therapy, 210-211, 214, 221-223, 232-233, 274
Potential capacities: 196, 274
Potentiality: 150, 274
Praxia: 143, 274
Precechtel, A.: 154-155, 203
Precentral fissure: 274
Prechtl, H. F. R.: 99
Preference: 34-35, 219
Premotor syndrome: 174. *See also* frontal syndromes
Prescott, J. W.: 132
Prevalence: 33, 219, 274
Primary learning disabilities: 97, 101-104, 105-113, 182-186, 274
Primary Mental Abilities: 251
Primitive signs (reflexes): 195, 210
Project Head Start: 130
Proprioception: 17, 24, 25, 28, 30, 40-41, 68, 187, 208, 211, 274
Pseudobulbar syndromes: 177, 274

Psycholinguistics: 24, 275
Psychological disturbances: 128-130. *See also* secondary learning disabilities
Psychomotor syndrome: 146, 275. *See also* minimal cerebral dysfunction
Psychotherapy: 255
Psychotic behavior: 129-130
Public Law (U.S.) 91-230: 16, 99
Public Law (U.S.) 94-142: 99, 100
Purposeful equilibrium: 24, 27, 78. *See also* equilibrium
Pursuit movements: *see* ocular movements

Q

Quirós, J. B. de: 77, 92, 103, 152, 165, 179, 228, 231

R

Rademaker, G. G. J.: 72, 73, 165
Ratjen, E.: 151
Raven's test: 176
Reactive behavior: 129, 275
Read, M. S.: 132
Reading and writing: grammar, 275; mechanics, 275; mechanisms, 246, 275; remediation, 240-252
Reciprocal movement: 214-216
Reflex: 52, 145, 275
Regard movements: *see* ocular movements
Relais: *see* synapse
Remediation: 205-223, 231-257; postural and psychomotor, 205-206, 232-233; psychoeducational, 236-240; reading and writing, 240-257; sensoriperceptive, 233-235; vestibular, 206-211
Remnant signs (reflexes): 195, 210, 275
Rendle-Short, J.: 130
Residual hearing: 125, 275
Restlessness: 107, 111, 228, 275

NEUROPSYCHOLOGICAL FUNDAMENTALS

The Authors

JULIO B. de QUIRÓS, MD, PhD, studied for his medical and doctoral degrees successively in Argentina, France, Germany, and the U.S. He lectured or led seminars at many educational centers (Northwestern University, Georgetown University, UCLA, Stanford University, etc.); at several Children's Hospitals (Washington, D.C., Los Angeles, etc.); at several County Schools (Montgomery, Fairfax, etc.); at various private educational centers (Arena School and Learning Center, The Center for the Study of Sensory Integrative Dysfunction, The Marianne Frostig Center of Educational Therapy, etc.). In Europe he lectured at universities such as the Sorbonne and Karolinska. In Argentina, his native country, he was Dean of the School of Sciences and Human Rehabilitation (Universidad del Museo, Buenos Aires) and supervised the Medical Center of Phoniatric and Audiologic Research up to the time of his death in 1980. He is author of 206 papers and 21 books published in various languages about subjects related to communication disorders and learning disabilities. Dr. Quirós was a member of numerous scientific associations all over the world. He worked intensively in Spain and Latin-American countries. He was the founder of the Latin-American Federation of Phoniatric and Logopedic Associations, and he organized many schools in different universities for the professional education of speech therapists and specialized teachers. In 1958, in Buenos Aires, he organized what may have been the very first postgraduate specialization for doctors (MD) dedicated to "Phoniatrics," the name which was subsequently changed in 1961 to "MD specializing in Communication Disorders and Learning Disabilities." This specialty demands three years

of postgraduate study and prepares doctors to work together with therapists, psychologists, special educators, teachers and others in remedial
programs. Up to the time of his death, he was involved in research concerned with new medical approaches and examinations in learning
disabilities.

ORLANDO L. SCHRAGER, MD, a specialist in phoniatrics, obtained
his MD in 1964 at the Faculty of Medical Sciences, University of Buenos
Aires, Argentina, and his postgraduate specialization in phoniatrics in
1969 under the guidance and supervision of J.B. de Quirós, MD. Since
1967 he has been an active medical member of the Medical Center of
Phoniatric and Audiologic Research at Buenos Aires. He has lectured or
led seminars in many remedial centers in his own country (Argentina),
and in Uruguay, Brazil, Venezuela, Chile, and Spain. He was Official
Reporter in 45 national and international conferences in Argentina and
other Latin-American countries. Dr. Schrager is author of 50 published
papers and has collaborated in seven books about subjects related to
communication disorders and learning disabilities. He belongs to several
scientific associations and was recently proposed for membership in the
College International de Phonologie Experimentelle. He is presently Vice-
Dean of the School of Sciences of Human Rehabilitation (Universidad
del Museo, Buenos Aires), is Director of *Fonoaudiologica* (journal of the
Argentine Association of Logopedics, Phoniatrics, and Audiology), and
is a member of the Board of the Latin-American Federation of Phoniatric
and Logopedic Associations. His present research concerns itself with
medical approaches to learning disabilities.